Cutting Along the Color Line

Cutting Along the Color Line

Black Barbers and Barber Shops in America

QUINCY T. MILLS

PENN

UNIVERSITY OF PENNSYLVANIA PRESS

PHILADELPHIA

Published by
University of Pennsylvania Press
Philadelphia, Pennsylvania 19104-4112
www.upenn.edu/pennpress

Printed in the United States of America on acid-free paper
10 9 8 7 6 5 4 3 2 1

Library of Congress Cataloging-in-Publication Data

Mills, Quincy T.
    Cutting along the color line : black barbers and barber shops in America /
Quincy T. Mills. — 1st ed.
        p. cm.
    Includes bibliographical references and index.
    ISBN 978-0-8122-4541-7 (hardcover : alk. paper)
    1. African American barbers—History—19th century. 2. African American
barbers—History—20th century. 3. Barbershops—United States—
History—19th century. 4. Barbershops—United States—History—20th
century. 5. African American business enterprises—History—19th century.
6. African American business enterprises—History—20th century. 7. African
Americans—Race identity—History—19th century. 8. African Americans—
Race identity—History—20th century. I. Title.
    HD8039.B32U647 2013
    646.7'2408996073—dc23   2013011244

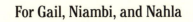

For Gail, Niambi, and Nahla

Contents

Preface

I WAS inspired to write this book while sitting in the Truth and Soul Barber Shop on the South Side of Chicago in the summer of 2000. I was not there to get a haircut—and despite the jokes of imminent attacks by rogue hair clippers, I never did—because I had just started growing dreadlocks one year earlier. But more about my hair later.

I was in Truth and Soul to observe the conversations and interactions among the barbers and customers. Melissa Harris-Perry (formerly Harris-Lacewell) employed me to do this work for her book *Barbershops, Bibles, and BET: Everyday Talk and Black Political Thought*. She was concerned that, as a woman, had she hung out in the shop, she would have altered the nature of the conversations. But even as a black male from the South Side, I have no doubt that I, too, altered the space in some way.[1] While she was interested in how African Americans develop their political worldviews through collective discourse, I could not help but think historically about the space. As I learned more about the owner, how he entered barbering, and how his entrepreneurial activities had shaped his political thought, I had more questions, and I had to go back farther in time.

That fall, I plunged into the archives and stumbled upon George Myers, a black barber in Cleveland, Ohio, in the late nineteenth and early twentieth centuries. He groomed William McKinley before he was elected president. In fact, Myers boasted of a large customer base of white, wealthy businessmen and politicians, and the Ohio Historical Society housed eight reels of microfilm of his personal papers. Why would a barber have such extensive papers? And why did he shave only white men in his shop? While few black barbers could say they had shaved a future president of the United States, as I discovered, Myers's practice of shaving white men was by no means an aberration.

Very early in my project, in September 2002, the movie *Barbershop* came out in theaters, striking a chord with millions of people, but not for the same reasons. Barber shops had long served as central institutions in black communities, so it was no hard sell to black moviegoers. The film grossed $20.6 million in the first weekend and ranked first at the box office. Yet, while many walked in with excitement and left after the movie's end with equal joy, others walked out of the theaters completely stunned. The film put civil rights leadership on trial for the world—particularly the white world—to witness. A controversy ensued, and black America found itself engrossed in heated debates about cinematic stereotypes and historical representation.

The controversial scene is iconic for its representation of barber shop talk, or the kinds of debates that take place in black barber shops among barbers and patrons. In many ways, these conversations are meant to be private. "I wouldn't say this in front of white folks," Eddie prefaced to the other barbers and customers in *Barbershop*, "but Rosa Parks ain't do nuthin' but sit her black ass down. There was a whole lotta other people that sat down on the bus, and they did it way before Rosa did." The barbers and patrons were completely outraged that he would challenge Parks's actions that led to the Montgomery bus boycott in 1955. Eddie's statement upset not only the shop patrons, but some black movie patrons as well. Although Eddie did not make his statements in front of white folks in the barber shop, they had front-row seats in the theaters. Earlier in the movie, Eddie proclaimed to Calvin, the owner, that the barber shop is "the place where a black man means something, the cornerstone of the neighborhood, the black man's country club." As the men in the shop sternly disagree with Eddie for his statements about Parks, Eddie questioned, "This is the barber shop, ain't it? If a man can't talk straight in the barbershop, then where can he talk?"[2]

The film lifted the veil of what happens in black barber shops, to the chagrin of many, but I grew frustrated that the public was still talking about barber shops in the same ways they had for decades. Though my research for this book was still in its early stages, I knew there had to be more to these shops than our public discourse has allowed to come into focus. Where did George Myers fit in this narrative about barber shops as the "black man's country club"? Surprisingly, there was no article or book on the history of black barber shops that I could consult. This question about the past and the present was critical in piecing together an untold history that might reflect a different story.

But, then, there was the question of my hair. Curious acquaintances, when they heard what I was working on, often made an observation along these lines: "It's interesting that you're researching barber shops and you have such long hair." In 1999, a year before I started this research, I vowed not to cut my hair and submitted my head to a friend's dexterous hands. She twisted my hair in sections to form what would become the birth of my dreadlocks. Year after year, those dreadlocks tangled, some merging to join as one. As each dreadlock grew longer and longer, I plunged deeper and deeper into the archives in search of African Americans who stood behind the barber chair to gain financial security. Nonetheless, it was not interesting to me that I was researching a business I was not patronizing at the moment. The historical research seemed much bigger than me, much more significant than my own hair. At no point did I feel less qualified or committed to represent the history of black barbers and the development of their shops in black communities.

But this question of my personal and professional connections to barber shops proved to be more than a curiosity as I continued my research. As I have written elsewhere, my encounters with southern barbers in hopes of an oral interview resulted in countless rejections but also a clearer insight into the connections between barbers and their shops. With sixteen-inch dread-locks sprawling down my back, I ventured to Atlanta, Georgia, and Durham, North Carolina, to interview black barbers who owned or worked in a shop any time before 1970. Much to my surprise, they were more interested in my hair than in sharing their histories in the profession. They raised a series of questions that were at once about my hair and the underlying functions of their business. In disapproving of my hair, they foregrounded the tenets of their profession. For example, "I'm in the grooming business," one barber offered his professional opinion, "and you don't look groomed." Another barber pointedly questioned, "What does it mean that you're here to talk to me about barbering, but you haven't cut your hair in I don't know how long?" Yet another barber stated, "If we were depending on people like you, we would be out of business." From my perspective, my hair was distracting. But from their professional perspectives, my hair posed a material threat to their livelihoods. This particular question gave me an opening to reframe our discussion about the past. "Well, you saw this in the 1960s and 1970s," I responded, "when Afros and Naturals emerged on the scene." I asked him, and other barbers I later interviewed, about this highly politicized era of hairstyles. One barber was quick to point out, "They were still coming in for shape-ups or some other service."[3]

I embodied barbers' challenges in the profession over time, which was a history I wanted them to share with me. These encounters had everything to do with how barbers saw their lives and labors. Self-sufficiency has been a key component of the meanings of black freedom since slavery. Barber shops have historically been one of the most accessible paths to business ownership and economic independence. These men thus took their roles as entrepreneurs very seriously. The popular idea that the barber shop is the place where men of all walks of life can talk freely may be partly true and endearing. I suspect homophobia is as much an issue in barber shops as it is in larger society. Barbers, however, kept their eyes on the bottom line. Both my research agenda and my physical presence failed to speak to the lived experiences of southern barbers. If I was attached to my hair, did that mean I was detached from the barber shop?

Cutting Along the Color Line is a product of archival research, interviews, and, most significantly, critical rejections. Because I listened when barbers refused to share their histories, this book will welcome readers into several black-owned barber shops throughout history that might be familiar and unfamiliar. Spending time in the shops revealed to me how over the years they have been both businesses and public spaces. Barbers labored in a service industry where they shaved men and cut their hair. They positioned their shops where they might capture a preferred clientele. With most areas of service consumption, relationships and personal connections matter. The service transaction, though, was rarely limited to an economic exchange. The social organization of barbers' labor to groom men included the value they placed on making men look good, presentable, and respectable. Grooming black men was a way of creating a respectable black masculinity. For the set of barbers I was looking to interview, a neatly groomed face and head could be the difference in getting a job or getting a date. Barbers thus took great pride in the role they played to groom the race, and they had planned to get paid for doing so. *Cutting Along the Color Line* unravels these connections over time and space to tell a story of black men's individual and collective interests in the barber shop—my own hair notwithstanding.

Introduction

IN October 1838, the *Colored American*, a black newspaper based in New York City, published a letter to the editor from a black man who, while traveling in Orange County, New York, had a disturbing experience at a black-owned barber shop in Newburgh. "I went out to get my hair cut and my beard taken off," he explained, "and for this purpose I called at the shop of Mr. . . . . [*sic*], a colored barber, and sir, he would not touch my face with the handle of his razor, nor my head with the back of his shears! When I entered Mr. . . . .'s shop, he had just finished shaving a white man. I asked him as politely as I could, if I could get my beard shaved off. He turned his eye with a slavish and fearful look toward the white man, and groaned out, 'no sir, we don't shave colored people.'"[1] Although the writer reproved other black barbers who had similar policies, he did not identify the barber in question and identified himself only as "Long Island Scribe." Considering New York had abolished slavery more than a decade earlier, in 1827, Long Island Scribe understood this rejection as an attack on his "right as a man, citizen, and a traveler" and was stunned at the barber's unmanly display of submission. "What a class we 'colored people' are," he exclaimed, "so black and degraded that we cannot touch each other! How can we condemn the whites, so long as such a state of feeling exists among ourselves."[2]

In an editorial appearing below Long Island Scribe's letter, Samuel Cornish, the paper's editor, defended the barber and excused this policy as one of racial and economic necessity. Cornish had been a long-time journalist and key figure in New York's abolitionist community, therefore Long Island Scribe probably did not expect the allowances Cornish gave to this barber.[3] He explained that black barbers were "delicately situated," without the "same independence that white men" enjoyed, and that therefore "we should feel more lenity towards them." Cornish's answer to this dilemma was to practice "a measure of policy and forbearance" and "when traveling, whether the barber be a white or colored man, make it a rule to shave ourselves . . . [then] we are always politely served with a good razor, box, and towel, without any hesitancy."[4] Cornish's response shed light on the practical necessities of navigating the urban and racial environment of the antebellum North. While New York had indeed abolished slavery, African Americans experienced a rather tenuous freedom.[5] Black travelers expected northern black business people to exercise their freedom by not capitulating to the wishes of white patrons and, in the case of some men, accommodate them with a hot towel and sharp razor. Cornish, though, urged readers to account for the limits of freedom in the antebellum period.

Long Island Scribe's experience in nineteenth-century New York runs counter to contemporary perceptions, made famous in popular culture such as the hit movie *Barbershop*, of black barber shops as public spaces where black men can congregate, socialize, and air opinions without repercussions.[6] Indeed, the shop from which Long Island Scribe was excluded bears little resemblance to the one that Joseph Bibb, a *Pittsburgh Courier* columnist, described in 1943. "The theme song of the colored American barber shop chord is a jingle of discontent," Bibb wrote in the opening lines of his article. "Well-trained reporters and news analysts well know that they can get a fairly accurate slant on how the masses are thinking by listening in on the arguments and discussions carried on in the countless tonsorial parlors that dot every colored community in America. It is there that the issues of the times are considered at all hours of the day and night." Bibb was not exaggerating. Reporters from the *Pittsburgh Courier* and *Chicago Defender* regularly printed debates and conversations they participated in or overheard at a barber shop in their respective newspapers, reflecting the democratic ideals of World War II and the realities of Jim Crow America. For Bibb, there were "evidences in the barber shops that there is a sort of resignation toward an ignoble fate. The philosophy expressed in these semi-private assemblies is alarming and disconcerting."[7] Bibb's assessment indicates that at least by the 1940s, the barber shop served as a public space where African Americans gathered to critique both white and black leadership.

Though the stories related by Bibb and Long Island Scribe may seem distinct and unconnected, *Cutting Along the Color Line* demonstrates that the two barber shops at the center of these stories, while a century apart, tell a larger story about how the history of black entrepreneurship in the service sector and the development of a black public sphere informed blacks' struggles for freedom. What accounts for these two vastly different experiences in African American history? And how did both profit motives and political ideals shape the public culture of the shop? Barbers were visible members of the black middle class in the nineteenth century, and their shops were among the most numerous of black businesses in the twentieth century. This book tells the story of multiple generations of black men who labored as barbers and traveled to barber shops for a shave, haircut, and social interaction in the northern and southern United States between the mid-nineteenth and the late twentieth centuries. It is at once about the rise of a profession, the evolution of a business, and the transformation of a public space.

The modern black barber shop joined black churches, beauty shops, and the black press to anchor the black public sphere in the twentieth century.[8] Describing the role of black churches at the turn of the twentieth century, historian Evelyn Brooks Higginbotham has noted, "Separate and independent of the state and also the market economy, the public sphere operated as a realm where all citizens interacted in reasoned discourse, even in criticism of governmental authority."[9] On the surface, the same might be said of black barber shops. Especially during the era of Jim Crow, black men had few spaces where they could congregate and deliberate freely and with a sense of privacy. When George Schuyler, a black journalist and critic, traveled to the South in the 1950s to gauge the mood of black southerners, he made a point of visiting barber shops even though he usually shaved himself. "The barber shop is a forum," he told an interviewer. "If you hit it when no one is talking that's unfortunate, but it's very difficult to hit a barber shop with any people in it when nobody's talking . . . as soon as two people show up, you've got talk in the barber shop."[10] Considering Schuyler's conservatism, his presence and political views would have sparked heated debates with liberal customers.[11] Nonetheless, Schuyler's expectations mirror many of our own. African Americans continue to frequent black barber shops, churches, and beauty shops because black culture guides the dynamics of these spaces.

This book departs from traditional discussions of the black public sphere because barber shops were not, to borrow Higginbotham's words, independent of the market economy.[12] Unlike churches, barber shops are profit-generating institutions that various classes of men enter, for grooming services or to socialize, without much at stake; no professions of faith or obligations of membership are required. At the end of the day, barbers must turn a profit to stay open, and we must therefore account for the influence of the market economy on the shop's culture. In this way, we can appreciate Long Island Scribe's experience as part of a longer historical narrative in which black commercial barber shops began as capitalist ventures but evolved into something more. The benefit of bringing the barber back into our discussions of barber shops is that a better understanding of the business of barbering not only increases our knowledge of the early history of the occupation and the shop, but it also deepens our understanding of how market decisions inform public discourse.

Historians have recognized the significance of barber shops in black urban life, but this recognition has been limited to passing references with one exception.[13] They have also chronicled the entrepreneurial presence of blacks in American history, especially in the areas of insurance, beauty care, and sports.[14] But historians must move beyond the blacks-made-money-too thesis in order to fully explore the challenges and tensions that capitalism played in visions of individual and racial progress within black communities. African American business history should highlight the dual economic and social or political functions of business activity.[15] The sheer number of shops, the relative permanency, and consistent patronage placed barber shops, like black churches and beauty salons, at the center of black public life.

Cutting Along the Color Line places barber shops within what I call the black commercial public sphere.[16] This sphere encompasses the private and public, individual and collective interests that organize these spaces. Barber shops are locations of economic exchange, but they are also spaces that facilitate public discourse. As businesses, barber shops operate as private spaces where grooming services are rendered. Yet, interactions between barbers and customers allow for public conversations between acquaintances and strangers. This book traces the conditions that allowed for such a sphere to develop at all. To consider the barber shop a commercial space means that we must take full account of the peculiar labor relations between owners and staff. Owners and employed barbers engage each other over "independent labor" issues such as booth rent, percentages, professionalism, and opening and closing times. Also, barbers and patrons form intimate commercial relationships based on trust. Patrons do not switch barbers often, unless forced to because of extended travel or a move to a new city. Any entrepreneur would relish the formation of community surrounding their business, yet businesses must make money to stay open. Barbers balance their profit motives with the public space of their shops. Black barbers in the United States joined barbers throughout the African diaspora as they sought ways to earn a living and control their time in urban areas.[17]

Barber shops have historically been grooming places where commerce, culture, masculinity, and politics intersect, and this book addresses larger questions about the multiple lives of men as entrepreneurs, workers, consumers, and leisure seekers. In order to unpack this complex terrain of the barber shop, this book turns on a pivot or, put another way, swivels with the barber's chair, to explore the varying expectations that men had of barbers as entrepreneurs and their shops as public spaces.[18] The grooming process, what I call "shaving-time," offers a useful framework in which to examine these roles, relationships, and expectations. Shaving-time—a term used to stand in for the barber's labor that also included cutting hair—involves three groups of people: the barber (owners and employees), the patron or customer in the barber's chair, and a waiting public.[19] This framework thus opens a window onto the interactions between shop owners and employees, barbers and patrons, and barbers and waiting publics. Whether owners or employees, barbers of all stripes used their grooming skills to become self-employed workers in pursuit of economic independence and self-sufficiency. Even if barbers did not own a shop, they were not typical wage workers who were expendable. The relationship between shop owners and employees reveals the interplay between the black business class and independent laborers. In essence, black workers did not have labor issues just in white-owned factories; they also had issues with their black bosses. Moreover, barbers established trusting relationships with their patrons that were specific to the barber not the shop. They performed a service for their patrons by making them look good for public presentation—a clean-shaven face and neatly trimmed hair. The power of their service production informed how barbers thought about their work. By paying attention to white patrons' consumer desires, black barbers understood the power and profit potential of customer service long before it became a central part of American business beginning in the 1880s.

At the same time, patrons sat in the barber's chair with the trust that their barbers would perform this service with great care and precision. In the black barber–white patron relationship of the nineteenth century, whites exercised their political power in the barber shop by dictating whom their barbers could shave. These power dynamics shifted in the twentieth century. With black customers, barbers wielded much more control over what happened inside their shops. Patrons ceded little deference to their barbers, but rather they sponsored them. Customers, in contrast, gave some deference to their barbers while also maintaining their own consumer power. White and black men constructed different meanings of what it meant to sit in the chair and get a shave or haircut from a black barber. This consumption side of shaving-time encompassed the multiple expectations patrons hoped to receive (a bolstered racial, class, or gendered identity). Travel revealed many of the consumer politics of barber shops. African Americans with means who traveled across the state or country, like Long Island Scribe, especially in the North, did not expect Jim Crow to follow. Barber shops are rather local places, but they do not exist outside of regional and national political landscapes. Whether close to home or miles away, black and white men considered commercial grooming a necessary part of their everyday lives. These layered interactions are critical in any discussion of the economy of barber shops.

While patrons submitted to their barbers, other men sat in a row of chairs, waiting their turn. As they waited, they read, talked, or played the numbers or chess. Traditionally, owners decided whether they would allow men to hang around without getting groomed, but the waiting public has always been central to the world of the barber shop. Thus, other figures populated the space: black newspapermen, numbers runners, and other petty entrepreneurs were there because they knew a group of idle people could be easily engaged. The waiting men also watched the barber shave his patron, which informed their impressions of the barber's skill and the larger barber-patron relationship. The wider public outside of the barber shop also formed impressions about what went on inside this space. What did black men think when they saw black barbers shaving white men in the nineteenth century? The grooming process organized these interactions, and shaving-time centers the grooming process within the relationships between men inside and outside of the shop. At different historical moments, barbers, patrons, and waiting publics jointly constructed and reconstructed black barber shops as businesses and public spaces through their racial, masculine, and economic exchanges.

A related theme of this book is the paradox of barbering as a service business. Specifically, black barber shops reveal the ambiguities of integration and commercial public spaces. Barbering was an occupation that assumed deference given the barber's dependence on the customers. Since the "product" was a service, black patrons held the sort of authority in the barber-patron relationship that was all too rare for them in other commercial exchanges. Blacks did not patronize black barber shops solely because they were shut out of white shops. Rather, they patronized black shops because they knew the barbers valued them as customers and understood black culture enough to produce their desired hairstyles. They also knew they could discuss racial politics with other black men. Ultimately, then, integration made little difference for the willing congregation that black barber shops fostered.

The public intimacy of commercial grooming defined the politics and economy of barbering, yet that intimacy depended on the selective privacy of bodily care and conversation among strangers. I argue that the public intimacy of grooming rendered barber shops private spaces in the public sphere, where the "hidden transcript" defined black barbers' entrepreneurial lives as political conduits among white patrons, and defined black patronized shops as spaces of economic, cultural, and political resistance outside of the purview of white society.[20] This is not to suggest that the world of black barbers and their shops should be read through the lens of oppression, or as essential private spaces where "infrapolitics"—the everyday acts of resistance that are outside the visible and public protests—can take shape. But rather racial autonomy and cultural practices and productions bound African Americans together in a collective that was neither a response to oppression nor prescriptively nationalist. Because black barbers owned their shops, they had the power to determine how their labors and their shops might be of service to black communities. Since these decisions were often mediated by market forces, the possibilities of collective action were not presupposed but were products of conscious political actors that produced both hidden and unhidden transcripts depending on the historical moment. Therefore, the labor of service work is a critical starting point for understanding the political engagement of barbers as entrepreneurs and their shops as public spaces. In this way, we can examine the historical paradox of why hundreds of black barbers shaved only white men in their shops and why many African Americans continue their weekend ritual, long after integration, of getting a haircut in a black barber shop on Saturday and worshiping the Lord in a black church on Sunday.

The barber's work of shaving men in public had much larger implications beyond the labor of removing stubble. Service work determined how people perceived the barbers' work. Barbers' act of shaving men represented a transformative act of grooming individual and collective identities. With the level of trust and public intimacy that existed in barber shops, black barbers were uniquely situated as conduits of racial politics. They overheard conversations about private and public matters and developed working relationships with their patrons and customers. Black barbers literally and figuratively had the ear of influential men. White patrons opposed sharing the barber shop or the barber's tools with black customers as equals. These were contested sites of social contact similar to swimming pools, which aroused whites' hysteria at the idea of being in the same pool with African Americans.[21] Therefore, whites, as shop patrons, demanded their consumer privacy that was defined by racism and segregation. Yet black consumers wanted their own racial privacy in barber shops, not because they wanted to exclude whites, but because they did not trust them. Because of this intimacy, barber shops stand apart from traditional debates about segregation and separation, which differentiates them from other spaces in the black public sphere. Black men sought out black barber shops because they wanted to willingly congregate with other black people out of the purview of white surveillance. Patrons and customers determined whom they wanted to bear witness to both their grooming and their conversations. At stake were alternative class formations and contested ideologies of race and manhood. The intimacy and exclusion within barber shops thus offer a more nuanced window into the rise and fall of Jim Crow America.

From the nineteenth through the twentieth centuries, black barber shops were spaces where men sought shaves and haircuts, made money and spent money, worked and rested, talked and listened, and defined (racially and economically) what it meant to be men. Black barbers occupied a tenuous position as they attempted to balance the social and political implications of forced segregation and willing congregation—in the shop and the city—with their own expectations of class mobility and autonomy.[22]

The expansive chronology and geography of this book opens a treasure trove of source material to reveal a historical narrative about the black service industry, black institutional life, and the pressures of individual and collective interests on equal rights campaigns. Autobiographies and manuscript papers from prominent nineteenth-century black barbers illuminate a rich and complex relationship between black barbers, their exclusively white patrons, and the black men, like Long Island Scribe, who were excluded from these shops as customers. Between 1870 and 1930, white barbers' competition for market share, their quest for labor and business reform, and black barbers' racial and business decisions to groom the black masses accounted for white and black visions of the modern barber shop in urban America. City directories point to the urban shift of black barber shops from downtown business districts to black neighborhoods. As these barbers catered to the growing black urban market in the early twentieth century, their shops emerged as central spaces where black men adjusted to the urban setting and caught their cultural bearings. Black newspapers and oral histories reveal the ways black barber shops functioned as businesses and public spaces in the urban North and South.

This book centers the grooming process to illuminate the work that race and deference did for service consumption in the public sphere. The act of shaving men, and cutting their hair, was more than a business transaction devoid of meaning. To understand how barbers groomed race, it is critical to centralize the functions of a service economy. The business and politics of deference—barbers' service to their patrons—undergirded the contests over black barbers' labors. The reciprocity of racial and gender production illustrates that patrons and waiting publics often drew their own competing meanings of the act of shaving and haircutting. In the nineteenth century, when black barbers shaved white men, the white men marked their barbers as inferior and unmanly servile workers. For barbers, deference made business sense, but it caused significant political ruptures within black communities. In other words, from the perspective of white patrons and African Americans who were excluded from black-owned shops, to shave white men meant to groom whiteness—how white men saw themselves in relation to blacks, but also how blacks saw themselves in relation to whites' perception of them. In the twentieth century, black barbers emphasized the artistry in their professional work to groom a respectable blackness. Similar to black educators, barbers envisioned their work to be in service to black communities.[23] Black patrons acted more like customers because they did not attempt to exercise the same power over their barbers as did white patrons. But hairstyles particular to black culture were no less contested. Barbers, patrons, and waiting publics thought differently about the act of shaving and haircutting, which reveals the complicated terrain of who actually did the work of grooming race.

To consider how race was inadvertently or purposefully groomed is to consider the production of racial ideologies. Race worked, or was reproduced, on three different levels inside of barber shops: biologically, socially, and culturally. Barber shops offered a number of services, but their primary service offerings were shaves and haircuts. Biologically, hair type varied between coarse, curly, and straight, each of which required different cutting methods. However, whites commonly marked coarse (or the commonly used term "kinky") hair as the inferior hair of black people. Socially, barbers associated race and hair type. Where barbers thought they could see race, they believed they knew the hair type. The race of the barber *and* patron determined how blacks and whites articulated race and hair type to exclude people from the shop. Culturally, patrons preferred the racial privacy of these spaces, where they could interact with other men of their same race and, in some cases, class. If race were a job, its division of labor operated on these three fronts simultaneously, demonstrating how race was produced and reproduced through service work and consumption.

Gender was inextricably bound with the process of grooming race. Gender worked "as a cultural process" through which men understood the act and business of barbering.[24] Production and consumption in the service economy informed how barbers, patrons, and waiting publics thought about manhood. In the nineteenth century, black communities had competing visions of manhood that were determined by class and race. White men feminized barbering because barbers had charge of one's personal presentation. By caring for and tending to the needs of other men, black barbers were grouped with other service workers, such as domestic workers. But it was not simply that barbering, or service work, was unmanly. Rather, it was the scores of slaves and free blacks who dominated the trade that made barbering unfit for a white man. Indeed, the labor movement to reform barbering drew on the gendered language of professionalization, skill, and exclusivity to make it more socially acceptable for white men. Black men who were not barbers feared that black barbers' continued racial dependence and service to white patrons would inform how whites thought about all African Americans. Barbers, however, countered these notions of their labor as subservient. They instead emphasized their skill, artistry, and "first-class" shops. Owning a barber shop and controlling their time brought them within the boundaries of nineteenth-century popular notions of republican independence and citizenship. This economic autonomy proved particularly critical during civil rights campaigns.

Discussions of gender in the nineteenth and twentieth centuries tend to focus on the linear shift from a producer to a consumer society.[25] This book argues that shift was not so linear. Barbers continued to base their manhood on the power of their production, yet they had to deal with their customers' ideas of manhood as consumers. In the twentieth century, the practice of "truth-telling" and "truth-stretching"—that is, of telling stories in the barber shop— determined the social production of manliness inside the barber shop's public sphere. As black men interacted with each other, they staked claims on their manhood by how well they held their own in verbal contests inside the shop. They attempted to establish authority in their conversations. Both truth-telling and truth-stretching fashioned a level of everyday authority. In the barber shop, a factory worker could be a philosopher, a postal worker could be a politician. The autonomy of the barber shop helped facilitate the production of authority.

This racially private space in a Jim Crow public gave black men refuge from the daily discrimination and humiliation they experienced.

Though the subjects in this book are principally men, the homosocial environment of barber shops has been overstated. Women have historically worked in barber shops as manicurists and barbers and, at certain times, entered as patrons. But even with the absence of women in many shops, men used feminine tropes to articulate the boundaries of manhood in the barber shop. Grooming race in the barber shop was indeed a masculine undertaking. Although black beauty shops have a much shorter history than barber shops, black beauticians did more to define the grooming industry. This book will draw on comparisons between the service-based work of barbers and the functioning of their shops along with the ways black beauticians leveraged a commodity-based industry to establish a beauty culture.

This book is framed chronologically and thematically, and is organized into two main parts. Part I examines barbering as a path toward personal and economic freedom, and the politics of black-owned barber shops as commercial spaces for white patrons between 1830 and 1920. Moving from slavery to freedom to Jim Crow, this section illuminates the tenuous position of black barbers as entrepreneurs subject to business relationships defined by paternalism in slave societies and patron-clientage in legally free yet segregated societies. It explores the ways in which slaves and free blacks perceived, capitalized on, and negotiated barbering in the antebellum North and South to gain more control of their time, to escape their master's surveillance, and to accumulate income and establish businesses. African Americans were not silent about barbers' racial policies. Black barbers' practice of shaving white men fueled a contentious debate within the black community about racial deference, manhood, and the kind of labor that befitted a free people.

After the Civil War, black barbers still shaved white men to gain better financial benefits, but their business decisions did not go unnoticed among black communities across the country. In the period between the end of the war and the turn of the century, black barbers carefully calibrated the social costs and the financial benefits of grooming exclusively the white elite. In particular, black barbers negotiated individual advancement and collective identity when black male communities called for "manly" resistance and white patrons called for deference. This was articulated in terms of the contested meanings of barber shops as private and public spaces in the struggles over the Civil Rights Act of 1875.

In addition, the first section of the book examines white barbers' attempt to professionalize, or modernize, the barbering trade and the resulting effect this had on black barbers. White immigrant and native white barbers, the organization of the barbers' union, technological innovations, and state regulations of barbers and barber shops all contributed to the displacement of black barbers from downtown business districts to black business districts.

Part II chronicles the transformation of black-owned barber shops into black commercial public spaces between 1890 and 1970. This process was tied to changes in black and white visions of the modern barber shop in urban America. Here, I focus on a new generation of African American barbers who envisioned a modern black barber shop that not only catered to black men, but also provided them a space to congregate. The Great Migration presented new opportunities in an expanding black urban marketplace, even as the Great Depression constrained consumers' disposable income. After World War II, barber shops were central sites in the larger goals of desegregating public places of accommodation. The movement to "desegregate" white-owned barber shops offers compelling evidence of the liberating functions of black shops and the underlying objectives of the freedom struggle. Drawing heavily on oral histories, I examine the ways in which barbers were active in the civil rights movement, and how men used barber shops to discuss racial politics and organize resistance campaigns. By looking at the changing hairstyles of the period, I also explore the business and cultural politics of hair as a method of understanding what barbers and patrons expected from the grooming process.

Throughout this book I employ "barber shop" as two words. In the nineteenth century, "barber shop" was the commonly used term. It signaled a commercial space where a craftsman or artisan did his work. While there are a very small number of early references to "barbershop," this one-word descriptor did not gain wide usage until the twentieth century. Today, "barbershop" dots the windows of most shops across the country. Except where I use a direct quotation, I will use "barber shop." While this might appear to be mere semantics, this decision reflects the larger aims of the book. Moving from the lexicon of "barbershop" to "barber shop" encourages us to bring the barber back into the shop. In other words, the iconography of the barbershop tends to centralize the conversations that take place there. This effort is by no means an attempt to minimize the consumerist framework of these spaces, but simply to reorder the language to put producers and consumers in conversation.

PART I

Barbering in Slavery and Freedom

CHAPTER 1

Barbering for Freedom in Antebellum America

IN his 1855 novella *Benito Cereno*, Herman Melville provides a vivid literary evocation of antebellum grooming. This tale about a revolt aboard the slave ship *San Dominick* is woven around the real-life American captain Amasa Delano's account of an actual 1805 event.[1] To heighten the symbolic meaning of the story, Melville changed the name of the ship from *The Tryal* to *San Dominick* in reference to the 1790s slave revolt in Saint Domingue. In the story, Delano boards the seemingly distressed Spanish slave ship to find a dejected and bewildered captain, Benito Cereno. After Delano leaves the ship and Cereno jumps after him, Delano learns that the slaves controlled the ship and Cereno the entire time. Moreover, Cereno's body servant, Babo, acts as the leader of the revolt.

In the figure of Babo, Melville presents the popular antebellum perceptions of loyal black servants and their potentially hidden agendas to strike against their owners. On the one hand, Babo is presented as the cheerful servant attending to his master. "There is something in the negro which, in a peculiar way, fits him for avocations about one's person," the narrator interjects. "Most negroes are natural valets and hair-dressers; taking to the comb and brush congenially as to the castanets, and flourishing them apparently with almost equal satisfaction. There is, too, a smooth tact about them in this employment, with a marvelous, noiseless, gliding briskness, not ungraceful in its way, singularly pleasing to behold, and still more so to be the manipulated subject of. And above all is the great gift of good-humor . . . a certain easy cheerfulness, harmonious in every glance and gesture; as though God had set the whole negro to some pleasant tune."[2] Babo feeds into the perception, but if Delano listened carefully, he would hear a more defiant tune. Amazed at Babo's "steady good conduct," Delano makes an offer in jest: "I would like to have your man myself—what will you take for him?" Babo objects that he would not part from "master" for any amount of money. This is an early sign that things are not what they seem. Babo plays the role of loyal servant to evoke the common perception of the paternal master-slave relationship. Yet, on the other hand, behind Babo's mask is the leader of the revolt who has forced Cereno to submit even though he can easily cry out to Delano.

Babo searches for a sharp razor to shave Cereno. Babo repeatedly strokes the razor "on the firm, smooth, oily skin of his open palm." He places the razor above Cereno's face as if to begin, but then suspends it inches from his throat while Babo's free hand dabbles "among the bubbling suds on the Spaniard's lank neck." Cereno shivers from fear at the sight of the sharp steel held at his throat. At this moment, Delano ponders this erratic behavior between master and servant. In Babo, he sees "a headsman," and in Cereno, a subject "at the block." The scene would have been familiar to northern and southern antebellum society: a black barber holding the razor to his white customer's neck. Delano acknowledges the "elephant" that white society refused to acknowledge—the unspeakable, though momentary, power that a razor-wielding black man held over his totally defenseless white customer. Cereno represents the white patrons who black barbers shave daily, while Delano represents the larger white public that views blacks as especially suited for service work. At this moment, however, Delano pictures a reversed role of power relations that are and are not what they appear. Eric Sundquist describes this scene as the figure of tautology where Babo slides into mastery and Cereno slides into dependency.[3] For Christopher Freeburg, Babo performs a "ruse of objectification" that reveals the failures of "absolute mastership."[4] This paradox creates a visual narrative for antebellum white society that calls into question the ideology of inferiority inherent in black service work in private and public spheres.

The revolutionary seed was never far from the surface. "Now, master," exclaims Babo as Cereno squirms in the chair, "You must not shake so, master. See, Don Amasa, master always shakes when I shave him. And yet master knows I never yet have drawn blood, though it's true, if master will shake so, I may some of these times." That time is not far off. Suddenly, Babo's razor draws blood from Cereno's throat. While the blood stains the white creamy lather under his throat, Babo, facing Benito with his back to Delano, pulls back the razor while still holding it up as the blood trickles down. Babo, "with a sort of half humorous sorrow," declares, "See, master—you shook so—here's Babo's first blood."

Benito Cereno reminded all slaveholders and the larger white antebellum public who relied on slave and free black service workers that, even if they had not drawn blood as Babo had, anger might be quietly brewing behind the "good-humored," "cheerful" slaves who cared for them. Thomas Wentworth Higginson, a Massachusetts minister and abolitionist, publically expressed these very concerns. "I have wondered in times past," he noted in an address to the American Anti-Slavery Society in 1858, "when I have been so weak-minded as to submit my chin to the razor of a coloured brother, as sharp steel grazed my skin, at the patience of the negro shaving the white man for many years, yet [keeping] the razor outside of the throat. We forget the heroes of San Domingo."[5] Even as Higginson advocated abolition, he recognized the simmering seeds of resentment and frustration. Melville's shaving scene captures the ambiguities between the appearance and reality of Babo's position in relation to Cereno and Delano, as well as other black barbers' positions vis-à-vis their white patrons and a larger white public.

While black barbers did not draw much blood from their customers, barbering between 1830 and 1865 opened much needed physical and economic mobility for both slaves and free blacks. Black barbers negotiated their position as captive capitalists in a slave society where their lives and livelihoods depended on shaving white men. Barbering symbolized both the possibilities and limits of freedom for African Americans in the antebellum period. Economically prosperous yet socially and politically marginalized, black barbers endured the stigma of servility to achieve a measure of independence. They capitalized on white patrons who imagined, and paid for, apparent servitude. But this perceived servitude was service in the minds of black barbers. The line between servitude and service informed the meanings of barbering as a trade and a business in antebellum America.

All black barbers were not owners, and all were not free. The antebellum black barber shop was a place where slaves and free blacks, capital and labor lived and worked together. As such, they all came to the barber shop for different reasons, but they all used their barbering skills and the shop as a route toward skilled work and freedom from slavery and wage dependency. African Americans worked as barbers and in other personal service occupations to gain more control of their time and livelihood. For slaves, becoming a barber was both a step away from the close supervision of the master and a step toward freedom. Barbers' entrepreneurial pursuits helped them acquire a modicum of wealth and attain social standing in black communities. They were actively involved in black politics and community life. In fact, because they worked among whites and lived among blacks, they were key conduits in abolitionist networks.

Despite barbers' work in assisting fugitive slaves and participating in local and national black political movements, black middle-class reformers could not overlook how barbers made their living. They encouraged black men to leave the service industry behind for more manly and respectable occupations such as industrial jobs. They viewed barbering for whites as signs of un-manly service work unfit for a free people in a free society. Black men's ideas of independence, manhood, and freedom were played out in their discourses on the respectability of barbering as a means of labor and entrepreneurship.

Black Barbers in a Slave Society

Antebellum slaves groomed men of the slave community and the master class. As early as the eighteenth century, slaves—untrained or trained barbers and hairdressers—spent Sunday morning grooming the hair and faces of fellow slaves in preparation for Sunday worship services. Worship services and holiday celebrations were about the only occasions when slaves could gather in leisure, and many slave owners monitored these activities as best they could. Therefore, the porch or yard outside the slave quarters served as their "barber shop" and "beauty shop." In March 1797, Benjamin Henry Latrobe, an architect who had emigrated from England and settled in Virginia the previous year, painted a scene he observed during his travels through Virginia of slaves tending to each other's hair on Sunday morning. Latrobe noted in his sketch book that once these men had completed the styling and shaving, they ended the "scene by mutually shaving and dressing each other."[6] It is possible that some slaves used their Saturday afternoon leisure time for grooming, along with other personal chores, before social gatherings later that evening; however, Sunday afforded much more time.[7]

These Sunday morning grooming rituals continued into the nineteenth century. In the early 1830s, Joseph Ingrham, a white New Englander traveling near Natchez, Mississippi, described slaves preparing for worship services as an example of a properly managed plantation. "No scene can be livelier or more interesting to a Northerner," he noted, "than that which the negro quarters of a well regulated plantation present, on a Sabbath morning, just before church hour. In every cabin the men are shaving and dressing—the

Figure 1. *Preparations for the Enjoyment of a Fine Sunday Evening.* 1797. Work on paper by Benjamin Henry Latrobe. Latrobe Sketchbooks/Museum Department. Image ID 1960.108.1.2.36, Courtesy of the Maryland Historical Society.

women, arrayed in their gay muslins, are arranging their frizzy hair, in which they take no little pride."[8] Where Ingrham witnessed signs of contentment, former slave James Williams of Alabama remembered discontent. "The only time the slaves had to comb their hair was on Sunday," he lamented. "They would comb and roll each other's hair and the men would cut each other's hair. That's all the time they got."[9] This time was not enough, especially considering the grueling work regimes they endured throughout the week. In this Sunday morning practice slaves groomed themselves as an act of control over their bodies and appearances.

Unfortunately, slave grooming practices were not limited to looking good for the Lord. Slave traders forced captives to be "dressed" for the slave auction to appear attractive for a master of a different sort. Former slave William Anderson recounted in his slave narrative the dressing process he witnessed while in a slave pen in Natchez, Mississippi. "The slaves are made to shave and wash in greasy pot liquor," he recalled, "to make them look sleek and nice; their heads must be combed, and their best clothes put on."[10] John Brown went through a similar process in a New Orleans pen when mulatto Bob Freeman "roused" the slaves in the morning to prepare for the day's auction.[11] Traders called on slaves who were not captives of the pen to groom the other slaves for sale. William Wells Brown first tried his hand at barbering when he was ordered to prepare "old slaves" in a New Orleans slave pen. Brown's owner ordered him to "shave off the old men's whiskers, and to pluck out the grey hairs where they were not too numerous; where they were, [I] coloured them with a preparation of blacking with a blacking brush. After having gone through the blacking process, they looked ten or fifteen years younger."[12] Considering Brown was not "well skilled in the use of scissors and razor," he believed he "performed the office of the barber tolerably." Brown blurred the line between the "tolerable" aspects of the barber's office. He referred to his inexperience as a barber and the decent job he performed with the scissors and razor. Yet the wrenching task of making slaves more attractive to be sold raised the stakes of what was "tolerable" for the barber's office, insofar as Brown made those on the auction block look younger and hence more valuable.[13]

Most slaves, however, picked up a razor in the service of their master's personal grooming and plantation economies. Barbers filled the ranks of skilled slaves who worked in various capacities and places throughout the South in the antebellum period. Enslaved men, as body servants to their owners, were charged with daily personal duties that included shaving. In a Works Progress Administration (WPA) interview in 1938, Bill Reese recounted his father's entry into barbering while a slave in Georgia. "As soon as he was big enough to be trained for a trade," Reese stated, "his master arranged for him to learn how to be a barber. High-class white folks liked to have their own barbers then and they wanted 'em well trained, and professional men like pa's owner liked to have at least one slave that could do what they called valet service now." As an apprentice, he learned all of the duties of operating a barber shop, such as "blacking" shoes, attending to customers, stropping razors, shaving, and cutting hair.[14]

Slaves who performed service work around the plantation did not generate income, but they were considered investment assets that could be hired out. Enslaved barbers who worked as personal servants could be shifted around in their masters' business plans to cover losses or generate new income. To leverage their skilled slaves and recover from slow economies, some owners moved these slaves to the field, but most hired them out for the extra money.[15] They either identified a shop and directly hired out their slaves, or allowed them to roam the city streets, find their own work, and hire themselves out. Enslaved boys, between ten and fifteen years old, worked as apprentices to free black barbers—and in some cases lived with them—for five to seven years, or until they reached the age of eighteen or twenty-one.[16] Isaac Throgmorton became a barber when he moved to Louisville, Kentucky. His owner was a peddler, and according to Throgmorton, "his servants were always out." "He put me at a trade with a free man and I lived with free people." Throgmorton served a seven-year apprenticeship before he "kept shop" for himself for two years, then "one year steamboating up the river."[17] Master and employer (or slave and employer in cases of self-hire) negotiated the terms of the contract, which included wages and length of service. On average, enslaved barbers in a city such as Natchez received $12 per month, and in New Orleans $20 per month.[18] After surrendering a portion to their masters, enslaved barbers saved or spent the remainder of their earnings.

Antebellum enslaved barbers were hired out to free blacks because the latter dominated the field. Barbering offered free blacks, in the South and North, employment in a high-demand industry with the potential to achieve economic independence. Free black barbers, journeymen and owners, in the antebellum southern economy worked either in downtown shops or on steamboats. Many seized the opportunity to become entrepreneurs in an industry void of white competition, with minimal startup costs and significant profit potential. Barbering lacked the kind of industry-specific labor organization that defined certain cities. Many slaves worked on the waterfront in port cities, like Charleston, South Carolina, for example. Barbering, though, was portable even if smaller towns and cities could accommodate fewer barbers than more populated areas. Free black workers in skilled trades faced the same labor restrictions as skilled slaves in urban areas. Blacks encountered strong opposition from white workers in skilled trades such as blacksmithing, carpentering, and caulking.[19] Barbering as a job classification—always ambiguous and politically and racially defined—regularly shifted among personal service, semiskilled, and skilled depending on one's position in the trade. These categories, however, were not mutually exclusive. Whether or not white workers wanted to admit it, barbering required skill. The average person could not shave with a straight razor without drawing blood. Barbering was one of the leading occupations for black men in the urban North, even though they did not have the same monopoly of the trade as their southern counterparts.

As white indentured servants moved steadily out of barbering after the American Revolution, the prevalence of black barbers reinforced the belief that barbering was unsuitable work for citizens.[20] But, if citizens shunned this service work, their identities were nevertheless groomed through its consumption. Having their wigs touched up was a moment when their gentility could be bolstered and they could remind themselves that, regardless of their station in life, they were not serving others. Only the fictions of republicanism could make this logic work: the financial remuneration from barbering made black barbers economically independent, yet the ties between citizenship and whiteness persisted. The eighteenth-century ideas linking barbering and blackness persisted into the nineteenth century and became stronger as slavery expanded westward.

The abundance of southern black men tending to white patrons informed opinions about barbering, service, and skill. In the nineteenth century, barbering and other service-related occupations had a stigma of servility in the South. As historian Ira Berlin argues, "The servile nature of the job drove away white competitors, while it encouraged the patronage of white customers who felt they should be served by blacks."[21] Where African Americans were relegated to certain occupations (personal and domestic service and manual labor), the occupation itself became racialized. As late as the early twentieth century, one historian observed, "A distinguished gentleman of Richmond, who in 1912 was eighty-four years of age, asserts that in all his life he never had a barber who was not colored to cut his hair or shave him."[22] Such long-standing southern traditions reinforced perceptions that blacks were made for barbering. The intimate service that barbers provided for their customers informed the social value and skill level whites attached to the trade. White barbers were rare fixtures in most southern cities until the late nineteenth century, leaving the trade almost exclusively to blacks.[23]

While the presence of black barbers was a familiar scene, white foreign travelers offered more detailed observations on the racial make-up of southern barber shops. When William Russell traveled throughout the Union and Confederacy from 1861 to 1862 as a war correspondent for the *Times* of London, he "descended into the barber's shop" in the Willard Hotel in Washington, D.C., one day to discover "all the operators [were] men of colour, mostly mulattoes, or yellow lads, good looking, dressed in clean white jackets and aprons, smart, quick, and attentive." He suggested that barbering appeared to be "the birthright of the free negro and coloured man" because they seemed skilled at their work.[24]

Russell's observation of the prevalence of mixed-race barbers points to the demographics of free black barbers. Barbers of mixed-race parentage stood out among the ranks of free black barbers because their white fathers were more likely to manumit them and help them establish themselves. In the early nineteenth century, skilled artisans and house servants were more likely to be manumitted. Richmond barber John Powell recalled that his antebellum boss, William Lyons, groomed his master, who was also his father. According to Powell, Lyons "got paid well for his work, soon was able to buy his freedom. And his father set him up in business."[25] The inconsistencies of racial classifications make it difficult to get an accurate count of the total numbers of dark- and light-skinned black barbers. For example, the 1850 U.S. census listed Reuben West, one of the leading black barbers in Richmond, Virginia, as a mulatto. However, the 1860 census listed West as black.[26] West was light skinned and one of the wealthiest barbers and businessmen in the state. The leading black barbers in the nineteenth century were of mixed race.

Barbers counted themselves as tradesmen and were part of the craft hierarchy that moved from apprentice, to journeyman, to master barber, to shop owner. Formerly enslaved, William Johnson learned barbering from his brother-in-law, James Miller, the "most widely patronized barber in Natchez, Mississippi." Johnson saved enough money to acquire a barber shop in 1828 in Port Gibson, Mississippi, fifty miles north of Natchez. He took in $1,094 in twenty-two months at this location by "Hair Cutting and Shaving alone." On October 14, 1830, Miller sold the unexpired portion of the lease on his Main Street shop to twenty-one-year-old Johnson for $300. In 1833, Johnson made a down payment of $1,375, half the purchase price, to acquire the building property and retired the note in less than two years. He charged 24 cents for haircuts and 12.5 cents per shave ($1.50 per month). In 1834, he erected a bathhouse at a cost of $170, charging 50 cents for a hot or cold bath. Most of his customers paid cash, but many secured credit.[27] Johnson made substantial improvements to his Main Street shop and expanded to new locations. The Main Street shop eventually contained six chairs, "two washstands, a coatrack and a hatrack [sic], a table and a desk, and two sofas, while the walls were ornamented by four mirrors and more than thirty framed pictures, including several horse-racing scenes." In the late 1830s and 1840s, he opened two small one-man barber shops: the "Natchez-under-the-Hill" shop and one located in the Tremont House, a small hotel around the corner from his shop on Main Street. Slaves or free black employees operated both shops. Johnson also traveled to customers' homes and businesses to perform barbering work. During his first three years in business, Johnson's expenses and income averaged $1,500 and $2,500, respectively.[28]

Johnson's successes may not be representative, but journeymen could move into the entrepreneurial class rather fluidly in barbering. When a steamboat captain cheated William Wells Brown out of his pay in the fall of 1835, Brown was forced to seek employment in nearby towns. While looking for work in Monroe, Michigan, between Detroit and Toledo along Lake Erie, he "passed the door of the only barber in the town, whose shop appeared to be filled with persons waiting to be shaved." Since there was only one barber in the shop, Brown figured he would draw on his barbering experience from shaving slaves at slave auctions and shaving white men on the steamer to earn money for the winter. The barber turned down Brown's persistent requests to work, even at low pay. Finally, a frustrated Brown threatened to open a nearby barber shop to compete with the barber. According to Brown, the barber showed no concern; after all, if Brown was looking for work, where would he find the money to open a shop? Moreover, as a newcomer to a small town, Brown would have a difficult time attracting customers. Brown reported that one day, as he was leaving the shop, "one of the men, who were waiting to be shaved," offered to help him set up a shop across the street and "promised to give me his influence." If this indeed was the only barber shop in town, with one barber, then perhaps this customer had waited too long, too often. Brown accepted the customer's offer to open his own shop.[29]

Brown became an entrepreneur by chance, but his move reflects the low barriers to entry to becoming a shop owner. He outfitted his small shop modestly, but he created an image—a "brand" in business terms—that was worth much more. "I . . . purchased an old table, two chairs, got a pole with a red stripe painted around it," he recalled, "and the next day opened." Brown did not mention it, but he, of course, would have needed such instruments as scissors, razors, towels, and shaving mugs—all inexpensive items. His most expensive piece of equipment was a sign over the door that read "Fashionable Hair-dresser from New York, Emperor of the West." He spread word that his competitor's shop "did not keep clean towels, that his razors were dull, and, above all, he never had been to New York to see the fashions." Brown failed to mention that he had not been to New York, either, and led his customers to believe that he was bringing big-city style to Monroe. According to Brown, he commanded the "entire business of the town," mostly white residents, in a matter of a few weeks.[30]

The structure of Brown's small-town barber shop was typical even among big-city shops, but the elite owners started with more elaborate equipment and extensive services. There were no fundamental differences in organization and location between northern and southern shops. Most black barbers opened their shops in or near commercial districts where businessmen and

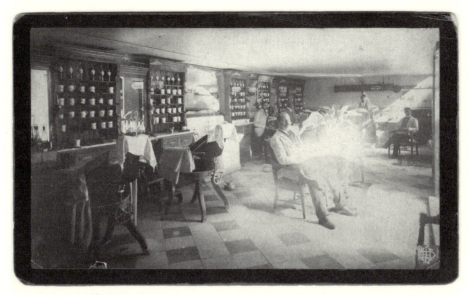

Figure 2. Barber shop with shaving mug racks, circa 1890. The shaving mug racks were standard in most barber shops in the 1800s. Meta Warrick Fuller Photograph Collection. Courtesy of the Photographs and Prints Division, Schomburg Center for Research in Black Culture, New York Public Library, Astor, Lenox and Tilden Foundations.

politicians moved about. They leased space in various office buildings and in leading hotels to attract middle-class visitors.[31] Lewis Woodson operated his shops in several Pittsburgh hotels, including the Anderson, the St. Charles, and the Monongahela House. Many residents considered the Monongahela House the finest hotel in the city and the region. Woodson joined John Vashon, John Peck, and Lemuel Googins as the leading black barber shop owners in the city.[32] Vashon opened his shop in 1833—which included a sign that read "Shaving, Hair Dressing, and Fancy Establishment"—inside a building on 59 Third Street, next door to his home. Located downtown, the shop served as a center of information among white male residents and travelers. The average barber shop was intimately structured to foster familiarity and trust among customers. Regular patrons could count on seeing their personal shaving mug on a rack. Barbers were assured of regular visits, and patrons grew accustomed to the personal attention.

    Barbers structured their shops to complement the business strategies of financiers who looked to accommodate their elite consumers' desires in luxury

hotels. These hotels employed what historian Molly Berger terms "technological luxury" to appeal to elite gentility.[33] A bathhouse was one such luxury
that the leading barbers incorporated in their service offerings. In the early
nineteenth century, few Americans bathed because of the scarcity of indoor
plumbing. Cities began to install public water and sewage systems based on
who could pay. Therefore, the wealthy received benefits of the system faster
than the general population. Yet indoor plumbing was still not widespread
even among the wealthy.[34] The public bath movement has its American origins in the 1840s when health reformers began emphasizing connections
between cleanliness and physical fitness. As the well-to-do became more accustomed to bathing, they used personal cleanliness as a mark of superiority
over the poor and working class. To be sure, bathhouses were not just for the
wealthy. In fact, urban reformers hoped to wash away the "moral depravity"
of the poor by convincing them to bathe more. While the most "elegant hotels
afforded their guests the pleasures of a bath," the middle and upper classes
could also avoid bathing with the lower classes by going to bathhouses attached to upscale commercial businesses such as barber shops.[35]

Barbers capitalized on the new technology and air of exclusiveness bathhouses brought to the public sphere. In 1833, Vashon opened the first public bathhouse west of the Alleghenies, on Third Street between Market and
Ferry Streets in Pittsburgh.[36] Men bathed on the lower level, while the upper
level was reserved for women. To maintain security and privacy for the upper
level, the entrances to each level were separate.[37] After several years, he made
major renovations and advertised its reopening:

CITY BATHS
The subscriber respectfully informs citizens of Pittsburgh, and
strangers visiting here, that his Warm, Cold, Shower Baths for
Ladies and Gentlemen . . . having undergone thorough repairs, and
being brilliantly illuminated with Gas Lights, are now open for the
season, every day, (Sunday excepted), from 6 o'clock, A.M. to 11:
o'clock, P.M. The subscriber feels grateful for the patronage so lib-
erally bestowed upon him by the public and will spare no pains to
merit a continuance of its favors.[38]

Vashon's barber shop and city bath were business and political clubs for the
city's white leadership.[39] In 1836, a Nashville barber, "Doctor Jack," advertised
his baths as a place where patrons could enjoy "the falling spray, the lucid

coolness [of] the flood." The bathhouse had separate facilities for women, staffed with female attendants.[40] William Johnson noticed that public baths were opening in various cities, so in 1834 he decided to open one of his own. While most of the bathing customers were men, who were probably also his barber shop patrons, he noted in 1840 that a "French lady" took a bath. The bathhouse was not profitable, but it offered patrons "relief from the heat and dust of the unpaved streets."[41] William Johnson's enormous success as a barber, like that of other black barbers, depended on the breadth of services he offered his patrons. St. Louis barbers Louis Clamorgan and Mr. Iredell highlighted the luxurious services of their shops. An 1845 advertisement noted their "Splendid Hair Cutting and Shaving Saloon" and a bathhouse with tubs of "the finest Italian marble, the rooms large, airy and elegantly furnished."[42] Barbers appealed to the sensibilities of their white clients to provide complete bodily grooming. These kinds of business decisions at once imagined barber shops as spaces to enjoy the serene landscape of bodily care and as places that provided multiple revenue streams for the owner.

Grooming the white public propelled many black barbers into the black middle class and elite, measured through wealth and status. Before the Civil War, black professionals, entrepreneurs, carpenters, tailors, waiters and cooks in ritzy hotels, and barbers made up the economic elite. Philadelphia's black elite intrigued white artists David Claypool Johnson, William Thackera, and Edward Clay enough that they created graphic racial caricatures of black society in public and private life. In the late 1820s, Clay produced a vicious series of colored prints entitled *Life in Philadelphia*. His lithograph series painted the black middle class as pretentious, uneducated, and on the brink of turning the city (with the help of white abolitionists) into an amalgamated society with interracial marriage and biracial children.[43] These and other prints portrayed whites' anxieties about black economic mobility at the time.

Anthony Imbert drew a wrapper illustration for the *Life in Philadelphia* series that depicted a well-dressed black barber prepared to shave a white customer. The barber, dressed in a fancy coat with an ornate collar, stands above his customer, who is dressed rather plainly, while his coat rests on a hanger labeled "plain body." The barber holds a razor, with "Magnum Don," which means "great gentleman," on the blade, thus making barbering the source of the class portrayal.[44] Imbert cast the barber in a pretentious image, or as a dandy, by dressing him in a fancy coat instead of his barber's smock or apron.[45] Most intriguing about this illustration are the particulars of shaving-time. The barber looks away from the customer, presumably at those looking

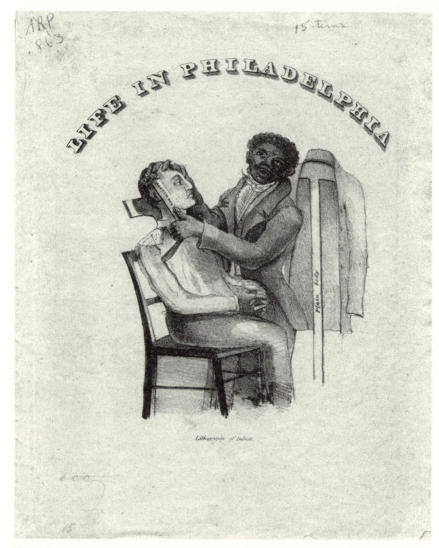

Figure 3. Anthony Imbert, wrapper illustration, *Life in Philadelphia* (1828), Bd 912 Iml 83. Courtesy of the Historical Society of Pennsylvania.

at him or the illustration, while he holds the razor on the side of the customer's lathered face. The customer looks rather relaxed, with a content face and folded hands.

Barbers composed a large segment of the southern black elite, in some cases because of their wealth, but in most cases because they had formed relationships with their prominent white patrons. In 1858, Cyprian Clamorgan published his survey of the St. Louis black elite in *The Colored Aristocracy of St. Louis*. For Clamorgan, the "colored aristocracy" referred to African Americans "who move in a certain circle; who, by means of wealth, education, or natural ability, form a peculiar class—the elite of the colored race." He particularly highlighted the large number of barbers in this group. "It will doubtless be observed by the reader," he noted, "that a majority of our colored aristocracy belong to the tonsorial profession; a mulatto takes to razor and soap as naturally as a young duck to a pool of water, or a strapped Frenchman to dancing; they certainly make the best barbers in the world, and were doubtless intended by nature for the art. In its exercise, they take white men by the nose without giving offense, and without causing an effusion of blood."[46] There was nothing "natural" about the predominance of mixed-race barbers in St. Louis or any other city. Barbers who catered to the white elite were indeed wealthy, but it is no surprise Clamorgan, a mixed-race barber himself, profiled a large number of barbers in his survey of the black elite. Nineteen of the thirty-two men profiled were barber shop owners or journeymen.[47] Clamorgan's book served as an advertisement of black barbers' capabilities as businessmen, but more particularly let customers know that they would not let the razor slip.

Not all black barbers were among the elite. In fact, a look at the shop level reveals a complicated interplay between owners and employees, slave and free. A precarious mix of free and enslaved black barbers attended to these bathhouses, opened and closed the shop, stropped the razors, and shaved customers. William Mundin, free born and of mixed race, served an apprenticeship with Reuben West alongside his slave apprentice in his Richmond barber shop.[48] Johnson had two free blacks working in his Natchez barber shops, far less than the five or six slaves he employed. He employed free black apprentices Wellington West and Washington Sterns, both of mixed race, to work intermittently in his shops. Johnson acted as employer and guardian to his slave and free apprentices. West and Sterns received an average of $25 per month, double the wages of slave apprentices. Occasionally, Johnson also gave his free apprentices food and clothing.[49]

Like most workers, free black apprentices wanted to improve their wages and well-being and took advantages of opportunities regardless of the race or goodwill of their employer. Free black barbers looking for more mobility, beyond the stationary downtown shop or traveling to customers' homes, found it on steamboats. Many slaves hiring their time as barbers, such as Isaac Throgmorton of New Orleans and Frank Parrish of Nashville, found work aboard steamboats, but according to historian Thomas Buchanan, free blacks made up most of the black workforce on the western rivers. Buchanan further suggests that only the larger boats commonly provided barbering services for their passengers. Barbers rented small shops at one end of the cabin, where they groomed passengers for fees and tips, unlike other steamboat workers, such as stewards, who were on the clerk's payroll. Steamboat barbering gave free black journeymen an opportunity to travel while maintaining their economic autonomy.[50]

When journeymen took to the river, they occasionally left inland shop owners in a bind. James Thomas understood the allure of barbering on steamboats because he had once been a steamboat barber for a year. As a shop owner in Nashville, he recalled, "In the antebellum times, when the large number of steamboats needed barbers, the shop keepers had hard work getting men to stick."[51] Farther south in Natchez, William Johnson agreed. On January 15, 1848, he recorded in his diary, "Bill Nix Commenced to run on the Steam Boat Princess as Barber." Over two years later, he noted, "My force at present in the shop is myself, Edd [sic] and Jim, for Jeff has left and taken the Shop on the S.B. *Natchez* and he is starting now for New Orleans."[52] In additional entries, Johnson noted that his free black barbers had left to work on a steamboat. In his diary, Johnson did not openly express disappointment or annoyance at his barbers for taking off, suggesting that free black journeymen had some level of independence and flexibility in their work schedules.

While free black employees might skip out on the shop for better opportunities, enslaved apprentices had to answer to an employer *and* a master. Although white masters left direct supervision of their slaves to black employers, masters, as absentee owners, maintained their power and paternalism in the master-slave relationship. Between 1835 and 1851, William Johnson hired about five apprentices. William Winston, John, Bill Nix, Steven, and Charles were slave apprentices in his shop for a number of years. On July 5, 1836, Johnson wrote that twelve-year-old "little William Winston came to stay with me to Le[a]rn the Barber trade." Winston's owner, Fountain Winston, provided in his will that Winston should be emancipated when he reached twenty-one years of age.[53] Johnson's slave apprentices regularly worked in his principal shop unsupervised. He allowed Charles to operate his "Natchez-under-the-Hill" shop, and Bill Nix to operate the one near Rodney, Mississippi. Major Young, the owner of one of Johnson's apprentices, informed Johnson that he wanted to help his slave set up a shop of his own. "I saw maj young this evening," Johnson wrote in his diary, "and he told me that he wanted to do something for charles and that he wished to give him a start in a shop to hisself. I told him very well, and he spoke of setting him free. And that if he did he thought it would be attended with some difficulty in regard to his coming back here again."[54] Young showed less concern with Charles becoming free than with his being forced to leave Mississippi. Young's benevolent aspirations guided his paternalistic guardianship for Charles's future. He entered the life of nominal freedom that many barbers knew all too well.

White masters, black employers, and the law determined the degrees of freedom slave barbers could enjoy. Matters of degree, however, are luxuries of distant historical analysis. Slave barbers in southern cities were "masterless" slaves, but they were nonetheless slaves. Ebenezer Allison "served his time in the barber's shop" in Richmond, Virginia. He was hired out from John Tilgham Foster, who, according to Ebenezer, was a kind master. His kindness, though, fell short of freedom, which for Ebenezer had no middle ground. "I had no right to leave him in the world," Foster reasoned, "but I loved freedom better than Slavery."[55] If living among freemen and earning wages was a privilege, having to relinquish a portion of their earnings and being sold to a more controlling owner reminded barbers they were not free. Isaac Throgmorton believed he lived a free life because he worked and lived among free blacks. "Only when he [his master] would send for me to come round," Throgmorton concluded, he would "let me know that I was not altogether free."[56] The moments when Isaac was called to "come round" were perhaps moments when his owner expected the agreed-on portion of Throgmorton's income. Being summoned and forfeiting a portion of the fruits of his labor represented critical aspects of Isaac's freedom. Barbering offered him the opportunity to live in relative freedom at least for intermittent periods of his life in the city. Quite simply, barbers similarly situated like Throgmorton wanted to be neither slaves on the plantation nor hired-out slaves living *relatively* free. Even as apprentices to free black barbers, there was no solace in their bondage in a "masterless" labor arrangement.

Free black employers did not just hire enslaved apprentices—some also acquired their own slaves. Free black barbers used their profits to purchase family members still in bondage. Since many southern states in the first half of the nineteenth century required freed slaves to leave the state within twelve months of their manumission, when free black barbers purchased relatives, they were registered as slaves instead of "freed." Richard C. Hobson, of Richmond, was emancipated in 1841. He used the profits from barbering to purchase his wife and son, but did not manumit them until 1850, when the court allowed them all to remain in Virginia.[57] Black barbers were among a contingent of free black slave owners who did not emancipate relatives they purchased because of state removal laws, and purchased slaves to work in their businesses.

Black slave owners purchased slaves for both benevolent and commercial reasons. Directing their skills toward urban consumers, free black entrepreneurs faced a limited labor supply. White workers generally refused to work for free blacks, while free black artisans had other opportunities.[58] Thus, black barbers addressed a glaring concern of a small labor supply by tapping the one large supply that existed in the nineteenth century: slave labor. The prosperity of black artisans allowed them to invest in human chattel, train them in the skills of their trade, and further increase the profits of their businesses.[59] In most cases, the slaves who worked in black barber shops were more than likely hiring their time. Black slave owners who were barbers owned between one and five slaves. Their slaves either apprenticed in their barber shops, were house servants, or both. Between 1840 and 1860, the six leading black barbers in Richmond owned one or two slaves.[60] During the 1850s, Reuben West owned a house servant who he later sold because of her "spirit of insubordination." James H. Hill, a contemporary of West's, asserted that West "owned two slaves, and that one of them was a mulatto barber" in his four-chair barber shop on Main Street.[61]

The labor relationships between black owners and enslaved hired-out workers, however, were not as fluid as those between owners and free employees. The master-slave relationship between free black barbers and their enslaved apprentices cannot be compared with the relationship between white masters and slaves. Even though black barbers held limited boundaries around their apprentices, they were still legally bound for a period of time, and they clearly understood they were not free. William Johnson fed and clothed his enslaved apprentices, provided for their education, and allowed them space to enjoy leisure activities with or without his free apprentices. They received passes to attend the theater, the circus, and parties given by local servants.[62] But, Johnson monitored their leisure activities. He outspokenly disapproved of their "ungentlemanly" behavior at every turn.

Johnson's experience reveals that the tension between black masters and black apprentices was less about labor than about leisure. In his diary, Johnson recorded his disappointments in some of his apprentices' behavior. Beyond the daily record, he disciplined them with beatings when they were too leisurely, quarreled, or engaged in coarse public behavior. On December 17, 1835, Johnson wrote in his diary, "William & John & Bill Nix staid out untill ½ 10 O'clock at night. When the[y] came they knocked so Loud at the Door and made so much noise that I came Out with my stick and pounded both of the Williams and J. John ran Out of the Yard and was caught by the Patroll, Mr. McConnell and Reynolds. I made Mr. McConnell give him 12 or 15 Lashes with his Jacket off." When John ran out of Johnson's yard, he ran into the public sphere of the institution of slavery. Johnson drew on the services of the state—making the patrol whip John—to signal that he could manage his slaves. On another occasion five years later, John and Winston went hunting by the lake, and Johnson "wrode up thare and caught both of them and gave them both a flogging and took away their guns—I threw away winston's as far as I could in the Mississippi [River]."[63] To be sure, most slaves did not carry guns. The mere sight would have sent the entire planter class into immediate hysteria, which explains why Johnson did not wait for them to return. But again, Johnson was likely more concerned about what white citizens of Natchez would think about allowing his slaves to have access to weapons of rebellion, even if used only for leisure.[64] If we read Johnson's diary against the grain—read the experiences of his barbering apprentices through his words—we get a more complicated narrative of how African American men barbered for freedom.

Johnson suggested in his diary that of all his enslaved apprentices, Steven gave him the most grief. Steven resisted Johnson's rules and control at almost every turn. He drank heavily and ran away often. The tension between Johnson and Steven began seven weeks after Steven entered an apprenticeship with him on January 2, 1836. "I had to Beat Steven this morning," Johnson recorded on February 23, "for taking the shop key away and was not ready to open the Shop."[65] Steven had the freedom to take the key and open the shop without supervision. Therefore, his infraction was not taking the key, but opening late. Perhaps this was Steven's form of resistance, a kind of work slowdown. If this was an offense that warranted a beating, Johnson wanted to make a point to Steven (and his other apprentices) about what was acceptable behavior. Johnson did not write about Steven opening the shop late again, but there were numerous entries about Steven's drinking activities during his leisure time.

From August 1840 to January 1844, Steven got drunk and ran away so often that Johnson mentioned his actions almost nonchalantly. Less than one month before Johnson began noting Steven's propensity to drink, he released a free black employee because "to be drunk ½ of his time would never suit me nor my customers."[66] Perhaps this made Johnson more attentive to the drinking habits of his other employees. His entries concerning Steven were as follows:

> August 10, 1840: "steven was twice whipped for being drunk. He ranaway."
> September 12, 1841: "hired steven out to mr. Gregory to haul wood in the swamp. Apparently he ran away, and stole a watch. Was whipped and sent back to Gregory."
> October 1, 1842: "steven ran off again."
> January 26, 1843: "steven ran away after getting drunk. I will astonish him some of these days if he is not Careful."
> August 14, 1843: "steven ranaway yesterday and was brot home to day by bill nix. I gave him a floging and let him go—no, I mistake, it was today that he ranaway."
> August 24, 1843: "I came very near cetching steven to night. He was in the stable ajoin[in]g mine but he jumped out and ran into the weeds somewhere."

Steven disappeared so frequently that Johnson had a hard time keeping track. On December 19, 1843, Johnson finally grew tired and frustrated at not being able to control Steven and contemplated selling him. "Steven is drunk to day and is on the town but I herd [sic] of him around at Mr. Brovert butlers and I sent around there and had him brought home and I have him now up in the garret fast and I will sell him if I can get six hundred dollars for him, I was offered 550 to day for him but would not take it. He must go for he will drink."[67] Although Johnson was clearly upset that Steven constantly ran away, he was more upset that Steven drank so often, and did so in public. Four years later, Johnson explicitly cited Steven's love for liquor as the principal reason he sold him. On January 1, 1844, he sold Steven to "the overseer of Young & Cannon" for $600. Johnson "felt hurt" because he "would not have parted with him if he had only have let liquor alone."[68] Johnson tolerated Steven's drinking for so many years because selling him was more complicated than releasing his free black barber.

Johnson's admonishments, then, reflected his concern about how his white customers and other white citizens in Natchez would perceive him based on his employees' public drunkenness. Steven did not need a drink to run away. Although Johnson characterized Steven's absences by writing "he ranaway," it is quite possible he did not run away as often as Johnson asserted, but that he simply refused to seek permission for his leisure time. Johnson's business was guided by a paternal, hierarchical relationship. White men wanted their black barbers to be submissive and deferential, and in return, black barbers would receive patronage and protection. Johnson acquiesced to this role and sought to teach his employees the mechanics of barbering and the necessary submissiveness that accompanied it. Steven clearly did not fit this mode. A group of barbers like Steven would transform the deferential model that white men expected.

Yet, Johnson was not entirely deferential himself. In fact, whites in Natchez accorded him a little respect. Johnson owned land and hunted. He was a horseman and marksman. Most strikingly, he gambled at the racehorse track and lent money to the city's white agricultural and business community. Socially, he enjoyed the outdoors; economically, he enjoyed making money. His diary is replete with accounting of loans issued, interest charged, and repayment terms. While it was common for black barbers to pose enough wealth to be lenders, it was uncommon for whites to respect them enough to enter into and honor such loan contracts. Nonetheless, Johnson was excluded from various areas of Natchez society. For example, he could not vote or sit next to white men at public gatherings. As his biographers suggest, "He was a part of the community and yet not a part of it."[69] Most importantly for Johnson, he stayed abreast of anything that could cost him money. Steven's drunkenness could do just that. Johnson's penchant for money is most vivid in two rather mundane diary entries the first week of October 1841. Just five days into October he noted, "Business is remarkable dull for this month." Four days later he penned a similar statement but added that he "Could not Collect any money from Any One."[70] Johnson paid attention to his money, and did not want his unsupervised slave and free apprentices contributing to "dull weeks."

Throughout the antebellum period, municipalities explored various regulations to control "unsupervised" slaves with considerable mobility like Steven. The restrictions on black labor, slave or free, tied access to skilled trades with a greater propensity for urban mobility. In 1822, the Savannah city council prohibited any black person from being apprenticed "to the trade of Carpenter, Mason, Bricklayer, Barber or any other Mechanical Art or Mystery."[71] According to Brenda Buchanan, "Mechanical Art and Mystery" referred to a craft leading to perfection of workmanship.[72] The ordinance sought to prohibit African Americans from learning skilled trades to decrease the likelihood of job competition, but also to limit slaves' mobility.

Some authorities realized they could not control the rising tide of skilled slaves navigating the city without supervision. In 1856, councilmen in Mobile, Alabama, proposed an ordinance to allow slaves to operate their own barber shops only if their owner paid a $10 annual fee. The proposed ordinance required slaves to receive twenty lashes if they operated barber shops without permission from their owners.[73] These ordinances attempted to reconcile the varied expectations of the different stakeholders in the institution of slavery. Slaveholders looked to maximize their income, and hiring out slaves could serve those purposes. Even though local governments could not control this practice, many urban dwellers remained ambivalent about it. In 1859, the *New Orleans Picayune* complained about the slave hiring-out system: "A species of quasi freedom has been granted by many masters to their slaves. They have been permitted to hire their own time, and with nominal protection of their masters, though with none of the oversight, to engage in business on their own account, to live according to their own fancy, to be idle or industrious . . . provided only the monthly wages are regularly gained."[74] As long as masters stood to profit from hiring out, city councils proved ineffective in stemming the tide of slaves roaming the city.

Enslaved barbers in the city capitalized on the white networks they developed during the course of their labors. They often entered legal arrangements with third-party white benefactors to prevent being sold to a less lenient master. The benefactor would legally own the slave, but the slave was allowed to live on his or her own or to purchase his or her freedom. This was the case with Frank Parrish, a mixed-race slave in Davidson County, Tennessee. When his master died, Frank, along with other property, was left in the care of his master's widow. Mrs. Parrish allowed Frank to hire out his time in Nashville, where he lived with four free blacks on South Cherry Street. Frank supported himself as a barber on steamboats and eventually opened a barber shop and bathhouse. Despite numerous successful years as a barber, at the age of forty-five Frank was still a slave. Upon the death of Mrs. Parrish, Frank was transferred to her heirs. This time, however, he did not leave his life to chance. To prevent his own sale at an estate liquidation, Frank asked for and received an agreement from his white benefactor, Edwin H. Ewing, to purchase him. No one else bid against Ewing, who, in 1853, allowed Frank to purchase his freedom.[75]

Frank trained another quasi-independent slave barber in Nashville, James P. Thomas. Thomas, also a mixed-race slave, was born in 1827 to Sally Thomas and Judge John Catron, chief justice of the Tennessee Supreme Court and later a U.S. Supreme Court justice. When Sally's owner died in 1834, she sought financial assistance from a white lawyer, Ephraim Foster, to purchase James's freedom out of fear that he might be sold. Foster lent her $50 to purchase James's freedom, but since he did not leave the state as the law required, he legally remained a slave and Foster remained his owner. Circa 1841, he hired out as an apprentice barber with Frank Parrish. In 1846, he opened a barber shop in his childhood home on the corner of Cherry and Deaderick Streets, where his mother still ran a clothes-cleaning shop. The shop was centrally located near the market square, banks, and the courthouse. His customers included businessman E. S. "Squire" Hall, preacher William G. Brownlow, former governor William Carroll, plantation owner William Giles Harding, and Davidson County lawyer Francis Fogg. James asked his owner to petition for his freedom, which he successfully did.[76] By the 1850s, southern attitudes and legal manumission codes had changed, increasingly closing off this avenue of freedom, particularly in the lower South.[77]

As the changing landscape of antebellum slavery altered the world of slaves, the world of free blacks also underwent dramatic shocks as they confronted state laws that required former slaves to leave the state after gaining their freedom. James Thomas lived several years operating a barber shop relatively free, though legally enslaved. Thomas could have arranged for his freedom before he actually did, but he would have come up against the Tennessee law that required freed blacks to leave the state. He enlisted his white benefactor, who was also a customer at his barber shop, to petition for his freedom and challenge the state law. The state granted Thomas's petition, which made him the first black person in the county to gain both freedom and residency.[78] Slave barbers like Thomas, who had established successful barber shops or had family members in the state, wanted to remain in the state after they were freed. Virginia, too, required emancipated slaves to leave the state within twelve months after gaining their freedom. This law prohibited free blacks from acquiring slaves, except slave spouses, parents, or slaves who were inherited. Later, free blacks could acquire any slave except descendants.[79] North Carolina denied freed blacks permission to enter the state. Southern legislatures enacted these laws in fear that free blacks might conspire to incite slave revolts or otherwise become indigents to the local economy.

Like Thomas, other black barbers in the lower and upper South petitioned the state legislature to remain in the state after they were freed to maintain business dealings and stay close to family members. In 1829, Natchez barber William Hayden petitioned the Mississippi legislature to maintain his residency after he gained his freedom. The 1822 act required him to leave the state, which he argued would "produce absolute ruin" to his business. He contended that he had "a good reputation, and own[ed] property" and therefore should be exempt from the state law. Similarly in 1837, Harrison Minton petitioned to remain in Virginia because he "[was] a barber and able to sustain" himself; in addition, his friends and family were currently enslaved in the state.[80] Petitioners usually referenced their industriousness, business acumen, honesty, and family ties in these appeals. In many ways, white citizens were motivated to keep free black service workers in the state to stabilize the service industry.[81] In 1852, Charles H. Reynolds complained to a justice of the peace that Joseph Rollins and the other barbers in his shop resided illegally in Louisiana. Rollins was a free black barber who operated a shop in the basement of the Planters' Hotel in New Orleans. The *Daily Picayune* reported, "Yesterday the well known Goins, Parsons, and five other barbers, all f.m.c. [free men of color], who have for years past smoothed the chins and curled the hair of thousands of our citizens, were brought before Recorder Caldwell, on the charge of being in the State in contravention of the law. Several of these men have been so long in this city, and have for many years kept such famous barbershops, that their arrest [resulted in] quite an excitement."[82] There is no evidence to suggest they were prosecuted.

If a barber's reputation could prove beneficial, his income could further his pursuit of freedom. On November 22, 1833, Joseph Hostler, a barber in Fayetteville, North Carolina, petitioned the state legislature that his late owner, David Smith, allowed him to purchase his freedom. Hostler reported that he paid his owner $96 per year from his earnings while he hired out his time over four years. In total, he paid his owner and his owner's estate $500.[83] The legislature granted Hostler his freedom. Slave owners, however, were notorious for reneging on verbal agreements. That Hostler had to petition at all suggests Smith's estate would not honor the purchase agreement. In the 1850s, Bird Williams allowed his slave James Maguire of Louisiana to hire out as a barber and hairdresser. Maguire received $20 per month, which allowed him to purchase his freedom for $850. After the purchase price was paid, but before he was legally manumitted, Williams died. With no record of the transaction, the firm Harral & Gill acquired Maguire and Williams's other property. Maguire lived with Mr. Harral and served as his personal barber. Mrs. Harral also had Maguire dress her hair regularly, but she preferred he perform his barbering duties in her "bed chamber" after Mr. Harral left for work. When Maguire refused directives, she threatened to "sell him onto a cotton plantation." He did not wait to see if she was bluffing. He fled.[84] Maguire was clearly concerned about being sold onto a plantation, but he was also afraid the appearances of grooming his mistress in her bedroom would lead to his death, which was not the kind of freedom he had in mind.

Self-hired enslaved barbers escaped if their relatively benign experience was altered through sale or the whims of their masters' relatives. Hiring out allowed enslaved barbers to live and work in cities among freemen and away from the master's gaze, which gave them the resources and the space to escape at will. Lewis Francis hired his time as a barber in Abingdon, Maryland. Each month he relinquished $8 from his earnings to his mistress, Mrs. Delinas. Yet she did not believe she was reaping enough from his labor, so she threatened to sell him. Francis did not take this threat lightly and escaped to Philadelphia.[85] Another slave, Richard Eden, hired out his time as a barber in Wilmington, North Carolina. He paid his mistress, widower Mary Loren, $12.50 per month and paid an additional twenty-five cents per month as a head tax to the state. Eden became quite vulnerable, though, when he married a free black woman, an "offense" for which he could have gotten thirty-nine lashes. Afraid he might be sold or that his mistress might renege on the purchase agreement, he and another slave talked of finding the Underground Railroad and made arrangements with the captain of a schooner headed for Philadelphia to stow away. The Philadelphia Vigilance Committee assisted them in getting to Canada, where Eden planned to open a barber shop.[86]

In many cases, enslaved barbers had known life beyond the direct control of their owners, and they seized every opportunity to realize complete freedom. Isaac Throgmorton revealed that he ran away because he had lived virtually free and had no intention of living otherwise. He stated in an interview:

> I will tell you the reason why I ran away. I had one or two reasons. In the first place, as I had been raised a barber and among freemen, it always seemed to me that I was free; but when I was turned over to another man, who kept close round, I saw I was not a freeman; that all the privileges were taken from me, that I had when I was working with freemen. Then, when I was moved from Kentucky to Louisiana, I saw so many cruelties that it sickened my heart, and notwithstanding I was treated well, there was no comfort for me. Then, secondly, although my master treated me well enough, when he got married, his wife and all her kin considered that I had been treated to[o] well, and I knew directly that his head was laid low I would be done forever. I came here in 1853. I had no particular

trouble in getting away. This man just wanted me to shave him and travel round with him. . . . Well, he came up to Kentucky to spend his summers, and he brought me there, and I saw it was a good chance.[87]

There were a small number of barber shops in most cities, but some white travelers preferred the convenience of having a personal barber to waiting in a shop. To meet these needs, enslaved barbers such as Isaac regularly accompanied their masters or white patrons in their travels to tend to their grooming needs. These travels presented them with numerous opportunities to escape. As a barber, Throgmorton was accustomed to the "privileges" of living with freemen, which proved to be an important vehicle in escaping white surveillance and eventually slavery altogether. For him, this lack of surveillance partly defined his level of freedom.[88] Throgmorton's journey to Louisiana proved to be his impetus and springboard to freedom. He disguised himself as a fisherman to escape, and ultimately made it to Canada.

While Throgmorton's southern travels as a barber opened space for him to escape slavery, northern black barbers who traveled south, particularly on steamboats, ran the risk of being accused of being runaways. Barber George Stewart could attest to the experiences of free black barbers who were under constant threat of being labeled fugitives, kidnapped, and sold into slavery. In the spring of 1837, while traveling on the Mississippi River, he was accused of being a fugitive slave and arrested in Baton Rouge, Louisiana. After nearly a year, William Huston, a "Licensed Intelligence" officer in New York City, submitted an affidavit confirming that Stewart was born in New York "of free parents." It is unknown if Huston was a former customer of Stewart's or if one of his customers enlisted Huston's help on Stewart's behalf, but this detail probably mattered little to Stewart.[89] Nineteenth-century law operated under the assumption that if accused, a black person was a fugitive until proven free. The testimony or legal assistance of whites was often critical in such cases.[90] Therefore, free black barbers cultivated relationships with their patrons, not just because it made good business sense, but also for their own protection. Even the most prominent barbers, butchers, caterers, and carpenters understood the importance of maintaining cordial relations with their white customers.

Huston vouched for Stewart, but there were scores of fugitive barbers who had to pass as free. They targeted areas with free black populations in the upper South and the North to achieve anonymity and obtain assistance from relatives and sympathizers. Since there were fewer free persons of color in the lower South, fugitives had less space to be anonymous. In the upper South, skilled and literate slaves had a good chance of posing as self-hired slaves or free blacks. Like other skilled and literate fugitive slaves, barbers also employed the method of passing as free by donning fanciful clothing and forging freedom papers.[91] It was a bold move indeed for fugitive slaves to escape slavery and earn a living shaving white men. But blending into free black barbering communities under the auspices of anonymity meant negotiating both the urban slave economy and the unequal relationships with white patrons. The presence of self-hired slaves allowed fugitives to seek apprenticeships with free blacks, and the profession of barbering was no exception. Whether posing as a slave hiring his own time or as a free person of color, what did it mean to pass as free by passing as a barber? Runaway mulatto slaves attempted to pass as white to lessen the chances of being challenged. Literate runaways forged freedom papers to pass as free persons of color because it was illegal in most states to teach slaves to read or write. Although most black shop owners were mixed race, to pass as a free black barber had less to do with education and color. Rather, runaways needed to don the mask of the deferential black barber. Generally, if they maintained good relationships with white patrons, they had a better chance of gaining their protection.

While being able to reach out to white benefactors could be useful, black barbers and the larger slave community had sharper and more reliable resources at their fingertips. In fact, when it came to running for freedom, everyone could be a barber where the razor and the shop facilitated critical instruments and spaces for protection. Enslaved barbers exercised their urban mobility and freedom from surveillance in the city, but neither urban nor rural slaves needed to be barbers to carry or use a razor. Slaves shaved themselves in the slave quarters and their urban environments, making razors readily available grooming instruments or weapons. When Charles Rodgers set out to escape from his master Elijah J. Johnson of Baltimore County, Maryland, his weapon of choice for protection was a "heavy, leaden ball and a razor."[92] It is unknown if Charles was a barber, but if he had to use the razor, lather and professional skill would have been unnecessary. William Grose also understood the dangerous journey ahead when he planned to leave his condition as a house servant in New Orleans. "I can't die but once," he reasoned, "if they catch me, they can but kill me: I'll defend myself as far as I can." Grose armed himself with an "old razor."[93] If blacks could use the razor to earn money, cultivate white networks, or cut a slave catcher, the barber shop served similar purposes.

Free black barbers did not strike white patrons who sat defenseless in the barber's chair, but these patrons were mistaken if they believed their power over their barbers was absolute. Despite the specter of redress from white patrons, free black barbers reached out to the slave and fugitive community, if not by day, then by night. John Brown escaped from slavery in search of freedom, which for him meant England. On his journey, he arrived in Paducah, Kentucky, "when few people were about," and specifically searched for a barber shop for refuge. "In the United States, the barbers are generally coloured men," he wrote in his published narrative, "and I concluded I should be in safer hands with one of my own race." After "peeping in at doors and windows," Brown saw a black man inside of a barber shop. The man opened the door for Brown, but immediately locked it behind him upon entering. He took this caution not only for Brown's safety but also for his own. He sensed Brown was a runaway and vowed to help him keep moving. According to Brown, the barber warned, "You mustn't stop here: it would be dangerous for both of us. You can sleep here to-night, however, and I will try to get you away in the morning. But if you were seen, and it were found out I was helping you off, it would break me up." Despite the risks, the barber gave Brown food, a place to sleep, and, after making inquiries, provided him with information on a steamer leaving for New Orleans the next day.[94] He did not realize England was the opposite direction. Nonetheless, when Brown recounted these events in his narrative, he did not identify the barber or the shop. This kind of assistance extended to the seas as well. Free black barbers along with other black men who worked on steamboats drew on their extensive networks in various river towns to act as conduits of information and assist fugitives. For instance, free black barber Shelton Morris coordinated escapes while he worked on an Ohio River steamboat.[95]

After slaves escaped to the North, they realized that the road to freedom would be neither smooth nor solitary. It required the help of many people at every turn. Free black barbers were active in the abolitionist movement as organizers and participants in sheltering fugitives in cities such as Philadelphia, Boston, New York, and Cincinnati. The political leanings of black barbers active in the abolitionist movement varied as much as the larger movement itself. In the 1820s, William Lloyd Garrison found strong supporters among black barbers. When James Forten learned that Garrison had established an abolitionist newspaper, the *Liberator*, he wrote Garrison to express support and suggested that Joseph Cassey would be a formidable agent in obtaining "many Subscribers." Cassey was a barber and the first *Liberator* agent in Philadelphia. Garrison acknowledged Cassey's early support in helping get the paper off the ground, noting "if not for [Cassey's] zeal, fidelity, and promptness with which he executed his trust, the *Liberator* could not have completed its first [year]."[96] Barbers were key agents for Garrison's paper. John Burr joined Cassey in distributing the paper in Philadelphia. It is likely they were not the only two of approximately sixty-two black shop owners to assist Garrison.[97] In the Northeast, Alfred Niger distributed the paper in Providence, Rhode Island, and Garrison had a host of barbers to share his abolitionist paper in Boston. Barbers were key individuals to distribute the newspaper because they came in contact with a number of people in their shops and in other networks of their lives.

Beyond distributing newspapers, many of the prominent barbers of the antebellum period worked actively with abolitionist societies and lent their shop space to the freedom struggle. In the 1830s, the abolitionist movement entered its radical phase where white abolitionists began shifting their position from gradual and compensated emancipation to immediate abolition.[98] Black barbers demonstrated they were far from mere bystanders in this more aggressive movement. The vigilance committees established in New York in 1835, in Philadelphia in 1837, and in Boston in 1846 operated openly to assist free persons of color and runaways. Some barbers actively assisted in such committees and organizations. For example, in 1833, John Vashon helped establish the Anti-Slavery Society of Pittsburgh.[99] Far more barbers, however, used their shops as spaces for the abolitionist struggle.[100] Shortly after Lewis Woodson arrived in Pittsburgh in 1815, he helped establish the Bethel A.M.E. Church on the corner of Water and Smithfield Streets—the first black church west of the Allegheny Mountains. Fugitives passing through Pittsburgh found refuge in the church and among its members.[101] Moreover, when slave owners traveled to Pittsburgh, they often stayed downtown at the Monongahela House and the Merchants' Hotel at the corner of Third and Smithfield Streets. Those traveling with their slaves unknowingly faced a very organized network of black service workers. Black workers in these hotels shuttled these slaves, who were looking to escape, from the hotel around the corner to Vashon's City Baths or John Peck's Oyster House. From here, they were sent north on one of the escape routes.[102] This kind of assistance was not limited to big cities. Fugitives who made their way through Sandusky, Ohio, between Cleveland and Toledo, found barber shop owner Grant Richie very active among the town's one hundred black residents to assist them on their journey to freedom.[103]

Many barbers, perhaps, calculated their level of involvement based on their customer base or the likelihood of economic reprisals. Northern barbers had three potential sets of customers: the small black male community and white male abolitionists who supported black equality and those who opposed it. Peter Howard's shop attracted black and white abolitionists, providing him more freedom to use his shop as a vessel to openly discuss the abolitionist movement and house fugitives. Other barbers risked the disapproval and loss of white patronage in their shops for aiding the Underground Railroad and vigilance committees. A majority of the participants were skilled and professional workers such as tailors, oyster dealers, carpenters, merchants, dentists, druggists, and ministers.[104] They exercised a little economic independence in their work day, and some of them owned spaces, such as barber shops and churches, conducive to housing or shuttling people through the city. Yet clergymen, judges, and professors faced economic reprisals from those in power who disagreed with abolitionism.[105] To be sure, unskilled workers were equally active in the movement by opening their homes and passing along information. Beyond the community of abolitionists in barber shops or the potential reprisals some barbers faced, the other segment of potential patrons included slave catchers and slave owners who traveled north in search of their "property" and took a minute to get shaved or simply search for information. The entire black and abolitionist community needed to work together, especially when the federal government tightened fugitive slave laws.

When Congress passed the Fugitive Slave Law in 1850, southern slaveholders received federal support to recover their property, forcing some blacks to flee and others to stand strong. Unlike the Fugitive Slave Act of 1793, the new law subjected law-enforcement officials to a $1,000 fine if they refused to arrest a runaway slave, and any citizen who aided a runaway slave was also liable for a $1,000 fine and six months in prison. Slave owners needed only to provide an affidavit as evidence, while the alleged runaway was denied trial and could not refute the charges. The law gave slave owners federal backing to travel with their slaves to northern cities without fear of losing them and to head north to recover runaways. The law also opened a market for slave catchers looking to profit from the rewards for returning runaways. Fugitive slaves headed farther north in droves, particularly to Canada and England, where they could be out of slavery's reach. The black and white abolitionist community stood poised to protect fugitives and resist the slaveholders and slave catchers.

Fugitive slaves who worked as barbers ran the risk that a white customer, perhaps one they had yet to form a close relationship with, would discover their status and inform authorities. In some cases, fugitives relied on the shop owner. In late 1850, George White had been apprenticing as a barber under John Vashon in Pittsburgh. Considering Vashon's work in the abolitionist movement and Pittsburgh's Underground Railroad, he was likely aware that White had escaped slavery. This, of course, was not a problem until White's former owner, Mr. Rose, came into shop looking for a shave. Rose traveled to Pittsburgh from Wellsburg, Virginia, on a business trip. While in Vashon's shop, he recognized White as his runaway slave who, on January 14, 1851, was subsequently apprehended. Vashon quickly stepped in to help White achieve his freedom. He purchased White for $200 only to then set him free.[106] Other barbers were not so lucky. In 1854, word spread that two men from Virginia had arrived in Manchester, New Hampshire, looking for fugitive slave Edwin Moore, who had established a barber shop in the city. After hearing of their arrival, Moore boarded a train to Canada with his wife and three children.[107] John Thompson spent his early years as a slave in Fauquier County, Virginia, but seized his opportunities for freedom. Thompson had twice escaped slavery; once after being sold to a Huntsville, Alabama, cotton planter, and again after being purchased by a slave trader from Richmond. In October 1857, the Philadelphia Vigilance Committee assisted Thompson on this second escape, sending him through the Underground Railroad; he eventually settled in New York and worked as a barber. Thompson reported to be "doing very well" as a barber, but in December 1860 he was forced to leave the shop and the city behind because someone had informed his master, who had been in the city searching for him, of his whereabouts. After this scare, Thompson was "obliged to sail for England."[108] The culprit who betrayed John Thompson could have been anyone, from a customer to someone simply looking for a financial reward.

Black barbers played central roles in communication networks because they were strategically situated to counter slave catchers emboldened by the Fugitive Slave Law. Barbers spent their work hours grooming and listening to white patrons, and their non-work hours in their black communities. Slave owners and catchers regularly passed through Ohio Valley cities like Cincinnati and Pittsburgh because they bordered the slave states of Virginia and Kentucky. They often stayed overnight in the city's hotels. Black barbers and hotel employees were among the first to be aware of their arrival, and these black workers were able to pass information to necessary channels.[109] Despite the presence of black barbers, white patrons talked freely about matters of race, slavery, and runaways.

Black barbers not only capitalized on the information white patrons exchanged, but also capitalized on their barber shop networks to protect their own freedom. The relationships between barbers and their white patrons proved critical in substantiating their freedom. In Petersburg, Indiana, slave catchers attempted to kidnap a black barber who had recently opened a shop. The kidnappers received a description of the runaway from a confederate in Washington, D.C., and had handbills printed that described him as a runaway from Tennessee. After he was captured and taken before the court, a friend of the barber delayed proceedings until a runner who was dispatched to Vincennes, Indiana, returned with a sworn statement from Robert Laplant. The statement confirmed that the barber had been born on his father's farm near Vincennes and that Laplant's parents had employed his parents. He was subsequently freed.[110] Because free black barbers were vulnerable to illegal enslavement, they had real incentives to form alliances with their white customers for protection.

White customers and the larger white community had the potential to protect their black barbers, as well as to betray them. George DeBaptiste, born of free parents in 1814 in Fredericksburg, Virginia, worked as a barber and personal servant before he migrated to Madison, Indiana, in 1838. While in Madison, DeBaptiste was an agent in the Underground Railroad. After he died in 1875, the *Detroit Advertiser and Tribune* recounted much of his heroism in southern Indiana. According to the newspaper, he regularly approached slaves traveling in Madison to convince them to run away, and routinely went into Kentucky to secretly meet with slaves to arrange for them to cross the river and head farther north. His customers from Madison and Kentucky jokingly accused him of assisting fugitives. Some even tried to bait DeBaptiste by sending slaves to him to ask for the way to Canada, but he never fell for such trickery. In response to his activity aiding fugitive slaves, he was targeted in two states. A reward was offered for his arrest in Kentucky and a justice of the peace ordered him to comply with the 1831 Indiana black code that required blacks to post a bond to remain in the state. He posted the bond and was not deterred by the warrant, but the pressure was mounting. He eventually left Madison and moved to Detroit in the 1850s where he continued his work in the Underground Railroad.[111] DeBaptiste's independence as an entrepreneur was limited by his dependence on white patronage.

The paradox of black barbers' economic and personal freedom also came to bear on the politics of deference inside the shop. Free black barbers may have operated successful barber shops and exercised a level of relative autonomy as entrepreneurs, but their white customers were quick to strip them of their sense of independence when they seemed to be "getting out of their place." Relationships between free black barbers and white patrons were neither paternal nor strictly patron-client. Rather, they were situated between the two. The intimate nature of grooming and the subsequent conversations that usually arose gave barbers a tenuous sense of comfort in the shop.

Barber James Thomas reflected on the nature of this relationship in his autobiography. When a white patron asked Thomas to accompany him to New York City as his personal barber and servant, Thomas initially declined. He explained that he had recently purchased a barber shop and did not want to be away for too long. "Don't tell me about your business," the patron shouted. "I'll buy it and shut it up." The patron's decision to bring Thomas to New York was not paternal. He was not doing Thomas, as a free person, a favor in allowing him to travel, but rather he wanted the use of Thomas's services. Although Thomas tried to exercise his independence by declining to travel, the patron's threat reveals the free black barber's ambiguous position. If Thomas expected a give-and-take relationship with white customers, he realized racial hierarchies required black barbers to do more giving than taking. "It was beneath the dignity of a gentleman to lose his temper," he reasoned, "when dealing with an inferior. The barber was safe so long as he showed a cheerful willingness to please. In that way he would secure a good friend."[112] He recognized his customers wanted him to be a white man's barber. Deference guided Thomas's interactions with his customers to the extent that he was forced to accept an inferior role.

Black barbers (and other service workers) understood the difference between the business and politics of deference. Racial deference entailed "a cheerful willingness to please" white patrons, which Thomas did for his own safety. Yet this proved to be a business strategy to "secure a good friend" who would offer resources and, if needed, protection. William Dabney, businessman and journalist, recalled advice his father, a successful caterer in antebellum Richmond, passed on to him about the world of race and service work. "All of your books haven't taught you never to let a white man know how much you really do know about anything except hard work," he recalled his father saying. "He don't care how superior you are in working, but for Gawd's sake, son, please listen, if you ever expect to get money or anything worth while out of a white man, always make him feel that he knows more than you and always act as if you think he is the greatest man in the world."[113] This advice could have been extended to barbers, who negotiated similar encounters and had to decide if the mask of deference was worth wearing for financial gain. Dabney's fatherly advice spoke to an incipient philosophy of customer service that blurred power relations in the service economy.

Thomas related two examples that illustrate how the black barber-white patron relationship could become strained when the barber was too inquisitive. "On one occasion," Thomas recalled, "there was a drum heard on the street and an old puffed up individual was sitting in the shop. He asked what they were beating the drum for. I told him they were going to bury an old veteran. He yelled back, his eyes snapped, What's that? What's that? It didn't take more than a breath for me to change it to going to bury an old soldier. Oh! He said and settled down."[114] This encounter occurred in the 1850s, but it is unclear what the politics were of using "veteran" versus "soldier" during this moment. Yet, it was certainly clear to the white customer that Thomas was out of place, and it was clear to Thomas that a slight corrective might be in order. This encounter demonstrates the mask that black barbers wore in order to defer to the sensibilities of their white patrons. The term *veteran* was comfortable, but Thomas understood the need to pacify his customer and understood the necessary language to do so.

Thomas, on another occasion, asked one of his customers about the opposition to the Wilmot Proviso—a proposed bill to prohibit slavery in territories acquired from Mexico during the Mexican war. "The Wilmot proviso," Thomas wondered, "it appeared, didn't suit the people at all. I attempted to learn what that meant and asked a young lawyer to explain to me what was understood by that proviso. The set back I got from him for asking such a question caused me to be careful as to who I plied questions to with regard to politics. Among other things he told me I had no right to listen to Gentlemen's conversations. But the next gentleman, a cultured Virginian by the name of Rice, explained the meaning to me."[115] Initially, he felt comfortable enough to talk politics with this particular customer. Yet, by intimating that a "cultured" gentleman explained the meaning of the Proviso to him, he revealed his perceptions of class and culture among whites. Thomas liked "the Southern people individually but collectively and politically 'Dam 'em.'"[116] While he submitted to a deferential position required of nineteenth-century barbers, his compliance might be read as a business decision rather than acquiescence to the racial order. That he "collectively and politically" damned white southerners suggests he grew frustrated with racial politics in the antebellum South.

African Americans conceded Thomas's tenuous position in the South, but northern barbers received much more criticism. Northern black activists launched scathing critiques at northern black barbers for depending upon white patronage at the exclusion of black customers. This was the very business decision that placed them among the black elite and in strategic positions to help fugitive slaves. The tension between black barbers and black reformers publicized barbers' dilemmas of making a living versus the imperatives of black manhood and respectability. Black skilled craftsmen and entrepreneurs fit the definition of republican independence, but race colored the boundaries of republican ideology. Free black barbers were marginalized from white definitions of republicanism as independent, respectable, and honest craftsmen who worked with their hands. They were excluded from republican virtue because even their most skilled occupations were stamped with low or servile status. Racial subordination in the workplace, particularly where white consumers interacted with black workers, reinforced white supremacy in social and political spheres.[117] But, could black barbers achieve the dignities of their labor, which republicanism denied them, outside of the barber shop?

Black Barbers and Black Politics

African Americans' racial identity was inextricably bound with their class and gender. Black middle-class reformers believed the meaning of black labor had tremendous implications for African Americans' struggles for citizenship. Reformers articulated this problem in masculine terms. African American leaders at once advocated that men assume the mantle of republican citizenship by becoming producers and encouraged laborers and entrepreneurs to leave behind occupations and practices that reinforced stereotypes of passiveness and submissiveness. In other words, they pushed for respectable, manly business leadership. A segment of the black middle class worried what whites would think of the entire race based on barbers' decisions to exclude black customers.

African Americans had reason to take notice because in the early nineteenth century Englishmen who traveling in America took note that blacks were excluded from northern shops. An English traveler, Henry Fearon, who witnessed a black customer being refused service at a New York barber shop, received a lesson on race and barber shop culture. Perplexed and taken aback, Fearon requested an explanation from the black barber. Only a stranger, the barber thought, would ask such a question. "Ay," the barber answered, "I guessed you were not raised here. Now I reckon you do not know that my boss [also black] would not have a single . . . gentleman come to his store, if he cut coloured men; now my boss, I guess, ordered me to turn out every coloured man from the store right away, and if I did not, he would send me off slick." That evening, Fearon shared the incident with three white American "gentlemen . . . of education and of liberal opinions." One respondent, vehement and reassured, replied, "Ay right, perfectly right, I would never go to a barber's where a coloured man was cut!"[118] When Isaac Candler, also from London touring America, was in a black barber shop in New York in the early 1820s, he recalled Fearon's experience, published in his 1817 narrative, and queried the barber on how common this might have been. He plainly responded that he "dare not shave one of his own race, for fear of losing the custom of the whites."[119] These may have been odd experiences worthy of note in a travel log for Fearon and Candler, but these were grave concerns for the northern black middle class determined to become independent of whites in the northern antebellum post-Emancipation period.

The movement to redefine the meaning of black labor and entrepreneurship appears most vividly in the mid-nineteenth-century debates over the racial and gendered meanings of barbering. This discussion took place primarily among northerners after gradual emancipation policies had run their course and disfranchisement and segregation had emerged. Southern slavery served as the backdrop because northern freedom was elusive. In his 1828 *Appeal,* David Walker warned black men not to be satisfied with subservient work. Walker did not object to menial work as a means of subsistence, but if blacks relied on such jobs as bootblack and barber, they would be relegated to a subservient status.[120] His charge was part of a larger call for slaves and free blacks to exert their manhood and resist slavery and degradation. While Walker was just one person who abhorred service work, he joined a cacophony of voices in organized bodies that argued for labor respectability.

Delegates at black state and national conventions called for blacks to shift from menial to more respectable mechanical and agricultural jobs.[121] Black conventions were organized political meetings among northern free blacks to address issues of political, economic, and civil rights. Convention representatives regularly proposed resolutions that bound labor politics with racial politics. At the 1848 Colored National Convention, of which Frederick Douglass was president, delegates debated and passed resolutions that addressed racial progress, but the list of resolutions began and ended with proclamations against unmanly occupations. Martin Delany, black physician and abolitionist, supported the second resolution that encouraged blacks to follow the same mechanical trades as white men because he believed bootblacks could not command the same respect as mechanics. One resolution declared, "The occupation of domestics and servants among our people is degrading to us as a class, and we deem it our bounded duty to discountenance such pursuits, except where necessity compels the person to resort therein as a means of livelihood."[122] The delegates charged black barbers, particularly, with further-ing regressive and unmanly policies of racial submissiveness. The last resolu-tion, adopted without discussion, proclaimed that black barbers encouraged prejudice against blacks when they refused "to treat colored men on equality with the whites." Such behavior made barbers "base serviles, worthy only of the condemnation, censure and defamation of all lovers of liberty, equality, and right." Unlike their opposition to domestic and other personal service occupations, conventioneers were not opposed to barbering as a trade or an enterprise. But they were vehemently opposed to barbers' success built on the foundations of white patronage at the expense of blacks' dignity.[123]

Other delegates attacked these labor resolutions as elitist and unrealistic. J. D. Patterson argued, "Those who were in the editorial chair and others, not in places of servants, must not cast slurs upon those, who were in such places from necessity."[124] Patterson suggested leaders of the convention were disconnected from the majority of black workers who worked in a racially restricted labor market. Barbers made up a large segment of the very middle class who critiqued their legitimacy. How they achieved and maintained their status occupied black leaders' attention. In a final address, convention leaders acknowledged the heavy focus on labor, but stressed its grave importance be-cause "to be dependent, is to be degraded. Men may indeed pity us, but they cannot respect us," until black workers achieved economic independence from whites.[125] In the end, Frederick Douglass encouraged blacks to gradually move from these "degraded" occupations as soon as "necessity ceases." There was one barber in particular whom he believed no longer needed to live by the razor.

In late June 1850, Frederick Douglass visited James Whitfield's barber shop in Buffalo, New York. In addition to shaving whiskers, Whitfield wrote poetry between customers. He had published several poems in the *North Star* before Douglass's visit. It is unclear if Douglass stopped by Whitfield's shop to visit him or to get a shave or haircut. (Based on photos of Douglass at the time, it does not appear that he received very many haircuts.) Upon entering the shop, he was surprised to find Whitfield, a "sable son of genius," behind the barber's chair. Douglass wrote of his anguish: "That talents so commanding,

gifts so rare, poetic powers so distinguished, should be tied to the handle
of a razor and buried in the precincts of a barber's shop . . . is painfully dis-
heartening." He believed Whitfield's contributions to racial advancement
would come not from the razor, but from the pen. "Come out of that cellar,
Whitfield!" Douglass wrote, "and let your bugle blasts of liberty careen over
our Northern hills. You are implored to do so by your enslaved and slandered
people."[126] He considered blacks' labors in barbering "the malignant arrangements of society" that hindered more than helped upward mobility.

Douglass was not alone in believing that Whitfield should spend more
time writing poems than shaving beards. In his 1852 book *The Condition,
Elevation, Emigration, and Destiny of the Colored People of the United States,*
Martin Delany suggested that Whitfield was "reprehensible" for laboring in
such a "humble position" when he was "one of the purest poets in America."[127]
Delany repeated many of his concerns from the 1848 convention that blacks
would only achieve equality and manhood when they assumed occupations
in business, trades, professions, and the sciences. He emphasized that "a
good business practical Education" presented the best means toward these
ends. For Delany, men should become producers or enter some avenue of
"importance," while women should take responsibility for educating future
producers or "filling places of usefulness."[128] His ideas on important men and
useful women shaped his perceptions of Whitfield and his creative talents.
The barber shop did not fit Delany's vision of a significant business enterprise.
Ironically, in the 1830s, Delany was mentored by Lewis Woodson, one of the
leading members of this "humble position" in the antebellum era. But, like
Delany, William Wells Brown, a former barber himself, agreed that Whitfield
was "intended by nature for a higher position in life."[129]

While these men lamented Whitfield's labors against his calling, Whitfield
had his own ideas for his life's work. His work as a barber allowed him the
time to produce a volume of poems entitled *America,* but he wanted to devote more time to a life of letters. Whitfield worked as a barber aboard the
steamer *Bay State,* and convinced one of his customers to buy his book. The
customer, an anonymous correspondent for the *Pennsylvania Freeman,* sent it
to the Book Notices editor along with a letter. In the letter, the correspondent
noted, "While shaving me, he asked me very modestly, if I would purchase
a . . . volume of poems of his own composition. . . . He told me the only time
he had for reading or writing, was in the intervals of labor; and as his business
required him to be in his shop early and late, it was difficult for him to get an
hour at any time, when he was not liable to interruption." According to the

correspondent, "The object of publishing that volume was to try to get means to support him while he should devote more time to the cultivation of his mind, and to writing, than he was able to do now."[130] Since Whitfield moved from an inland shop to a steamer, it is possible his business was not doing well. The correspondent described him as a "man of nearly pure African blood." Light-skinned barbers generally fared much better in business than dark-skinned barbers. Perhaps Whitfield also wanted to come in contact with a wider base of customers to sell his volume. This strategy proved unsuccessful, because he returned to his Buffalo shop and shifted his energies outside of the barber shop to promoting emigration.[131] Whitfield preferred to spend more time reading and writing because he was passionate about poetry and shaved men only to earn a living. Yet, when Douglass lamented seeing him behind the barber's chair, his admonishments of barbering may seem more like collateral damage, as he went to great pains to support and encourage Whitfield to spend more time writing poetry. But Douglass's distaste for barbering extended beyond Whitfield-the-poet, and included any black man who labored in service jobs for white patrons in a free society.

Black conventioneers at the Ohio Colored Convention of 1852 were equally critical. They condemned any "colored who refuses to shave a colored man because he is colored" as "much worse than a white man who refuses to eat, drink, ride, walk, or be educated with a colored man . . . for the former is a party *de facto* to riveting chains around his own neck and the necks of his much injured race." At the same convention, however, they called upon black men to equal white men in wealth and enterprise.[132] This may have posed no paradox for the conventioneers, but it certainly did for black barbers. From conventioneers' perspective, barbers willingly chose their customers, and if black barbers chose to shave black men, barbers would be more independent and manly. Yet they had succumbed to the wishes of their white clients. Conventioneers were undoubtedly aware of this precarious position among black barbers, but, for them, it was irrelevant. They assumed barbers could still successfully operate their shops serving black men.

For much of the 1850s, Douglass spoke out against "degraded" jobs such as barbering. He believed black barbers were losing the battle of competition with European immigrant and native white barbers. In his article "Learn Trades or Starve," Douglass argued that the increase of Irish immigrants in the 1850s in barbering and other "employments and callings, formerly monopolized" by blacks demonstrated that even among menial occupations, African Americans' dominant position was vulnerable and should no longer be the path to economic independence for black youth. "A few years ago," he lamented, "a *white* barber would have been a curiosity—now their poles stand on every street."[133] Unlike southern black barbers, northern black barbers faced Irish and German immigrant competition. Between 1840 and 1860, Irish and German immigrants entered northern labor markets in New York, Boston, and Detroit, willing to work in the domestic and personal service industries where black workers were traditionally resigned. As European immigrants increasingly became domestics, porters, dockhands, cooks, waiters, and barbers, they made fluid the racial stigma of "black jobs." In New York in 1855, 854 of the total 997 barbers were foreign born. There were 608 German barbers, 68 Irish barbers, and 78 black barbers.[134] Henry Ward Beecher, a minister at Plymouth Church in Brooklyn, New York, noted in an 1862 sermon that black barbers were being replaced as fast as white barbers could be found. In Boston between 1850 and 1860, the proportion of foreign-born barbers and hairdressers increased from one-fifth to one-third in the city.[135]

For Douglass, not only were white barbers displacing blacks, but barbering was not a respectable calling for black youth. Douglass's critiques of barbering rested on the social and racial organization of service work. For example, he dismissed barbering as a skilled trade compared with mechanical and agricultural trades. "We must find new methods of obtaining a livelihood," he proclaimed, "for the old ones are failing us very fast." Douglass reasoned that barbering may have been one of the preferred occupations during slavery, but in freedom, black barbers embraced a false sense of economic security. Douglass envisioned the mechanical arts, or "high industry," as the path to black economic elevation and respectable citizenship. Douglass argued that menial occupations as service workers to wealthy whites led "those engaged in them, [to] improvidence, wastefulness, [and] a fondness for dress and display. Catering to the pride and vanity of others, they become themselves proud, vain and foppish."[136] Douglass, like other middle-class reformers, was concerned about the moral, social, and political consequences of blacks holding such positions. He believed black barbers and other personal service workers imitated the customs and fashions of their white patrons. He cautioned against the perils of city life through leisure and consumption that he believed were on display in the barber shop. How black service workers spent their earnings and used their leisure time diverges from Douglass's moral indictment of service work.

Like Martin Delany and David Walker, Frederick Douglass used masculine terms to criticize those engaged in barbering and other personal and domestic service occupations. For Douglass, the larger implications of service work for the white elite led to the "cost of their manhood and respectability," and it was not worth the financial benefits of laboring in a degraded profession. "To shave a half dozen faces in the morning, and sleep or play the guitar in the afternoon—all this may be easy; but," he questioned, "is it noble, is it manly, and does it improve and elevate us?" Many readers wrote to the paper in support of Douglass's charge that in order to operate on equal footing with white citizens, black barbers, cooks, and waiters needed to stop serving them.[137] He charged black barbers to break the cycle of unmanly labor by trying to encourage their sons to rise above the degraded positions their fathers had occupied.

Barbers defined their labors differently. They argued there was self-respect in any occupation. Uriah Boston, a black barber and prominent figure in the black community of Poughkeepsie, New York, wrote a letter to Douglass's paper in 1853 to defend barbers from these "attacks."[138] While Douglass initially refused to publish Boston's letter, he eventually relented. Boston argued that barbering was not degrading and servile, but a respectable business with intelligent businessmen. He reminded Douglass that barbers represented "a very large class of business men among our people."[139] He suggested that if Douglass advocated for the rise of a black middle class, he must account for the large number of black barbers who made up the current black elite. This group also included Lewis Woodson, black barber and prominent abolitionist of Pittsburgh, who stressed the importance of wealth in racial advancement. "Our efforts to obtain wealth," he argued, "have not been equal to our efforts to obtain knowledge."[140] While education and wealth were not mutually exclusive, these barbers wanted to make it clear that their profession could indeed be in service to racial progress.

Ironically, Boston and Woodson were but two of the many barbers who were very active in the abolitionist movement and the struggle for the franchise. After Pennsylvania struck black citizens from the voting rolls in 1837, black barbers were among the activists who organized on local and statewide levels to push for a reversal. In 1841, John Peck was elected president of a group of Pittsburgh black residents organized to regain the franchise. In August of the same year, barbers John Vashon and Lewis Woodson assumed leadership roles in a statewide convention on the franchise. In the Northeast, barber Alfred Niger, as vice president of the Rhode Island Anti-Slavery Society, fought for black voting rights in the 1830s and 1840s.[141] Boston was a leading figure among black activists in New York to expand black suffrage. From 1840 to 1846, he led the Dutchess County Suffrage Committee, which coordinated petition drives and worked with black leaders throughout the state. In 1855, he established the Poughkeepsie Political Suffrage Association, an auxiliary of the New York State Suffrage Association, which led the local battle for the franchise. Moreover, he was a regular at black state conventions, and occasionally at black national conventions. In fact, when Boston missed a convention in Troy, New York, in September 1855, the report on the convention in *Frederick Douglass' Paper* asked, "But where is Boston—Uriah Boston! There is a vacancy in our Convention when Uriah Boston is not present." Boston also led the annual Emancipation Day celebrations in August to commemorate the British abolition of slavery.[142] These barbers defied simplistic labels.

Did Boston live two lives, one at the barber shop in downtown Poughkeepsie with his white patrons, and another among black activists in the city and around the state? We do not know very much about Boston's barber shop, except where it was located, and that white patrons frequented the shop. Upon his death in 1889, his obituary in the *Dutchess Courier* stated, "Year after year the various questions of the day and especially that of anti-slavery, were discussed at Boston's 'tonsorial rooms.'" It also went on to say that Boston "always took an intelligent part." It appears that many of those white customers were anti-slavery advocates such as David Lent and Theodorus Gregory. Boston thought very highly of himself, even signaling his own labor respectability. For example, his advertisements in the Poughkeepsie city directories in the 1850s and 1860s proclaimed that he offered "scientific hair cutting" and, in several cases, stated "NO SHAVING DONE."[143] These advertisements juxtaposed his manly, professional skills with the unskilled, intimate work of touching a man's face. Shaving was tied directly to the wider perceptions of barbering as a natural, servile occupation for blacks. It is also striking that in the city directories, Boston was not listed as black. African Americans listed in the directories had a "c" for colored next to their names, but not Boston.[144] He was not passing for white—he was listed as black in the census—but he may have established such a reputation that he convinced the publisher not to mark his race in the directory. Therefore, Boston knew of what he spoke when he suggested that Douglass was grossly misguided. But the larger story, from Douglass and Boston, hinged on the manliness of entrepreneurship and independence.

Men dominated the kinds of jobs that Douglass believed would propel black workers into a new era of self-respect. Certainly he mentioned that black women needed to move out of domestic service, but he failed to suggest what kinds of jobs they might pursue to achieve economic independence. If Delany and Douglass perceived entrepreneurial pursuits as a masculine endeavor, Eliza Potter surely shattered that model. Potter was a successful black hairdresser who traveled with elite white women. Along with other black entrepreneurs in the grooming industry, Potter represented her hairdressing work as an empowering position of social critic and counselor to women of the white aristocracy. She likened her work to that of physicians and clergymen, other professionals who had intimate relationships with their patrons.

In 1859, Potter published an account of her experiences dressing white women's hair in the North and South. She did not simply provide a woman's voice in black entrepreneurial activity alongside her male counterparts. She completely recast the role of black entrepreneurs in the service industry in the antebellum period.[145] As Potter listened to her patrons' conversations, she was in a position to judge. She mentioned very little about the business of hairdressing, save for a few passages on her lucrative income. But her account counters the manly rhetoric of entrepreneurial activity and the degradation of service work.

Beauty shops had not yet lined urban business districts, but black women did labor as private hairdressers to elite white women. From the colonial period to the 1830s, the prevalence of wigs in American society blurred the gender line between hairdresser and barber. In fact, the average person and even city directories used the two terms interchangeably. Men, many of them trained as wigmakers, groomed men's and women's hair. Commercially, black men serviced white men and women. As wigs grew out of fashion and men wanted more frequent shaves, male hairdressers shed the responsibilities of styling hair and focused on shaving, trimming, and cutting hair. Although black women had always groomed one another's hair, the shift in men's work opened opportunities for black women to groom white women's hair in the commercial sphere. In the 1850s, Eliza Potter traveled extensively with her white clients, combing their hair and that of other ladies in high society in Cincinnati, Saratoga, New Orleans, and Paris. In fact, Potter learned the art of hairdressing in Paris when she traveled there with a family.[146] While in Cincinnati, she serviced a majority of her clients in the Burnet House hotel.

The intimate relationship between black barbers and their white male patrons paralleled the relationship between black hairdressers and white female patrons. Eliza Potter wrote in her account that "the hairdresser is everywhere chatted with, and confided to." Potter did not always care to hear some of the conversations that reached her ear, but, she reasoned, "I could not tell ladies to shut their mouths, and hence I was much oftener the receptacle of secrets than I desired to be." The hairdresser, according to Potter, received a great many tales of envy and contempt. She was less concerned about what they did and with whom, and more concerned that they "paid me my wages."[147] Armed with intimate stories of society life, Potter shared many of these "anecdotes" in her book.

Potter's patrons may have thought she was a mere servant, but she exercised her power in this relationship. On one occasion in New Orleans, she was combing a "lady's" hair in her room at the St. Charles Hotel. The lady had traveled with her four children and several servants. Much to Potter's surprise, a "gentleman" walked into the room, sat down, and began talking with the lady in French. The patron reassured her male guest that Potter did not speak French because she was "from the upper country." They talked about scheduling a secret rendezvous, until she rushed him out of the room in anticipation of her husband's return. Potter wasted no time in telling her client that even if she was "rich and highly educated," she should not treat anyone, even the hairdresser, with contempt. Potter exclaimed there were "many simple looking people, and poor people, who understood more than those who were speaking of them."[148] Potter refused to be invisible. Like barbers, hairdressers listened to the conversations between their white customers. Potter, however, went beyond spectator status not only to defend her presence, but also to offer advice and counsel.

Despite the debates among men about the manliness of entrepreneurial activity and the dependent nature of service work, Potter was probably more convincing than barbers in shattering these hollow discussions. Johnson's and Thomas's relationships with their patrons were paternal. Potter's relationships with her customers, in contrast, were not paternal, and neither were her customers her patrons; they seem to have truly been her clients. Region partly explains the differences between Potter's work and Johnson's and Thomas's work. As free blacks in the South, Johnson and Thomas had to negotiate the limits on their freedom dictated in a slave society. Potter traveled south to dress hair, but she was not dependent on a southern clientele. Moreover, Johnson and Thomas worked in stationary shops, while Potter moved around. Her mobility allowed her to be much more independent. Potter's account encourages us to question, if not completely read, the silences in barbers' personal accounts of working with white patrons and negotiating the line between racial and business deference in service work.

*   *   *

Barbering in the antebellum South provided a work culture where the re-muneration and mobility gave barbers multiple paths toward legal and eco-nomic freedom by grooming the white southern aristocracy. Despite the hundreds of white necks passing under their razors, black barbers gave their white patrons what they paid for: a shave, luxurious treatment, and defer-ence. Since slave societies depended on racial deference, enslaved and free black barbers faced similar challenges in relating to their white patrons. White patrons' paternalism paid off for barbers looking to secure some level of independence. Barbers allowed white patrons to believe they had control, and to some extent they did, if only because of the structures of the larger southern economy and political sphere. Barbers controlled the barber shop; their deference was a matter of politics and business. They did not execute the revolutionary power of the razor, but they did shed the mask after closing time. Grooming white patrons also informed the work relationships between enslaved and free black barbers. Northern black barbers had similar experi-ences; however, black reformers held them to more stringent standards of respectability because they lived and worked in a free society.

Antebellum black barbers negotiated the racial stigma of the trade and the racial and social demands of the white public in order to realize their en-trepreneurial strivings. The antebellum experiences of northern black bar-bers served as precursors to the economic, political, and social struggles that northern and southern black barbers faced after the Civil War. Members of the black middle class and working class who were denied shaves continued to question black barbers' manhood and the larger implications of barbering in the attainment of civil rights. For black barbers after the Civil War, their exchange with white customers was transformed to a patron-client relation-ship, retaining many of the major points of contention from the antebellum period. At shaving-time in the North and South, black barbers wore a mask of deference and servility to establish businesses. White men sat in the bar-ber's chair for immaculate service. While they relaxed and got shaves, they produced white racial superiority. Yet for the black public, shaving-time was often a shameful moment when the perceived inferiority of black barbers was projected onto the lives of all black men.

CHAPTER 2

The Politics of "Color-Line" Barber Shops
After the Civil War

IN the summer of 1918, Harlem Renaissance writer and anthropologist Zora Neale Hurston earned money to pay for tuition at Howard University by manicuring the hands of white politicians, bankers, and members of the press who frequented George Robinson's barber shop on 1410 G Street, N.W., in Washington, D.C. She worked alongside another manicurist, ten barbers, and three porters, all black. This Virginia-born mixed-race barber, according to Hurston, owned nine shops in the city, but only one was in the black community.[1]

One afternoon that summer, a black man entered the shop, which caused confusion before he uttered a word. Nathaniel Banks, the manager and the barber with the chair closest to the door, overcame his surprise and asked the man what *he* wanted in *this* barber shop. "Hair-cut and shave," he replied. Banks, astonished, still tried to be helpful, or so he thought. "But you can't get no hair-cut and shave here. Mr. Robinson has a fine shop for Negroes on U Street near Fifteenth." The U Street corridor was a vibrant black business and entertainment district in the Shaw neighborhood, which was considered the center of black life and culture before Harlem assumed this designation in the 1920s. In fact, Robinson lived on U Street. The man understood there was a black side of town, but he referenced the Constitution of the United States to claim a seat in Robinson's shop downtown. As Banks began to gently escort the man out of the chair, he attempted to frame the issue around hair type. "I don't know how to cut your hair, I was trained on straight hair. Nobody in here knows how." Refusing to accept this premise, the protester shot back,

"Oh, don't hand me that stuff! Don't be such an Uncle Tom. These things have got to be broken up," he continued as he tried to force his way into another barber's chair.[2]

The barber was probably indeed trained on straight hair, because most of the leading black barbers from the Civil War to the early twentieth century groomed only white men in their commercial shops. But it is unlikely the barber could not cut this man's hair. With the decision to serve white men, Robinson and other black barbers, like their antebellum counterparts, had to deny service to black customers because many white men would not be shaved with the same razor or cut with the same shears that touched the face or head of a black man. More important, white men objected to any perception of social equality this practice might portray. Black critics often labeled barbers like Robinson "color-line" barbers for shaving white men at the expense of black men. These "color-line" barbers traded deference for dollars; however, they worked in a less than free market economy that left them in a precarious position. By 1918, color-line barbers were no longer predominant among black barbers, but many of them were still in business. Hurston described how the rejected black man refused to submit until the black barbers, porters, and white customers threw him out of the shop and into the middle of G Street. Hurston neither reprimanded the protester nor participated in the "melee." "But," she admitted, "I wanted him thrown out, too. My business was threatened."[3] Hurston was not a neutral observer; she stood to lose money along with the male workers in the shop.

This incident was emblematic of how color-line barber shops stood as contested sites of public space, racial intimacy, and economic freedom. Incidents such as this had occurred many times over in several southern and northern cities after the Civil War and into the twentieth century because the meanings of freedom contained individual and collective interests. Barbers' relationships with their customers after Reconstruction evolved into a socioeconomic exchange characterized by unequal relations where white patrons' control was less direct and more ambiguous. This patron-clientage encompassed an informal system of reciprocity organized in a public-private sphere that mirrored social relations that white society attempted to recreate in slavery's image between white and black men in the larger public sphere. In other words, barbers served as clients in their own shops where white men exercised much more power as patrons. Clients depend on their patrons for some tangible or intangible resource. Patrons dictated the rules and clients were benefactors if they maintained what historian William Chafe called an "etiquette of civility" or acceptable behavior.[4] White patrons tacitly recognized black barbers' independence, yet they required the barber shop to be an exclusive space for the white elite. They consumed personal grooming services, but in a way that reproduced antebellum images of racial superiority. By catering to the white elite, color-line barbers attempted to balance their own class ambitions with black collective struggles for respectability and civil rights.

As potential patrons, black men were not a part of the waiting public inside the shop; they were waiting on the outside looking in. Yet they contested these barbers in their shops, in the political sphere, in newspapers, and even in fiction, in the process revealing the larger implications of color-line barber shops for African American freedom. Color-line barbers' negotiation of the patron-client relationship underscores the larger systematic targets of civil rights struggles, particularly when barbers' self-interests deviated from the interests of the larger black community, such as the struggles over the Civil Rights Act of 1875.

Black barbers, white patrons, and the American public drew different conclusions on the intersection of race, class, and manhood during shaving-time, a moment in the shop when race relations were betwixt and between. Black barbering in the post-Emancipation period thus suggests that the struggle for equality was both an inter- and intraracial struggle, the latter hinging on competing visions of racial solidarity, class mobility, and black manhood.

Black Barbering in a Free Society

All workers cherished reaping the fruits of their labor, but it was especially so for black southerners released from the inhumanity of bondage. The end of slavery left blacks and whites battling over the meanings of freedom, and economic independence was chief among the claims that freed people deemed central in moving away from the dependency of slavery.[5] While the major battles over economic autonomy centered on land ownership and the injustices of the sharecropping system, black skilled, personal, and domestic service workers also tried to remake their economic lives to their own benefit in nonagricultural work in urban areas or resort towns.[6] Those who had worked skilled jobs during slavery continued in these employments, while others sought apprenticeships. Black urban workers faced sharp difficulties obtaining industrial and highly skilled jobs because of white labor competition. However, the semi-skilled, unskilled, and generally less desirable jobs were left wide open: waiter, cook, domestic servant, porter, barber, and a host

Table 1. Total Number of Barbers in Select Cities by Race, 1880

	Black	% of Total	White	% of Total	Total
Atlanta	73	92	6	8	79
Charleston	115	96	5	4	120
Nashville	101	80	25	20	126
Richmond	137	93	11	7	148
Chicago	130	13	893	87	1,023
Cleveland	55	22	198	78	253
New York	106	3	3,177	97	3,283
Philadelphia	430	21	1,661	79	2,091

Source: U.S. Census.

of other occupations. Many freedmen and freedwomen transformed their marketable skills into businesses in the post-Emancipation period.

In the decades after the Civil War, the demographics of the barbering industry looked radically different in the North and South. Black barbers continued to compete with German and Irish immigrants in the North, but they dominated the trade in the South. According to the 1880 U.S. Census, first- and second-generation Germans accounted for 41 percent or more of the barbers classified as white in northern cities. While Cleveland had just over half the number of black barbers that were in New York City, blacks in Cleveland actually accounted for a higher percentage of the total barbers in their city. Most striking about the northern census data is the large number of black barbers in Philadelphia compared with other cities. As early as 1856, the number of black barbers in the city was high (248) and continued to grow.[7] Unlike in the North, black barbers dominated the industry in the South. Southern whites still perceived domestic and personal service work as "Negro jobs," because former slaves had performed such work, and it required a level of deference.[8] Unaffected by white competition, southern black barbers had a sense of economic security.[9] Black barbers saw opportunities that white men would not allow themselves to see.

Although black barbers constituted a minority in the North and a majority in the South, shaving only white men proved to be the prevailing practice in both regions. Northern barbers who contemplated serving black men faced a small market because a majority of the black population resided in the South. Southern black barbers, in contrast, targeted white customers to maximize their income potential. If barbers had committed to a black market, they would have faced a considerable challenge in attracting white customers. Personal service entrepreneurs—barbers, caterers, tailors—who catered to wealthy whites were still considered the elite among black workers and entrepreneurs, which placed them among the small northern and southern black middle class. African Americans who had been free before the Civil War generally remained at the top of post-Emancipation black society in the South.[10] Barbers who were among the black elite were typically of mixed race or very light skinned, born free or freed before the war, and maintained contact with white benefactors.[11] White patrons who submitted their chins to their black barbers certainly hoped they had the skill to shave them without incident.

Some black boys entered barbering because they had worked in their father's or uncle's shop to contribute to the household economy. Bill Reese practically grew up in the barber shop. In 1869, six-year-old Reese worked in his father's shop in Athens, Georgia, during a period when "colored children learns [sic] to work mighty early." Reese performed such tasks as "taking pa's meals to the barber shop, sweeping out the shop, washing spittoons, and shining shoes." He worked there throughout his childhood and relinquished his earnings to his mother to cover household expenses. By the time he was twelve he "made from a dollar-and-a-half to as high as three dollars in one week." This was very little money at the time, but it does not appear that Reese worked full time or received full pay. Although he did not state how he was paid, since he turned over his earnings to his mother, his father probably allowed him to keep the tips. He had also been working in his uncle's shop, where he might have received a portion of his intake and tips.[12]

Not all barbers had prior ties to family shops. Many actually entered barbering as one of the available skilled trades in their search for work in urban areas. At age eighteen, John Merrick, born into slavery in 1859, left Sampson County, North Carolina, to look for work in Raleigh. Although he found work as a bricklayer, he had to make up for the downtime in the winter. The barber shop provided more secure, steady employment. He worked as a bootblack and porter in W. G. Otley's barber shop, where Merrick's eventual business partner, John Wright, worked as a foreman. After spending considerable time in the shop, Merrick began to learn barbering.[13] Not all rural blacks waited to get to the city before taking up the razor. Alonzo Herndon was born in 1858 in Walton County, Georgia. At age twenty, he moved to Covington, Georgia, where he worked as a farmhand and also cut hair on Saturday afternoons. He rented a small space in the town's black section to learn the trade.[14]

Wage and seasonal workers also saw the same security that agricultural workers saw in barbering, which was just as worthy as the professions. George Myers was born in the free black community of Baltimore on March 5, 1859. His father, Isaac Myers, a formidable predecessor to twentieth-century black labor organizers Frank Crosswaith and A. Philip Randolph, urged black workers to organize black cooperatives and fought against segregation in unions. George later developed a more conservative stance on black union organizing. He attended public school in Providence, Rhode Island, a preparatory school of Lincoln University in Chester, Pennsylvania, and completed high school in Baltimore. While his father wanted him to continue his education to study medicine, his formal schooling ended when he realized blacks could not enroll in Baltimore's city college. Instead of training his hands to use scalpels, in 1875 he first apprenticed as a house painter, then as a barber. At the age of twenty in 1879, Myers moved to Cleveland and secured a position as foreman in James E. Benson's barber shop at the Weddell House located between Superior and Bank Streets. Benson, a thirty-year-old mixed-race migrant from Virginia, had recently assumed the lease there.[15]

Beyond escaping wage labor and sharecropping, some black journeymen used barbering as a platform to other, more desirable, labors. For example, several black politicians during Reconstruction had been barbers before entering politics. According to historian Eric Foner, fifty-five southern black barbers held local or national office during Reconstruction. A majority of these barbers were elected to office in South Carolina, North Carolina, Alabama, Georgia, and Mississippi. Thirty-eight of these men were mixed race, and thirteen were black. Forty-two of them reported being literate. Seventeen were born free, and ten were born slave but were freed before Emancipation.[16] To be sure, black laborers and veterans made up a large component of elected officials in Reconstruction politics. The black men who occupied leadership positions in the antebellum period (such as ministers, barbers, and abolitionists) may have sustained these positions after the Civil War by helping to organize black political conventions, which put them in positions to be elected to political office. However, considering the status and wealth that black barbers held in the antebellum period, fifty-five former barbers elected to political office are not many. Black southerners had redefined political leadership after the Civil War, where wealth and status no longer held a symbiotic relationship with racial leadership. This applied particularly to barbers, who had established their careers grooming the white southern aristocracy, compared with the black Union Army veterans who fought for freedom and the death of slavery. This is not to suggest that some black barbers, particularly elite barbers, did not assume leadership positions. Rather, black southerners had begun to redefine the basis of black community leadership at the local and the national levels, including women, laborers, and veterans.[17] That many of these barbers left the trade behind as they entered politics, perhaps, suggests their own understandings of racial advancement in free societies.

If barbering was a fine temporary occupation for some, it was a clear path to business ownership and economic independence for others. In 1877, Reese's uncle sold him the shop, placing him in the ranks of the entrepreneurial class at the youthful age of fourteen. The racial makeup of his uncle's clientele is unknown, but Reese explicitly noted that he "catered to colored people." If his uncle groomed white patrons, Reese's change of clientele would have been a major overhaul of the shop. Reese described 1870s Athens as a "little village" with one business street.[18] There were likely only a few shops in this small town where most black residents went to Reese's shop—that he mentioned he catered to black customers suggests that this was not the norm—and the white residents went to another black-owned shop.

This young business owner would have had a steep learning curve in managing the shop. But the only difference between being a journeyman and an owner was that a journeyman gave a percentage of his earnings to the owner. Owners paid their barbers a percentage of the barber's receipts. Reese worked on the "check system" and received fifty cents of every dollar he took in. After shaving or cutting a customer's hair, Reese and the other barbers wrote out a ticket for the payment before submitting the money to the owner. On Saturday night, the owner checked the week's gross income against each barber's tickets. Reese preferred this system because "the man that brings the most business to the shop gets the most money."[19] He did not indicate his average weekly income, but during this same period, George Knox, of Indianapolis, paid his barbers between $11 and $15 per week.[20] Unskilled wage laborers earned as low as eighty-six cents per day, or just over $4 per week. W. E. B. Du Bois, in his study of Philadelphia in the 1890s, reported that a cementer received "$1.75 a day; white working men get $2–$3."[21] Given the population difference and urban setting, a barber in Athens would probably have earned less than one who worked in Indianapolis. By the turn of the century, barbers received a weekly minimum guarantee plus a commission, or a percentage of the receipts of their chair exceeding a stated figure. This stated figure covered shop expenses, while the "over money" amounted to profits each barber generated, which the barber and shop owner shared. Thus, a barber might receive $15 to $25 per week plus 60 percent of the receipts he brought in exceeding $35.[22]

Barbers were not the only employees the owner kept on payroll. Barber shops consisted of a wide range of employees to attend to the various needs of the shop and its customers. A foreman managed the daily activities of the shop, including opening and closing, and ensured that customers were serviced well and barbers maintained high morale. A porter collected patrons' coats and hats to hang up, gathered the tips, and brushed loose hair off their clothing. At smaller shops, one person performed the work of foreman and porter, but larger shops of fifteen or more chairs hired different men for these duties. Employees for non-grooming services included bootblacks who shined shoes and attendants of the bathhouses for shops large enough to offer such services before plumbing became common in American homes. Many barbers actually started out in these positions before learning the barbering trade. Larger shops also hired female manicurists.

Barbers with visions of entrepreneurship had a realistic opportunity to establish their own shops because of the low economic and racial barriers to entry. Although journeymen barbers received low wages, the time and cost to move from a journeyman to a proprietor were minimal. In 1899, W. E. B. Du Bois surveyed 162 black barber shop owners nationally for his *Negro in Business* report. Their average startup capital ranged from $100 to $500, and they invested an average of $1,200 in their shops.[23] Other, more prominent barbers opened their shops with $2,000 to $3,000. The average shop was furnished with two to three wooden barber chairs and sitting chairs for waiting patrons. The owner also needed essential tools such as mirrors, soap for softening beards, shaving cups and brushes, razors, and combs.[24] In addition to wages and equipment costs, owners had to consider rent. In the small town of Athens, in 1877, Reese paid $4 per month for a "little upstairs place." Four years later, he moved downstairs to the first floor of the same building on Jackson Street and paid $10 per month.[25] A street-level shop was in greater demand because it benefited from the foot traffic. Reese was probably correct in believing his income would increase at a greater rate than his rent. Barbers in larger cities could expect to pay substantially more than Reese for the monthly rent.

Barber shops attended to the grooming needs of their customers, but the array of services they offered varied based on their capitalization, location, and customer base. White men still frequented barber shops for shaves

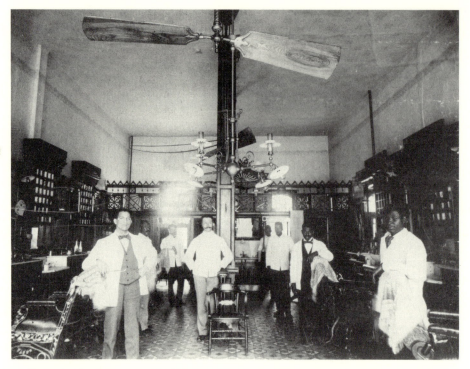

Figure 4. Alonzo Herndon's barber shop at the Markham House Hotel, 1895. Herndon is standing in the center of the shop surrounded by his fellow barbers. Courtesy of The Herndon Foundation.

because the average person lacked the skills to strop and use the straight razor at home. Although it was easier and cheaper for a friend or family member to cut a man's hair, middle- and upper-class men paid for these services. The average price of a shave was five to ten cents, a haircut was fifteen to twenty cents, and a shampoo averaged fifteen cents.[26] Based on barber Alonzo Herndon's 1902 account book, many of his customers visited the shop daily, most likely for shaves, but also for other services.[27]

Southern black barbers capitalized on the growth of New South cities, such as Durham and Atlanta, which brought moneyed men to town. Barbers saw opportunities to service the gentility of the Lost Cause.[28] White men and women enjoyed being served by blacks as one of the reminders of the genteel privileges of the Old South. Julian S. Carr and Washington Duke (organizer of the American Tobacco Company) traveled to Raleigh for shaves and haircuts because of "unsatisfactory" service in Durham. Instead of continuing to travel to their barber, they brought their barber to them by encouraging Merrick and his senior colleague, John Wright, to open a shop that "wealthy white men deserved" in the New South city. In 1880, Wright seized the opportunity to continue grooming these industrialists and recalled that he and Merrick "struck Durham about the time she was on her boom." Duke and Carr were key to this boom, particularly in the tobacco and textile industries.[29] Six months later, Merrick purchased half interest, and they worked as partners until 1892, when Wright sold his share to Merrick before moving to Washington, D.C. Merrick went on to open several more shops across the city. Like Merrick, Herndon migrated to an emerging city to groom its elite. In 1883, he had settled in Atlanta, where he worked as a journeyman barber in William Dougherty Hutchins's Marietta Street barber shop. Hutchins was one of a few black barbers who owned a shop in Atlanta predating the Civil War. When Herndon arrived there, the city directory listed twenty-eight barber shops; twenty-three of them were black-owned. Henry Rucker, Robert Yancey, and Robert Steele were among the wealthiest black barbers operating in Atlanta.[30] Within six months, he purchased a 50 percent interest in Hutchins's shop.[31] Herndon eventually opened his own shop and partnered with other barbers while he established himself and became settled enough to handle the expensive downtown rent.

Merrick and Herndon learned early on that grooming former confederates and carpetbaggers required a public deferential demeanor.[32] While it is difficult to know exactly what patrons thought, the racial and paternal politics of the period suggest that the line between competent businessman and affectionate servant was blurred. "I came to Atlanta with the determination to succeed," Herndon noted, "and by careful conscientious work and tactful, polite conduct." Being "polite" and "tactful" was essential to servicing a white market.[33] White southerners highlighted these qualities when speaking of black barbers. The *Atlanta Constitution* acknowledged William Betts's death in November 1901. Betts had worked as a barber in Atlanta for over forty years, and he partnered with Herndon to own shops on both Whitehall Street and Lloyd Street. The newspaper fondly recalled that Betts was "polite and appreciative. He had no false ideas about the greatness of his race. He looked upon the man he shaved as his friend and gave himself entirely to his occupation. . . . Always polite to the white man, and never obtruding upon his superiors."[34] Robert Steele used similar language to advertise his services. An ad for his Marietta Street shop in the city directory read: "Polite Attention,

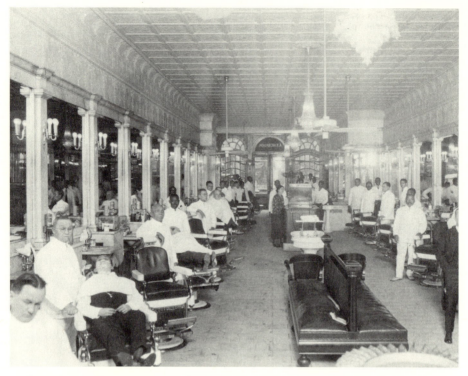

Figure 5. Alonzo Herndon's Crystal Palace Barber Shop at 66 Peachtree Street. Courtesy of The Herndon Foundation.

First Class Work Always At Bob Steele's Barber Shop."[35] Being polite seems central to any service business; however, whites perceived politeness and deference when attached to black service as signs of inferiority. In fact, this was part of the fantasy white patrons paid for. If former confederates and carpetbaggers sat in black barbers' chairs for shaves and had an inflated sense of themselves as superior men, then black barbers stood above them poised to take their money.

While black barbers exercised tactfulness toward whites, they negotiated the limits and benefits of these business relationships. One year after Herndon had opened the first A. F. Herndon Barbershop, he accepted an offer from the owner of the Markham House Hotel to become the sole proprietor of its shop. Adjacent to the Union Depot, it was among Atlanta's prominent hotels. Herndon's two-year lease allowed for "water for said baths and barbershop whenever the same runs and there is heat upon the building sufficient, but they are not to run the heat for that especial purpose."[36] He was required to have a white person, merchant John Silvey, guarantee the lease at seventy-five dollars per month. His next two-year lease increased to eighty-three dollars, but did not require Silvey's guarantee. On May 17, 1896, a massive fire burned the entire block where the hotel and barber shop were located. Herndon relocated to the Norcross Building on 4 Marietta Street. Unfortunately, on December 9, 1902, a fire that started around the corner destroyed Herndon's and other businesses on his block. Yet, he recovered quickly. By the following Saturday, Herndon opened another shop on 66 Peachtree Street, named the Crystal Palace, which grew to become his flagship location. By 1904, he owned three barber shops in Atlanta, which at one time employed seventy-five people.[37]

Like their southern counterparts, northern elite black barbers often got their start through white connections. George Myers opened his shop in the new Hollenden Hotel in Cleveland in 1888 with several loans for his $2,000 startup capital. Liberty Holden, the hotel's owner, lent him 80 percent of the money, and he also received assistance from many future business and political leaders of the city, who were his patrons at his previous shop, such as Leonard C. Hanna (Senator Marcus Hanna's brother) and Tom Johnson (eventual mayor of Cleveland). James Ford Rhodes, historian and eventual president of the American Historical Association, was also among Myers's sponsors. They maintained regular communication outside of the barber shop. In fact, Myers later reminded Rhodes of his kindness, but he refused any credit. "You are mistaken," he wrote to Myers, "in your notion that I put up any money to start you in business. I did say some good words to Mr. Holden but . . . 'talk is cheap.'" Myers shared his ledger with Rhodes that accounted for his financial sponsors and noted, "Suffice to say that I paid every one of you gentlemen and through my successful conduct of business and integrity I held the confidence and esteem of all who have passed to their reward."[38] Myers's note to Rhodes provides an early example of how he eschewed long-term debt, financial or otherwise, which was a recurring theme in how he managed relationships.

Although barbers were constrained more by custom than contract in deciding the racial market they would target, they received such considerable business and connections that they were still well represented among the black business leaders in many cities in the late nineteenth century. Color-line barbers' social status emerged from the potential favors and benefits they might extract from this patron-client relationship—favors and benefits many

African Americans hoped barbers would deliver to their communities.[39] The tension between barbers' individual aspirations and black communities' expectations provided rich material for black literary writers. Charles Chesnutt, novelist and political activist, published *The Colonel's Dream* in 1905 and "The Doll" in 1912, with color-line barbers as central characters that complicate the everyday tenuous class and gender experiences of these men. Chesnutt reflected on his contemporary moment through literature to render visible the limits and possibilities in the barber shop.

The Colonel's Dream, Chesnutt's last published novel, tells of a retired white merchant, Colonel Henry French, southerner by birth and northerner by achievement, who returns to his old southern town of Clarendon after the Civil War. This New South novel emphasizes the tension between French's liberalism and the southern traditionalism of Clarendon's white residents. Chesnutt explores the limitations of French's northern liberalism through his nostalgia for the Old South, which is piqued through his interaction with black characters. William Nichols, a mixed-race barber, represents an aristocratic figure who serves only white men in his southern barber shop, yet occupies a leadership position in the black community. Through Nichols's relationship with French and Clarendon's black community, Chesnutt suggests that color-line barbers in the New South redefined their relationships with white patrons and capitalized on the racial economy of southern traditionalism for class mobility.

Chesnutt establishes Nichols's elite class status within the black community by emphasizing the resources that accompanied his occupation and wealth. A former slave, Nichols took advantage of a foreclosure and purchased French's childhood mansion for $500 after Emancipation. French realizes a black family resides in his childhood home when a "neatly dressed coloured girl came out on the piazza, [and] seated herself in a rocking-chair with an air of proprietorship."[40]

Nichols is cautious and deferential with French, but at the same time he has confidence in his own class mobility and economic resolve. When French sits in Nichols's chair, Nichols engages in pleasantries to gauge his mood; as the narrator suggests, "knowing from experience that white gentlemen, in their intercourse with coloured people, were apt to be, in the local phrase, 'sometimey,' or uncertain in their moods." Nichols introduces himself as one aristocrat to another. "I feels closer to you, suh, than I does to mos' white folks, because you know, colonel, I'm livin' in the same house you wuz bawn in."[41] Nichols is deferential yet, in this same breath, he makes a connection—a clever suggestion of social equality—that is forbidden, and legislated against, in southern society. French had fought in the Confederate army to defend the institution of slavery. And the barber, a former slave who is lathering his face and attending to his grooming needs, resides in *his* home. But, Nichols reveals this news at the very moment he is holding a razor.

After this bombshell, Nichols tells French, "For I loves the aristocracy; an' I've often tol' my ol' lady, 'Liza,' says I, 'ef I'd be'n bawn white I sho' would 'a' be'n a 'ristocrat. I feels it in my bones."[42] In reality, for a black man to publicly suggest that he can imagine himself not only as a white man but also as an aristocrat would be an affront on whiteness regardless of class. His affinities for whiteness and upper-class status, he suggests, are not mere chance but natural. Nichols's sentiments about the mansion weigh heavy on French's mind, so he immediately offers to purchase the house at any price. Although Nichols originally had no intention of selling, he is indeed an opportunist and requests $4,000 for the house, to which French agrees, clearing Nichols a handsome profit. French explains his sudden and impulsive purchase to a friend, Laura: "The barber complimented me on the family taste in architecture, and grew sentimental about *his* associations with the house. This awoke *my* associations, and the collocation jarred—I was selfish enough to want a monopoly of the associations" (emphasis in original).[43] Laura seems mystified that French would dare live in the house after a "coloured family" had lived there. While complimenting the Nichols family as decent people, French still reminisced about the "old" South. "It is no less the old house because the barber has reared his brood beneath its roof," he argues. "There were always Negroes in it when we were there—the place swarmed with them. Hammer and plane, soap and water, paper and paint, can make it new again . . . surely a good old house, gone farther astray than ours, might still be redeemed to noble ends."[44] In this paternalistic moment, French still desires the "old" days in the "old" house. He suggests that Nichols—not Nichols the person who was rather upstanding in his view, but Nichols the black barber who cannot possibly keep up the mansion as befits an aristocratic family—cannot bring nobleness and honor to the ownership of such an estate. French, however, is confident he can wash the blackness away.

Chesnutt further complicates our understanding of race, class, and work by reiterating Nichols's ties to Clarendon's black community. Nichols grooms white men and grows wealthy through a shrewd housing purchase, but uses his profits from the house to build a row of small houses for black residents. Nichols also acts the part of the elite. For example, although French's friend,

Laura, is mystified that he would live in a home after blacks had resided there, she is secretly employed by the Nichols family as a piano teacher for their daughter. Nichols is party to segregation in his shop, assists black residents with work and housing, and employs a white woman in his home in the late nineteenth-century South. Chesnutt presents the character of a barber whose mask of deference generates resources that ironically permit him to defy southern custom. Individual and group interests are not necessarily irreconcilable: Chesnutt paints the black barber as one who submits to racial deference to sustain his business but is not marginalized from the black community.

While Chesnutt used *The Colonel's Dream* to illuminate the benefits of class mobility among color-line barbers, he critiqued the competing notions of manhood in "The Doll." Originally submitted to *Atlantic Monthly* in 1904 but not published until 1912, the story unmasks shaving-time to conceptualize the tenuous position of color-line barbers.[45] Colonel Forsyth, a southern white politician visiting the North for a political convention, seeks to prove his theory of race—that blacks are naturally inferior and submissive—to a northern, white, liberal colleague, Judge Beeman. Forsyth chooses the barber shop in his hotel as the proving ground. He sits in the chair of the black proprietor, Tom Taylor, requests a shave, and proceeds to talk, directly to Beeman, but indirectly to Tom, about his racial ideologies—the natural way of things, eugenics, Darwinism. Tom ignores him until he speaks of killing a black man to "teach him his place." Forsyth tells the story of a black girl who was accused of misconduct as a servant in his mother's home. The girl complained to her father, who in turn confronted Forsyth's mother and Forsyth himself when he entered the room. Not backing down, the black man continued to defend his daughter until Forsyth shot him.

To Tom, the story sounds eerily familiar. He realizes it was *his* father Forsyth shot and now this man's neck rests under his razor. Tom is placed in a position he has longed for. He had heard this story before, but a different version. "In his dreams," according to the narrator, "he had killed this man a hundred times, in a dozen ways."[46] While continuing to shave him, Tom thinks about how he will slice his throat—at what point, at what angle. He also thinks about the consequences of his actions should he take Forsyth's life. He considers himself a "representative man, by whose failure or success [the entire race] would be tested." He also considers his responsibility to his profession, his shop, and his barbers. Ultimately, he knows he will also suffer; he cannot escape justice, as Forsyth did after killing his father. Tom is on the verge of taking Forsyth's life until he sees the doll his daughter had given him to get repaired. Instantly, Tom thinks of how his violent reaction will affect her life and his own. Forsyth leaves—little does he know, escapes—the chair and the shop, gloating to Beeman, "I never had a better shave in my life. And I prove my theory. The barber is the son of the nigger I shot."[47]

Chesnutt, as Melville did with *Benito Cereno*, paints shaving-time as a moment to illuminate the visible and hidden dynamics of manhood in a public space among barbers, patrons, and waiting publics. Chesnutt problematizes the appearance or performance of deference and humility that was paramount to the livelihood of color-line barbers and other personal service entrepreneurs. Tom's Victorian sensibilities of manliness are defined by independence, character, and restraint, while Forsyth equates resistance with manhood. Because Tom does not resist, according to Forsyth, Tom is cowardly, inferior, and unmanly.[48] Chesnutt attempts to complicate the relationship between racial deference and manhood. As a barber, Tom has the ability and opportunity for revenge, but he has no refuge if he does. In turn, he and other color-line barbers learn to survive in a world of racism and segregation. Tom understands manhood as driven by restraint and responsibility. He emphasizes this notion of manhood and citizenship compared with Forsyth's notion that Tom's lack of action was cowardly and unmanly. Although white middle-class men reoriented how they thought about themselves as men, from manliness to masculinity, black middle-class men held onto Victorian definitions of manliness to lay claims to American citizenship. Chesnutt underscores the tensions in race and manhood as identities at the turn of the century.

This barber shop is the site of manly contest; however, the source of Tom's manly restraint is his responsibility to protect his daughter. Tom's manhood is read through his patriarchal responsibilities. Forsyth's blood would stain the other barbers and make it difficult for them to shave other white men. It would send chills down the spines of every white patron who submitted to a black barber's razor, completely altering the trust in the barber-patron relationship. Yet, Tom's decision to take it on the chin instead of carving it on Forsyth's throat went beyond a heavy burden of racial responsibility. The doll represents the central force of his manly responsibility. Even in this homosocial space, in the absence of women, a little girl proves the weightiest anchor that defines Tom's manhood.

"The Doll" also offers a fictional portrait of black-owned barber shops as white public spaces. Forsyth and Beeman talk freely about racial matters inside Tom's shop, appearing to pay little attention to the black barbers. Since we know Forsyth's motivations, we know that he is indeed aware of the barbers. Through Forsyth's discourse and because of his racial ideologies, he at once disavowed Tom's presence and implicitly challenged and monitored his manhood.[49] Like *Benito Cereno*, power relations in "The Doll" are blurred. Barber and patron say very little to each other, but each perceives shaving-time through a racial, gendered lens; not only of the characters, but also of the author. Melville's Babo and Chesnutt's Tom decide not to cut their white patrons' throats. Babo drew blood, but he needed Cereno alive to continue to mask the revolt. Tom, in contrast, was more constrained. Ultimately, Chesnutt did not have the same creative freedom in Jim Crow America that Melville had as a white writer, to craft black, razor-wielding barbers initiating violent revenge on whites. In "The Doll," the racial discourse was staged even though the events were true, but, as Chesnutt underscores, Tom walked the line of invisibility and restraint as he observed the conversation and determined how he would wield the power of the razor at that moment.

As Chesnutt's fiction indicates, color-line barbers were uniquely positioned to overhear white racial discourse, a fact that was not lost on barbers or customers, even if they seldom admitted it. Catering to white politicians in Greenfield, Indiana, George Knox built a profitable barber shop across the street from the courthouse. White businessmen and particularly politicians frequented his shop for shaves and to talk politics. "The Democrats would sometimes come into my shop and hold their little councils and caucuses," Knox recalled. "I would be working away apparently paying no attention to what they would say." As "apparently" revealed, Knox paid attention. To be sure, he was a staunch Republican attuned to local and national politics. "Some said that I was taking too much interest in politics," he stated in his autobiography, "it would not be good for my business; I would lose my trade, but I kept right on."[50] That he "kept right on" suggests that he entered the conversations to some extent, unlike the protagonist in "The Doll." While local politicians may not have welcomed Knox's participation, they knew he listened. In 1875, Henry Wright, a candidate for Hancock County auditor, approached Knox for information on his opponent. "One morning he [Wright] came to me and asked if I had any news that would do him any good. I said if you will come back to my shop at six o'clock in the evening, I think I will have the news you want. He was a strong Democrat and a customer of mine and I always desired to help those who helped me, regardless of their politics. One of the principles of my life has always been to hold old and add new friends."[51]

Despite the political views and maneuverings in Knox's barber shop, he cultivated political relationships in a way that did not affect his business.

Men were not the only political conduits inside barber shops. A host of black women also listened to the political discourse of white patrons while manicuring their hands, and in some cases grooming their faces. Zora Neale Hurston's white patrons at George Robinson's shop on G Street in downtown Washington, D.C., included bankers, government officials, and members of the press. These men sat at Hurston's table and talked about "world affairs, national happenings, personalities, the latest quips from the cloak rooms of Congress and such things," Hurston recalled. "While I worked on one, the others waited, and they all talked." She believed that they talked so freely because they considered her safe. Other patrons attempted to enlist Hurston's help in gleaning information. One member of the press, according to Hurston, handed her a list of questions to ask particular patrons and to report back their answers. "Each time the questions were answered," according to Hurston, "but I was told to keep that under my hat, and so I had to turn around and lie and say the man didn't tell me." She lied to one white man to protect another to ultimately protect herself. Not passing on information was far less egregious than betraying a customer's trust, but the reporter would not rest. "I never realized how serious it was," she recalled, "until he offered me twenty-five dollars to ask a certain southern Congressmen something and let him know as quickly as possible." He even tried to seal the deal by offering Hurston a quart of French ice cream. When the Congressman came to the shop the next day, Hurston felt uneasy about the arrangement because he had begun to tell her "how important it was to be honorable at all times and to be trustworthy." "Besides," she reasoned, "he was an excellent Greek scholar and translated my entire lesson for me, which was from Xenophon's Cyropaedia, and talked at length on the ancient Greeks and Persians."[52] The reporter never asked again. The intimacy and trust allowed Knox and Hurston to occupy similar positions despite the gender and temporal differences. Yet, they also witnessed sharp critics of the shops and racial policies that facilitated their positions as conduits.

Color-line barbers and manicurists may have been in unique positions to observe the conversations of white businessmen and politicians, but this was no solace to northern and southern blacks who confronted these barbers in person and in print to demand an explanation for excluding black men. In 1873 in Xenia, Ohio, black men protested a local color-line shop. According to the *Xenia Gazette,* at "about 9 o'clock at night they [blacks] gathered in front of the shop and held a council of war. Finally one of them went in while the others stood guard outside. The leader, who had thus advanced, then planted himself in one of the great chairs and asked the proprietor if he was going to shave him; to which innocent interrogatory the brave barber replied 'no.' With this the ruffian let fly a rock at the proprietor, which took effect on his left arm, slightly. There was then a lively hustling about, amongst hands, for a few minutes, and the conflict was over."[53] These men knew they would not be shaved but refused to submit to his policy and were willing to engage in fisticuffs. For protesters, this policy was more than a shameful mark of ra-cial disunity; it was an unmanly display of inferiority that burdened the race. As black men repeatedly challenged black barbers on their racial exclusion policies, their responses revealed the economic dilemmas of race. In 1874 a group of black men was rebuffed after demanding shaves in a Chattanooga, Tennessee, barber shop. After they were asked to leave, they questioned if their money was not as good as a white man's. The barber answered, "Yes, just as good, but there is not enough of it."[54] Certainly, white men, on the whole, had more disposable income than black men. From a purely economic per-spective, black barbers were forced to choose between two separate markets, and one was more lucrative than the other.

Color-Line Barber Shops and Reconstruction Politics

Though protests of color-line barber shops existed before the Civil War, the debates over the Civil Rights Act of 1875 raised the political stakes of their existence. Senator Charles Sumner introduced the supplementary Civil Rights bill to grant African Americans equal access to public accom-modations, public schools, common carriers, churches, and cemeteries.[55] The lengthiest debate occurred in the forty-third Congress, where all seven black congressmen spoke vigorously about their experiences of indignation on train cars, in hotels, and in restaurants. Opponents, armed with the re-cent 1873 Slaughterhouse decision, rejected the bill as an unconstitutional at-tempt to interfere with states' rights and regulate social intercourse between blacks and whites.[56] In a lame-duck session, Republicans passed this last act of the Reconstruction era, which guaranteed African Americans equal ac-commodations in "inns, public conveyances on land or water, theatres, and other places of public amusement."[57] It had to be enforced during the return of white conservative Democratic leadership, however, who had begun to roll back the gains of Reconstruction.[58] The Civil Rights Act of 1875 may have passed, but the struggle was hardly over.[59]

Barber shops were not mentioned in the House debates and were not explicitly listed among the schedule of public places, but this did not deter black travelers. On March 4, 1875, John Hunter, a "rather stout black man," enjoyed drinks with a friend at the bar of the Willard Hotel in Washington, D.C., located on Pennsylvania Avenue. After they finished drinking, they went into Carter A. Stewart's barber shop inside in the hotel for a shave. In Stewart's absence, his employee turned Hunter and his friend away because only "gentlemen" were shaved at this shop. Moreover, the employee proclaimed, "Waiting on colored men would injure the business of the establishment." Without argument, Hunter marched to the Police Court and requested a warrant against Stewart for violation of the provisions of the Civil Rights Act enacted three days earlier. The Police Court twice refused to issue Hunter a warrant on the grounds that barber shops were not included in the schedule of public places and therefore did not come under the law.[60] The Civil Rights Act was intended to prohibit proprietors, usually white, from discriminating against black consumers in public places of accommodation. However, Carter Stewart was no white proprietor. He was a prominent forty-six-year-old mixed-race barber. He was also among the first black men elected to public office in Washington, D.C., in 1869, representing the first ward in the Board of Common Council.[61] But none of this mattered to Hunter, who believed he had the recently passed federal act on his side.[62] Having drinks before entering the shop, perhaps, gave Hunter and his friend a moment to collect themselves before seeking a shave and testing the act in Stewart's shop.

African Americans like John Hunter believed a barber shop was no different from a theater or inn, while whites, like authorities in the Police Court, either interpreted the act verbatim or ideologically placed the barber shop as a private business with no charge to public enjoyments. Hunter was among a host of African Americans across the country who immediately tested the new law.[63] The week the bill passed, a *New York Times* editorial noted the changes that Virginia proprietors began making to "evade the law." The editorial also mentioned, "It is worthy of remark that colored barbers refuse positively to wait on men of their own race. In Richmond several fights have resulted from this refusal."[64] African Americans believed the new Civil Rights Act guaranteed them equal access in white restaurants as well as black barber shops. The act lacked enforcement powers, which left the onus on African

Americans to file suit. Proprietors wondered how the law would affect their patronage, and consumers wondered how legal authorities would use their power to define public and private in absence of any clear markers. African Americans questioned the "rights" of private parties and whether or not a business that served the public qualified as a private entity. Reconstruction era debates around the public and private sphere were mostly about political inclusion and white men's efforts to protect white womanhood.[65] But the spaces between the ballot box and the home were also battlegrounds for rights and citizenship. It was not long before framers of the Civil Rights Act were called to address its intent with respect to barber shops.

Massachusetts representative Benjamin Butler, a key architect of the bill, addressed "confusions" about the line between private businesses and public spaces. "The trade of the barber is like any other trade, to be carried on by the man who is engaged in it at his own will and pleasure," he wrote to *Harper's Weekly* on March 18, "and the Civil Rights Bill has nothing to do, and was intended to have nothing to do, with its exercise. A barber has a right to shave whom he pleases as much as a jeweler has a right to repair a watch for whom he pleases. . . . These are not public employments, but private businesses, in which the law does not interfere."[66] Butler believed the bill was meant to enforce rights and privileges already granted under common law in places of public amusement, public conveyances, theaters, and inns as businesses *for* the public. Butler would have been hard pressed to explain how a barber shop or a jewelry shop was not *for* the public. He understood state definitions of public businesses as enterprises that were licensed by the state. "The theatre and like public amusements," he argued, "were licensed by the public authorities and protected by the police." As Butler worked to protect the rights of black consumers, he also worked to protect proprietors, but the public and private rights of both parties were not made any clearer as he attempted to explain them. He opposed "to the utmost of my power any attempt on the part of the colored men to use the Civil Rights Bill as a pretense to interfere with the private business of private parties."[67] He cast his remarks within a narrowly legal framework that addressed venue, but in the debate over the bill itself, he correctly identified the core of the issue. On the House floor before the bill's passage, he had argued: "There is not a white man at the South that would not associate with the negro—all that is required by this bill—if that negro were his servant. He would eat with him, play with her or him as children, be together with them in every way, provided they were slaves. There never has been an objection to such an association. But the moment that you elevate this black man to citizenship from a slave, then immediately he becomes offensive. That is why I say that this prejudice is foolish, unjust, illogical, and ungentlemanly."[68] Despite these sentiments, Butler was not as forthright and candid after the bill passed.

Where protesters read their exclusion as a denial of their civil rights, whites read blacks' agitation as a desire for social equality. Opponents of the Civil Rights Act argued that Congress had no authority to legislate social intercourse. They believed it was a private matter who whites sat next to on a train, in a restaurant, or in a barber shop. European travelers to the United States in the late nineteenth century commented on this lack of social interaction. James Bryce, a Scottish professor who visited America to study its political system, noted, "He [a black man] is not shaved in a place frequented by white men, not even by a barber of his own color. . . . Social equality is utterly out of the question."[69] But just what "social equality" meant to blacks and to whites was a matter of debate.

African Americans rejected claims that they were seeking social equality. They stood firm that they could not care less about sitting next to a white person, but simply wanted the right of equal movement and accommodation in the public—for them, social equality was the language used to rally whites to stem civil rights gains. Representative John R. Lynch, an African American congressman and lawyer from Mississippi, addressed this issue on the House floor. "No, Mr. Speaker," he proclaimed, "it is not social rights that we desire. We have enough of that already. What we ask is protection in the enjoyment of *public* rights. Rights which are or should be accorded to every citizen alike."[70] Similarly, in 1891, Reverend J. C. Price of Virginia put it plainly: "When a person of negro descent enters a first-class car or restaurant . . . he does not do it out of a desire to be with white people. He is seeking simply comfort, and not the companionship, or even the presence of whites. . . . There is no social equality among negroes . . . culture, moral refinement, and material possessions make a difference among colored people as they do among whites. . . . The social-equality question is now brought forward because it is considered the most effective stroke of policy for uniting the anglo-saxon people of the country against the manhood rights of the negro."[71] African Americans understood social equality as a society without class distinctions. Whites would not have disagreed that class mattered, but race and gender also guided their use of the term.[72] Reverend Price's suspicions were shared by many African Americans, and were violently played out in many southern cities, as seen in the Wilmington riot of 1898 and the Atlanta riot of 1906.

White barber shop patrons drew on the rhetoric of social equality to object to interracial public intimacy and consumer equality. Black barber
shops were spaces of consumption and leisure where whites exercised their
power as whites, men, and consumers. For them, the plane of social equality
stretched horizontally—between consumers—as opposed to vertically—
between the consumer and producer, or barber. By marking the barber shop a
private space, white patrons protected the social intimacy they enjoyed while
hanging out there. Yet, one person's privacy equaled another person's exclusion. By adhering to white patrons' desires of racial exclusivity, color-line barbers ran the risk of blurring the line between business and racial deference.
Barbers advertised their services to a white public, who made no distinctions
between the requisites of a service transaction and the requirements of servitude. White consumption in a leisure economy was undergirded with privacy
claims to promulgate the fears of social equality. By opposing the Civil Rights
Act, color-line barbers guarded their individual economic interests under the
umbrella of privacy claims, which proved highly toxic to African Americans'
collective interests in equal rights to public space.

The 1875 federal law was so widely disregarded and contested on the streets
and in the courts that in 1883 the United States Supreme Court was forced to
rule on its constitutionality.[73] The court overturned the 1875 federal act and
shifted the responsibility of protecting African Americans' civil rights to the
states. It held the act unconstitutional because Congress could prohibit racial
discrimination only by states, not private parties.[74] This decision partially assured southern states that the federal government and the court would not
interfere with their maneuverings around the Reconstruction amendments,
and in many ways it set the stage for the Jim Crow laws of the 1890s. Ironically,
Tennessee was the only southern state to enact a civil rights law after the 1883
decision and the first of the southern states to pass a "bona fide Jim Crow law."
Tennessee's Civil Rights Act of 1885 excluded barber shops in its schedule of
public places.[75]

In contrast to the South, many northern states passed civil rights laws
to fill this void: Ohio, Iowa, Connecticut, New Jersey (1884); Michigan,
Illinois, Minnesota, Indiana, Rhode Island, Nebraska, Massachusetts (1885);
Pennsylvania (1887); New York (1893); and Wisconsin (1895).[76] Connecticut
and Rhode Island passed moderate laws that prohibited discrimination only
in public conveyances and places of public accommodation and amusement. Illinois and Minnesota passed more comprehensive laws that explicitly
spelled out a long schedule of public places that fell under the civil rights law.

Notably, unlike the 1875 federal law, the Illinois, Indiana, and Wisconsin state legislatures explicitly included barber shops in the schedule of public places. Northern states may have been progressive in passing civil rights laws that included barber shops, but racial custom proved too powerful to be curtailed by law.[77]

Notwithstanding this tension over the intents and purposes of the federal act of 1875 or the state acts post-1883, African Americans in the North had no idea they would have to invoke it against black proprietors. Black protesters in Ohio thought it was ironic that if civil rights laws were actually enforced, it would hurt blacks' position in the barbering trade.[78] "I am a colored man myself," William Ross of Cincinnati proclaimed, "but can't shave negroes, and that is the reason I don't like the Civil Rights bill."[79] While Ross was mixed race, he did not make this color distinction. He seemed torn between racial affinities and how the state act would cause him to lose his white customers. The irony suggested that civil rights laws were passed to prevent whites from discriminating against blacks in public places. However, black barbers were also discriminating against black men, and theoretically, enforcement of the civil rights laws would have required them to serve black customers, thus driving their white customers away. The struggles for civil rights transcended individual actors, but targeted a larger system of racial exclusion and injustice. In the 1850s, Frederick Douglass predicted this very quandary when he urged blacks to move out of dependent occupations. Whether one was for or against racial exclusion policies in black barber shops, legislation prohibiting discrimination in public places of accommodation demonstrate the paradox inherent in black barbers' ideologies of self-interest during a period of exclusion and the emergence of Jim Crow.

Color-Line Barbers and the Rules of the Trade

In this highly charged political context, many color-line barbers argued they had no choice but to exclude black men because white men would not patronize a shop where black men were shaved. Barbers often identified this practice as the "rules" or "policy" of the trade. When Reverend J. Francis Robinson arrived in Auburn, New York, just west of Syracuse, in 1889, he was refused a shave at several black-owned barber shops. It is unknown where he traveled from; a year later he assumed the pastorship of Mount Zion First Avenue Baptist Church in Charlottesville, Virginia, which suggests that he may have traveled from the South. He would have been used to the color line in southern barber shops, but perhaps he expected northern barbers to be less constrained. Although he was accompanied by Reverend F. D. Penny of the local Second Baptist Church, who offered the proprietors one dollar to shave his friend, it was useless. "I refused to shave him because it is against the rules of the trade to shave a coloured man," one barber explained.[80] This rule was based on the racial custom that prohibited symbols or signs of social equality. Hence, these were rules made not by the barber, but by the white customers. The language black barbers used to justify these rules, however, created the impression that it was indeed *their* rule.

Barbers also cited differences in racial characteristics and physical traits to justify this policy. However, they articulated this racialized language to rationalize their policies that made them appear more in control of their business than they actually were. In 1884, a reporter from the *Cleveland Gazette*, a black newspaper, went to a number of black-owned barber shops in Cincinnati to survey black barbers' attitudes on "shaving colored men." That a newspaper investigated this issue illustrates its significance among African Americans in the late nineteenth century. The *Gazette* staff was conscious of black barbers' policy of exclusion because the staff undoubtedly made their own decisions on where to get shaved. However, in receiving protest letters from black residents, the paper endeavored to provide color-line barbers an opportunity to explain themselves.

The reporter asked the barbers two questions: "Do you shave colored men here?" and if not, "Why?" Most respondents said they did not serve African Americans. Some cited the demands of their white customers, while others cited racial differences between blacks and whites. Strikingly, these respondents used racialized language to explain their policies. Richard Fortson, a mixed-race barber from Alabama who leased a shop at the Palace Hotel, replied, "No, sir; we have no colored soap, no shears that will cut the wool from the scalp of the coon." William Handy, a Georgia-born mixed-race shop owner, answered, "No, sir. I am a colored man myself, but can't allow colored men in my shop. . . . If I shave a colored man white men will not patronize me." Handy could have let his economic explanation rest. He prefaced his response with a shared racial identity and alluded to a market that was beyond him. But he did not stop there: his immediate response was for a black public, his subsequent reasoning was for whites. Handy continued, "and then again, colored men are harder to shave. You see, when he goes two days without shaving the wool turns back to the skin, and so, you see, we would have to cut each hair twice where we cut a white man's once." The reporters "fled" to what they considered a more "congenial" neighborhood, but they received the same uncongenial responses.[81]

According to the reporter, William Ross seemed to run a tight ship in his shop as his barbers stood stoic next to their chairs with their neat white barber's smocks. Ross answered the question as many had before him, "No coon gets shaved here. We have no black soap, and when I went into this business I put up a sign which you can read for yourself: '*No Nagurs need apply.*'" "Color soap" or "black soap" is not to be read literally. They refer to the informal codes of social segregation that personal care products, like soap, were too intimate to be shared between black and white bodies. George E. Hayes proclaimed he shaved black men only if they could pass for white. Unlike the other respondents, Hayes revealed his willingness to negotiate the "rules" of the trade. The *Gazette* reporters left with the conviction that "the colored man of Cincinnati must shave himself or grow a beard."[82]

These responses reveal the precautions color-line barbers took to protect their business in the face of white surveillance. Perhaps white customers were present when the *Gazette* reporter came around with questions. If so, the barber would have to remain cautious. Yet, the highly racialized language they drew on suggests they may not have responded any differently in whites' absence. The public nature of the encounter was much too risky for them to respond otherwise, even to a black newspaper reporter. If their white customers did not believe their barber was loyal, then white men's confidence would be shaken and the barber's business might be lost. The power of de facto segregation and racism lies in its ability to work without laws and without direct supervision. It can both exist and not exist at the same time and in the same space. Black barbers operated in a racial public space where their entrepreneurial ambitions were bounded by racial custom.

Perhaps these Cincinnati barbers actually believed that African Americans' hair was inferior. Fortson, Handy, Watson, and Ross were all of mixed race, and from the South (except Ross). Because of their mixed racial parentage, their own hair might have been straighter, more similar to their white patrons' than to that of other black men. These barbers acted on a perceived economic rationality that suggested it was more cost efficient to serve white men because of superior racial and physical characteristics. Whatever reasons, racial and social constraints on their independence hindered them from acting on their own free will.

Black critics pointed out color-line barbers' hypocrisy, especially barbers who made claims about their own blackness or black identity. An 1883 article in the *Detroit Plaindealer*, a black newspaper, argued, "Though they [barbers] participate in the demands of the race, they hesitate to, and often will not accommodate their fellow man with a shave in their tonsorial parlors. An individual cannot command respect until he respects himself, nor is he entitled to respect until he respects others. Our barbers are unanimous in the cry for equality, but they forget that when they refuse to accommodate a man of their own race they make a shameful and degrading confession *that they and their fellowmen are inferior* and unworthy of the treatment that the white man receives at their hands." Suggesting a hard-enough bout against racial prejudice, the article pointed out: "White men take pleasure in calling attention to these facts and ask, 'you do not count yourselves worthy of equal considerations, why should we consider you so.'"[83] This critique had a wide reach that addressed both intra- and interracial conflicts. The writer called for black barbers to be held accountable for their policies. The larger issue was the implications this had for racial progress. As publisher of the *Indianapolis Freeman* newspaper, George Knox faced a barrage of criticism for claiming to fight for equal rights while excluding black men from his barber shop. Levi Christy, the editor of the *Indianapolis World*, a rival paper, regularly used his newspaper to charge that Knox had been selected by white political leaders in his barber shop to represent African Americans throughout the state on various racial matters. Christy thought Knox was a poor excuse for a race leader. Christy claimed that he took a "colored gentleman of refinement and ability" to his barber shop, but Knox would not accommodate him when "white men were being entertained." For Christy, business and racial politics were not mutually exclusive. In an 1892 article in his newspaper, he declared that Knox had a right to choose his patrons, but that "he must be told that he cannot discriminate against his own people and at the same time demand their support. A white man's 'nigger' has no place in the respect of decent colored people."[84] The black public understood the racial and class dilemmas of color-line barbers, but many rejected the idea that barbers' hands were tied.

The opposition, and even the supporters, anchored their critiques in the history of race and capitalism. A Youngstown, Ohio, citizen reminded readers of the *Cleveland Gazette* "that the object of all men in business is to make money. . . . His patrons were those who owned the country and had all the money, and who would not tolerate for a moment the *right* of the colored man to enjoy the same privileges with themselves. . . . Therefore there was left to the colored man no alternative but to run his business to suit his customers or starve out" (emphasis in the original).[85] This respondent argued that

altruistic motives had no place in economic exchanges, and race consciousness could not displace profit motives. Some black businessmen who sought
to build profitable enterprises on white money accepted the racial constraints
on their business decisions. He considered black businessmen "captive capitalists."[86] He posited a notion of economic pragmatism that accepted an unfair
society, especially when one's individual profit was at the collective expense of
African Americans. While he urged black readers to be sympathetic to capitalism's constraints, another Youngstown resident foreshadowed capitalism's
greed. In response to the letter in defense of color-line barbers, this person
prioritized the masses over the individual. "No man who has the interest and
advancement of his race at heart would conduct his business in a manner that
would be detrimental to their interest and progress for the sake of money," the
letter began. "Principle, our love for our people and our desire for their elevation should overbalance our greed for gold." This person went on to remind
readers of one of the world's greatest atrocities at the hands of capitalism.
"The motive that actuated those that were engaged in buying and selling our
people was the desire for money. The men who do not recognize our rights
to-day because of their financial interests are as much our enemies as were
the slave dealers of the past."[87] Comparing color-line barbers to slave dealers
could not have a driven the point home any harder. But could barbers actually
reconcile the incongruence of profit motives and human interests?

Reports from the North, from newspapers and barbers themselves, noted
that more shops were beginning to open their doors to black customers in the
late 1880s through the early twentieth century. The *Western Appeal*, a black
newspaper in St. Paul, Minnesota, reported in 1887 that "colored barbers in
different parts of the country are exhibiting manhood enough to obliterate
the color line in their shops. The discriminations which colored men have
made in their establishments against colored men, have been one of the biggest stumbling blocks in the way of our obtaining civil rights. No other race
of people on Gods green earth treats its members as some of ours do each
other."[88] The article failed to indicate in which cities these changes were taking
place; presumably St. Paul and Minneapolis were among them. The changes,
however, were likely more black-owned shops that welcomed black customers as opposed to shops that boasted an interracial customer base. Well into
the early twentieth century, barbers would begin to acknowledge an interracial clientele. According to the *Michigan Manual of Freedmen's Progress*,
published in 1915, Henry Wade Robinson of Ann Arbor, Michigan, serviced
the black and white elite and "has completely negated the popular fallacy that

in order to be successful in the barber business the boss was required to draw the color line in his patronage."[89] Class and region were important markers for black barbers who served both black and white customers in the same shop. These shops were often referred to, or even advertised, as equal rights shops. Middle-class men were likely the only black men who managed to get a shave in these shops, which was likely the case at George Myers's shop in Cleveland.

Myers was known for shaving the white, not black, business and political elite. Harry Smith and T. Thomas Fortune, editors of the *Cleveland Gazette* and *New York Age,* respectively, called Myers the "color line barber" who "refused to shave colored men not guests of the [Hollenden] hotel."[90] However, Richard Robert Wright, president of Georgia State Industrial College, wrote Myers to counter this "libelous" statement and noted, "While passing through your city and not a guest at any hotel, I was shaved in your barber shop. . . . I do not wish to see an injustice done a good man."[91] It is unclear if the letter was published elsewhere or if Wright simply wanted to privately show him support. Myers mentioned to friend John Green that "in our cosmopolitan shop 'all customers look alike to us,' the rich the poor, the high, the lowly, all meet upon a common level and all receive the same prompt polite and courteous treatment, we absolutely make no distinctions."[92] Despite this contention, Myers's manuscript papers suggest that only whites and a few black elite men visited his shop.

Moreover, references or claims to serving black and white customers usually came from black barbers in the North. These northern references to mixed barber shops did not translate well in the South. While visiting the South, European traveler George Campbell related how, during a satirical play in Richmond, a "civil rights man" told of a "civil rights" barber shop in New York where both whites and blacks were shaved. He noted in his journal that the audience appeared to be greatly amused.[93] It was uncommon for a white and black man to be shaved side by side.

This southern story was not lost on Paul Laurence Dunbar when he explored the complicated world of the barber in *The Sport of the Gods,* published in 1902. Joe Hamilton, an eighteen-year-old barber, lives with his parents and younger sister in a small southern town. The narrator describes the Hamiltons as "aristocrats," with a "neatly furnished, modern house, the house of a typical, good-living negro."[94] His father and mother are both employed as a butler and housekeeper by one of the town's most prosperous white families. Joe earns his living as a barber for white men and, as the narrator suggests, he "rather too early in life bid fair to be a dandy" because of ideas he gleaned from customers. When the patriarch is falsely accused of stealing from his employer and is subsequently imprisoned, the family is completely ostracized by both the white and black communities, which eventually forces them to migrate to Harlem. Although this is ultimately a migration story, Dunbar also examines Joe's movement between white and black cultures as a barber.

Prior to the false imprisonment of his father, Joe does well serving whites and even justifies his choice of clientele by drawing on racialist language to articulate the unattractiveness of a black market. Yet, Joe's status and livelihood are vulnerable to the whims of racism and his own use of racist ideologies. When his father is convicted, Joe is forced to leave his job at the barber shop because of the "looks and gibes" from his fellow barbers. It seems odd the narrator does not mention the reaction of his white customers. Perhaps it is more important for Dunbar to illustrate that Joe is forced to leave by his fellow employees because readers will understand that his white customers will neither sit in his barber's chair nor patronize other barbers in the shop. Joe laments, "Tain't much use, I reckon, trying to get into a bahbah shop where they shave white folks, because all the white folks are down on us."[95] Left with few options, he relents: "I'll try one of the colored shops."

Joe had once cast fellow black men as the "other," too lowly to be lathered and shaved by his hands. When he seeks a position at a black-owned and patronized shop, the barbers, in dialect that Dunbar was known for employing in his fiction, remind him of his history of shaving only white men. "Oh, no, suh," the proprietor responds, "I don't think we got anything fu' you to do; you're a white man's bahbah. We don't shave nothin' but niggahs hyeah, an' we shave 'em in de light o' day an' on de groun' flo'." Another barber grinningly bellows, "w'y, I hyeah you say dat you couldn't git a paih of sheahs thoo a niggah's naps. You ain't been practisin' lately, has you?" The proprietor reminds Joe, "I think that I hyeahed you say you wasn't fond o' grape pickin'. Well, Josy, my son, I wouldn't begin it now."[96] Joe had hurled these racial epithets at black men attempting to get shaved in the shop where he worked. The narrator put it best: "It is strange how all the foolish little vaunting things that a man says in days of prosperity wax a giant crop around him in the days of his adversity."[97] Barbers in the "colored shops" make it clear that Joe has already cast his lot.

Dunbar portrays Joe as a color-line barber in an unstable position in white and black worlds. Although Joe is powerless in negotiating the inter- and intraracial dynamics of the barber shop, the narrator paints Joe's situation as ironic, not tragic. For Dunbar, Joe's self-interest to serve white men is of his own volition because the other black barbers in the novel shaved black men. Joe's character symbolizes the tenuousness of black "elitism," especially when it was dependent on white support. Dunbar highlights the limitations of catering to a white market and the potential backlash of alienating surrounding black communities. Many barbers separated their work between these two worlds.

Color-line barbers spent a good portion of their days shaving white chins, but their "work" extended beyond the barber shop. Their lives as entrepreneurs were tied to their lives as men and their race. John Merrick, Alonzo Herndon, and George Myers, three of the most financially successful and nationally recognized color-line barbers at the turn of the century, capitalized on the economic and political resources from their barber shops to assume leadership roles within black communities. Their work outside of their shops illuminates their regional strategies of racial advancement to contribute to the expansion of black economic development and political patronage. Merrick and Herndon established insurance companies in the South, while Myers was very influential in Republican politics in the North. Their work on behalf of black communities also allowed them to express their manhood, through independent leadership, in ways they could not inside their shops. They left their client positions in their barber shops and entered patron positions in their insurance companies and political work. Merrick and Herndon represent the shift in the black business leadership class from sole proprietors with white patrons to larger, cooperative enterprises [98]with black customers. Myers's work in the Republican Party highlights new relationships black business leaders had, as racial representatives, with white elites, particularly within the Republican Party and urban political machines. Collectively, their work outside of their shops exemplifies how these color-line barbers used their financial and political resources to support black communities.

Color-Line Barbers and Patron-Client Politics

Northern color-line barbers were much more engaged in electoral politics than their southern contemporaries principally because black southerners were violently disenfranchised.[99] George Myers's patron-client relationship that centered on the economy of the barber shop was transformed into a patron-client relationship within the Republican political machine. In the mid-1890s, the Republican political machine enlisted Myers to rally black voters in Ohio behind the Republican Party in state and federal elections. He used his position as a racial broker to secure patronage positions and push the administration to address the concerns of black voters. In the barber shop, Myers had the ear of political leaders as he shaved the stubble from their faces. In electoral politics, he had the ear of the same political leaders, but, here, as a representative of black voters.

Myers's involvement in the Republican Party arose from his relationship with Marcus Hanna, Cleveland millionaire businessman, and Governor William McKinley, who were customers at his Weddell barber shop. Hanna selected Myers to serve as an alternate delegate at the Republican National Convention of 1892, the typical role blacks served at national conventions during this period, of which McKinley was chairman. In this instance, however, the regular delegate became ill, and Myers used this voting power to help nominate McKinley for president. Myers was not alone in his nomination, as McKinley, though not a presidential candidate, received forty-five of Ohio's forty-six delegate votes as a "favorite son." The significance of Myers's position at the convention was his deciding vote, twenty-three to twenty-two, which placed Ohio McKinleyite William Hahn on the Republican National Committee and led to the establishment of the Hanna-McKinley machine. Myers credited this moment as his thrust onto the "national political" scene.[100]

During the 1896 campaign, Hanna asked Myers to organize black voters behind the Republican Party, which brought him considerable influence with northern and southern blacks.[101] Myers was instrumental during the Republican National Convention in St. Louis in organizing black delegates from southern states, particularly Louisiana and Mississippi. He provided the only entertainment available to black delegates because the hotels refused to house them. Myers's involvement extended beyond major events to behind-the-scenes work to ensure black representation in the party. He questioned Charles Kinney, candidate for governor, about rumors that, if elected, he had no plans of appointing any black Republicans to office. Kinney denied the rumor and assured Myers that if elected, he would grant black appointments.[102] Ultimately, Myers was concerned about the "possibility of the colored line being drawn in this organization."[103] Through his visible work during the convention and his behind-the-scenes activities, Myers embodied the archetype of a race representative in Republican politics. Ralph Tyler, a black journalist and close friend of Myers, observed, "All Afro-Americans who came knocking for entrance at the McKinley door referred to Mr. Myers, his word was law, his decision final."[104] Myers's entry into politics symbolized a lateral move from a "client" position in his barber shop to a similar "client" position in politics. In both arenas, he deferred to white patrons, which curtailed forthright and independent movement to express direct opposition in any sustained form. Ironically, his client position to his white political patrons placed him in a patron position to the black electorate. They, and especially a growing number of disfranchised black southerners, relied on Myers to help them secure local political appointments.[105]

Myers leveraged the white political resources that grew out of his barber shop to assist African Americans, but John Merrick would have to rely on economic resources in his southern environs. Merrick believed that bringing economic security to millions of African Americans through life insurance would best serve the masses. Black and white folklore surrounds the impetus for John Merrick to organize North Carolina Mutual in Durham. Whites suggest Merrick simply followed the advice of his most prominent patron, Washington Duke, to capitalize on the untapped black insurance market. Blacks, in contrast, suggest Merrick grew tired of black men entering his barber shop to collect donations for funeral services. Regardless of Merrick's reasons, the connections he made with white patrons from his shop, the wealth he generated from it, and his general eye for unmet needs put him in a position to lead a team of black businessmen to organize the insurance company. Merrick's biographer—an African American who published this work in 1920, one year after Merrick's death—suggests he received his business education in the barber shop from Durham's business and political elite, but Merrick had enough business acumen, as evidenced by his six barber shops.[106] Merrick developed his business experience and established contacts in his shop, but the blueprint rests more with black mutual aid societies.

North Carolina Mutual had evolved out of Merrick's membership in the Grand United Order of True Reformers and the Royal Knights of King David. The True Reformers was a fraternal society whose aim was to unite African Americans in finance and brotherhood. The society provided life insurance to members, and in 1907, to provide a depository for insurance premiums, it organized one of the first black-owned banks in the United States.[107] In 1883 Merrick, former agent with the True Reformers, joined with other black business leaders in Durham to organize a new fraternal insurance society, the Royal Knights of King David. William Gaston Pearson, a co-founder of the Royal Knights, recalled in the 1920s that "these [fraternal] societies were the trailblazers of Negro business. The Royal Knights of King David trained John Merrick. . . . It pioneered the way for the North

Carolina Mutual."[108] Since most white insurance companies were reluctant to provide coverage to African Americans, a consumer market and a consumer need made black insurance companies necessary and viable.[109]

Merrick's initial vision of the company combined traditional death benefits to surviving relatives and charitable ambitions that tied the company to Durham's black working class. The organization and vision reflected men's conception of business and black capitalism as a male responsibility, where Merrick and the other directors set out to "preside, provide, and protect."[110] On the evening of October 20, 1898, John Merrick called a meeting of seven men at Dr. Aaron McDuffie Moore's office. Merrick outlined the purpose of the meeting as an effort to "aid Negro families in distress" and establish in Durham "an insurance association similar to the two organized by Negroes in Richmond in 1893 and 1894." Each man pledged fifty dollars to the insurance association, and they presented the charter as a bill before the State Assembly. The North Carolina Mutual and Provident Association, according to the charter, had "the object of . . . relief of widows and orphans, of the sick and of those injured by accident, and the burial of the dead, and . . . a certain per centum of the proceeds to be fixed by the board of directors, shall be turned over to the Colored Asylum at Oxford, North Carolina."[111] This was a vision his barber shop could not fulfill.

The founding of North Carolina Mutual provided hope of black economic progress, but the riot in Wilmington, North Carolina, only weeks after the insurance company was formed, left despair that black political rights would be curtailed. In the 1896 election, a coalition of white Populists and black Republicans defeated the Democrats for control of the state legislature. Since their defeat, the Democrats vowed to retake state government in the 1898 election. The Democrats and their supporters looked to energize their base by appealing to white voters' fears of black men endangering white women. The *Wilmington Messenger* reprinted a year-old speech by Rebecca Felton that charged white men with allowing black men to move around the city too freely, which she believed put white women in danger of being raped. In response, Alexander Manly, black newspaper editor of the *Daily Record*, wrote an inflammatory editorial in August in his newspaper, which demystified black aggression and recast black and white sexual contact as normal. Manly challenged the virtue of white women and the clandestine nature of illicit interracial sex. He argued that sex between black men and white women was no less immoral than sex between white men and black women. "You set yourselves down as a lot of carping hypocrites," he wrote, "in fact you cry aloud for the virtue of your women, when you seek to destroy the morality of ours. Don't think ever that your women will remain pure while you are debauching ours."[112] He suggested that some white women chose to engage in relationships with black men, which challenged the myths of hypersexual black men and the purity of white women.

White Wilmington residents, outraged at Manly's article, used it to rally whites to retake control of government and the public sphere. For white politicians, Manly's article resulted from African Americans' political and economic success. On November 8, Democrats were voted back into local offices and control of the state legislature. The following day, Democrats called a mass meeting where they ordered a committee to compose a declaration that, among other things, whites would "never again be ruled by men of African origin." The committee threatened black leaders to respond to the declaration by the next morning or some action would be taken. With no response on November 10, 1898, a mob burned Manly's newspaper office and marched through the city randomly beating and killing blacks on site.[113] Black political officeholders, the black press, and black mobility in the city threatened white racial control in the postbellum South.

North Carolina Mutual and the Wilmington race riot symbolized African Americans' turn from politics to business. Merrick saw not cowardice but manliness in this strategy of racial uplift. "Had the Negroes of Wilmington owned half the city," Merrick explained, ". . . there wouldn't anything happened to compare with what did. Let us think more of our employment and what it takes to keep peace and to build us a little house and stop thinking we are the whole Republican Party."[114] Merrick followed the philosophy of Booker T. Washington that racial progress would be realized only through economic progress, which required a certain amount of compromise. For Merrick, there was power and manliness in property ownership; it was a more subtle form of resistance. But Merrick left unanswered if black residents would have been *allowed* to own half the city and exactly how their property ownership would have given them the power to prevent a riot. Merrick's barber shops made only indirect contributions to a black economy. His foray into the insurance business, however, marked his larger goals of business ownership and his new focus of targeting black consumers.

While Merrick turned his attention to building his insurance company, many African Americans, in both North and South, did not let the Wilmington matter rest, including George Myers. President McKinley failed to respond, which outraged southern and northern blacks. Because they directed their disappointment at the Republican Party, Myers was strategically positioned to push the administration.[115] Blacks appealed to the McKinley administration to denounce the massacre. An anonymous Wilmington black resident wrote McKinley, alluding to blacks' support of the Spanish-American War, and asked, "Is this the land of the free and the home of the brave? How can the Negro sing my country tis of thee? As one of the mourners in a strange land with no protection near . . . I cannot sign my name and live."[116] T. Thomas Fortune, editor of the *New York Age*, a black newspaper, told delegates from the Afro-American Council, an organization he founded in Rochester, New York, to oppose lynching, disfranchisement, and racial discrimination, "McKinley is a man of jelly who would turn us loose on the mob and not say a word."[117] "Representative colored men" wrote numerous letters to Myers to express their concern about the president's silence and its effects on black Republican constituents. Reverdy C. Ransom, a prominent black minister from Chicago, wrote Myers, "There is quite a strong sentiment among Illinois republicans against the administration . . . and it has been openly asserted that they will not support him." "McKinley has almost tore his drawers with me," Ralph Tyler complained in a letter to Myers. "His action relative to the Carolina affair will cost him a many thousand colored votes, when he runs again. The country is aflame with indignation and . . . my guess, when he runs again, that the colored vote of Ohio, Indiana, and New York, where the sentiment appears strongest, will be cast against McKinley in 1900."[118] This calamity and African Americans' dissatisfaction with the party presented Myers, as a racial broker, with the charge to advise the party to respond and inform party officials of black public opinion.

Myers maintained his dual allegiance to both the Republican Party and black voters. He wrote Senator Hanna and advised him on settling the tensions between blacks and the party. He suggested appropriate legislation to investigate the Carolina matter that would also give the president some intervention power. It is noteworthy that Myers alluded to the federal government's lack of power to intervene in state matters. In his letter to John P. Green, a black former member of the Ohio House and Senate and current government stamp agent, appointed by McKinley, Myers pointed out, "I . . . by all means at my command to stir 'Uncle' up to the immediate action, if he does not move, I shall have the satisfaction of knowing that I done my duty, first to the 'Race' and second calling his attention to the impending crisis. If the administration will have this measure introduced immediately, it will demonstrate to the negro, that his confidence has not been misplaced."[119] Myers was on a

middle ground between the party and black voters. He understood the dual-
ism of his position—he had both a "duty" on behalf of the "Race" to confront
party officials and a responsibility to the party to assess the potential effects
on black votership. Although his actions may seem conciliatory, in a personal
letter to Green he mentioned that "the outrages perpetuated upon my people
in the South makes my blood boil."[120] Hanna responded to Myers's letter and
assured him the attorney general was investigating.[121] There is no evidence
of such actions being taken. Nonetheless, Myers continued to raise the issue
among party officials while still organizing black voters.[122]

After McKinley's reelection, Myers wrote him a letter to request his immediate attention to the growing movement to disfranchise southern black
voters. Myers reminded him of blacks' opposition in the recent campaign
and requested he give attention to black disfranchisement in the South.[123] He
noted McKinley's silence on the Wilmington riot "in the South at the time we
all looked and prayed for you to make appropriate recommendations to congress." Myers discovered that a second black faction in the party—Benjamin
Arnett, Henry Cheatham, and Judson Lyons—advised McKinley to take a silent position.[124] Arnett was a prominent A.M.E. minister in the state, chaplain
of the state legislature and 1896 Republican convention. In fact, many considered him to be a closer advisor to McKinley than Myers. McKinley appointed
Cheatham, of North Carolina, to Washington recorder of deeds and Lyons,
of Georgia, to register of the treasury over Myers's recommendations. This
trio advised McKinley that a presidential statement might embolden whites
to increase their attacks in defiance.[125] Most African Americans were not of
like mind. Myers, on the other hand, spoke for many African Americans
across the country who believed McKinley, as president, needed to take action. Myers compiled information about McKinley's positions, as expressed
in his first inaugural address and speeches to Congress on lynching and disfranchisement. "My motive in writing," Myers explained, "is to entreat you
[McKinley] to seriously consider the matter of disfranchisements . . . calling the attention of congress to this all-important matter to us."[126] For Myers,
disfranchisement was a northern as well as a southern problem. He subtly
warned McKinley that if he failed to address black voters' concerns, they may
turn their votes away from the Republican Party.

Myers positioned himself as a broker for African Americans and the party.
He made known his own activities, in the midst of such opposition, to "bring
the Northern colored men into line," resulting in McKinley securing a sizable northern black vote. "One other thing," Myers noted in his long list of

complaints to McKinley, "there was a strong feeling of resentment through-out the entire North, among the colored people that, in view of the fact that they voted, and their votes were counted, and in many states thereby victory was assured and gained, they were entitled to a share of the representative positions. I write you these facts, not because I desire an office (for you know I am an immune) or that I have any friends I want taken care of, but because I am interested in the success of your administration and the betterment of the condition of my race."[127] He was disappointed that the president failed to empathize with his black supporters and expressed restraint: "It is only my devotion to friends holding office . . . that makes me keep silent."[128] Though not an official politician holding public office, Myers understood the respon-sibility placed on him by his larger black constituency to utilize his access to the white political networks to provide political suasion for equal rights.

Myers was not elected to political office, but he was nothing short of a pol-itician. He managed his political relationships similar to his barber-patron relationships, remaining loyal to all parties he represented. He privately took the administration to task for its lack of response to racial violence and other concerns of black voters. Yet publicly, he emphasized the political constraints of the federal government to protect African Americans' civil and political rights. In 1904, Myers organized a meeting of sixty prominent black men in Ohio to better align the "colored organizations . . . and the republican party." He addressed the delegation and shared his perspective on the role of the gov-ernment and its responsibility to black citizens to condemn racial violence.

> Every intelligent person knows that the present administration has done all that can be done under the constitution and laws to pre-vent these crimes and to punish those who commit them. There are many persons, white and colored, of more than ordinary intel-ligence, who honestly believe that a national administration can, if it will, protect every person in the enjoyment of life, liberty and property. But those who understand our system of government know better. Under the constitution and laws of the United States, as construed by the supreme court, the protection of the individual in the enjoyment of life, liberty and property comes under the po-lice regulations of the state and that if the state cannot or will not, afford this protection, the individual is without a remedy. This is one of the defects of our governmental system which I hope will some day be remedied.[129]

Myers argued that black voters had been looking for redress in the wrong places. Since the end of the Civil War, African Americans had held the federal government responsible for protecting their civil rights. Myers entered the national political scene during the rise of Jim Crow, which reassured southern states that the federal government would not interfere with how they managed race relations in the post-Reconstruction era. Based on his private correspondence, he believed the administration should have done more in the wake of the Wilmington riot, and sweeping disfranchisement policies in the South. Although Myers acted as a racial broker, the Republican machine elected him, not black voters. His role was to represent black voters, but his loyalty restrained his reach of resistance and protest.

Despite Myers's political activities in local and national Republican politics, his white social networks remain curious. Paradoxically, Myers referred to Hanna as his "friend," but addressed him by the nickname "Uncle." This was rare because whites usually called loyal black men "uncle."[130] Compared to other cities, race relations were relatively fluid in nineteenth-century Cleveland where African Americans had access to integrated schools and economic opportunity.[131] This unusual landscape opened space for Myers to develop a close friendship with James Ford Rhodes and use "uncle" as an endearing name for Hanna. But this relationship proved to be more significant to Myers than Hanna. Though Myers considered Hanna a friend, he remained politically independent of him and his political machine. He took pride in his responsibilities of organizing black voters. However, Hanna did not value Myers or black voters as much as Myers believed. In Hanna's writings on the 1896 campaign, he did not mention the role that Myers or black voters played in McKinley's election.[132] Myers believed he was banking political favors by refusing to accept an official position in the administration. He figured Hanna would be compelled to look favorably upon his political patronage endorsements. Nonetheless, to Hanna, Myers was a mere pawn in the game of politics. Myers fell short of building a black political base. African Americans could overlook his business decisions of shaving white men in his barber shop if he could use his white political networks to benefit black communities. Within the patron-clientage power relationship, his clientage afforded him independence and influence but little real power. Because he was a client inside the shop and within the Republican Party, he lacked the requisite power outside of Ohio to afford any substantial changes or political security to African Americans.

Because color-line barbers in the South lacked access to political resources during the rise of Jim Crow, they capitalized on black consumers' economic needs. John Merrick and Alonzo Herndon organized the two largest insurance companies in the South. Merrick, Dr. Moore, and Charles Clinton Spaulding were the "triumvirate" responsible for North Carolina Mutual's growth and development as an anchor of Durham's black business community. Between 1901 and 1902, the company was plagued by losses that far exceeded premiums. Merrick and Dr. Moore contributed their personal cash to help keep the company afloat. Between 1902 and 1905, their monthly premium intake consistently grew and put the company on better financial ground, which encouraged Merrick to devote his energies full time to the insurance company. Merrick and the other executives did more than secure the financial health of their insurance company; they also secured the financial health of Durham's black community. North Carolina Mutual added new revenue streams and provided a greater diversity of financial enterprises to serve black residents. Between 1908 and 1926, Merrick and other company executives helped organize a number of financial services companies: Mechanics and Farmers Bank (1908), the Bankers Fire Insurance Company (1920), Mutual Savings and Loan Association (1921), and Southern Fidelity and Surety Company (1926). The office of Mechanics and Farmers Bank was located on the first floor of the North Carolina Mutual building on Parrish Street. By the 1920s, North Carolina Mutual had become the center of black enterprise in Durham, and Durham had been heralded as the "Capital of the Black Middle Class" or the "Black Wall Street of America."[133]

Merrick placed the success of North Carolina Mutual squarely within the context of a black economic sphere. In a 1903 article in the *North Carolina Mutual* newspaper, he wrote that by purchasing insurance products from North Carolina Mutual, black consumers were protecting themselves with life insurance and protecting black labor by keeping the company afloat. Although the black working class benefited from access to insurance, the labor that consumers would be protecting made up the new professional class of middle managers. Merrick believed North Carolina Mutual provided a model for a black economy that would help create racial self-sufficiency. "I hope that my children and yours will be in better condition," he added, "and will have this company to point to with pride."[134] Unlike Merrick's barber shop, black working-class patronage determined North Carolina Mutual's success and Merrick's economic position among the new black elite. In his appeals to black consumers, he attempted to connect entrepreneurs, business entities, and the working class together under the rubric of a mutually beneficial black economy.

Like Merrick, Alonzo Herndon of Atlanta employed the wealth and influence he derived from shaving the city's wealthy and politically connected white patrons to organize a successful insurance company for black Georgians. In 1904, Reverend Peter Bryant, pastor of the Wheat Street Baptist Church, organized the Atlanta Benevolent Protective Association as a mutual aid society to provide benefits to the city's black working class in times of illness and to cover funeral costs. Bryant acted as president and public spokesperson, while Reverend James Hopkins managed the daily operations from his home until the organization obtained office space in the Rucker Building at the corner of Auburn and Piedmont. On July 6, 1905, a bill was introduced and later passed the Georgia legislature, which required insurance companies to deposit five thousand dollars with the state treasurer by January 1, 1906, to guarantee that claims could be paid in the event the company failed. Bryant and Hopkins did not have the capital to meet the state's requirement, so they searched for a suitable buyer. According to Hopkins, "When there were bids by white institutions, [we were] fully decided to let this institution remain as it began, a race institution." Alonzo Herndon, the wealthiest African American in Atlanta, did have the capital and the interest. His history as a barber to the white elite put him in a commanding financial position to bail out and reorganize Atlanta Benevolent. Herndon purchased Atlanta Benevolent for $140, along with two other insurance companies, the Royal Mutual Insurance Company and the National Laborers' Protective Union, and merged them into the Atlanta Mutual Insurance Association. Herndon obtained a charter on September 6, and on September 19, 1905, he deposited the required five thousand dollars with the state.[135] Atlanta Mutual was the first company, black or white, to comply with the new state insurance law.

Herndon's business experience more than compensated for his lack of experience in the insurance industry. He assumed the presidency of Atlanta Mutual and staffed the board with black insurance executives who had a proven track record of leadership in the industry.[136] As a mutual company, the policy holders were empowered with ultimate legal control of the management of the company, but they were not in fact involved in selecting its leadership until 1910. At the first meeting of Atlanta Mutual policy holders in May 1910, they elected its board of directors: Herndon, Edward Howell, Charles Faison, Edgar S. Jones, and Solomon Pace. All but Howell were barbers,

Figure 6. Founding meeting of the Niagara Movement, 1905. Alonzo Herndon (top row, second from left), Norris Herndon (second row, second from left), W. E. B. Du Bois (second row, fourth from left). Courtesy of The Herndon Foundation.

which suggests a certain level of confidence black Georgians placed in these men and their position in the black community.[137]

During the same summer Herndon organized Atlanta Life to secure insurance products for African Americans, he participated in the founding meeting of the Niagara Movement, organized by W. E. B. Du Bois, to address civil and political rights. On July 11, 1905, Herndon joined twenty-eight other black men at the Erie Beach Hotel in Fort Erie, Ontario. The mostly educational and professional elite gathered to mount an organized movement to demand full citizenship and counter the accommodationist rhetoric of Booker T. Washington. Herndon, however, was older than most of the participants and not formally educated, and the nature of his successful barbering business was very much in line with Washington's economic philosophy. Indeed he seemed a bit out of place; even Du Bois suggested Herndon lacked "broad sympathies and knowledge of the world."[138] Historian Carole Merritt suggests that Herndon's wife, Adrienne, played an indirect role in her husband attending the Niagara meeting. Adrienne was a drama professor at Atlanta University, where Du Bois also taught and supported her art. Du Bois served as Adrienne's stage carpenter in the William Gillette production of *Sherlock Holmes in the Adventure of the Second Stain*. Adrienne and their son, Norris, were at Fort Erie, but women were not allowed in the Niagara meetings.[139] Despite Herndon's presence at this founding meeting, he was not one of the group's outspoken members. Perhaps he erred on the side of caution out of concern that his barber shop patrons would be displeased with his positions on civil and political rights. His presence illuminates his interest in collective organizing to address the social and political concerns of African Americans, but his silence reveals his careful attention to how his work outside of the shop could affect his economic base inside.

During a period when public pronouncements of racial uplift were the order of the day, Herndon preferred to let his business and charitable activities define his racial leadership. The *Atlanta Independent* noted, "He has sought to prove his faith in his people by providing opportunities for them in home and education for their families that they may find useful and profitable employment. He thinks he can do the race more good by creating jobs for them and furnishing them opportunities to help themselves than by discussing the race problem."[140] Leadership through representation and charity, while laudable, could be paternalistic endeavors. In Edward Carter's 1894 biographical account of leading African Americans in Atlanta, he described Robert Steele as the "prince of barbers." But he was compelled to explain Steele's profession.

"His patronage is white, and consists of the best of that race in this city," but "it must not be inferred . . . that Mr. Steele is not a race man. To his people he is kind, benevolent and generous, exercising a great deal of charity toward them."[141] Herndon's economic success, however, could not shield him from racial tension.

Despite Herndon's elite status within the black community and amiable relations with Atlanta's business and political elite, his barber shop did not escape the path of the Atlanta race riot of 1906. The riot was fueled by white fears of black economic success, increasing rhetoric by white politicians for disfranchisement, and unsubstantiated public discourse of black criminality and loitering around Decatur Street. Black businesses along Marietta and Forsyth Streets received the lion's share of bricks and stones hurled through their windows and front doors. White men smashed the front windows of Alonzo Herndon's barber shop on Peachtree Street. The shop was closed at the time, and Herndon and all but one of his employees escaped mob violence. Fred Walton, a bootblack in Herndon's shop, was pursued by a mob of white men and killed. Walter White, thirteen years old, was accompanying his father on mail delivery rounds that evening and witnessed Walton's murder. Because White and his father were light enough to pass for white, they navigated the streets unscathed that evening. "We saw a lame Negro bootblack from Herndon's barbershop," White noted as he recalled the horror he witnessed, "pathetically trying to outrun the mob of Whites. Less than a hundred yards from us the case ended. We saw clubs and fists descending to the accompaniment of savage southing and cursing. Suddenly a voice cried, 'There goes another nigger!' Its work done, the mob went after new prey. The body with the withered foot lay dead in a pool of blood on the street."[142] Other black bootblacks sought refuge in the Kimball House barber shop located on the Wall Street side of the hotel. The mob noticed the men inside the shop and hurled rocks at the window.[143]

Part of the mob headed west on Marietta Street toward the post office. Yelling "Get 'em, get 'em all," they rushed upon a black barber shop across from the federal building on Marietta. Two barbers were working at their chairs when the mob threw bricks and stones through the front windows and glass doors. The barbers' pleas to cease the attack were met with a brick in the face and gunfire. The mob beat, kicked, and ultimately killed the two barbers. Before dragging their bodies to the street, the mob completely destroyed the shop. They tore the clothing from the two dead barbers lying in the street, and twirled these rags above their heads to rally more participants to join the riot. They left the barbers' mutilated bodies in the alleyway near the gas and electric building.[144] The mob also attacked a black barber shop at 47 Decatur Street, known as "The Detroit," which was patronized by black customers. The mob of white men rushed the shop with rocks, but the barbers and customers escaped through the back door.[145]

Many African Americans in Atlanta believed white barbers who were members of the mob spearheaded the attacks on black barbers and their shops. An anonymous black Georgia resident suggested white barbers used the mob as a cover to destroy their black competitors because they were unable to successfully penetrate the white consumer market that black barbers controlled.[146] Henry Lincoln Johnson, Herndon's black lawyer with the firm Johnson & Malone, convinced the chief of police to issue an order closing every black barber shop, restaurant, or "other place where negroes are likely to collect."[147] Ironically, Herndon's shop was excluded from this order because "negroes didn't collect" there. Herndon joined Johnson and other black leaders, as racial brokers, in meeting with city officials to help quell the violence. Herndon's compromise with the city to close "places where negroes . . . collect" hurt black businesses that served the black working class. This act to "protect" the black working class actually patronized them and a segment of the black business class because they, not the white mob, had to retreat from the public sphere. Despite Herndon's leadership in brokering peace, he helped broker a raw deal that highlighted the distance between him and the black proletariat.

Herndon, Merrick, and Myers could have left their barber shops and remained highly successful and influential, but they remained barbers. "Both Mr. Hanna as a friend, and Mr. McKinley as President, repeatedly offered and desired to take care of me politically," Myers wrote his correspondent, James Ford Rhodes, "but fortunately being in a business that was far more remunerative than any position that either would have given me, I declined. The too short political careers of both, justified my conclusion to stick to business, and I voluntarily retired from the game after Mr. Hanna died."[148] Although Myers had already demonstrated his loyalty, had he accepted another appointment, he would have further indebted himself to the political machine. Merrick's and Herndon's barber shops, though, were not "far more remunerative" than their insurance companies. In fact, in 1908, Herndon and his wife Adrienne began building a stately mansion in West End Atlanta, which would be a towering symbol of their success.[149] Regardless of the number of business ventures they entered, Herndon, Merrick, and Myers were barbers at heart.

Figure 7. Portrait of Adrienne, Alonzo, and Norris Herndon, 1907. Courtesy of The Herndon Foundation.

These three men, like many other black personal service entrepreneurs, built their careers on grooming the white elite at the expense of black men and charges of racial betrayal. Yet, they channeled these resources and connections to black communities in other ways.

By the time color-line barbers across the country had been thoroughly criticized and North Carolina Mutual and Atlanta Life had gotten off the ground,
African Americans' individual and collective interests were difficult to reconcile in a politically and economically restrictive Jim Crow society. In her autobiography, *Dust Tracks on a Road*, Zora Neale Hurston unsympathetically
recalled her feelings on the summer ruckus of 1918, mentioned at the beginning of this chapter, when a black man insisted on being groomed in George
Robinson's shop. But the incident was only part of the story. Hurston went
on to analyze, or rationalize, her own thoughts on the matter. "I wanted him
thrown out," she recalled, because of the "threat of our living through loss
of patronage." She realized, however, she was "giving sanction to Jim Crow,
which theoretically, I was supposed to resist. That was the first time it was
called to my attention that self-interest rides over all sorts of lives." Attempting
to make sense of the incident, Hurston highlighted the complicated role black

Figure 8. The Herndon Home. Courtesy of The Herndon Foundation.

barbers played in black communities. "You might say that we fifteen Negroes should have felt the racial thing and served him," she reasoned. "He was one of us. Wrecking George Robinson like that on a 'race' angle would have been ironic tragedy. He always helped out any Negro who was trying to do anything progressive. . . . So, I do not know what was the ultimate right in this case. I do know how I felt at the time. There is always something fiendish and loathsome about a person who threatens to deprive you of your way of making a living. That is just human-like, I reckon."[150]

For many color-line barbers, Hurston said it best when she observed that "self-interest rides over all sorts of lives." George Robinson's self-interest centered on his barber shop and his economic decision to target the white elite. His "other lives" included his blackness and manhood. Although Robinson "always helped out any Negro who was trying to do anything progressive," he felt forced to negotiate his personal and collective interests. If color-line barbers' "self-interest" included their commitments to white patrons, then their other "lives" included their work outside of their barber shops. This line was difficult to negotiate, but many color-line barbers before and after the Civil War leveraged their businesses to deliver economic and political resources to black communities. If the emerging white barbers union had any say, color-line barbers would be relieved of this dilemma. From 1890 to 1930, color-line barbers, especially nonelites, faced direct competition from immigrant and native white barbers who claimed the white elite should be serviced by the new professional barber of the modern era.

CHAPTER 3

Race, Regulation, and the Modern Barber Shop

FANNIE Barrier Williams, a black social worker and reformer in Chicago, insisted in 1905 that white men were organizing to displace "easy-going" black barbers. "When the hordes of . . . foreign folks began to pour into Chicago," Williams asserted, "the demand for the Negro's places began. White men have made more of the barber business than did the coloured men, and by organization have driven every Negro barber from the business district. Thus a menial occupation has become a well-organized and genteel business with capital and system behind it."[1] Two decades later William Dabney, a black newspaper editor in Ohio, echoed this opinion when he described how white barbers successfully competed against black barbers in Cincinnati by introducing modern business practices to their shops. "White men came into the barber business," he began. "The Negro laughed. More white men came. Less laughing. The white man brought business methods. . . . He gave new names to old things. Sanitary and sterilized became his great words, the open sesame for the coming generation. . . . Old customers died and then their sons [emerged] 'who know not Joseph.' . . . Negro barber shops for white patrons melted as snow before a July sun. White barbers became 'as thick as autumnal leaves in Valombrosa' [sic]."[2] Dabney and Williams witnessed similar trends and believed black barbers had been on the wrong side of the industry's transformation. Though both gave considerably too much credit to whites' business acumen, they were right that a new generation of barbers and customers had called into question the old color-line barber shop. White barbers envisioned a new modern shop for the white public, but black barbers, in the North and the South, were not as complacent as the black middle class suggested.

Black barbers faced new challenges as the nineteenth century drew to a close. Increasingly they were obliged to cater to changing business practices, which, in industrializing cities especially, emphasized business efficiency and modern equipment, and to changing styles, as Americans developed a taste for European fashion, food, and luxury. Indeed, the entire industry during the Progressive era assumed a new shape. Immigrants entered the trade in large numbers and formed an international union, technological innovations and modernization changed consumption patterns, and the Progressive-era emphasis on state regulation and professionalization redefined who would be a barber and how barber shops would be managed. Unionization and professional standardization were especially influential in this regard. Through these efforts, it became clear that blacks were positioned outside the boundaries of white barbers' visions of the modern barber profession.

New Competition

At the turn of the century, black barbers' leading competitors were first- and second-generation immigrant workers. Writing in the *New York Age*, a black newspaper, in 1891, Henry C. Dotry reminded black workers that "usually one of the first things foreigners learn after entering upon these shores is prejudice against the Afro-American, and they strive to bar him from various branches of labor."[3] Although northern black barbers had been competing with immigrant barbers since the 1850s, a new expanding economy in northern cities brought even more competitors from Old World countries. In their quest to assimilate into American culture and the American economy, immigrants allied themselves with native white barbers against highly successful color-line barbers for control of a clientele that included white businessmen, merchants, and politicians.

German and Italian immigrants were the fastest growing population of workers entering barbering in the North. Some had been barbers in their native countries, while others entered barbering when they arrived in the United States. If other jobs were scarce or not available, immigrants had little trouble learning to cut hair or shave, and they saved the necessary capital to open their own shops. German immigrants entered barbering in increasing numbers from 1870 to 1900 (Table 2), with a large presence in New York, Illinois, and New Jersey. In 1880, German-born barbers outnumbered U.S.-born barbers 1,604 to 1,508 and represented nearly half of all barbers in the city. In Chicago, Cincinnati, and Pittsburgh, they accounted for one-third of the total barbers.[4]

Table 2. Total Number of Barbers by Nationality and Race, 1870–1910

	1870	1880	1890	1900	1910
United States Nationality	22,756	41,949	82,157	125,801	172,946
U.S.-Born	16,377	29,585	42,639	45,253	72,164
Black	Not Available	Not Available	17,697	18,964	19,441
German	4,814	7,668	10,999	24,183	Not Available
Italian	162	Not Available	3,325	12,201	Not Available

Source: U.S. Census

Note: Figures for U.S.-born barbers for 1870 and 1880 include native white and black barbers. Subsequent census reports made distinctions. For the 1890–1910 federal census, U.S.-born only includes native whites.

Federal census reports include second-generation foreign workers in the "U.S. born" category, which misrepresents the presence of "native" white barbers. If second-generation foreign barbers are included with foreign-born barbers, the number of nonnative white barbers significantly overshadows that of native white barbers in northern cities (Tables 3 and 4). Native white men avoided barbering for two reasons. First, they considered barbering an unskilled, servile occupation. Although the close association between blackness and barbering was not as pronounced in the North as in the South, northern white workers attempted to distance themselves from such service-oriented work. Germans saw entrepreneurial opportunities where white Americans saw disdain.

Black barbers had to compete with the growing number of German barbers who were considered more skilled at cutting hair. In *The Tonsorial Art Pamphlet*, published in 1877, Manuel Vieira noted, "We find many number one shavers among the colored workmen, but in hair cutting they are deficient to a certain extent. The Germans display a great deal of taste in hair cutting and hair dressing, and there are more number one German barbers in this country than of any other nationality, they naturally take to the trade. The Germans take more pains in trying to please their customers."[5] In Vieira's estimation, African Americans' expertise in shaving made them great shavers, but Germans' expertise in cutting hair made them great overall barbers. He drew a line between the skilled and unskilled duties of barbers.

While black barbers had to contend with the German competitors, Italian immigrants posed no real threat to their positions in the city. Italians

Table 3. Total Number of Barbers in Select Cities by Nationality and Race, 1890

	Total	Native White- Native Parentage	Native White- Foreign Parentage	Foreign White	Colored
Boston	1407	261	278	734	134
Brooklyn	2216	76	532	1553	55
Chicago	2675	636	647	1163	229
Cincinnati	808	90	309	259	150
Cleveland	527	88	181	178	80
Columbus	282	96	67	32	87
Detroit	456	98	110	137	111
Indianapolis	347	123	60	33	131
Kansas City	583	236	72	90	185
New York	4971	149	868	3843	111
Philadelphia	3032	596	850	1163	423
Pittsburgh	593	66	217	205	105
St. Louis	1270	148	446	383	293

Source: U.S. Census.

Table 4. Total Number of Barbers in Select Cities by Nationality and Race, 1910

	Total	Native White- Native Parentage	Native White- Foreign Parentage	Foreign White	Black
Boston	2561	155	285	2066	55
Brooklyn	5087	69	405	4559	52
Chicago	5681	1118	1140	3100	319
Cincinnati	1019	319	273	303	124
Cleveland	1297	290	267	631	109
Columbus	586	350	97	54	85
Detroit	1066	283	250	454	78
Indianapolis	772	463	95	36	178
Kansas City	915	578	97	61	179
New York City	9155	129	470	8311	226
Philadelphia	4602	568	826	2827	374
Pittsburgh	1389	234	392	563	200
St. Louis	1985	574	510	605	294

Source: U.S. Census.

immigrated to the United States in large numbers after the second wave of German immigrants. However, native whites marked the "new immigrants" from southern and eastern Europe—Italians, Jews, and Slavs—as degenerates who were incapable of assimilating.[6] Prior to 1890, Italians were not well represented numerically in the barber trade in the North (see Table 2). The huge increase of Italian barbers from 1890 to 1900 reflects a larger Italian immigration flow, which peaked in 1907. Significantly, 58 percent of all Italian barbers in the United States lived in New York, and after a single decade, they outnumbered all barbers in the state. Additionally, the number of Italian barbers in the United States grew to half that of black barbers. The federal census also shows that the number of black barbers increased from 1890 to 1910, but at a slower rate than immigrants and native whites.

With the sudden influx of over 7,000 Italian barbers in New York during the 1890s, German and native white barbers grew increasingly concerned about competition. In New York, they lumped Italian and black barbers together as culprits of cut-rate shops. For example, in reports on the enforcement of the Sunday law in New York, the *New York Times* singled out Italian and black barbers for unfair labor practices and for undercutting prices.[7] American nativist barbers were vehemently "outraged" that Italian barbers charged five cents for shaves, below the market price. In June 1895, one hundred "boss barbers" of Brooklyn formed the Boss Barbers' Association to limit competition. "We are barbers first," one barber declared, "but we are Americans always!" These white barbers denounced Italian and black barbers as "un-American" because they "take off as much stubble for 5 cents as they [whites] do for 10 and 15 cents, and they concluded that it is a good thing to prevent this competition on at least one day in the week [Sunday]." A "vigilance" committee was appointed to police Italian and black barber shops on Sunday and report violations to the authorities.[8] The charge against Italians went beyond pricing structure. Many barbers believed Italians conspired to secretly take over the trade. The *New York Times* noted, "The Italian barbers, it is said, have adopted a secret trade mark, which they make on each customer's head or face. A small tuft of hair is cut shorter on the back of the head, and another secret mark is made on the face, and thus an Italian barber can tell whether the man he is attending to has been previously handled by an Italian or not."[9] Whites did not view blacks as industry threats because of their small numbers, but they were grouped with Italians for charging lower rates, and thus being "un-American."

To be sure, blacks were equally worried about Italian (and German)

Table 5. Total Number of Barbers in Select Southern Cities
by Nationality and Race, 1890

	Total	Native White-Native Parentage	Native White-Foreign Parentage	Foreign White	Colored	Colored Percent of Total
Baltimore	1182	162	423	280	317	27%
Louisville	427	66	153	88	120	28%
Memphis	191	24	16	28	123	64%
Nashville	248	32	9	14	193	79%
Richmond	220	11	7	7	195	87%
Atlanta	176	11	1	2	162	92%
Charleston	162	9	2	3	148	91%
New Orleans	672	88	251	133	200	30%

Source: U.S. Census

Table 6. Total Number of Barbers in Select Southern Cities
by Nationality and Race, 1910

	Total	Native White-Native Parentage	Native White-Foreign Parentage	Foreign White	Black	Black Percent of Total
Baltimore	1,508	344	392	491	279	19%
Louisville	592	235	167	70	120	20%
Memphis	492	187	35	47	223	45%
Nashville	320	110	7	11	192	60%
Richmond	361	66	23	61	211	58%
Atlanta	420	184	15	18	203	48%
Birmingham	373	111	12	26	224	60%
New Orleans	1,148	312	320	227	289	25%

Source: U.S. Census.

competition in a profession historically dominated by blacks. Black south-erners were concerned that immigrants would eventually move South and displace black domestic and service workers. The *Richmond Negro Criterion* warned, "The foreign immigrants will turn in the direction of the South. When they come, woe, woe to the Negro. The time is fast approaching when domestic employment for females of our race will be as far gone as that of the barber."[10] This concern reflected African Americans' outlook on systematic discrimination and their vulnerable stake in the market economy. According to the 1880 federal census, German barbers increasingly surfaced in Baltimore and Louisville. In fact, by the 1890s, foreign-born barbers outnumbered black, and native white, barbers in these two cities. Although most southern cities did not witness this trend, one or two immigrant barbers were enough to constitute a rhetorical presence, or a way to articulate the beginnings of a potential market shift.

Black southerners' fears of being pushed out of the barbering industry were not only targeted at immigrants, but also encompassed a growing contingent of white southerners. Southern states witnessed dramatic increases in native white barbers in the first decade of the twentieth century. In Georgia, the total number of native white barbers quadrupled from 66 in 1890 to 253 in 1900, only to triple to 1,025 by 1910. The number of black barbers increased as well, but at a significantly lower rate. In a twenty-year period, native white barbers in Georgia went from representing 7 percent to 42 percent of the barbers in the state. In North Carolina, the number of native white barbers nearly quadrupled, from 47 in 1890 to 179 in 1900, only to quadruple again in 1910 to 778. They went from representing 9 percent to 45 percent of the barbers in the state. While the number of black barbers decreased in some cities, such as Baltimore, their numbers actually increased in most cities and states. But, because these increases were at a much slower rate than native white and immigrant barbers, the percentage of black barbers to the total number of barbers decreased dramatically. For example, African Americans made up 92 percent of the total barbers in Atlanta in 1890, but twenty years later they made up only 48 percent. Native whites accounted for these percentage changes.

Regardless of their numbers, white barbers still faced the task of convincing white patrons to frequent their shops instead of black shops. A white barber in Durham admitted that they met "a great deal of competition from the Negro Barbers. It was difficult to change the habits of whites that had grown accustomed to particular black barbers. We found it impossible to get them to change to our shops. However poor white men who moved into Durham from the country much preferred our services to that of a Negro, and especially a Negro who was more or less wealthy."[11] In many southern cities at the turn of the century, white supremacists charged that black barbers were taking jobs that "belonged" to white men.[12] The traditional southern association of blackness and barbering was beginning to wane. In 1908, Alfred Holt Stone, a white Mississippi cotton planter and racial theorist, argued in *Studies in the American Race Problem* that despite the southern prejudice for black personal servants, few southern men patronized black shops after "having once tried white shops." He further believed that white southerners would eventually displace blacks in other service occupations when they learn, "as the Northerner did long ago, that the Negro is not the only race on earth engaged in such occupations."[13] The black middle class, in both the South and North, was convinced that immigrants and native whites "crowded" out black barbers because they failed to exercise efficiency in business management. White men grew more interested in personal service work, but they first wanted to redefine what it meant to service the public.

Facing new competition from immigrant and native-white barbers, color-line barbers with the available resources made extensive and elaborate improvements to their shops. In 1885, the *Cleveland Gazette* announced the opening of William Ross's new Cincinnati shop, which cost $3,000. This was the same Ross who opposed the Civil Rights Act of 1875 and Ohio's 1884 Civil Rights Act, and was among the respondents in the *Gazette's* investigation into Cincinnati's color-line barbers a year earlier.[14] After his lease at Burnett House expired, he opened his new shop at 158 Walnut. From their "reportorial purview," the reporters "saw that it has seven of the latest patent barber chairs, finished in deep cardinal silk velvet, with an elegant French mirror dressing case in front and a marble-top washing apparatus attached, furnishing both hot and cold water. The floor is covered with black and white square marble slabs, and in the rear is a large two hundred-dollar anthracite stove of the latest patent, and whose heat makes December as pleasant as May."[15] Ross employed seven men and averaged $200 per month in expenses.

George Myers of Cleveland responded to white competition in the late 1890s by improving the decor and service of his shop. "You see, when I started in the barber business," he recalled, "there were so many things needed to make shops more sanitary and to serve patrons better, that it wasn't hard to make improvements." He employed a female manicurist, a chiropodist, and a stenographer for busy professionals. He also installed modern sanitary equipment, comfortable chairs, and even a telephone near each chair. "I used to notice that a man would often become nervous after he had been in the chair a few minutes, as though he had suddenly thought of some important matter that should be taken care of right away," he explained. "It seemed, too, that many men regretfully took the time to have their barber work done. With the individual telephone, a man can have his barber work on him as long as may be desired without losing a minute. Our operator calls his numbers for him, either local or long distance, giving him the same service that the busiest man has in his own office."[16] With these business decisions, his shop was exceptional among black and white proprietors and earned him a notable reputation. Elbert Hubbard, a journalist, proclaimed the shop "the best barber shop in America," a phrase Myers adopted and painted across the wall. Myers's shop was indeed a model of the new "modern," efficient barber shop.[17] However, there were few shops across the country where a customer could get a haircut, make a call on his individual telephone, and dictate a memo to a stenographer, all without leaving the barber's chair.

Southern barbers may not have replicated Myer's telephone service, but they joined him and others in making capital improvements to better appeal to their patrons' modern desires. Barbers accomplished this by equipping their shops with furniture and fixtures imported from Europe to invoke the cosmopolitanism of sartorial consumption.[18] At the first National Negro Business League conference, held in Boston in 1900, barber Daniel W. Lucas of Kansas City addressed the convention about the improvements black barbers had accomplished in his city. In his address, titled "Tonsorial Artists," he noted the large investment he poured into the furnishings and fixtures in his barber shop. Noting the trend to update barber shops, he argued, "The modern up-to-date barber shop of America has a Turkish bath house in connection, and is designed for the pleasure, comfort and luxury [of a] high toned barber shop, with Turkish bathrooms . . . destined to become more and more like the old Roman baths, a gathering place for luxurious care of the body or person. The possibilities for a colored man in the barber business are great . . . if he will see to it that he has nothing but what is the best and give better service than any one else."[19] Catering exclusively to local white customers and traveling men, Lucas emphasized modern improvements to recast the barber shop from a place of necessity to one of luxury. In 1913, Alonzo Herndon remodeled and enlarged his shop on Peachtree Street in Atlanta. The new shop included white marble, bronze chandeliers, gold mirrors, and sixteen-foot front doors made of solid mahogany and beveled plate glass. This enormous (24 by 102 feet) barber shop extended an entire city block with twenty-five barber chairs and eighteen baths with tubs and showers on the lower level.[20] He used this opportunity to reintroduce whites to all three of his shops by placing an advertisement, with photos, in the *Atlanta Constitution*. Whether black barbers purchased new fixtures and furnishings in response

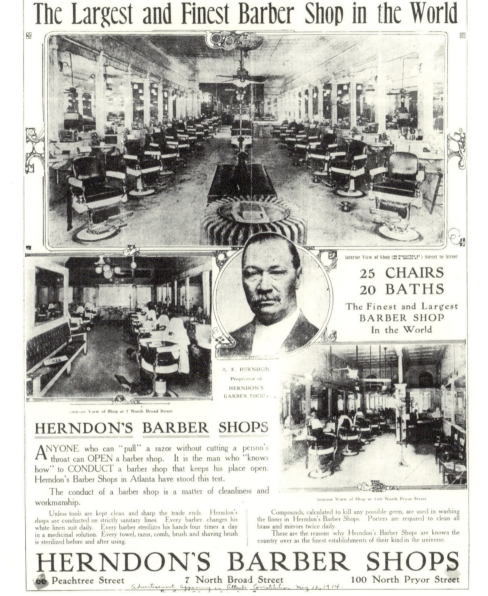

Figure 9. "The Largest and Finest Barber Shop in the World," *Atlanta Constitution*, May 12, 1914. Courtesy of The Herndon Foundation.

to the prevailing language of business efficiency and progress or to keep pace with white and black competitors, only the elite barbers could afford large-scale capital investments.

Despite the major improvements of a few, the average shop owner did not import European fixtures or house a bathing room. At a time when professionalization and efficiency were the buzzwords of modern business, the average barber likely stood out for his lack of progress. Booker T. Washington, founder of the Tuskegee Institute and a prominent black leader in the late nineteenth and early twentieth centuries, consistently pointed out what he thought black business people needed to do to compete with whites. As the foremost booster of black business development, Washington censured blacks, in his 1901 autobiography, for failing to improve barbering while whites "put brains into it." "Twenty years ago every large and paying barber shop over the country was in the hands of black men, [but] today in all the large cities," he claimed, "you cannot find a single large or first class barber shop operated by colored men. The black men had had a monopoly of that industry, but had gone on from day to day in the same old monotonous way, without improving anything about the industry. As a result the white man has taken it up, put brains into it, watched all the fine points, improved and progressed until his shop today was not known as a barber shop, but as a tonsorial parlor."[21] He was well aware of Myers's shop and had heard Lucas's address on "Tonsorial Artists" at the NNBL conference a year prior. Washington ignored the several black "first class" shops in major cities to focus more on industry-wide competition. His counsel to barbers was consistent with his larger messages to African Americans, particularly southern agricultural workers, to "cast down your buckets where you are." He believed black barbers failed to capitalize on technology to secure their place in an industry that few whites historically wanted to enter. The Progressive-era gospel of efficiency lent the black middle class a language with which to explain the influx of white immigrant and native white barbers. But, there were other industry improvements, or "fine points," to use Washington's words, that affected the terrain on which blacks competed with white barbers.

New commercial shaving equipment for use at home disrupted men's weekly visits to barber shops. Before the twentieth century, most men went to barber shops for shaves rather than haircuts. It was more cumbersome to use the straight razor at home because it was difficult to keep sharp, and most shaving soaps failed to work up a good lather. King Gillette, a Chicago businessman, sought to satisfy the men who did not want to frequent the barber shop daily to save time or money. "There [was] no razor on the market," he recalled, "that was of such low cost as to permit . . . the blade being discarded when dull and a new one substituted."[22] Gillette did not invent the first safety razor, but in 1903 he streamlined its production and made it more efficient and cost effective.[23] The disposable safety razor threatened to make a trip to the barber shop a luxury rather than a necessity. In the 1930s, African American John Moore of Raleigh, North Carolina, assessed how it was affecting his shop: "I believe safety razors have hurt us more than anything else. Looks like all men have safety razors and they shave at home. Shaving used to be the biggest part of our business. We have to depend on cutting hair for our living now."[24]

The commercialization of the safety razor inadvertently broke the link between blackness, service work, and unskilled labor. With the popularity of the Gillette safety razor, men went to the barber less often for shaves, and more attention was placed on cutting hair. This is not to suggest that barbers did not cut hair prior to the twentieth century. However, the changing popularity of hairstyles dictated the frequency of haircuts.[25] White barbers considered cutting hair more of a skilled task than shaving. Now, instead of labeling the barber an unskilled worker, white barbers made distinctions between the barber's skilled and unskilled duties. This new articulation of the social meanings of barbering offered possibilities that can best be described as "reskilling" the industry. As white barbers attempted to reskill the industry, or to define themselves as skilled professionals, these job classifications, and who performed them, carried more weight. With less emphasis on the intimate contact of handling a man's face, barbering gained prestige among white men as a skilled craft. Thus, technological innovation contributed to the whitening-up of barbering and shaped the primary work of the barber and the emphasis on his "skill." The rise of a service ideology provided the preconditions for such notions to take shape. An emerging consumer capitalism, between 1880 and 1915, facilitated the new modern consumer service that corporations, such as department stores, used to invoke ideas of desire and luxury. Merchants recognized that the American marketplace had been undergoing a shift from a production- to a consumer-based society. By 1915, service became a necessary business strategy or, as William Leach notes, "the benevolent side of capitalism," that would propel profits with customer satisfaction. Yet employees wanted to maintain their dignity in this new project of consumer service.[26] For individual white barbers, understanding their labor as skilled work was dignifying, and it made them feel better about engaging in service work. In the larger barbering industry though, white barbers took grander measures to establish professional dignity and authority to position themselves as service workers for an expanding consumer society.

The Industry Organizes

While immigration and the safety razor helped to redraw the demographics of the barbering industry, German journeymen barbers organized to articulate their labor issues. In May of 1869, Fred Tourell led a group of barbers in organizing the Journeymen Barbers' Union in New York to decrease working hours from fifteen to twelve, observe Sunday as a day off, and increase their two-dollar daily wage. They held several meetings at the German Assembly Rooms in New York throughout the year to encourage German barbers to join this local union.[27] This effort grew into the Journeyman Barbers' International Union of America (JBIUA), founded in 1887 in Buffalo, New York. JBIUA organizers vowed to "make national a reform movement for the correction of abuses," including "long hours and low wages, Sunday work, and 5 cent shops." The barbers' union was unique among trade unions because, in addition to working conditions, it was equally concerned with prices. The union conceded that owners could pay them decent wages only if prices were at market rate. Therefore, it railed against shops that charged "5 cents" for a shave because union shops could not compete for customers, and owners might use this as an excuse to pay lower wages. Many barbers shared these concerns, but the JBIUA was focused on establishing an exclusive body. In its first year, only fifty barbers joined the union, but between 1890 and 1902, membership rose dramatically, from 800 to 16,000. They obtained a charter from the American Federation of Labor, in April 1888, which was yet another move to associate barbering with a skilled occupation. The AFL firmly believed in craft autonomy and allowed affiliated unions to manage their internal affairs without interference.[28] For the JBIUA, this decentralization would be critical for its southern locals.

Southern unionizers had a strong incentive to see black barbers organized into the JBIUA. In the North and South, white locals reached agreements with boss barbers on hours, wages, and prices. In a given city, all white-owned barber shops that acknowledged the union agreed to a set wage and price scale. The national body issued union shop cards to these owners to display in their barber shops to foster solidarity among union members in other industries. Owners who did not allow their barbers to organize or agree to the union's standard conditions, particularly pricing, could essentially undercut its price scale, woo customers away from union shops, and potentially hinder organizing efforts. Organizing black barbers was critical in most southern cities because they still outnumbered white barbers at the turn of the century. Yet, organizers were not concerned with all black barbers, only those with a white clientele.

At the union's ninth convention, held in Memphis, Tennessee, on November 8, 1898, its first convention in a southern state, delegates decided they needed to make a concerted effort to organize black barbers.[29] The JBIUA sent general organizers on a "tour" of northern and southern states to organize white and black barbers. Whether the organizers attempted to organize one local or separate locals depended on the willingness of both white and black barbers. For instance, black barbers in Mobile, Alabama, resisted organizing with white barbers because black barbers claimed they were already charging higher prices than the white union shops.[30] A higher price level would certainly appease the union, but working hours were also central to their efforts. It is also possible that the black barbers who spoke with the union organizer charged lower prices but simply were not interested in talking with him or cooperating with the city's white barbers. In 1898, there were separate locals in Nashville, Tennessee, and Galveston and Houston, Texas.[31] Some organizers attempted to establish one local, but most yielded to local racial politics between white and black barbers and organized them in separate locals. Other organizers simply focused on setting up all-white locals, even if they were a minority.

In 1900, the AFL revised a section of its constitution, Article XII, Section VI, to allow central unions, local unions, or federal unions to issue separate charters to black workers if "it appears advisable."[32] In the *Journeyman Barber*, the AFL defended its policy and efforts of organizing black workers in the South. They claimed that if black workers were denied admission, it was because of their character, not their color.[33] In 1903, the JBIUA put forth the same decentralized policy on southern black membership as it did for its northern locals. "Our policy of equality for all skilled members of the craft, irrespective of class, creed or color, has resulted in their [blacks'] organization into unions of their own in the South."[34] Their policy also prohibited northern unions from excluding black members. In Detroit, black barbers were admitted to the local in 1889, but when the local was reorganized after a dormant period, it was all white.[35] There were an estimated 1,000 black members of the union in 1903, out of total membership of 20,800.[36] Reports in the *Journeyman Barber* monthly journal claimed that black barbers were sometimes denied admission, but not because of discrimination, since "white men are more often treated in a like manner."[37] In fact, the union heralded its policy as proof that "complete equality" existed in its branches and wondered why the estimated 26,000 black barbers not unionized could not see this.[38] To regulate black competition, the union actively attempted to organize black barbers where there were a significant number of black-owned shops effectively competing with white shops.[39] Like that of the AFL, the JBIUA's national policy of equality had different results in southern cities. The wording suggested the union accepted the separate-but-equal doctrine that defined southern racial politics at the turn of the century.

While in Savannah, Georgia, in 1912, organizer A. C. Mendell noticed the difficulty of organizing in the South. He stated in his monthly report, "I had made up my mind that I was going to organize the white barbers of the town if it took me a month." Mendell's energy targeted the few white barbers in the city, instead of the black majority. "The conditions of our craft in this city have been such that it has made it difficult to organize," he continued. "Many of the first-class shops have been conducted by colored help, some of them owned by white men who still insist in hiring colored men for various reasons. They claim they cannot secure white help enough at any time they need them, but I think the main reason is because they do not want to pay them enough. The colored men are still in a majority in that city and they undoubtedly could be organized, but I made no effort owing to the conflict between the two races."[40] Mendell realized the difficulty in organizing a city with black barbers in the majority. A small white local would have been ineffective in Savannah. Moreover, some white barbers played on the racial preferences of the city's white elite by employing black journeymen to staff their shops, highlighting the difficulties in organizing there. Ultimately, black barbers kept their distance because they were suspicious of the union's motives.

Some southern organizers successfully created separate black locals. In Selma, Alabama, John Hart organized a white local and "all black barbers working on white patrons."[41] Even though W. O. Pinard, a general organizer, noticed the barbers "here are mostly colored," he successfully organized blacks in Savannah, Georgia, with thirty charter members. Establishing a black local with a few charter members was half the battle. In cities where black barbers were in the majority, organizers needed to convince them of the benefits of operating on the same hours and wage scale as the few white shops.[42]

Despite the international body's aims, black and white locals rarely worked in concert with each other. Locals 152 (white) and 197 (black) of Little Rock,

Arkansas, never agreed on work hours or prices. While white shops affiliated with Local 152 operated on a twelve-hour day, a white barber claimed barbers affiliated with Local 197 "open as soon as they get to the shops and remain open until they get ready to close, which is always from thirty minutes to an hour later than the real union shops work." He lamented that white barbers were unable to compete with "scab shops" that displace the union shop card because customers would simply patronize these shops for lower prices. What he referred to as scab shops were actually union shops that apparently disagreed with the JBIUA's hours and prices, but members of Local 152 seemed less concerned with the working conditions of the black journeymen who were working these "extra hours." Since only journeymen were eligible to join the union, Local 152 failed to align with black journeymen to pressure the owner to decrease hours. Similar issues existed in Jackson, Mississippi, and Shreveport, Louisiana.[43]

According to a survey by the Tennessee Bureau of Labor in 1896, black and white barbers in Nashville worked the same thirteen-hour days, six days per week, but black barbers were paid less than white barbers. Black journeymen earned an average wage of nine dollars per week on the percentage plan. These black-owned shops charged ten cents for shaves and twenty-five cents for haircuts. White journeymen, in contrast, earned an average wage of ten dollars per week. The report accounted for seventy white barbers and fifty black barbers, but it is unclear how many of these black barber shops served a white clientele.[44] Since the shops in Nashville's black local catered to white men, and the black and white locals had the same wage scale, it is likely the black shops that catered to black men brought down the average wages of black barbers.

Despite the wage disparity between black and white barbers in Tennessee, barbers in some cities organized into interracial locals. In 1899, Pinard gathered white and black barbers in Chattanooga into one local. Next, he went to Knoxville with "strong hopes of forming one big local," but was forced to form separate locals.[45] Generally, the national organizing body supported incorporating black barbers into white locals. However, organizers usually deferred to the wishes of local white barbers to form separate locals. There were some black and white locals that cooperated to improve working conditions. For example, as the depression of 1893 deepened through the decade, many Nashville barbers ignored the customary practice of closing on Sunday. The black and white locals, however, successfully worked together to pass a local ordinance prohibiting Sunday barbering. This interracial cooperation did little against the numerous barbers who decreased prices to deal with the depression.[46]

Organizer Leon Worthall summed up the challenges of organizing black barbers in the South: class solidarity could not overcome racial tensions.

> We, as part of this great American labor movement, have a rather perplexing problem before us with the colored workers, and I further believe that the only solution is either to organize them with us, or not to bother with them at all. If the colored element is a competing factor in the industry, as such it behooves us to give them a place in our already organized white local and if one is not organized then to organize them into a mixed local, where they can be properly educated into the principles of trade unionism. True that we have places where two locals, one of white and another of colored, are successfully conducted, but even there the sailing is not at all smooth. I hope that the day is not far distant when we as trade unionists will cease to be narrow along economical lines and deal with the colored question on its merits.[47]

Worthall considered the presence of black barbers a "perplexing problem." He seemed less concerned with black journeymen increasing their wages and gaining better working conditions. Rather, black journeymen and color-line shop owners were roadblocks to the labor movement, an apparent "problem" that black scholar and activist W. E. B. Du Bois captured eloquently at the time. "Between me and the other world," Du Bois suggested, "there is ever an unasked question: unasked by some through feelings of delicacy; by others through the difficulty of rightly framing it. All, nevertheless, flutter round it. They approach me in a half-hesitant sort of way, eye me curiously or compassionately, and then, instead of saying directly, How does it feel to be a problem? they say, I know an excellent colored man in my town; or, Do not these Southern outrages make your blood boil? At these I smile, or am interested, or reduce the boiling to a simmer, as the occasion may require. To the real question, How does it feel to be a problem? I answer seldom a word. And yet, being a problem is a strange experience."[48] Many southern black barbers distrusted the organizing efforts of the union, particularly the movement behind barber shop regulation, because African Americans were often posited as a "competing factor," "perplexing problem," or "negro problem."

Black workers were skeptical of most labor unions because they perceived them as organized conspiracies by foreigners to drive them out of tradition-ally racialized occupations—as barbers, painters, waiters, and coachmen. In 1903, an editorial in the *Colored American* stated, "The first thing they do after landing and getting rid of their sea legs is to organize to keep the colored man out of the mines, out of the factories, out of the trade unions and out of all kinds of industries of the country."[49] Many black barbers partially blamed the JBIUA for their decline in the profession. George Myers commented to his friend James Ford Rhodes that there were "no unionists" among his twenty-eight employees. "I have little use for Organized Labor," he proclaimed. "It is inimical to the Negro."[50] He believed class-consciousness among white labor-ers was an effort to "crowd out" blacks from certain occupations. Like other black leaders, such as Booker T. Washington, Myers associated unions and radicalism with foreign-born workers, which, in his view, threatened the eco-nomic progress of black workers.[51] He viewed unionization and reform as a disguise for white control. But the JBIUA looked to establish its control by aligning itself with the professional class rather than the working class.

In the late nineteenth century, occupations such as medicine, law, social work, and education initiated formal entry requirements into their fields, which protected their exclusivity and prestige. In the mid-nineteenth century, almost anyone could become a doctor. These "doctors of the people," historian Robert Wiebe noted, "roamed the land at will." In the 1890s, doctors began joining local medical organizations and pressured the American Medical Association (AMA) to reorganize in 1901. AMA membership, 8,400 in 1900, rose to over 70,000 by 1910. Other organizations also demanded "modern" scientific safeguards that would limit entry into the field. Also during the period a cadre of new doctors transformed public health into a "profession within a profession."[52] Barbers would soon join the crowd of reformers intent on protecting the public but obsessed with consolidating power and authority in their industry.

The Struggle over Professionalization

The JBIUA was not an association like the AMA, and the ancient days of the beard-shaving, bloodletting, barber-surgeon were long past, but the bar-bers' union was equally concerned with professionalizing its field and drew on public health to do it. JBIUA leaders followed suit with the AMA and American Bar Association to create entry requirements where none had pre-viously existed. In the process of professionalizing the trade, they demanded

greater emphasis on scientific knowledge of disease, which they believed
would enhance the industry's image. In addition, by addressing public health
concerns, they increased the likelihood that Progressive-era reformers would
support their regulation movement to protect the public from unsanitary
barber shops.

By 1900, a number of scientific articles linked certain diseases with unsanitary barber shop practices. In 1903, *Scientific American* praised New York's
law regulating barber shops, which the Board of Health enforced.[53] In 1905,
Isadore Dyer, M.D., published an article, "The Barber Shop in Society," warning physicians of the contagious diseases lurking around American barber
shops. Dyer argued that various skin and other infectious diseases—syphilis,
ringworms, and pus infections, to name a few—could spread to other customers through the brush, comb, razor, shears, or towel.[54] One towel was usually
used for every twelve customers. He praised Missouri's 1899 barber law, but
argued it addressed only cleanliness, not disease prevention. He concluded
that the "barber shop is a commodity and as such should be regulated," and
the "public has so long deserved some protection."[55] While considering the
shop a commodity was technically inaccurate because men paid for shaves
or haircuts, not the shop, Dyer probably meant that purchasing a haircut
was not like buying a prepackaged good—and that the tools barbers used to
groom one patron (towels and scissors) were also used on another. Most critical for Dyer and other concerned scientists was to ensure that diseases not
be passed from customer to customer inside the shop. To this end, reformers
relied on government regulation to safeguard public life in a growing urban
environment.

Race, public health, and sanitation anchored proposed barbering regulations. In Atlanta, disease and public health were the medium for framing
tensions with labor and race relations. Black washerwomen were marked as
carriers of contagious disease, particularly tuberculosis. Since they washed
white people's clothes in their own front yards, reformers were concerned
that the "unsanitary" conditions of black neighborhoods were a breeding
ground for disease that could spread to whites through their clothes. Health
reformers and politicians regulated washerwomen, initiating licensing laws
and bimonthly examinations.[56] Through the guise of professionalization,
black women's "lives and labors" were policed. Measures to safeguard public
health and professionalize domestic work were means of establishing order
in the public sphere. Protecting the public, however, meant protecting the
white public. Barber shop reformers were equally concerned with protecting

the white public from contagious diseases. By showing a concern for public health, the union hoped to find allies among Progressive reformers. Black barbers believed this discourse of public health and sanitation was a facade for driving them out of the field. Since color-line barbers were in the majority in most southern cities, labor organizers made a more concerted effort to organize black barbers catering to white men and build alliances with state legislatures to secure the passage of state licensing laws.

The JBIUA saw regulation as a central component to their larger vision of professionalizing the trade. In 1896 a union officer investigated the training system of barber schools in Chicago. "I found it worse than I had anticipated," he reported. "I then wrote an article for our Journal, describing the school and advocating laws to provide for examination and licensing of barbers. That was the beginning of the agitation for license laws."[57] This training system was described as a "schemed system" that made an aspiring barber "believe that a six or eight week course would sufficiently fit him for a first-class position, or make him a practical and competent boss barber."[58] He referred to the Arthur Moler Barber College, considered the first barber college in the country, founded in 1893. Moler opened other barber colleges in Cincinnati, Minneapolis, and New York. Students paid a $25 fee for a two-month program that allowed them to gain experience with volunteer customers.[59] The Greater Richmond Barber College charged the same tuition rate, and an additional fee for room and board if needed.[60] A 1908 barbers' guide described the beginning of legislation as a concern for the public who might "stumble" into unsanitary shops managed by "incompetent" barbers who graduated from run-of-the-mill barber schools. The guide further compared law and medical schools to barber schools in an effort to draw a connection to the "proper" training needed for specialized professions.[61] Since the union disdained barber colleges and the saturation of barbers in the market, it would have a hard time convincing the state that regulation made sense.

In 1897, Minnesota was the first state to pass a law regulating the practice of barbering. Minnesota's law was similar to those proposed by ten states who followed suit by 1902. The key section in the law was a three-member board of examiners to be appointed by the governor: one member recommended by the union, one "employing barber," and one "practical barber."[62] That the JBIUA was allowed to recommend a member of the board of examiners became a highly contested issue in other states. The central component of the law required all barbers to go before the board to obtain a license. The JBIUA's involvement received greater scrutiny in states with a larger number of black barbers and significant black political influence. In 1900 Minnesota had 2,528 total barbers; 1,731 were native white, 517 were German, and 196 were black. Opponents in other states mounted stronger opposition against proposed barber bills.

Reports of pending licensing bills in northern state legislatures focused on the "sweeping power of regulation" held by the proposed registration board. The *Philadelphia Tribune* noted that under the proposed state law, "the board would have the power to revoke any certificate of registration and thus bar from barbering any person for conviction of crime; habitual drunkenness; having or imparting any contagious disease; for doing work in an unsanitary manner; or for gross incompetence, following a hearing on charges."[63] While stressing the importance of the legislation and denouncing opponents, *Mack's Barbers' Guide* professed, "For if they do not [want legislation], why don't they rise up, out of that shiftless, unpretentious manner and oppose it in a body."[64] In Ohio, black barbers did just that.

On January 23, 1902, Representative Clarence Middleswart, Republican from Washington County, introduced House Bill 180 in the Ohio General Assembly "to establish a board of examiners for barbers and to regulate the occupation of a barber in this state, and to prevent the spreading of contagious disease." No one contested the bill's public health provision. The power of the board of examiners, however, received opposition. George Myers, Ohio's prominent African American barber, believed the JBIUA agitated for this bill because it would have required barbers to take examinations before a review board—a board with the potential to discriminate against black barbers. The union's direct involvement with the bill—the secretary-treasurer of the JBIUA actually wrote the bill—gave Myers further cause for concern. The distrust of the union went beyond Myers's abhorrence of unions. Few black barbers belonged to the union, and those who did were treated with contempt. The "black barber bill," as Myers called it, threatened barber shop owners by potentially reducing their labor supply of black journeymen. The average black journeyman barber, however, lacked political connections and had more at stake. The board would have the power to deny a license to applicants without "good moral character," promulgate rules as "necessary," and revoke a barber's license for not complying with such rules.[65]

Myers led the opposition by calling on his associates in Ohio's Republican political machine. By 1902, Myers had fully established himself a major businessman and political figure in African American life. He had helped organize black voters for the Republican tickets in federal elections. He had pushed the party bosses to consider African Americans for patronage positions. Most important, he stayed in the governor and president's ears about racial violence that had been picking up steam throughout the country. In the ten years since attending the state convention in 1892, he had cultivated a number of political networks that he now had to call on to protect his livelihood. But, since he was less than successful in placing a significant number of blacks in patronage positions, and since neither Governor Asa Bushnell nor President McKinley heeded his advice on addressing racial violence, it was unclear how far his state Republican associates would go to bat for him to oppose the barber bill.

Myers wrote letters to several senators and the governor to solicit their support as personal favors against House Bill 180. He structured his argument around discrimination and the debt the Republican Party "owed" black voters. If the bill became law, Myers argued, "it will be the means of driving every colored boss-barber in Ohio out of business."[66] He claimed the pending bill would mean "a reenactment of the Black-Laws of Ohio" by a Republican legislature "against its most faithful and loyal allies, the colored voter."[67] Myers was right: blacks held a balance of power in midwestern states such as Ohio, Illinois, and Indiana.[68] And white leaders knew it. Joseph Benson Foraker, a prominent white Ohio Republican in the 1880s, recalled, "The Negro vote was so large that it was not only an important but an essential factor in our considerations. It would not be possible for the Republican party to carry the state if that vote should be arrayed against us."[69] Members in the General Assembly, too, understood the political climate. It helped that there was an African American, George W. Hayes, serving in the state House of Representatives. Ralph Tyler reported to Myers that he visited Hayes at "the House," and Hayes had assured Tyler that he would see to it that the bill was delayed. According to Tyler, Hayes heard some fellow representatives say "that if the bill would hurt the colored voters they [Republican leaders] would not stand for it."[70] Hayes also complained that other barbers besides Myers had not shown enough public protest. To be sure the General Assembly understood the magnitude, Myers presented a petition signed by 105 black citizens, presumably barbers, of his county, Cuyahoga. House Bill 180 was defeated, 60 to 36.[71] Proponents did not give up, but the arguments on both sides, and the results, played out just the same. Barbering regulation would not succeed until 1933, three years after Myers's death.[72] Ohio was among the last remaining states to pass a barber licensing law.

Black barbers in Ohio blocked the law from passing because of the political influence of key black leaders such as George Myers and Representative H. T. Eubanks, from Cuyahoga County. They were also successful because of the position of the state's black population as a balance of power in electoral politics. Myers's political influence was unrivaled because of his past work with the political machine. But it was unlikely the black electorate would bolt from the party if they passed a barber licensing law. This legislation was certainly more pressing for Myers and other barbers than for the average black citizen. In essence, Myers persuasively made the case that he could sway the mood of black voters if this bill had passed. White barbers made little effort to rally black barbers in support of licensing legislation, perhaps because of their low numbers. Ultimately, black barbers dealt a blow to the licensing movement here not because of numbers, but because of their political connections.

The southern landscape was the complete opposite. Here, black barbers lacked political influence, but they outnumbered white barbers. Organizing black barbers proved more central in the union's southern strategy to lobby for licensing legislation. If southern black barbers questioned the union's motives in setting up locals, they grew more suspicious when the union proposed regulation. In 1906, Victor Kleabe of Austin, Texas, an active member of the union, acknowledged, "We have been told that some colored barbers think the law is for the purpose of driving them out of business. That is not the case. We are all alike in the eyes of the license law."[73] Yet, considering the racial politics in the early twentieth-century South, blacks had no reason to believe the license law would operate any differently from other laws administered by the state that left them few protections, for example, from lynching or the convict lease system.[74] Southern organizers failed to make these connections. By 1939, Maryland and Virginia were the only two southern states that had not passed a law regulating barbering, a reality that local white barbers desperately wanted to change.[75]

Union organizers in Virginia believed that the more black barbers they brought into the union fold, the less trouble they would have securing the passage of a state licensing law. They saw varying degrees of success as they surveyed large and small cities. Organizers established black locals in Portsmouth in 1913 and Bristol in 1921.[76] In Bristol and Newport News, blacks were the only barbers organized into a local. The largest white shops in Newport News were members of the white local in Norfolk. The three white and eleven black shops in Suffolk were not interested in joining the union. In Roanoke, all the white shops belonged to the union, but the black shops were not organized. Organizers faced this dilemma so often that they usually referred to it as the "white and colored half-and-half." Unorganized black barbers of Norfolk posed a major threat to the white Local 771. In July 1917, organizers successfully established a black local in the city.[77] C. F. Foley, general organizer, described Alexandria as the "best organized town in Virginia—100 percent organized, both white and colored, and harmony prevailing between both." Norfolk and Richmond were two key cities for the union to create alliances with black barbers and state officials to lobby for regulation. While in Richmond, organizers often hit a wall in their efforts to establish a black local. One organizer ended his Virginia tour in Richmond and concluded, "Then came the color line, which is drawn very tightly in this city, the same as in all other southern cities. One will have nothing to do with the other."[78]

Despite the union's limited success in small towns, its failure to organize black barbers in Virginia's major cities proved to be a critical stumbling block to convincing the legislature the state needed a law to regulate barbers. In 1924, Senator Howard Smith presented a barbering bill to the General Assembly, which passed the Senate and House Committee on Laws at the last session of the year. The proposal had some key political supporters, such as Harry F. Byrd, longtime state senator who was elected governor in November 1925.[79] Byrd's support was curious considering his championing of limited government.[80] Among the bill's provisions, it proposed that barbers be required to enroll in a six-month barbering course, work as an apprentice for eighteen months, and pass a physical examination before receiving a license to practice barbering in the state.[81] It also called for the creation of a state board of examiners to oversee its provisions. Black barbers were undoubtedly concerned about its numerous requirements. The law would consolidate the power of determining one's entry into the field in the hands of a state board. This initial bill raised a few eyebrows, but it did not amount to a major issue. White and black barbers were undoubtedly steeped in the proposed legislation because they already had a contentious relationship and they were certainly aware of similar laws that had passed in other states. The bill was defeated in the House, which prompted white barbers to form the Virginia State Journeymen Barbers' Association to further the passage of a barber bill. They focused on lobbying at the state capitol and trying to win over the chief opponents of the bill: black barbers.

With six years to regroup, the union targeted the 1930 state legislative session to mark the beginning of a long battle between white barbers, black barbers, and the state over public health, state regulation, and the modern barber shop. In 1929, white journeymen and master barbers met in a convention in Norfolk to discuss the best means of securing the passage of a license law at the 1930 session of the legislature. W. C. Creekmore of Norfolk, chairman of the legislative committee of the Virginia Federation of Labor, stressed the need for lobbyists at the state capitol. He urged delegates: "If a candidate for the legislature asks for our support, find out if he is in favor of the license law. If he isn't don't support him, but if he is give him your vote whether he be a Democrat, Republican, or Socialist."[82] H. B. Hubbard, secretary-treasurer of the Norfolk local, acknowledged the "large delegation of colored barbers from Richmond who were very instrumental in defeating our bill last time." Hubbard left convinced that these black barbers at the Norfolk meeting saw the light of regulation: "We showed them where they were wrong, and they expressed their willingness to help us next year."[83] Hubbard's perceptions could not have been more misguided. In fact, on January 22, 1929, black barbers organized the Barbers' Protective Association of Virginia (BPA) to oppose the legislation. Perhaps Hubbard and other organizers believed they could organize enough black barbers *outside* of Richmond to demonstrate to the state legislature that only black barbers *in* Richmond were concerned. Whatever their strategy, at the 1930 session of the state legislature, members of the Barbers' Protective Association made their voices heard.

On January 20, 1930, well over two hundred spectators, including a delegation of eighteen black and thirty-five white barbers, packed the legislature. By several accounts, Benjamin W. Taylor, vice president of the Richmond chapter of the BPA, was the surprise of the day. He gave a passionate, patriotic, nativist appeal: "I was born, bred and expect to die in America. We are American citizens and I think, Mr. Chairman and gentlemen of the committee, that you are too board-minded [*sic*] to allow outsiders, some of whom can't even speak our tongue, to come in" and dictate the welfare of the state's residents.[84] The "outsiders" Taylor had in mind were the German and Italian barbers who organized for the union. He strategically made this an issue between American citizens and immigrants, as opposed to one between whites and blacks, to sway white legislators to concentrate on nation rather than race.

Taylor also thought it was odd the union advocated for this bill as a health measure, especially since Dr. Ession G. Williams, state commissioner of health, opposed it. Williams argued it was simply unnecessary for the state's health.[85] Senator J. Belmont Woodson, physician and superintendent of the Piedmont Sanatorium, vocally opposed the bill, telling the Senate it was a poor excuse for a "health measure" and was an "insult to the intelligence of the Legislature of Virginia." The Senate killed the bill, but a substitute was offered. It eliminated the examining powers of the board and left physical examinations to the Board of Health, which would only give the barber board licensing powers. Weeks after the original bill was defeated, fifty delegates from across the state attended a BPA convention to oppose the bill's new incarnation.[86] Black barbers simply distrusted the union and the white barber's association because they did not accept blacks as equal members. Therefore, blacks were left with no other reasoning than to believe that the motive behind regulation was to "eliminate . . . from the field of competition the Negro barber who serves white trade."[87] Health officials, members of the Senate, such as Woodson and others, and both city newspapers echoed these concerns of race and exclusion.

Not only did the barber bill occupy a major portion of the General Assembly's agenda, it also filled the pages of the *Richmond News Leader* and the *Richmond Times-Dispatch* for thirty years. Both papers opposed the bill and identified its racial motivations. White journalist Virginius Dabney was a vocal critic of the licensing measure in the *Times-Dispatch*. Virginians were well aware of the issues, but Dabney reached out to a wider readership. In July 1930, his article in the *Nation*, a liberal journal, placed the bill in a larger national and racial context. First, Dabney equated the union's efforts to regulate Virginia barbers with their successful efforts to pass legislation in most states west of the Mississippi, and the beginnings of this movement in the South. He attributed the unions' difficulties in the South to "the large Negro population and the widespread belief that barber bills below the Potomac are designed to eliminate Negroes from the trade." Although he indicated that only four southern states had passed licensing laws, in fact eight southern states had such laws on the books.[88]

Most strikingly, Dabney broadened the discussion of the proposed barber board to draw similarities to racial bias in other state administrative bodies. Opponents of the board believed a white-dominated board with the power to decide who would be granted a license would effectively spell the end of black barbers servicing a white market. Dabney suggested the board might exercise this discriminatory power through the kinds of questions they posed on the examination. He shared sample questions that were published in the *Square Deal* in 1929. "Here are some of the questions," he wrote. "How many hairs are there to the square inch on the average scalp? Where is the arrector pili muscle located and what is its function? How is a hair connected with the blood stream and nerve system? Describe the function and location of the sebaceous glands. What is the scientific name for hair which shows a tendency to split . . . imagine the glorious opportunity which such questions afford a board of white barbers who wish to eliminate troublesome Negro competition."[89] Without explicitly referencing it, Dabney conjured images of disenfranchisement and the administration of the literacy tests in southern states. Southern state voter registration boards required citizens to read passages from various state or federal documents and answer questions related to government. They asked blacks more difficult and obscure questions, however, and sometimes flat-out said they did not read a passage correctly when they had done so. In the end, these boards rejected many literate blacks and registered illiterate whites.[90] From the beginning, the white press consistently placed race at the center of their discourse on the battle over the bill.[91] Dabney had written critically on the bill in the *Richmond Times-Dispatch* since 1930, and continued to do so after he became editor in 1936. He also published articles denouncing the poll tax and urging the passage of a federal anti-lynching law.[92] For Dabney, and most important for the scores of black barbers who had been denied the franchise, the proposed barber board reeked of this "race-neutral" entity and examination policy that would essentially be implemented along racial lines.

The JBIUA had to contend not only with black barbers, but also with white Virginians who viewed proposed legislation as a threat to their southern way of life. The public discourse reflected whites' competing ideas of the modern barber shop. In a letter to the *Times-Dispatch* in 1932, Dan O'Flaherty, a white Richmond citizen, charged the JBIUA with attempting to displace "pleasant" and "efficient" black barbers whose "equipment is as good and as sanitary as any." O'Flaherty opposed the call for whites to displace blacks in barbering because he believed whites could not be as cheerful and pleasing when serving the white South. "We in Virginia," he asserted, "know that the colored man is the best servitor in the world. . . . He is furthermore an integral part of the courteous background of Virginia life. The colored barber who waits on white men is invariably a higher type of citizen of his own race than the white barber is of his race. Many Richmond colored barbers were brought up with and by our good families."[93] O'Flaherty emphasized the importance of black personal service work to southern traditionalism. He spoke for many southern white men who bound blackness and cheerful service as a well-managed racial order. They perceived this as a society where black service workers accepted an inferior position in the public and private sphere.

O'Flaherty's nostalgia for a servile black citizenship reflected larger southern attitudes toward black service workers. In 1926, the white barber's union convinced the Atlanta city council that black barbers should be prohibited from serving white patrons. Many council members thought it was yet another segregation measure, gave it little thought, and passed it. Not long after the council passed the ordinance, it received a flood of protests from white citizens asking the council to reconsider or the mayor to veto it. Civic, religious, and business organizations wrote letters to the mayor and a supportive *Atlanta Constitution* editorial board. White opponents based their protests on three arguments. First, this ordinance was a ploy from white barbers to get around black competition for white patrons. Second, and most startling, the ordinance was an unjust affront on American democracy. They applauded barbers' work ethic and applauded themselves for "protecting" black citizenship.[94] The *Constitution* went so far as to claim, "Georgia shows as much justice and as much fairness to the negro as any state in the union— and a great deal more than some."[95] As ridiculous as this may sound—given the Atlanta race riot twenty years earlier, disfranchisement, and segregation in public accommodations, just to name a few areas in Jim Crow's reach— these white citizens truly believed they were fair to black citizens because they believed they were deeply connected to their black servants, which for them included barbers.

Hence, the third argument got to the heart of white southerners' protests; messing with black barbers meant messing with black service workers, and southern tradition. If black barbers could be prohibited from grooming white patrons, whites questioned, feared even, what would prevent the state from telling them "who shall occupy our kitchens, drive our automobiles, wait on our tables, and nurse our children?" An Atlanta resident wrote to the *Constitution* praising its support of black barbers. "I have had a colored barber since I was old enough to receive that service," he fondly remembered, "and am old-fashioned enough to want to continue it, nor do I believe the good citizens will consent to any such unfair discrimination."[96] M. Ashby Jones, a moderate white pastor who worked for interracial cooperation, put the matter succinctly in his article titled "The Negro Barber Shop and Southern Tradition." He too went down memory lane, recalling a time when he "sat on the high stool" as a youngster "while the kindly voice of old Jim, the barber, told me folk-stories," and at the University of Virginia, where "Bob" was the "wise adviser of every student," and in later years, "Phil . . . who counted his friends in the old capital of the Confederacy by the scores and hundreds." "These are not mere personal memories," he proclaimed. "*They are the memories of the south*" (emphasis added). By declaring black barber shops a southern institution, he made a grand gesture to a tradition of black subservience, which, he reminded readers, "we have inherited from our past."[97] If slavery could no longer exist—southerners lost that battle—then they would fight hard to hold onto the vestiges of the Old South. Whites clung to black domestic servants, or their old mammys, in similar ways.[98] For many whites who rendered their protest in public forums, this would not be a Lost Cause. The council did reconsider by offering a public hearing, out of which came a "compromise." Under the revised bill, black barbers would be prohibited from serving only white women and children under fourteen. The Atlanta Chamber of Commerce pressed on and was successful in getting an injunction. Finally, in September 1927, the Fulton County superior court declared the ordinance unconstitutional.[99] For their twisted support of black barbers who groomed white patrons, a writer for the *Chicago Defender* said it well that this episode illustrated "the truth that the 'd' in Dixie will always stand for dirt."[100] While Virginia's approach to licensing was not as directly race-based as Atlanta's plan, the underlying message and meanings of black service work to the South were quite similar.

W. C. Birthright, general secretary-treasurer of the JBIUA, wrote a letter of response to the *Richmond Times-Dispatch* editor to deny O'Flaherty's charges that the licensing law was intended to discriminate against black barbers. Birthright proclaimed, "In our desire for better barbers, white or colored, in this *modern age*, we are convinced that the barber must know something of a human body on which he operates. The barber business is a science when the interest is shifted to the proper study of his work" (emphasis added). Birthright's notion that the barber "operates" on a human body was consistent with union reformers' nostalgia for the "professional" days of the old barber-surgeon. "It affects white and colored barbers alike," he continued, "and legislates no one out of business, as charged, but requires the future barber to be better prepared for the service he will render, and the present barber to conduct a scientific barber shop and to fit himself physically so he will not transmit disease to patrons."[101] Birthright's response reflected the union's vision of modernity, which emphasized the advanced, scientific skill of new professional barbers and the need to protect public health. Despite his claims of racial neutrality, Works Progress Administration workers in the 1930s acknowledged that the bill "has thus far been successfully warded off, due in no small part to the favor with which white Virginians regard Negro barbers and also to the efforts of the Barbers' Protective Association."[102]

Although the state legislature did not pass a licensing law in the 1930s, proponents maintained a dual state and city strategy. Where statewide strategies failed, reformers were successful on the local level. Norfolk (1932) and Richmond (1935) passed city ordinances to regulate barbers. It required every person applying for a certificate of registration to include a statement from a licensed physician "declaring that he is free from any contagious, infectious or communicable disease." The ordinance also required that barber shops be inspected on a regular basis to ensure proper sanitary condition.[103] The Department of Public Health required barbers to take the Wassermann test before they could apply for a license. August von Wassermann and Albert Neisser, at the Robert Koch Institute for Infectious Diseases, developed the Wasserman test in 1906 as a diagnostic blood test for syphilis. Richmond's ordinance included a similar public health component requiring regular sanitation inspections, but a physical examination requirement, "to prevent the spread of syphilis," did not pass.[104]

The Sanitation Division in the Department of Public Health assumed responsibilities for enforcing the new law, which disproportionately affected black barbers. When Joseph A. Panella, second-generation Italian and secretary of Local 771, was appointed Norfolk's inspector, he assured barbers it "makes no discrimination as between races, and will give a certificate of registration to any barber now in practice who is physically fit."[105] Black barbers were surely concerned with ambiguous language in the ordinance such as "physically fit." Panella noted in his second annual report that forty-four black barbers and thirteen white barbers tested positive for syphilis. In the first year of Norfolk's ordinance, thirty-nine barber shops were closed, while nine were closed in the second year.[106] According to Richmond's chief city sanitary officer Arthur B. Ferguson's annual report in 1936, inspectors made 3,207 visits and cited operators for combs, razors, mugs, and windows.[107] The following year, inspections reached a racial fever pitch in the city. The Sanitation Division directly targeted black barber shops for inspection to enforce the ordinance, such as requiring hot and cold running water in their shops. Inspectors ordered twelve black barbers to comply with the city sanitary code by making various upgrades or improvements to their shops. For example, an inspector ordered Richard Howard, at 552 Brook Avenue, to install a new water heater or receive a $25 fine each day the alleged violations persisted. Unfortunately, Howard's newly installed heater exploded, causing injuries to himself, his shop, and a customer. While there is no evidence indicating the condition of Howard's water heater, it is ironic that this incident occurred as a result of Howard complying with the city. K. C. Sargeant, one of the three inspectors who conducted the investigations, testified that black barbers heated water on a stove or grill. Sargeant acknowledged, "There are about seventy-five Negro barber shops and beauty parlors in Richmond and we are rigidly inspecting all of them." Yet, Ferguson insisted, "there is absolutely no discrimination being made against the Negro barber in our effort to enforce the code."[108]

Despite the vigorous city inspections, Richmond's white barbers were not satisfied without a physical examination provision, which the City Council approved in August 1939.[109] The new ordinance required barbers to prove they were free of any infectious diseases, particularly venereal diseases and tuberculosis.[110] There were approximately 207 barber shops (122 white, 85 black) and 585 barbers (313 white, 272 black) in the city. When the Ordinance Committee specifically asked Roscoe B. Greenway, legislative chairman of the Central Trades and Labor Council, what black barbers thought of the new requirement, he said they had been "informed and acquiesced to its passage."[111] Within the first five months, inspectors "uncovered" eighty-nine cases of venereal disease and five cases of tuberculosis among barbers, beauticians, and manicurists. The venereal disease cases amounted to 5.5 percent of the total of the three groups.[112]

Whites' obsession with containing contagious diseases through occupational laws encouraged some in the medical community to better inform the public. On October 31, 1939, Dr. Joseph E. Moore of Johns Hopkins University delivered a speech at the New England Post Graduate Assembly of Harvard University to address the misconceptions of syphilis and communicable diseases. According to Moore, the examination of barbers, beauticians, domestics, cooks, and waiters to determine if they had syphilis was unjustified because "ninety-nine and nine-tenths per cent of all infections with syphilis are acquired by means of one or another form of sexual contact and by this means only." Education awareness campaigns tended to target African Americans. White employers and state agencies used these campaigns to "exercise their prejudice against Negroes," forcing them out of work.[113] Although Norfolk inspectors found that forty-four black barbers tested positive in 1935, ultimately there was no danger of them passing the disease to their customers. As historian Pippa Holloway points out, Virginia's venereal disease program in the 1930s demonstrated how whites attempted to employ the state and public policy to regulate sex and manage race and class relations.[114] In whites' attempts to regulate the barber shop by policing the space for sexually transmitted disease, black women were indirectly implicated in this "public health" project. The barber bill forced many to wonder who needed to be protected and from whom. No one, not even Dr. Moore, dared ask what kind of sexual activity would be happening inside barber shops that the public needed protection from any sexually transmitted diseases. Questions of sex did not enter the public discourse on the bill, but even the general concern of public health did not go without question and critique.

White barbers' success on the city level encouraged them to keep pushing for a state law. And, they pushed for three solid decades. The bill was introduced and rejected so much the press called it the "customary barber bill."[115] Senator Alexander Bivins, a supporter of the legislation, made it known that he patronized a black barber shop and would continue to do so if the bill passed. Opponents, barbers and senators alike, identified the bill's hidden, and potentially far-reaching, agenda. In 1938, Senator Gordon B. Ambler pointed out the irony that the state board of health opposed a bill that proponents claimed was a health measure. He was not critiquing the health board, but rather was skeptical of the bill. He charged the union with introducing this legislation to displace black barbers and increase prices. "In some sections of Virginia," he noted, "Negro barbers have charged 25 cents for haircuts and their shops have been picketed by labor to force them to raise the price. We are faced with one thing in this country—protection of our democratic institutions."[116] White barbers were far more concerned with employing the state to help them protect their jobs, even beyond the competition with black barbers. For example, after Richmond passed its 1939 ordinance, white barbers took issue with city firemen who occasionally gave free haircuts to children. John Lloyd filed a complaint with the city, noting that this practice "placed them under the provisions of the barber ordinance."[117] Who knows what Lloyd would have thought of a father cutting his son's hair at home, but this surveillance informed the underlying protectionist motives of regulation.

Architects of the bill continued to shape it to increase its chances of passing the Senate, but they had not learned much because they continued to press for the same issues. They attempted to address the racial concerns by guaranteeing one of the three state board positions, for barbers and beauticians, to an African American. This hardly addressed the core concerns of many citizens in the state. For many years, proposed barbering bills made it out of committee and passed in the House, but not the Senate, because its members could not be persuaded to support the health component and the state board.[118]

In this long campaign to regulate barbers in multiple state congressional sessions throughout the 1940s and 1950s, southern white congressmen stood before their peers and openly defended black barbers. To be sure, others simply opposed the new administrative capacities in the bill. Their support should not be mistaken for racial liberalism. Senator Ambler's sentiments about the "protection of our democratic institutions" rang hollow within the context of African American life in Jim Crow Virginia. Ambler was much more progressive than many of his colleagues, but he did not have far to go in this regard. In 1940, Ambler unseated Richmond's mayor, J. Fulmer Bright, who had held office since 1924 and championed segregationist policies in municipal government.[119] In 1944, the General Laws Committee invited several African American leaders from the state to a hearing to give testimony on the potential effects of barbering legislation.[120] That African Americans got a "hearing" in the political sphere when most black citizens in the state were disenfranchised was at once disingenuous and encouraging.

White supporters stood up for black barbers because they firmly believed that African Americans served the nation best by serving white people, thus defining second-class citizenship. White elites perceived the barber bill as a populist attempt to control, or redefine, how they managed race in Virginia.[121] This long fight amounted to a battle between white unionized barbers and color-line barbers over white patrons and prices. Advocates of the bill cared little about the health of black residents. Health officials stopped short of disagreeing on health oversight, but they believed this was their function, not that of a group of appointed barbers on a new state board. White public advocacy for black barbers centered on their history of service to a white public. In Dabney's defense of black barbers, he noted, "The Negro barbers are among the most valuable elements of Negro citizenship." As "liberal" as Dabney may have been and as significant as barbers were to black business development, servicing the white public hardly equated to the value of citizenship. For Dabney and scores of other white Virginians, grooming white men meant grooming a racial ideology of black citizenship. Even black barbers staked their claims against the bill on their service to white patrons. Thomas Chappell, secretary of the Barbers' Protective Association, testified at the 1944 hearing that he had groomed some of the "best white trade in

Richmond" and preferred to keep it that way. So did his "white trade"—but for very different reasons.[122]

By the early twentieth century, white patrons began to shift their patronage from black to white shops. In 1908, a black barber in Columbus, Ohio, noted, "A white man came into a barber shop and pulled off his coat ready to have some work done, when, looking around, he notice that all the barbers were colored. A look of surprise and disappointment came over his face. He put on his coat again and walked out without saying a word."[123] While visiting two black locals in Memphis and Little Rock in 1911, union organizer A. C. Mendell noticed many black locals were growing smaller. He believed, "The white barbers are getting in control of all the business which formerly were conducted by the colored men."[124] In June 1924, an editorial in the *Louisville Courier-Journal* lamented, "Along with the old-time negro hotel porter, the negro barber that shaved 'white folks' has about passed." In Louisville and other southern cities, many blacks maintained their positions as barbers for whites at least until the Great Depression.[125]

Elite black barbers who managed to hold on to their white customers faced challenges from other state authorities and local realtors. George Myers maintained his white clientele throughout his career principally because of long-standing relationships. In the mid-1920s, however, the management of the Hollenden Hotel, home to Myers's barber shop, informed Myers that upon his retirement white barbers and manicurists would replace his all-black staff. He held off retirement for a few years so his employees would not be replaced, but he eventually sold out to the hotel.[126]

Being a modern professional barber required knowledge of science and public health. If there was ever nostalgia for the ancient image of the trade when barbers were surgeons, it certainly began in the late nineteenth century. White barbers argued that in order to protect the public from infectious diseases, the modern barber needed to know about those diseases and the proper way to sanitize his shop. By the 1920s, barber colleges included elementary chemistry, bacteriology, and anatomy in their curriculum.[127] Barbering textbooks of the mid-twentieth century read much like medical books. Their titles also reflect the emphasis on science: *Modern Textbook of Barbering: A Practical Course on the Scientific Fundamentals of Barbering for Students and Practicing Barbers; Art and Science of Barbering; Practical and Scientific Barbering.*[128]

White barbers envisioned a modern barber shop with uniform prices and licensing regulations with sanitary standards, and ultimately barber shops were seen as spaces where skilled craftsmen performed their artistry on white men in urban America. Color-line barbers were targeted as direct competitors, but they fought back in various ways to protect their positions in the market. Yet, black barbers were not passive victims in white barbers' modernity project. A new generation of black barbers emerged, and they also envisioned a modern barber shop: one that looked radically different from the color-line shops whites tried so hard to disrupt.

PART II

Black Barbers, Patrons, and Public Spaces

CHAPTER 4

Rise of the New Negro Barber

I N 1904, Paul Laurence Dunbar published *The Heart of Happy Hollow*, a collection of short stories that included "The Scapegoat," the first in a long line of twentieth-century works of fiction by black writers to explore the role black barbers and barber shops played in black communities. In the story, Dunbar captures well the changing currency of barber shops in the black community. Robinson Asbury, the protagonist, starts out working as a bootblack in a barber shop and moves up the ladder to become a porter, messenger, and barber, eventually purchasing his own shop. Dunbar was conscious of the racial politics surrounding color-line barbers who did business downtown to serve the white elite and the protest against these shops. Asbury opens his shop where "it would do the most good," which was in the town's black community as opposed to downtown. In locating Asbury's shop within the black community, Dunbar provides a keen contrast to the color-line shops of old. The narrator explains:

> The shop really became a sort of club, and, on Saturday nights especially, was the gathering place of the men of the whole Negro quarter. He kept the illustrated and race journals there, and those who cared neither to talk nor listen to some one else might see pictured the doings of high society in very short skirts or read in the Negro papers how Miss Boston had entertained Miss Blueford to tea on such and such an afternoon. Also, he kept the policy returns [numbers gambling], which was wise, if not moral.[1]

The shop's success establishes Asbury as an influential member of the black community; he comes into contact and establishes relationships with a number of prominent men and has access to the latest news and information. For these reasons, the local white political machine selects Asbury to manage the black constituency. He will "carry his people's vote in his vest pocket," and party managers will give him money, power, privilege, and patronage. Asbury is catapulted to a leadership position not simply because he was a barber, but because his barber shop was a gathering place for black men and potential voters. Although Asbury is fictional, men like him and shops like his became important fixtures in black communities throughout the twentieth century.

In addition to increasing competition, professionalization, and regulation, black barber shops also underwent dramatic internal changes between 1900 and 1940. The typical black shop in 1900 included three to four black barbers shaving white patrons, while a set of other white men sat in the waiting chairs talking or reading the newspaper. Those patrons were likely middle- to upper-class men who preferred to be groomed by a black barber to reinforce their own racial and class identities. Deference organized the barber-patron relationship that barbers had to negotiate to maintain trust. Trust in this case meant that white patrons did not think their black barber was capable of slicing their throats or serving black patrons when the shop closed. The black barber-white patron relationship of the nineteenth century was impersonal, paternal, and based on patron-clientage; in short, these were business relationships. By 1940, these businesses that capitalized on a white clientele had been transformed into black commercial public spaces. Now, black barbers openly trimmed the locks of black men. Black shop owners no longer stood among the wealthiest members of black communities, but barber shops and beauty shops nevertheless led the list of successful black businesses in most cities. In the process, barbers' social standing changed and became tied to their customer base in the same way that a preacher was significant primarily because of his congregation. For black customers, the regularity of shaving-time, or more accurately haircutting-time, allowed a relationship to develop that was akin to the doctor-patient trust. This relationship was personal and often generational, as a barber might groom multiple generations of men and boys in one family. By the mid-twentieth century, conversation and congregation were hallmarks of most black barber shops.

This most dramatic of transformations in the first four decades of the twentieth century reflected not just white barbers' efforts to realize their visions of a modern, professional barber shop, but also black barbers' historical experiences. Black barber shops were products of both the rise of Jim Crow and Progressive-era labor reform, as well as blacks' increasing support of the concept of black autonomy. Crystallized during the first large-scale black migration, the concept of autonomy within the black barber shop was both an institutional principle and an ideological orientation of race and masculinity. Color-line barbers' shift in location and customer base was not solely a product of displacement. Rather, a new generation of African American businessmen—the first to be born after the Civil War—put less emphasis on catering to the white elite and paid more attention to the black urban market. This new generation of black barbers recognized that they had more options than adhering to the color line in their shops. Instead, blackness and black culture could be produced and reproduced in a commercial space that brought black men of various class levels to the same shop. Work and leisure defined the boundaries of the making of the modern black barber shop, which allowed entrepreneurship, black identity, and public discourse to flourish.

Black Barbers for Black Clients

This new generation of barbers had been born into freedom between 1870 and 1880 and entered the field during the rise of Jim Crow and increasing competition between white and black barbers. The era was marked not only by increasing segregation and racial violence, but also by a rising tide of black resistance and protest.[2] Unlike their predecessors, these new barbers were not committed to white customers. Instead, they catered to a small but growing black consumer market. Like other black entrepreneurs, political leaders, and social reformers of the era, this generation of "New Negro" barbers began to focus on the internal needs and wants of black communities, in the process becoming significant fixtures in those communities.

The turn of the century was a transitional period in barbering, and color-line barbers of the old generation still had significant influence as New Negro barbers established themselves. As businessmen, both generations believed African Americans should control their own economic freedom. Color-line barbers like George Myers agreed with the general economic philosophy of Booker T. Washington that business and economic development was the best path to racial advancement. Myers believed African Americans would have to make money to rise above their subjugated status.[3] At a 1905 banquet for Washington in Cleveland, Myers proclaimed, "For a Negro to go into business means a great deal. It is indeed a step in social progress."[4] It was a masculine presumption that individual economic progress would stimulate collective racial advancement. Barbers of all ages would have agreed with Myers, but economic self-sufficiency has been used as a conservative and radical philosophy within black political thought.

The old and new generations disagreed, however, on the role that race should play in business marketing and promotion. The emphasis on appealing to black consumers and creating a separate economic sphere ran counter to the business philosophies of color-line barbers of the old generation. Since establishing the National Negro Business League (NNBL) in 1900, Washington extended numerous invitations to Myers to speak on the barbering profession at the League's annual conventions, but Myers declined every time.[5] These national conventions provided a forum for African Americans from across the country to report, or more often boast, of the business activity taking place in their cities and sound the call for mutual cooperation between black entrepreneurs and consumers.[6] Myers, however, urged black entrepreneurs to appeal to both black and white customers without racial distinctions. "Many of our people in business and practicing the professions seek to make color an asset," he stated. "Don't be a *colored* business man. Don't be a *colored* professional man. It's an admission of inferiority."[7] Myers was one of Washington's most loyal allies in the North, even though he fundamentally disagreed with Washington's philosophies. The racial politics of barbering prevented Myers and barbers like him from appealing to white and black customers, but a younger generation of barbers viewed a black market differently.

By 1915, the black elite occupational structure shifted from personal service entrepreneurs to professional endeavors and financial services entrepreneurs. Black doctors, lawyers, and teachers began their ascent to racial leadership. Financial services entrepreneurs—such as accountants, realtors, and insurance agents—defined the new black business community of the twentieth century.[8] These professions may have been more prestigious, but they also required significant start-up costs. The new generation of barbers would not achieve the same wealth as Myers, Alonzo Herndon of Atlanta, or John Merrick of Durham, but a haircut would always be in demand, and the costs to enter the field would remain low. Even though barbers faded out of the black elite occupational structure, shop owners were still a part of the business class.

Barbers were among a group of businessmen and -women who stood apart from the new black business and professional class. Unlike black grocers or tailors, black barbers, beauticians, and undertakers did not compete with their white counterparts, who generally did not want to handle black bodies. Moreover, black customers made conscious decisions to patronize black barber shops. Black consumers may have questioned whether white-owned grocery store chains stocked a better quality of breads at a lower price than local black grocers did. Black patients may have questioned if black physicians were as qualified to treat them as white physicians. But, black men seldom questioned whether white barbers provided a better haircut or closer shave. Additionally, black consumers could neither congregate in a white barber shop nor discuss racial matters in the company of white patrons. African Americans needed spaces where they could not only get a haircut but also gather in public, without the usual surveillance that accompanied other public spaces like parks, groceries, and street corners, to make sense of the changing social, economic, and political landscape around them. Since barbers did not have to compete with white businesses in the same ways as their peers, the masses of black men who migrated to southern and northern cities during the Great Migration increased their consumer base many-fold.

The Great Migration marked a central turning point in the growth of black barber shops, and it was during this era that they first began functioning as black public spaces. During the first four decades of the twentieth century, black barbers welcomed thousands of new black consumers as a result of Jim Crow repression in southern rural areas and labor shortages in northern cities. Robert Horton, a shop owner in Hattiesburg, Mississippi, spent a week with his daughter in New Orleans while she was enrolled at Straight College. During his brief stay, he cut hair in a shop and became engrossed in the constant talk about the migration. One day a labor agent came in to convince people to go north to fill labor shortages.[9] According to historian James Grossman, Horton had "occasionally received letters from a brother who had moved to Chicago in 1898,"[10] so while this was not news to him, he sensed a tide was turning.

Like Horton, many African Americans sought information from others as they weighed the possibilities of such a move, and many turned to the *Chicago Defender* as an authoritative source in describing job opportunities and living conditions in the city. Indeed, the *Defender* was sold, or at least available to read, inside barber shops "to supply topics for barber-shop discussion." Many readers also wrote to the paper, asking about housing and job opportunities. While most of these inquirers sought industrial jobs, barbers also wondered what the "Promised Land" held for them. "I am a barber of 20 years experience," a barber from Starkville, Mississippi, wrote to the *Defender*. "I am now in the business for white but I can barber for white or color[e]d. ... Also I am a preacher. ... I would like for my children to have the advantage of good schools and churches." Black churches, especially in rural areas, could not afford to pay their preachers substantial salaries. Therefore, preachers usually worked jobs that gave them considerable income and flexibility, like barbering, to carry on their pastoral duties.[11] A barber's wife from Greenwood, Mississippi, also wrote to the *Defender* for the sake of her children; she was concerned, like her husband, that businessmen would not fare as well as laborers.[12] Although these barbers appear to have been migrating for better educational opportunities, they lacked confidence that they would find jobs in a barber shop up north. These kinds of letters from barbers were rare, but they reveal the uncertainties of transferring their skills to a new region.

The *Defender* could have promised both Mississippi barbers that the scores of other black migrants to the North would certainly need haircuts. Robert Horton saw these business opportunities. When he returned home to Hattiesburg, he sold his shop and convinced his customers to migrate to Chicago with him, his wife, and children. In 1917, he had secured a group discount on the Illinois Central Railroad for him and his party. If blacks were going to move north, Horton wanted to capitalize on their grooming needs. It is also possible that his own customers had been debating whether or not to go north, and Horton simply did not want to be left behind. He earned on average $25 per week, his wife did not work, they had two children, and they owned their home. Horton believed he could substantially improve his business and his family's well-being.[13]

Between 1910 and 1930, approximately 1.5 million rural migrants settled in southern and northern cities, and as they did so they were forced to live in segregated neighborhoods.[14] Moreover, as property values increased and white business owners competed for prime real estate in central business districts, black businesses, including barber shops, were forced to relocate to segregated districts. Black urban migration and institutional racism thus contributed to the development of black business districts in American cities.[15] Black business districts were centers of black commerce and recreation where barbers could position themselves close to black consumers. Because of their concentration and size as well as wartime labor demands and the higher wages their residents commanded in the factories, black communities in these large cities were better able to support black-owned businesses.[16] Before the World War I–era migration, black business districts were located adjacent to central business districts along a particular street: Auburn Avenue in Atlanta, Parrish Street in Durham, Greenwood Avenue in Tulsa, and Beale Street in Memphis. During and after the migration, business districts developed along major streets within black neighborhoods.

City directories show a shift in where black barber shops were located: from downtown city centers in the 1880s to emerging black pockets (wards or blocks) by the 1920s. In most cases, the movement of barber shops reflected the residential patterns of black residents, which varied by region and city. African American migrants in the urban South settled in several neighborhoods, but were confined to particular city blocks. Between 1880 and 1890, the black-owned shops listed in the Atlanta and Richmond city directories were mostly located downtown, in Atlanta's Five Point area and on Broad Street and Main Street moving away from the Capitol Square in Richmond. In both cities, black barbers had been opening shops outside of downtown by the 1920s. Black businesses in Atlanta were forced out of the central business district as a result of the race riot of 1906 and the efforts of the city council to restrict black businessmen and -women from leasing downtown commercial space. Consequently, they established an adjacent black business district on Auburn Avenue (formerly named Wheat Street). The "Old Fourth Ward" on the East Side supported the development of Auburn. This street became the center of black consumer activity as businesses that served white patrons now primarily served the black community. In 1913, the city council enacted a zoning ordinance to legalize residential segregation, which resulted in the black community expanding to the west of the central business district to the West Side near Atlanta University Center.[17] Two years earlier Richmond's city council passed a similar racial zoning ordinance that designated black and white neighborhoods.[18] By 1920, black barber shops were moving with their new customer base. Particularly, many barbers in Atlanta opened their doors along Auburn, where Alonzo Herndon headquartered Atlanta Mutual and Henry Rucker (former barber and politician) opened his Rucker Building, which provided office spaces. Strikingly, many of these barber shops were just doors from each other. In 1930, seven African Americans owned shops very close to each other on Auburn (at 223, 231, 240, 250, 270, 280, and 291). This kind of clustering did not happen along Second Street in Richmond, the center of black commercial activity in Jackson Ward; rather, shops were more dispersed throughout the ward. While the number of black shops declined on major downtown streets in these two cities, a large number of blacks remained downtown to groom white men, a practice that continued through the 1960s.

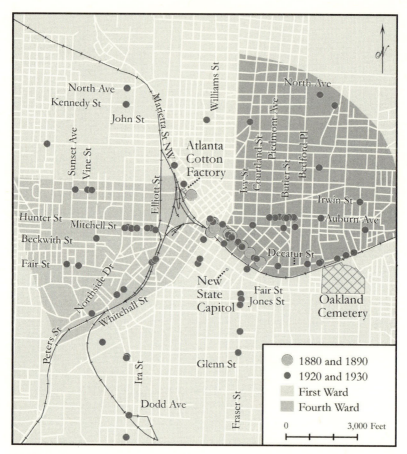

Figure 10. Black barber shops in Atlanta, Georgia, in 1880, 1890, 1920, and 1930.
Cartography by Boundary Cartography. Source: *Sholes' Directory of the City of
Atlanta for 1880* (Atlanta: A. E. Sholes, 1880); *Atlanta City Directory for 1890*
(Atlanta: R. L. Polk and Co., 1890); *Atlanta City Directory, 1920* (Atlanta: Atlanta
City Directory Company, 1920); *Atlanta City Directory, 1930* (Atlanta: Atlanta
City Directory Company, 1930).

The urban North showed similar movement relationships between black
shops and migrants, and patterns away from downtown city centers. These
cities absorbed the lion's share of southern migrants. By 1920, nearly 40 percent of African Americans in the North resided in eight cities, which included
Chicago, Cleveland, New York, and Philadelphia.[19] Southern migrants initially settled in neighborhoods where family and friends were located. Denied

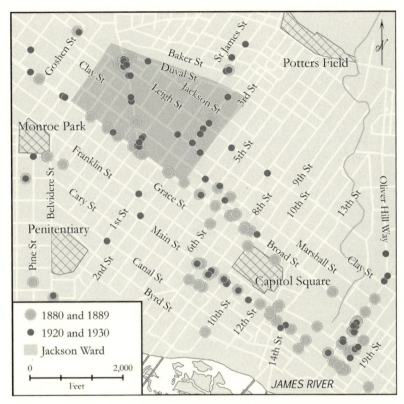

Figure 11. Black barber shops in Richmond, Virginia, in 1880, 1889, 1920, and 1930. Cartography by Boundary Cartography. Source: *Chataigne's Richmond City Directory for the Years 1880-'81* (Richmond: J. H. Chataigne, 1880); *Chataigne's Directory of Richmond, VA., 1889* (Richmond: J. H. Chataigne, 1889); *Hill Directory Co.'s Richmond City Directory, 1920* (Richmond: Hill Directory Co., 1920); *Hill's Richmond, Virginia, City Directory, 1930* (Richmond: Hill Directory Co., 1930).

opportunities to live in other areas, they had little choice. Black migrants to Cleveland settled in the central area of the city, from Euclid to Woodland and 81st to 105th Streets; however, black barber shops made a slower eastward movement from downtown to this area, which was east of 55th Street (formerly named Wilson Street).[20] The shops in 1880 and 1890 were concentrated downtown, but by 1910 began moving east along Central Avenue. The black barbers, such as George Myers, who were still downtown in 1910 or 1920 had likely been there since the 1890s.

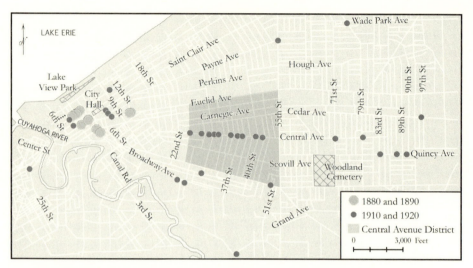

Figure 12. Black barber shops in Cleveland, Ohio, in 1880, 1890, 1910, and 1920. Cartography by Boundary Cartography. Source: *The Cleveland Directory for the Year Ending June, 1881* (Cleveland: Cleveland Directory Company, 1880); *The Cleveland Directory for the Year Ending July 1891* (Cleveland: Cleveland Directory Co., 1890); *The Classified Business and Director's Directory of Cleveland, Ohio, 1910* (Cleveland: Whitworth Brothers Co., 1910); *Cleveland Directory for the Year Ending 1921* (Cleveland: Cleveland Directory Co., 1920).

Unlike in Cleveland, shop movement in Philadelphia was less unidirectional. As residents, blacks were evenly distributed in the south, north, and west sections of the city.[21] While many barbers opened shops in each of these sections between 1870 and 1920, a majority of them located their shops south of Market Street. Most revealing is that there were very few black-owned shops near Market between the Schuylkill River and Independence Square after 1900. By 1910, many of these shops were located in North Philadelphia and farther south, in the western section (west of Broad Street) of the seventh ward.[22] The seventh ward was a major area populated by predominately black residents and businesses. This was the famed district that W. E. B. Du Bois researched for his 1899 book *The Philadelphia Negro*. Yet, by 1920, those shops continued to move farther south of South Street, outside of the ward boundaries.

When black men migrated to southern and northern cities, they searched for housing, work, a place to worship, and a place to get a haircut. Recent migrants either randomly visited shops in their neighborhoods or visited shops

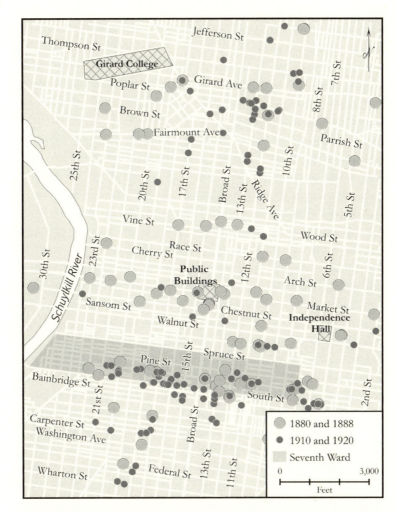

Figure 13. Black barber shops in Philadelphia, Pennsylvania, in 1880, 1888, 1910, and 1920. Cartography by Boundary Cartography. Source: *Gopsill's Philadelphia City Directory for 1880* (Philadelphia: James Gopsill, 1880); *Gopsill's Philadelphia City Directory for 1888* (Philadelphia: James Gopsill, 1888); *Boyd's Philadelphia City Directory, 1910* (Philadelphia: C. E. Howe Co., 1910); *Boyd's Philadelphia City Directory, 1920* (Philadelphia: C. E. Howe Co., 1920).

recommended by family or friends. After Horton arrived in Chicago, for example, he opened the Hattiesburg Barber Shop on 35th Street near Rhodes, which was just a few blocks west of the black commercial activity on "The Stroll" on State Street. In fact, of the fifty barber shops listed in the 1915–1916 *Colored People's Guide Book for Chicago*, thirty were located along State Street between 15th and 55th, but most were near 35th. Horton likely wanted to distance his shop from the bottleneck on State Street. Horton's shop became a gathering place for migrants from Hattiesburg and surrounding areas to collect their cultural bearings as they adjusted to city life, and a contact point for blacks in Hattiesburg still considering the move.[23] As a prominent figure who left Hattiesburg, Horton "became the recipient of numerous letters of inquiry about conditions in Chicago."[24] At the barber shop, people could connect with other southern migrants and longtime residents to gather information on city life and politics, such as employment, and black community life, such as night life and schools. Barbers did not need to look for customers; customers found the barber shop. Color-line barbers placed far more advertisements in white newspapers in search of white customers than barbers placed in black newspapers looking for black customers. Word of mouth was less expensive, and more effective, in a Jim Crow setting.

As a new black business and professional class emerged, they saw their livelihoods tied to a growing working-class population.[25] Black financial institutions (such as banks, insurance companies, and building and loan associations) and black fraternal and societal associations anchored black business districts. They not only provided financial stability to these districts through loans and real estate holdings, but they also provided spaces for black residents to hold meetings, organize social gatherings, and congregate. However, there were usually more barber and beauty shops located in black business districts than any other business, and they regularly accommodated the working and middle classes. For example, in Chicago in 1938, the twelve black barber shops and eleven black beauty parlors led the field in number of businesses on 47th Street.[26] Barber shops located in black business districts benefited from the foot traffic of black shoppers and workers on lunch breaks. African Americans could visit the barber shop before or after they attended to other business or recreation in the district. For Charles Herndon and Julia Lucas, black tobacco workers from the American Tobacco Company and Liggett and Myers were a large segment of their customer base in their barber shop on 121 Mangum Street near downtown Durham.[27] Yet, black consumers could accommodate only a small fraction of the total number of black barber shops in a given city, which means most shops were dispersed throughout black neighborhoods.

As black barber shops increasingly welcomed a black clientele, black women had begun to establish their leadership in an emerging beauty industry. The rise of the beauty culture industry paralleled this population shift and the inward focus of black business culture. In the early twentieth century, Annie Turnbo-Malone, Madam C. J. Walker, Anthony Overton, and Sarah Washington produced hair preparation and cosmetic products for black women. Turnbo-Malone and Walker did more than create and sell products—they were instrumental in creating an industry to sell a system that included hygienic and hair care products, employment, opportunities to open salons, and philanthropic and political engagement with black communities.[28] The industry developed based on commodity products, which provided black women the capital and opportunity to establish beauty shops as permanent spaces to facilitate their work as beauty culturists. While women found new opportunities in the beauty industry, they also found opportunities in the barber shop.

Women knew that they could use these shops, instead of or along with beauty shops, to their advantage in various ways. Black women worked in barber shops more often as manicurists partly because there was less competition for male customers. Color-line shops provided this service to their white customers, and Zora Neale Hurston provided rich detail of her work in Washington, D.C. But, black men also placed their hands across the table for their nails to be buffed and filed. Before Bessie Coleman embarked on an amazing career as a pilot, she worked as a manicurist in at least two barber shops in Chicago's Bronzeville neighborhood. One of her biographers asserted that her male customers "appreciated her looks and charm," but at least one customer looked beyond her appearance. While working at the White Sox Barber Shop, her brother, a World War I veteran, sat in the shop talking about how French women could fly airplanes. Coleman was intrigued, and received considerable encouragement in her interest from a regular customer, Robert Abbott, founder of the *Chicago Defender*. With Abbott's encouragement and her savings, she attended aviation school in France, which was the catalyst for her groundbreaking contributions as a pilot.[29] Coleman used her position as a manicurist to her benefit. This is not to suggest that she became the first black female pilot *because* she worked with and around men, but she did take advantage of her networks.

Most male customers did not help manicurists secure other employments;

in fact, most were simply titillated by their mere presence. Black newspapers often facilitated a masculine voyeuristic culture surrounding black female barber shop workers. A short notice in the *Defender* extolled, "An added feature of Holland's tonsorial parlor, 15 West 51st street, is a dainty manicurist—and oh, boy, she sure can hold your hands. Well, I know they've bought some more chairs for the boys."[30] The paper reduced this manicurist to a "dainty" "feature," or some object that black men in Chicago's Black Belt should observe. "Yes, we have a Manicurist," Ernest Joyner of Pittsburgh noted in the *Pittsburgh Courier*, "and I think she's here to stay." In the newspaper, John Clark applauded Joyner for adding a manicurist in his shop on Wylie Avenue. "With this addition as a part of the regular organization," Clark proclaimed, "Archeal's Barber Shop is complete as one of the most instructive and

Figure 14. Harlem barber shop, circa 1929. Courtesy of the Photographs and Prints Division, Schomburg Center for Research in Black Culture, The New York Public Library, Astor, Lenox and Tilden Foundations.

interesting barber shops in the city. All are excellent mechanics and artists as well as conversationalists."[31] By celebrating the addition of a manicurist to expand the services offered in this particular shop, Joyner and Clark intimated a new vision for modern black barber shops. For all of the manly excitement of having a feminine service in the barber shop, black men are silent in the available sources on what might have been perceived as a feminine act of *getting* manicures. Nonetheless, grooming men was not solely a male barber's job, and barbers groomed more than just men.

Female customers who sought barbers' skills for a new hairstyle joined manicurists in these predominately male spaces. In the 1920s, more women sat in the barber's chair for the first time during the bobbed hairstyle craze. The bob was so popular that some communities held "bobbed hair contests." Women participated in the emerging consumer culture of the early twentieth century, where gender identities increasingly became bound with mass consumption and leisure. Their mothers may not have worn such short hairstyles or sat in a barber shop, but these "new women" opted to define for themselves how long or short they would wear their hair, and where they would get it cut.[32] The number of beauty shops had been steadily increasing, but the large demand for bobs far outpaced the number of beauty parlors. In fact, many parlors opened their doors to welcome this growing demand, while black and white barbers scrambled to learn how to cut the "Boy Bob." One man was convinced that half the barbering patronage in Chicago was "composed of women and girls."[33] Black beauty culturists understood that if black women went to barber shops for their bob, then that was one service not performed in the beauty parlor. Roberta Creditte-Ole, a black proprietor of her own School of Beauty Culture in Chicago's Black Belt, warned women the bob was an artistic cut, and they should be careful not to submit to an incompetent barber.[34] In December 1926, Gertrude Smith won a bobbed hairstyle contest held at the Manhattan Casino on 155th Street and 8th Avenue in New York City. The *Pittsburgh Courier* noted that Smith, a manicurist in Marcia Lansing Beauty Shoppe, "wore a long mannish bob cut by Leroy Stokes, of the Elite Barber Shop, and dressed by Ethel Biard, of Ethel's Hair Parlor," suggesting that even though barbers cut bobs, they lacked the skill, and perhaps the interest, to style it.[35] The bob may have facilitated an intriguing moment when women regularly moved between the barber and beauty shop.

Many black barbers opened new, elaborate shops to accommodate women. J. C. Cooper entered barbering at age eighteen in Marion, South Carolina, but "on account of the exodus" north, he made his way to Hopewell, Virginia, then soon after to Richmond. After surveying various sections of the city, Cooper "decided I could do the best for myself, where I was most needed," which was at 619 Brook Avenue in Jackson Ward. He later moved a few doors down to another space adorned with:

> Hot and cold water baths, electrical massages, latest devices for anti-septic shampoos, together with a special department for ladies, where bobbing hair, trimming, shampooing, massaging and special hair treatment with the latest sterilizing outfits will be found available. Coupled with this may be found the most improved and expensive electric lights, seven in all ordered direct from Germany, and a customer, under the cooling breezes from the large electric fan in summer may be as comfortable as he will be from ample heat furnished. We carry also a full line of cosmetics for both male and female trade.[36]

Cooper envisioned the modern barber shop as his predecessors had, adorned with up-to-date equipment and extensive service options. Even though many black barbers were still grooming white men in Richmond in the 1930s on Main and Broad Streets, barbers like Cooper carefully considered the sartorial wants of a diverse black clientele. Cooper expanded the basic understandings of black consumption and modernity to reimagine the barber shop as a parlor that welcomed men and women—a proposition that the bob made possible.

The bob may have brought barbers more business, but their male customers were much more ambivalent. Men viewed women's entry into the barber shop as an intrusion on their space. African American writer and editor Chandler Owen claimed that men disliked bobbed hair. He cited the theory that opposites attract; men liked women who wore dresses, not knickerbockers, and long hair, not short hair. "All in all," he wrote, "the bobbed hair craze seems to be but a reflection of the general tendency of the women to become more masculine and the men to become more feminine, both of which square with the fundamental law that unlike poles attract and like poles repel. The feminine woman will like the masculine men, while the masculine men will continue to like the feminine women."[37] While Owen did not speak for all men, his thoughts on gender were quite common.

Owen's comments were not restricted to the bob as a masculine style, but rather it mattered that it was styled in a traditionally male space. If men did not want women inside barber shops, there was little they could do about it, though they tried. White men—particularly barbers—balked at the idea of white women going to black barber shops. Many African Americans across the country believed Atlanta's proposed 1926 ordinance to ban white women from black barber shops was a response to the popularity of the bob. An article in the *Pittsburgh Courier* noted that white barbers "skillfully took advantage of the craze for bobbed hair and had much to say of the shocking sight" of seeing black men cut white women's hair.[38] White barbers had been pushing for years to capture the white male patronage by lobbying for various kinds of regulation. This ordinance was challenged in the courts, which ruled the provision applying to children was unconstitutional.[39] The bob may have concerned white men who abhorred the idea of white women occupying the same space with black men, which was what segregation ultimately was

Figure 15. Metropolitan Barber Shop, 1941. Two barbers grooming men at 4654 South Parkway in Chicago. Courtesy of the Library of Congress.

Figure 16. Oscar Freeman, owner of the Metropolitan Barber Shop, 1942. A woman (note the stockings) appears to be getting a facial in the same shop where a year earlier a photographer took a picture of two men getting a shave and haircut. Courtesy of the Library of Congress.

meant to minimize. But, in all, the bob did not elicit a crisis in white or black masculinity.

Men accepted women as producers (manicurists and barbers) much better than women as consumers. Technically, female consumers were less permanent than manicurists or barbers; however, women exercised their power as consumers on equal footing with men when they frequented barber shops. As barbers, women had to confront the gender politics of skilled work. Had scores of women entered barbering, this shift may have threatened male barbers, but male customers were actually intrigued. In 1935, reporter Enoc Waters, Jr., interviewed Margaret West, a successful barber on the South Side of Chicago. Before getting to the particulars of West's history in the profession, Waters contextualized the gendering of barber shops. "When women began patronizing [barber shops] at the outset of the bobbed hair era," Waters recalled, "what a hullabaloo was raised by the male clientele which felt that the last stronghold of masculinity was going sissy. Then right behind the women patrons came the manicurists with all their feminine fripperies which sent raw blooded he men, who had for years chewed their plug tobacco and discussed 'manly' topics with abandon, scurrying to those places which had not been violated by the invasion of militant feminists."[40] To Waters, women intruded on barber shops. As customers and manicurists, or workers performing feminine duties, their presence was not considered legitimate. But as barbers, as Waters suggests, they performed the same work as men and were somehow less intrusive. "Now comes the lady barber," he quipped, "a dainty feminine morsel who wields the razor and handles the clippers with the dexterity of a man, but brings in addition a feminine touch to which men are peculiarly susceptible."[41] Although most women who entered the personal grooming service industry became beauticians, a small percentage of women opted to become barbers.[42]

Margaret West could attest to the ways the sighting of a female barber elicited curiosity in the barber shop and the press. West learned barbering from her father and brother before moving to Detroit to open a shop with her brother, Baby West. Although the shop prospered, in 1929 she moved with her brother to Chicago. Baby West was popular in Chicago, but was something of a wanderer. He left Chicago for New York and opened a shop in Harlem. Margaret remained in Chicago, working at Henry Brown's shop at 35th Street near South Parkway (now Martin Luther King Drive). Paid on a percentage basis, her income averaged $20 to $23.50 per week. West had a large male customer base, which she suggested may have resulted from their sense of "novelty" of being groomed by a female barber. This may have been true of spectators but not customers. If West was not a skilled barber, the novelty of gender would have worn off after a few poor haircuts. Waters reported that Margaret's presence in the shop "rid it of the undesirable traits usually associated with such places. Mr. Brown, the proprietor, has found no reason to post signs reading 'Please Do Not Use Profanity' often found in barber shops."[43] Although Waters initially acknowledged West's skills with the razor, he privileged her gender as her greatest asset.

Waters was not the only person at the *Defender* to focus on the physical appearance of female barbers. After graduating from Tyler, Billie Kirkpatrick cut hair in her husband's barber shop in Sherman, Texas. The *Defender* published her picture with a caption, "It is no mystery that her presence in the shop has accelerated business."[44] Women had to at once substantiate their

presence inside this male space and prove their barbering skills to each customer to convince them to return. Many women capitalized on their gender
to get the opportunity to prove their skills. In Monroe, Louisiana, Dollye Vaz
was the only female barber in the very popular Red Goose Barber Shop.[45] In
Cincinnati, Agnes Richardson was the only known black woman to own a
licensed barber shop.[46] There was nothing manly about being a barber, but
being a barber was commonly defined by being a man.

In an attempt to increase their prospective customer base even further,
barbers tried hard to dismiss class divisions as a show of solidarity. Although
it was a hard sell, George Myers tried to convince a friend he was part of
the working class. In 1920, George Myers still groomed white men in his
Cleveland barber shop, and in his correspondence with historian James Ford
Rhodes, former patron and friend, the two debated Myers's identity as a capitalist or proletarian. Rhodes proclaimed that Myers, because of his financial
success as a barber, "cut entirely loose from the proletariat and [is] now in the
capitalistic class."[47] Myers replied, "While still identified with the proletariat,
I shall at least be able to keep the wolf from the door in my 'sere and yellow
days.'"[48] He placed himself, as a barber, in a petit bourgeoisie position not far
removed from the black working class. Myers further stated, "While it may
be (if success in business counts) that I am classed with the capitalistic class, I
am far from a capitalist, and still identified with the proletariat. No barber to
my knowledge ever became wealthy enough to get away from them."[49] Myers
was far from a proletarian, and how much wealth one needed to "get away
from them" is unclear. Still, he understood the unstable position of the petit
bourgeoisie. Myers did little to actually identify with the working class and
identified with the proletariat only through his prospective leadership of it.

W. E. B. Du Bois extended this relationship between black capitalists and
laborers much further. "The colored group is not divided into capitalists and
laborers," he argued in 1921. "Today to a very large extent our laborers are our
capitalists and our capitalists are our laborers." He suggested black entrepreneurs and professionals not only became affluent through manual toil, but
also were a generation removed from a laboring class.[50] Barbers with black
customers exemplified this notion that the boundaries between black laborers and capitalists were blurred. Barbers could boast of being businessmen,
independent of an employer, which was no small feat. But while their income
did not significantly set them apart from the black working class, it was their
status as entrepreneurs who controlled their own time that marked the difference. William Jones, a sociology professor at Howard University, conducted a

study of black recreational activities in Washington, D.C., in the 1920s, which included barber shops. He described the barber shops from Fourth Street and Florida Avenue to Fourteenth and U Streets as commercial institutions that satisfy "the cravings for leisure-time activity." The focus on social interaction led Jones to conclude that "as a social and recreational institution it plays a greater role in the Negro community than it does as a pure commercial agency."[51] Yet commerce and labor were always bound together, which was apparent during the Great Depression.

Cutting Hair During Hard Times

As unemployment rose in the 1930s, African Americans, who were barely able to afford necessities like food and clothing, cut back on expenditures such as haircuts. Yet, next to funeral parlors, barber and beauty shops had come the closest to being recession-proof businesses. Men would always need to be groomed, but the major question was whether, and how often, they would get a haircut in a barber shop. Besides worrying about losing customers or pressures to lower prices, shop owners had to contend with their employees' demands for better hours and higher percentages of receipts. The growth of a black male urban population encouraged more barbers to open their own shops, but the economic hardships of this population also encouraged them to find ways to weather the storm.

While agricultural and industrial jobs were scarce in the 1930s, African Americans capitalized on the everyday practices of the familial economy that often reproduced gender roles. African Americans with larger families saved money on hair grooming by cutting and styling each other's hair at home. Many men and women learned hairdressing and barbering during these grooming sessions. Joseph Richburg of Summerton, South Carolina—southeast of Columbia—started cutting boys' hair in the community under a tree and on the front porch. "I started around say in 1930," Richburg recalled, "cutting one and another's [sic], my brother's hair. See we had a lot of boys, and my daddy, he would work the sawmill during the winter months and 'boy, you've got to help me do this, you've got to help me do that' and we got a pair of clippers. Mama use to do it with a pair of scissors before and he got a pair of clippers. Then I had to cut the boys' hair and they'd cut mine." But he did not actually enter barbering professionally until he needed money, because he was "courting, you know, going to see the girls so I went to a little place down on Davis Crossroads and I rented a little shop and I cut hair down there for ten, fifteen cents."[52] Work defined the coming-of-age stories for many African American children, especially in the rural South. For Richburg, learning how to cut hair not only allowed him to escape grueling agricultural work, but also allowed him to exercise a producerist notion of masculinity by earning enough money to date girls.

If Richburg wanted to learn barbering more formally, by 1933 he had the option of traveling to Texas to receive training in a black college. H. M. Morgan opened Tyler Barber College in Tyler, Texas, "to teach scientific barbering" to African Americans. This was the first barber school for African Americans. Instructors introduced students to the following subjects: Bacteriology, Hygiene, Sanitation, Biology, Histology, Anatomy, Pathology, Pharmacology, Light Therapy, and Electricity. Morgan reported "twenty-five chairs in the practice department, a laboratory for mixing drugs, chemicals and lotions for the treatment of the hair and scalp and beautification of the skin; lamps that produce the Infra-Red Ray and the Violet Ray, and . . . apparatus for producing galvanic and faradic currents, and class rooms." The college had separate dormitories for men and women, suggesting they had a sizable female enrollment. Their numbers increased over the years so that by 1944 women represented two-thirds of the 126 enrolled students. Between 1935 and 1944, Tyler graduated approximately 1,635 barbers.[53]

These graduates entered the field when fewer people could afford regular visits to barber shops. Some owners responded to the effects of the Depression by joining forces with the white-dominated Associated Master Barbers of America (AMBA) to prevent the price of haircuts from plummeting. In Birmingham in 1935, the local Barbers' Association, including black barbers, organized to discuss uniformity in prices.[54] In 1937, the Illinois Master Barbers Association won a superior court decision that upheld the minimum price for haircuts at fifty cents and the minimum price for shaves at twenty-five cents. Some members of the association violated the agreement and charged below the minimum price.[55] A black barber in Chicago believed barbering would be more profitable if his competitors cooperated on prices and standards:

> The only competitors I have are Negroes, and the reason the barbering business is not more profitable . . . is because of the "chiselers"—apprentice barbers who are operating small shops and cutting prices. The average registered barber having a large following can only earn around $22 a week. We have no Negro barber college because

young Negro men have no interest in spending their money quali-
fying to become barbers. The barber standard is low because of the
small compensation received for one's work and because a certain
shiftless type of individual has represented this profession.[56]

He was a member of an association of black barbers in Chicago that cooperated with state and city law enforcement agencies to arrest unregistered
barbers and owners with "unsanitary" shops. He complained that he had
to work longer hours to compete with other black barbers who drove down
prices, which, he argued, "deprived me of the opportunity for amusement"
or leisure.[57]

In 1935, twenty-five black barbers in Philadelphia established a separate
chapter of the AMBA, Chapter 829. They elected Sidney H. Jones, of North
Philadelphia, president of the chapter. Members had to be a manager or proprietor of a barber shop and pay a monthly fee of $1.50. This black chapter
cooperated with the three white chapters to lobby for revisions in the city
ordinance regulating the field.[58] The barbers affiliated with Chapter 829 were
a small fraction of the total black proprietors in the city. However, the chapter signaled a shift in interracial cooperation and organization among proprietors. The Depression encouraged this cooperation because some barbers
accommodated their customers, who also faced economic hardships, by low-
ering prices. These associations resembled unions, but instead of pushing for
better wages, they fought for better prices.

The 1940 United States Business Census reveals the state of black barber
shops and the level of competition they faced within black communities during the 1930s (Table 7). There were still a few color-line shops in the South,
but most shops targeted black patrons. The 6,656 black barber shops collectively grossed $8,273,000, employed 5,266 men and women, and paid them
a total of $2,448,000. The ratio of shops to employees suggests there were
a significant number of shops where the owner had no employees. Larger
markets like Chicago, New York, and Philadelphia had the most black barber
shops, but upper-South cities such as Baltimore, Washington, D.C., and St.
Louis were close behind. The ratio of barber shops to the black male population shows very little uniformity by region or market size. In Richmond,
there was one black barber shop for every 316 black men, whereas in
Birmingham, there was one shop for every 1,241 black men. A high shop-
to-consumer ratio suggests more competition between shops than in cities
with lower ratios. Richmond, St. Louis, Baltimore, Cleveland, New Orleans,

Table 7. Black Barber Shops, Receipts, Personnel, and Payroll
for Select Cities, 1940

	Black Male Population	Black Barber Shops	Receipts (thousands of dollars)	Employees	Total Payroll (thousands of dollars)
United States		6,656	8,273	5,266	2,448
Atlanta	46,027	61	128	144	54
Birmingham	50,493	41	44	38	18
New Orleans	68,829	137	132	64	31
Baltimore	80,683	179	191	109	52
Memphis	56,778	92	85	59	24
Richmond	28,125	89	197	148	84
St. Louis	51,762	130	144	125	46
Washington, D.C.	88,672	175	419	349	195
Chicago	130,588	250	379	238	124
Cleveland	41,096	85	124	67	39
Detroit	74,485	105	208	129	83
Pittsburgh	31,056	46	79	41	21
Philadelphia	118,859	214	238	88	44
New York	205,727	266	570	338	187
Brooklyn	47,744	70	125	53	26
Manhattan	133,930	166	398	267	152

Source: United States Department of Commerce, Sixteenth Census of the United States: 1940 Census of Business; Sixteenth Census of the United States: Population Statistics.

Washington, D.C., and Chicago had higher shop-to-consumer ratios than the other cities.

The financial data for these barber shops highlight the hardships they endured during the Depression. On average, black barber shops grossed $1,243 in 1939. Of the cities in the sample, only in Washington, D.C, Richmond, New York, and Atlanta did the average shop gross over $2,000. As hard as the Depression hit most people, black residents were surprised to see barber shop owners doing well. A black resident in Jackson, Mississippi, noted, "Most of us were really struggling, but some Negroes were doing well. One Negro man, Barber Jones, drove a Rolls Royce. We didn't know how he got the money because he only serviced Negroes in his barber shop."[59] He indicated that had Jones serviced whites, people might better understand how he could afford a Rolls Royce. Shop proprietors exercised their consumer power by purchasing a fashionable car. In an oral interview, Julia Lucas recalled meeting her first husband, Charles H. Herndon, a barber thirty-two years her senior, in Durham, North Carolina, and noted his Buick was the biggest car she had ever seen. When Lucas finished college in 1938, she started working as a bookkeeper in Herndon's shop.[60] On average, owners paid their employees $465, which was 30 percent of total receipts. Atlanta, Memphis, and St. Louis were the only cities in the sample that paid their employees below the average. However, the average owner in New Orleans, Baltimore, Memphis, Philadelphia, and Pittsburgh distributed less than 30 percent of receipts to employees. For example, for the average black barber shop in Philadelphia, the payroll was only 19 percent of total receipts. It is likely that there were more one-person shops in Philadelphia than other cities because these shops would bring the percentage down. However, the larger significance is that black shop owners believed prices were depressed and journeymen barbers believed they were not paid enough. As a result, both owners and employees organized in their own interests.

In the 1930s, shop owners increasingly supported journeymen barbers in the labor movement.[61] Like other black workers during the 1930s, a growing number of black journeymen barbers overcame their skepticism toward the labor movement and entered the "house of labor."[62] In 1939, members of the Barber and Beauty Culturists Union, Local 8 of Harlem, affiliated with the Negro Labor Committee, actively attempted to organize black journeymen barbers to pressure shop owners for better commissions and working conditions. Frank Crosswaith, chairman of the Negro Labor Committee (NLC), worked with Local 8 on their strategies to organize more barbers into the union and push for a city ordinance to regulate barbering. Crosswaith and union members posted numerous flyers to encourage local barbers to attend weekly NLC organizing meetings at the Harlem Labor Center at 312 W. 125th Street. They articulated their labor issues in terms of manhood rights. "A NEW DAY IS NOW DAWNING for Harlem Barbers," one flyer proclaimed while encouraging barbers to attend a meeting on March 21. "A day that will see us rise like men out of the swamps of depending upon tips and a commission onto the high ground of manhood enjoying a decent wage, reasonable working hours, union protection and our self-respect."[63] White barbers and black caterers had also been debating the tipping system since the early

1900s. They argued that tips degraded their status as skilled workers by tying their masculinity to the value of their production.

The union organized a meeting with the Master Barbers to discuss a contract that addressed decent wages and larger issues of their exclusion from Social Security. A flyer announcing a meeting asked, "Is there any reason why barbers should be left out of the Social Security Act? Is there any reason why a barber should not know how much he will take home to his family after a week's work? Is there any reason why a barber should earn less than a W.P.A. worker?"[64] The Social Security Act covered regular wage workers (non-mobile or seasonal) in large industries or companies, with at least four employees, whose contributions could be easily collected.[65] Barbers were not regular wage workers because a portion of their wages was a percentage of their receipts.

On November 30, 1939, delegates from Local 8 attended a City Hall conference with Mayor Fiorello La Guardia and Newbold Morris to discuss the pending barbers' license law that had been before the City Council for six months. George DeMar, special organizer for Local 8, suggested that a license law would eradicate many of the "unwholesome" conditions in barber shops. He believed the bill would "go far in eliminating vice and crime together with generally improving the conditions under which Barbers' work and public health suffers." Union organizers abhorred shops that allowed gamblers to operate their racket from the barber shop, and they appealed to journeymen with similar objections.[66]

The economic hardships that spurred the black working class to join unions and fight for higher wages also encouraged black business owners and intellectuals to increasingly advocate for a separate black or group economy, a "Negro market," or a nation within a nation. The separate economy consisted of two segments of businesses. The first included local, small proprietorships such as barber shops, beauty shops, grocery stores, and tailor shops. Service businesses comprised the largest number of black proprietors. Barber shops and beauty shops made up over 40 percent of these service businesses. The second segment included businesses that participated in capital-intensive industries such as banks, insurance companies, and real estate firms.[67] Booker T. Washington and later Marcus Garvey had long championed the development of a black commercial sphere. In the mid- to late 1920s, the NNBL urged black consumers to "Buy Something from a Negro Merchant!" Through its local chapters, the NNBL sponsored a number of programs, such as the "National Negro Trade Week," to channel the growing black consumer dollars to black-owned businesses.[68] These pitches for separatism were largely seen as black extreme political views, which were either a conservative retreat from political pressure or a nationalist call for racial solidarity. The increase and concentration of urban black populations and the economic crisis created the conditions for a renewed interest in black self-help. Barbers were active in Washington's NNBL and supported business development, but they did not have to convince black consumers to get a haircut from a black barber in the way a grocer had to join the NNBL in its clarion call to "Buy Something from a Negro Merchant."

Despite the passionate and pragmatic visions of a separate black economy as a strategy of survival in the 1930s, black consumer activists and intellectuals failed to see black barber shops as a critical component—along with beauty shops and funeral parlors—of a group economy. W. E. B. Du Bois argued that a new economic solidarity was paramount in the age of economic crisis during the Great Depression. All workers felt the pain of economic hardship, but black workers felt it harder and its effects more permanent. In offering a solution, Du Bois and other advocates of a group economy believed African Americans could capitalize on a captive market that resulted from segregation. "Separate Negro sections will increase race antagonism," he conceded, "but they will also increase economic cooperation, organized self-defense and necessary self-confidence." He recognized his opposition to Booker T. Washington's economic strategies of uplift decades earlier, but reasoned that new economic hardships required new survival strategies.[69] To be sure, black entrepreneurs and intellectuals were at the forefront of encouraging a separate economy. Black consumers simply wanted jobs, fair wages, and fair prices. The black working class launched "Don't Buy Where You Can't Work" campaigns in various cities.[70] This revealed the "paradox of early black capitalism."[71] While these were economic boycotts, they were also social movements that addressed issues of access and respect. If these campaigns were successful, and the slogans taken literally, black consumers' and workers' increased access could translate into a decrease in sales for black businesses. Many black businesses, however, saw the opportunity and increased their marketing appeals to keep consumer dollars within black communities. Yet, African Americans could work in black barber shops, and these shops did not have to convince black consumers to patronize them. In many ways, the businesses of grooming the living and the dead were at the heart of a separate black economic sphere that other business owners had hoped would develop.[72]

Black barber shops could not provide the economies of scale that advocates of a separate black economy had in mind, such as hiring large numbers of black workers. In fact, many of the early critics of a "separate Negro
economy," such as E. Franklin Frazier, pointed to these small, service-based
enterprises as evidence that "black" business was a myth propagated by the
black bourgeoisie to bolster their own class status.[73] But black culture was the
value that barbers and their shops offered—to their customers and the idea
of a group economy— that took more of an effort for commodity-based businesses to replicate. Black consumers patronized black barber shops not simply because they were black, but because black barbers were skilled at cutting
black men's diverse hair types. In the 1930s, black consumers did not attempt
to patronize white barber shops, unlike their attempts to eat in white-owned
restaurants and stay in white-owned hotels. Personal service work required
an intimate relationship where the patron trusted the barber to make him
look good. If he were pleased with the barber's work, he would likely continue to patronize this particular barber, thus becoming part of the regular
waiting public in the shop. Working-class men typically filled barber shops
on weekends because they had time off work. On a Saturday, men from the
surrounding neighborhood could be found in the barber shop getting a haircut or shave for the evening's outing at a juke joint and for Sunday morning's
church service. Some men frequented the shop not just for a haircut—or not
for a haircut at all—but also to hang out with friends. As men waited for their
turn in the barber's chair or stopped by the shop to occupy idle time by talking with other men, black barber shops became more than places of business;
they became public spaces.

Congregation and Conversation in the Shop

Black men coped with the Great Depression in many ways, and the barber
shop functioned as a central place where they could socialize and talk with
friends and strangers. Black barber shops were among the few public spaces
where African American men could congregate, socialize, and talk outside
of white surveillance or a large female presence. The racial and gender privacy of the space enabled a level of *truth-telling* where black men could critically discuss racial politics. It also enabled a level of *truth-stretching* where
they could fashion themselves as men in ways that would draw more opposition in a Jim Crow society. Black male congregation and conversation, then,
defined the culture of modern barber shops. Black entrepreneurs, such as

gamblers and the black press, also tapped into this barber shop culture, thus contributing to the commercial public sphere.

The public and private nature of black barber shops made them attractive legal businesses where illegal businessmen could operate their underground economy. In 1933, for example, Arthur Gholston, real estate owner and member of the Chicago Police Department, accused Thomas P. Weathersby, former owner of the Vendome barber shop, of conducting a den of commercialized vice inside his shop on 127 East 47th Street. Gholston told the police he had been walking along 47th Street when two girls stopped him at Prairie Avenue. He said they "took" him to Weathersby's barber shop and went to the basement, where they purchased beer. Gholston reported that he later discovered $33 missing from his pockets. He alleged the girls placed "knock-out" drops in his liquor. Gholston later filed a complaint in municipal court claiming that Weathersby was a "keeper of a disorderly, common, ill-governed house for the encouragement of idleness, gambling, drinking, fornication and other mis-behaviors." Weathersby was tried and found not guilty, but he was unable to establish another business because his license was revoked. He later sued Gholston and police officials for slander and libel.[74]

Barber shops, along with cigar stores, were common places for African Americans to play the numbers or "policy," an underground lottery run, because gambling operators used these legal businesses as public fronts to divert suspicion of their illegal activities inside. Many African Americans played the numbers to weather the Depression years. Customers and passersby made their picks with the runner at the barber shop, for example, for as little as a penny. James Mallory and R. Butler of Pittsburgh were arrested for operating a lottery inside Butler's barber shop. The judge released Butler but fined Mallory twenty-five dollars and gave him a lecture for not upholding his "Godly" principles as deacon of the North Side church.[75] The police arrested barber Joseph Sharper of Addison Street near 17th Street in Philadelphia because they alleged he "would suggest a winning number after trimming each customer's hair."[76] In Washington, D.C., Needham Turnage, United States commissioner, ordered forty-six-year-old William Hooper, a barber on 486 L Street Southwest, "held for the action of the grand jury on charges of writing numbers and possessing slips."[77] The very nature of the underground economy required a level of privacy outside the boundaries of authoritative surveillance. The barber shop provided the ideal combination of a private space in the public sphere, where anyone could play his or her numbers outside of the presence of law enforcement.

During the interwar period, numbers running was the largest black business in the informal economy, and its connection with key black businesses in the formal economy gave it legitimacy. To be sure, the African American working class did not view playing the numbers as an illegal operation, in contrast to law enforcement—at least those not being paid off. Many African Americans saw the numbers game and its operators as positive forces in black communities because they employed people and used their profits to build institutions.[78] A black resident of Detroit noted, "Everyone played either the numbers . . . or policy or both . . . it offered its players daily chances to pick up on a few quick bucks without any questions asked. It was very popular . . . because it was inexpensive and convenient."[79] Players sometimes placed their pick with a "walking writer," but players were concerned the writer would run off with their money. An established business or "policy station" was much preferred.

Business owners wanted to provide as many services to their customers as possible. Many barber shops and other small businesses stayed solvent because of their association with numbers running. Station owners were allowed to keep 25 percent of the gross business they wrote. A Chicago restaurateur reported, "Two years ago, my business was so bad that I thought I would have to close up. Then I thought of a policy station. I divided the store, and I find that I make more money from the policy than from the lunchroom."[80] Players who did not want to frequent illicit spaces to place their daily pick could stop in the local restaurant, grocery store, or barber shop. Some barber shops had a back room where the station operated. St. Clair Drake and Horace Cayton noted that in a selected area of Chicago's Black Belt in the 1930s, there were fifty policy stations. Thirty-three stations had no front; five were in shoeshine parlors, four in barber shops, and two each in beauty parlors, candy stores, cigar stores, and delicatessens.[81]

In addition to numbers operators, the black press also partnered with black barber shops. In fact, the waiting public embodied the ideal market for disseminating news and increasing readership. Southern rural residents, in particular, could leave news of local happenings at the barber shop to be picked up by a *Chicago Defender* agent and included in the next edition of the paper.[82] In Chicago, the *Defender* maintained bulletin boards at Lowis' Drug Store, on 47th Street and South Parkway, and the Metropolitan Barber Shop, on 4652 South Parkway, to inform black residents of the latest developments on the Ethiopian war front in the 1930s, and to display photos of "nationally famous characters" that appeared in the newspaper.[83] The black press was very creative in distributing its papers to its readers by arming the Pullman Porters with copies to distribute on their routes and making them available for sale in barber shops.[84] Northern and southern African American men purchased the *Defender* and other black newspapers from the local barber shop and often discussed its contents.[85]

Barber shops were ripe for conversation and debates among gathering men, but it was the privacy and security of the shop that allowed such gatherings to take shape. In a three- or four-chair shop, waiting customers occupied their time in various ways. Most men talked or argued about issues of the moment. It is not surprising that a group of people—sitting, waiting; if not comrades, then reasonably acquaintances—collectively discussed various issues of the day. African American men congregated in barber shops and discussed sports, racial and electoral politics, and the everyday news and events that occurred in their local communities. "The barbershop was a place where they gathered and talked about a lot of things," Julia Lucas remembered about her barber shop, "and [they] knew that it was secure with the people with whom they were talking. We didn't have that many private places, other than churches, where we could discuss anything that concerned black people's advancement and where they felt secure. A place does make a difference in how you express and when you feel free to express something that you know is controversial. But the barbershop was one of the places that people could go."[86] And people went, and talked, regularly.

In barber shop forums, as they were often referred to in the 1930s, African Americans could be found discussing the "mighty prowess" of the "Brown Bomber," Joe Louis, exhibiting the racial pride that emanated from his performance. In the 1930s, Louis became a black folk hero for African Americans, giving them hope of vengeance against segregation. But, Louis was not a distant folk hero out of reach from those men who discussed his success, because he also patronized black barber shops. In early September 1935, Louis went inside Elie's Barber Shop in Harlem for a trim. Word quickly spread that he was in town, and within ten or fifteen minutes, reporters claimed there were "5000 people crowded between 135th and 136th streets on Seventh avenue, blocking traffic, breaking the windows in the parked autos, and causing his body guards to call the police reserves for help." Another reporter noted, "When he stops in a barbershop the barbers neglect the other customers to get a close-up of their idol and the way crowds rush into the shop, in front of the doors and windows, is almost beyond the imagination."[87] When Louis dropped into a barber shop on the North End of Boston, word quickly spread among young children of the area, who rushed to the shop to see their idol. Louis treated a few of them to lessons on the correct boxing stance.[88] At the barber shop, African Americans could get close to Louis in a way that his celebrity status otherwise made impossible. Even if onlookers missed the opportunity to talk with Louis because of the large crowds peering through the shop window, he became a "real" person who visited everyday spaces where African Americans regularly congregated.

Black communities were not lacking in organized political, social, or economic meetings at local churches or fraternal halls. However, conversations inside barber shops were not organized and participants were not preselected. On average, they were not at the shop for a meeting or to discuss any particular issues. They were there for a haircut or to socialize with friends, barbers, and other customers. And those customers were not all men. Charles Herndon had a pool table, for recreation not gambling, in back of his Durham shop. Julia Lucas recalled that when workers from surrounding businesses and the tobacco companies had a lunch or dinner hour, they "would come down and play pool, get their hair cut, or a shave. It just became a place to meet people and I was right in the middle of it." And so was the female barber who worked in the shop. Because of Lucas and the female barber, women "felt comfortable" going to this shop, and even playing pool in the back. Lucas remembered that "people talked about everything in the barbershop . . . from who went out with whom, where you go to church, who are good church people, and who are the nothings."[89] Barbers or customers might engage in conversation with one or two people, which might invite others to offer input or counterarguments. Although typical barber shop conversations were not organized, there were a few established protocols that most men adhered to inside the shop. The shop customers accepted any protocols or interventions made by the owner. The owners left the multiple, separate conversations among groups of two or three men to be organized among them. When everyone in the shop discussed the same issue, the owner typically facilitated discussions by making sure speakers were not interrupted. Barbers, then, were key facilitators of the social interactions in the shop.

The networks of people who frequented barber shops made them important spaces for news and information in the black public sphere. An argument in a New York barber shop turned into a breaking-news story for a black newspaper reporter, Ralph Matthews. Two men in a barber shop got into an argument about whether Father Divine had gotten married again. Father Divine was an African American spiritual leader who founded the International Peace Mission Movement with a significant following in the black community. "One said Father Divine was talking 'spiritually' when he said in a sermon he had just married the 'Lamb of God.' The other thought [maybe] he was married 'sho' nuff.'" Overhearing the argument, Matthews followed up on the scoop, "discovered the term 'legal' in the sermon, and wrote a speculative story." Reverend Albert Shadd confirmed he had officiated the nuptials of Father Divine and Edna Rose Ritchings, a twenty-one-year-old Canadian white girl.[90] The Divine argument was not the first time a discussion from a barber shop was further explored in the *Chicago Defender*.

In 1944, George McWhorter, a customer in a Chicago barber shop, sought the assistance of reporter Lucius Harper to help him answer a perplexing question that arose during "one of those famous 'barber shop arguments.'" A former Louisiana resident "stumped" everyone in the barber shop when he argued that during slavery, free blacks purchased and owned white men. McWhorter said, "From all sources and sides our Louisiana friend was howled down." McWhorter posed the question, though a much broader one, to Harper regarding evidence of southern or northern free blacks purchasing white or black men during slavery. Before answering the question in his *Defender* column, "Dustin' Off the News," Harper identified the importance of barber shops as spaces of political discourse. He wrote:

> As we observe, this question arose in the barber shop, one of America's greatest open forums. Here, amid the clatter of scissors, the hum of electric clippers and the like, more questions of local, national and international moment are brought to light, debated and settled forthwith than are discussed on the floors of congress in probably two weeks. Our American barber shops are the only places where anyone can immediately become "Speaker of the House" without the benefit of ballot. However, it is one of the most cosmopolitan institutions in our community life. Around its chairs were molded into thought and actual life some of America's largest and most prosperous Negro business enterprises.[91]

Harper reported that some free blacks owned slaves, but they did not own white men. However, he did report that in 1833 George White, "the Negro town crier," purchased a white wanderer at a public auction under the Illinois vagrancy law. Harper suggests that barber shops were egalitarian institutions where everyone had equal authority regardless of social standing. He also intimated black men's engagement in politics and political discourse outside of parties and polls. Being "Speaker of the House" in the barber shop gave one the authority to be heard, make claims, and draw conclusions.

Whether barber shops were egalitarian or not often rested with the shop owners. They alone could determine how political, democratic, or radical the conversations could play out. During the 1930s, barber shops served as private spaces to discuss labor politics. In Charles Herndon's shop, the black tobacco workers were proud to be in the union and they, "especially the younger men and women," enjoyed talking about it. Herndon's wife and partner noted, "they talk about what they were going to organize and what they were going to ask for. It was the beginning of a revelation to me, how blacks would say, 'I'm all fed up, and I can't take it no more. We're going to do something about it.' And they would discuss it."[92] They were comfortable discussing labor politics because of Herndon and Lucas. But Lucas's presence in particular was critical for this shop to be a truly egalitarian and democratic space, with men and women engaged. After Herndon died in 1941, Lucas took over the shop and renamed it the Palace Barber Shop.[93] Few shops could boast of such an atmosphere, but some might have preferred a shop without a large presence of women. Even Lucas noted women would not go in certain barber shops. Shops with predominately male barbers and customers still provided a space to discuss issues men preferred not to discuss elsewhere.

From New York to Alabama, black men who joined the Communist Party would share party rhetoric and news with others in barber shops. Al Jackson was a black communist and barber shop owner in Montgomery, Alabama. Undoubtedly because of his leftist affiliation, communist leaflets were often left in his shop "for organizers who regularly came by for a trim."[94] This is not to suggest that all of Jackson's customers were communists, but any affiliation with the communist party was a subversive act in the eyes of white authorities. Yet, Jackson was able to publicly share communist literature in the privacy of his barber shop. As a communist, he knew what he was talking about when the issue came up. Having solid information, or knowing more than others about an issue, could establish authority but also stilt conversations. After attending a ten-week course at the Workers School in New York in 1934, Hosea Hudson returned to Birmingham, Alabama, eager to share his new insights on imperialism, fascism, and socialism with fellow black residents. The barber shop beckoned. "I'd be discussing socialism in the barber shop," he recalled. "We'd start the conversation off, then we'd talk about socialism, and how the workers' conditions would be improved under socialism. . . . They'd sit down there and wouldn't no one ask no questions, wouldn't interrupt what

I'm saying. They wanted to see what I had to tell."[95] Hudson could be quite persuasive, so it is not surprising few people challenged him. As a steel-mill worker and union official, he regularly extolled the virtues of radical resistance to economic exploitation, and he had a crowd sitting around the barber shop listening to him sound the drum.

In barber shops, the waiting public not only could receive a political education, but could also participate in the political fabric of the electoral process by discussing campaigns and legislation. Charley Cherokee, in his "National Grapevine" column in the *Defender* in October 1944, recommended as "election time" reading such articles as "Citizens of Negro Blood," by Wendell Willkie, a white liberal Republican politician, and "How Will the Negro Vote," by Walter White, black executive director of the National Association for the Advancement of Colored People (NAACP). Cherokee suggested this reading list "will give you ammunition for some fine barber-shop arguments."[96] Willkie had a short-lived bid for the Republican presidential nomination in 1944—short-lived in part because the GOP believed he was too liberal. In 1942, he publicly said the armed forces should be integrated, and he addressed the NAACP convention. It was here that he met, and became close with, Walter White. With his election-time reading list, Cherokee was facilitating political discourse for the waiting public of barber shops. The calls for knowledge and authority implicitly challenged men who claimed authority without adequate support.

Barber shop forums, conversations, or arguments became verbal competitions. If a man did not have enough "ammunition" to prove his arguments, a loss of authority meant a loss of manhood. The higher the stakes of a topic, the more one needed authority. When men talked about legislative issues and racial politics, the stakes were indeed high and men cited their authority. The highly contested Mitchell Bill, proposed in Congress in 1935 by Illinois representative Arthur Mitchell, was one such issue debated in a Chicago barber shop that had both proponents and opponents not only claiming authority, but also mapping out the best course of action for black political and economic progress.

Mitchell was the first black Democrat elected to Congress. The Chicago Democratic machine selected Mitchell to run against black Republican Oscar DePriest for Congress to deflect claims that the party neglected Chicago's black population.[97] Mitchell's bill called for an "Industrial Commission on Negro Affairs" to address African Americans' economic and general well-being. Enoc Waters, a black newspaper reporter, listened to barbers and customers give the bill both unyielding praise and a "good roasting."[98] Only one customer defended the proposed bill against an entire shop of opponents. The shop owner acted as facilitator to ensure that the lone Mitchell supporter was heard.

The men inside the barber shop had been critiquing black politicians as representatives in name only. They argued that black politicians such as DePriest and Mitchell could propose beneficial legislation only after they "had cleared up the business of their bosses." One customer used the Mitchell Bill to further his argument against the lone black congressman's legislative agenda. The only Mitchell proponent in the shop defended the bill as "the most sensible bill that's been introduced in congress in 20 years." The entire shop challenged him. When he failed to defend himself quickly enough, one customer sneered, "When it comes to proving it you don't know what to do." After gathering his thoughts, the proponent urged everyone to separate their feelings for Mitchell from their view of his bill. "First of all," the proponent told the men in the shop, "there ain't no use in everybody condemning the bill just 'cause you don't like the man who proposed it. That's the trouble with most of you. You think just 'cause Mitchell suggested it, it ain't no good. If a white man suggested it, you'd say it was all right." Growing impatient, the men attempted to interrupt the speaker.[99]

Over the rumble of jeers, he continued to discuss the benefits of having African American officials in positions of power dedicated to the problems of black communities. "Now I ain't got nothing to do with [you] not liking Mitchell. Maybe he ain't been perfect, but this bill redeems him for anything wrong he may have done. This bill gives our men a chance to handle the problems of their own people. Certainly we know our own problems better than the white man does." Objectors continued to interrupt him, but the shop owner insisted they "let the man have his say. Ain't no hurry. Your turn's coming." Appreciative and confident, the speaker continued, "and another thing, we've been ignored up there too much. When the colored folks bring up a problem there, they just overlook it. This way it would get some consideration. Call it Jim Crow all you want, but the only way for a Negro's problems to be handled is to let a Negro handle 'em. I'll bet if DePriest suggested the bill you'd all be arguing different just 'cause you like him. It's not the bill you're opposed to but the man, and that ain't fair." After the speaker "had his say," the shop erupted into competing conversations about his perspective.

According to Waters's account, the barber shop owner was the first to express his opposition to the bill and immediately addressed inconsistencies in the proponent's argument. The owner pointed out that white politicians had previously introduced a similar bill, which African Americans did not support. "We don't care about Mitchell," the barber proclaimed, "we're arguing against the bill."[100] The barber acted as spokesperson for everyone who had been grumbling, interrupting, and waiting for a chance to refute the Mitchell supporter. The barber also clarified that he and others could assess the merits of the bill irrespective of their opinions of the congressman.

"And another thing," the barber continued, as he pointed his shears at the proponent, "there ain't no group of Negroes nor any other race which can solve ALL the problems of the Race. Why do you think they got so many departments to the government? It's because no five or ten men can handle the whole thing. Now we have problems in all the departments of the government and these men—even if they were all Booker T. Washingtons—couldn't solve them." Even though the barber overstated Washington's political achievements, he admired Washington as one of the few black leaders who had been able to influence white politicians. He believed the commission would become a feel-good agency that would seek to accomplish multiple goals and end up accomplishing nothing. "In the next place the right men wouldn't get the jobs," he said matter-of-factly. "They would appoint Negroes who helped elect the administration. Those Negroes would become so high and mighty you couldn't reach them no way you tried. You know I'm speaking the truth."[101] According to the barber, patronage politics and bureaucracy limited the vision of African American politicians to actually improve the lives of black constituents. He was "speaking the truth" about where he thought real change would *not* come from: the government.

The barber's critique, though, was not limited to race and the American political system. Still checking off his many problems with the proposed bill, the barber cautioned listeners to question white-supported programs targeted specifically toward African Americans. "If you don't read the paper you can't know what's happening and I read them. They all say the bill is no good. The white folks are glad enough to pass that bill and when you find them anxious to pass something to help the Negro and nobody else you can bet your life there's something wrong. I'm against everything these white folks do for the benefit of us alone. All of us should be if its something for the good of all the people, we get ours. But this special stuff is bad."[102] The barber's position was neither conservative nor paranoid. The federal government failed to pass countless bills that would improve the lives of African Americans—anti-lynching legislation, for example.[103] For the barber, white political silence was the huge seam that ran through the bill. Why were "white folks"

supportive of this bill? He remained skeptical because ultimately the commission would have no power or authority to implement or enforce anything.

The barber addressed the bill's flaws, but Mitchell and his motives also drew
fire. The barber rejected the notion that the bill "redeemed" Mitchell. "Let me
tell you something brother," he asserted, "that Negro ain't done a thing since
he's been in Washington and just to exercise the privilege he has of presenting
a bill and also to make the folks back here think he's really doing something,
he cooked this commission idea up. He's been yeaing and naying all year, now
he wants to earn his salary."[104]

The barber shop provided non-elite men the opportunity to critically discuss the strengths and weakness of the Mitchell Bill. The owner's position
in the shop reflected his position in the conversation as well. He had an
authority to ensure everyone had an uninterrupted opportunity to have his
say. But he also exercised his power to privilege his own voice by speaking
for the opponents. More significantly, Enoc Waters, the reporter, privileged
the barber's voice in this "forum." Other men entered the conversation, but
the news article did not include them because they "expressed similar issues." Moreover, the article included an illustration of a spirited barber shop
scene, with a caption that recognized the barber's authority. In the shop,

Figure 17. Illustration of barber forum. *Chicago Defender*, August 10, 1935.

the barbers and the waiting public sliced through the fat of the bill to address the underlying concerns, hidden agendas, and probable outcomes. The barber spoke to the waiting public like a preacher to the congregation. Perhaps his call, "you know I'm speaking the truth," yielded a response that substantiated his critique and authority. The barber shop gave these men an opportunity to engage in participatory democracy by engaging in political discourse.

While truth-telling was central to the democratic sensibility of the barber shop, truth-stretching was central to the authority and legitimacy that undergirded an individual's claim to participation in barber shop conversation. Everyone in a barber shop may have had an equal opportunity to be an authority on several matters, but this authority did not go unquestioned and unchallenged. As men took various positions on arguments and told tales to the audience of the waiting public, barber shops assumed a masculine aesthetic of boasting and bragging. Andrew Dobson captured this masculine aesthetic in the barber shop in a poem he published in the *Chicago Defender*. The editor referred to Dobson as a "Bert Williams, Edgar Guest and a Will Rogers of the Race all rolled into one." Dobson contributed song and poetry on station WJJD under the assumed name "Uncle Joe Dobson." His weekly column in the *Defender*, "From Uncle Joe Dobson's Journal," featured this barber shop poem in 1935:

> I driv[e] to town las' Saddy—
> Fer to git a keg o' nails;
> I drapped in Ephum's barber shop
> And dere I hea'd some tales.
>
> De young ones doin' de listenin'
> De old ones doin' de lyin;
> De old ones doin' de drinkin'
> De young ones doin' de buyin'.
>
> Dey told 'bout cheap likker,
> With steak five cents a pound;
> How many suits dey used to have—
> De wimmin jus' run 'em down.
>
> Nobody had to work, dey sed,
> Mos' any one would [illegible];

If things got tight, change President[s]
All police was yo' friend.

It [illegible] 'fore I got full,
I had to talk or bust—
I never could stand a 'ceitful liar
De old ones is de wuss.

I looked 'em all right in de eye
And den I had my say:
"Fools: what you used to [be] us don't count
It's what you is today."[105]

In Dobson's poem, masculinity played into the economy and politics of
the barber shop. The poem's young customers participate in the economic
exchange of the shop by getting haircuts. During their time spent waiting for
the chair, they become an audience for the older members of the waiting public. Dobson portrays this group of men, the ones doing the "lyin and drinkin,'"
as participants in the social and political exchange of the shop. The narrator,
though, grows restless with the masculine bravado expressed by the "'ceitful
liars." He ends the poem with his own masculine challenge. That he "looked
'em all right in de eye" prefaces his physical challenge in countering what he
considered embellishments. He needed to look them in the eye *before* he had
his say. His final words in the poem suggest these were indeed the last words
in the shop, or the last words that mattered, at least to him. According to the
narrator, these men were reminiscing about yesteryear. The poem highlights
the intergenerational tension of the barber shop and the open conversational
forums, but this openness raised questions of truthfulness. It became popular
perception that men would lie to paint themselves in a better light. African
American writers like Dobson drew on these popular perceptions of black
barber shop "forums," conversational patterns, and their confident, boastful,
manly personalities. As this masculine aesthetic became associated with barber shops, it transformed into a barber shop aesthetic.

The barber shop aesthetic extended beyond the shop itself and was mani-
fested in the popular usage of barber shop "characters." Marcus Garvey labeled W. A. Domingo a barber shop "rat" or "philosopher" for his criticisms
of the United Negro Improvement Association membership. Jamaican-born
Domingo was a black socialist and the first editor of Garvey's newspaper,

Negro World. Garvey fired him because he feared Domingo's left-wing political affiliations would make the UNIA vulnerable to governmental attacks. In *The Crusader*, Domingo argued that most of Garvey's followers were "voteless" because they were not citizens or refrained from voting to adhere to Garvey's teachings that they not participate in the American democratic process. Domingo also argued that the UNIA worldwide membership was much smaller than Garvey claimed. Garvey countered that Domingo was simply bitter because he was dismissed from the UNIA. Garvey contended, "He is what commonly is called a 'barber shop rat,' who talks the kind of philosophy indulged in by frequenters of the tonsorial artist."[106] He also dismissed Domingo as a "barber shop philosopher." Garvey's derogatory designation of a barber shop philosopher suggests a practice of truth-stretching meant to dismiss Domingo's claims as a bunch of lies and untruths, acts that he linked to the everyday practices of barber shops.

A "barber shop politician" was another character that drew on the common practice of black men who critically discussed the American political system inside barber shops. In 1944, Charley Cherokee wrote in his weekly "National Grapevine" column in the *Chicago Defender* that African American southerners needed to organize a third political party, a "Negro Party," in order to realize any sense of salvation. He believed "intellectuals and barber shop politicians will pooh-pooh the idea" that a third, black political party would be effective.[107] A barber shop politician acted as an authority on electoral politics when political conversations took place inside the barber shop. The presence of barber shop characters reflects the images that arose from black barber shops that functioned as public spaces. Many black barber shops had common characteristics, which allowed people to draw on the masculine aesthetic that took shape inside the shop and become associated with it. The usage of barber shop characters was based on a shared experience and image of the ways in which black men were able to escape the shadows of urban anonymity by reshaping their masculine identities through congregation and conversation in the barber shop.

By 1940, barber shops had become commercial public spaces within black communities. Black men could get haircuts, play the numbers, and read the newspaper. If they could not afford a haircut, they could at least spend idle time talking to other men inside the shop. Barber shops became sites of information exchange to an extent that even newspaper reporters benefited from the daily discourse. In 1932, Carter G. Woodson, preeminent African American historian, argued that barber shops were doing a better job than schools in providing a space for African Americans to discuss racial politics. "They [barbers] sit around during their leisure, discussing largely things which take place among their people," Woodson wrote in the *Chicago Defender*. "They read Negro newspapers, and readily buy books on the Negro. . . . The cause of the Race can get a hearing in the Negro barber shop more easily than in a Negro school. In the barber shop the Negro has freedom; in the school the Negro must do what somebody else wants done."[108] Barber shops gave black men the physical space to discuss racial or electoral politics in public with a larger community, but also in the racial privacy of a black patronized space. The public and private nature of black barber shops allowed political discourse to take shape. Barbers and customers determined how these commercial public spaces would be used in struggles for freedom and equality. Declaring barber shops as sites of freedom runs the risk of flattening out the rich significance of these spaces. The freedom and space to discuss racial politics was only a small part of African Americans' conceptions of freedom. Within the context of getting a haircut, they also wanted the freedom to patronize any shop of their choice, especially when they traveled away from black neighborhoods.

CHAPTER 5

Bigger Than a Haircut

Desegregation and the Barber Shop

WHILE visiting Chicago in November 1942, Bayard Rustin, civil rights activist, remarked to associates of the Congress for Racial Equality (CORE) that he needed a haircut. When someone told Rustin where he could not get one, the University of Chicago barber shop, he proceeded to test the waters. Rustin entered the Reynolds Club shop shortly before James Robinson, a white CORE member. The barber bypassed Rustin and offered to groom Robinson, but both activists insisted that Rustin be served first. The barber denied Rustin his haircut, but a Divinity School professor witnessed the exchange and subsequently formed a committee of Divinity School faculty and CORE members to desegregate the shop. After threatening a boycott, the committee convinced the campus shop to desegregate.[1] What did it mean to travel in the Jim Crow era and seek a haircut in a white barber shop? Where did the desegregation of white barber shops fit within the larger black freedom movement?

Exclusion from white barber shops was off the radar of most black activists; in refusing to cut African Americans' hair, white barbers had the convenient excuse that they lacked the training to cut "kinky" hair. In doing so, however, they relied on biological racism, drawing on ways of seeing race through hair type, to turn customers away. Men who were excluded understood the arbitrariness of this policy, and when black college students were turned away from campus barber shops, progressive white students rallied in support of their classmates. The largest of these campaigns took place on or near northern rural college campuses with small black neighboring populations. While these desegregation campaigns complemented other campaigns to open access to public places, many wondered if this was a black cause—or if liberal white students were establishing their own interpretation of civil rights.

Yet the struggle against segregated barber shops on campus was not simply an issue of adjustment to college-town living; black domestic and international travelers found themselves challenging Jim Crow's color line as well. A black barber shop was not on every corner in American cities and small towns, and black travelers loathed having to go far out of their way to find a black barber. Moreover, African diplomats in the United States encountered the same humiliation of being refused service from white barbers, which caused international embarrassment to the United States during the Cold War. As the issue grew from a local to a national problem, protesters relied on civil rights and labor legislation, as well as appeals to the State Department, to desegregate white shops. That the evidence of segregation in this period comes from college students and domestic and international travelers suggests that traveling for school and leisure brought with it certain class expectations: black middle-class travelers expected to be able to travel freely and be accommodated at their convenience. In the years after World War II, black encounters with Jim Crow's barber shop had to do with extended travel away from black neighborhoods, in contrast to the daily lives of black laborers and domestics. In short, what would African Americans do when they were away from the familiar space of black barber shops?

The College Town Barber Shop

As activists in the black freedom movement struggled to break the back of Jim Crow in places of public accommodation across the nation, students in northern college towns, and some urban college campuses, targeted white barber shops on and around campus to address racial discrimination in their backyards. College students across the country, particularly in the North and West, noticed that segregated barber shops were affecting both African American students and African exchange students in the post–World War II period. Some towns had no black barber shops, and white colleges and universities certainly had none on campus. This left the small number of African, African American, and Caribbean students to drive several miles to a black barber, cut their own hair, go to a fellow student with haircutting skills—or go to the campus barber. For many, the last option was certainly most convenient, but white shops on or near campus proved less than welcoming.

College student protests of white barber shops reflected a coalition of white and black students, many affiliated with their campus chapter of the NAACP or other student organizations, who found in these campaigns an opportunity to participate in the black freedom movement. At the University of Illinois at Urbana-Champaign, it took a popular black athlete to spark a campus-wide protest of white barber shops near campus.[2] On October 30, 1953, Lee Ingwerson denied a haircut to James Caroline, the university's star halfback, even though the barber displayed Caroline's picture in the shop window along with a welcome sign on the door.[3] A week later, on the afternoon of the Illinois-Michigan game, students affiliated with the Student-Community Human Relations Council (S-CHRC) distributed flyers to football fans to raise awareness of the issue. Illinois ranked fourth in the Associated Press (AP) poll coming into the game, so protesters were sure to see a huge crowd. One flyer read: "'J.C.' Caroline, brilliant star halfback of the fighting Illini, whom you'll see in action today, ran into an obstacle greater than any Ohio or Purdue line could produce. The obstacle, a campus barber; 'J.C.' was flatly, and rudely refused service, due to the fact that he's a Negro! Yes, 'J.C.' Caroline, potential All-American cheered by thousands each Saturday *cannot get a haircut on his own campus!* Here is a strange example where Americanism is displayed on Saturday afternoons and vicious, active discrimination during the rest of the week. Is this the American way?" (emphasis in the original).[4] The protesters identified a problem that black athletes and entertainers knew all too well: white business owners lauded their talents but deplored their bodies, frequently resulting in discrimination.

Local white barbers cited two major reasons for not cutting black customers' hair. First, barbers claimed they lacked the skill and "special equipment" to cut "Negro hair," which they believed took longer to cut than whites' hair. Second, they feared losing white patrons by serving blacks. The Racial Equality committee of the campus YMCA had been assisting with the protests and refuted these excuses by referring to a University of Chicago barber who, after Rustin's stand and subsequent protest, opened his doors to all patrons.[5] According to the committee, the barber had not lost business since he changed his policy, his barbers learned to cut blacks' hair without special training, and he did not need to invest in new equipment. Although the Illinois campus area barbers claimed their policy was not based on prejudice, they pressed that the time was not ripe for a nondiscriminatory policy in their shops.[6]

Despite barbers' reluctance, the S-CHRC mounted a layered campaign that included public pressure and legal action. The YMCA Racial Equality committee drew up petitions that read, "I will continue to obtain my haircut in a barbershop which will cut hair of individuals regardless of race, color, or creed." The committee presented approximately 2,000 male signatures to the barbers as a kind of guarantee that they would not lose business. The committee also organized a legal action committee to gather evidence against barbers, which was taken to state attorney John Bresee. Bresee was slow to act, but Robert Johnson, a black student in his senior year and a member of S-CHRC, filed suit against Ingwerson, with financial backing from the YMCA Committee. The committee also enlisted public opinion and successfully encouraged the University Student Senate, the Men's Independent Association, and the Student Committee on Discrimination and Academic Freedom to pass resolutions on the matter. The YMCA Committee even requested assistance from the American Civil Liberties Union (ACLU) in Chicago. Earl S. Rappaport, student co-chairman, wrote a letter to the ACLU describing the campaign, and framed it in terms of American foreign relations. Rappaport wrote, "I would also like to point out the fact that the Champaign-Urbana area is visited by so many outstanding individuals and students of foreign countries attend the University that this discrimination may have many bad repercussions on the nation as well as the international scene."[7] They believed the muscle of a national organization such as the ACLU would be too much for local barbers to bear. Edward H. Meyerding, executive director of the ACLU in Chicago, declined to get involved because two attorneys had already taken Johnson's case and the ACLU had a policy of not competing with the NAACP or duplicating its work and services if they decided to get involved on appeal.[8] With continued pressure and protest to change their policies, local barbers appeased the protesters in a very calculating way.

On Saturday, May 1, 1954, campus barber shop proprietors announced they would take steps to accommodate black customers. However, their steps toward desegregation came with caveats and conditions that either left them power to turn away potential clients or transferred the quality of haircut received onto the customer. Rules posted in two shops near campus noted these qualifications:

1. we do not cut unusual styles of women's haircuts.
2. we do not cut curly, kinky, wooley, types of hair.
3. we reserve the right to determine our qualifications, or ability, to administer service. Any party insisting on service, assumes the liability of the results.

4. under the state law we are prohibited from serving any person who has an infectious disease or contagious disease.
5. the above regulations are applicable to all members of the public, regardless of color.[9]

With these rules, white barbers essentially formalized what they had already been doing. The rules at once emphasized barbers' skills and their underlying preference to keep blacks and women out of their shops. It is unclear what "unusual styles" the first rule referenced: in the 1950s no hairstyle brought women into the barber shops in large numbers, as the bob did in the 1920s. Rules 2 and 3 "officially" excluded anyone who appeared to have hair that white barbers marked as other-than-straight (curly, kinky, wooly). Although these "regulations are applicable to all members of the public, regardless of race," black men were more likely to be marked as having "curly, kinky, wooley" hair. Since the late nineteenth century, white barbers who were associated with the barbers' union commonly used public health or a concern for the spread of contagious diseases to secure regulations that would marginalize black barbers. But here, white barbers employed the barbers' licensing law, passed in 1919, and the public health provision as a tool to exclude black customers. In all, these rules would have been woefully inadequate under any circumstances, but they left an opening for students to at least get inside the shops.

And they did, with help. By October 1, the S-CHRC reported that all shops had opened their doors to black customers—including Ingwersen's shop, which, a few days earlier, had fallen in line. The students at Illinois successfully obtained equal access to white barber shops; equal treatment, though, was another matter. Some students were satisfactorily served and others "assumed responsibility" for their haircut. Albert Porter said he was humiliated in Val Rund's Barber Shop. "After about three minutes of close-cutting with the clippers," Porter reported, Rund "slapped some lather on my head and rubbed so hard I thought I would start to bleed. He took the stuff off; I paid him; he threw the change in my hand, and I left."[10] Some black students received butchered haircuts that would have made them the laughingstock of campus. According to John Langdon, acting co-chair of the S-CHRC, a barber "played a game" with a black customer, "spinning around on his heels and taking swipes at the customer's head with the clippers as he turned."[11]

Campus barber shop politics also inspired the white liberals who lived in many college towns. For example, the residents of Yellow Springs, Ohio, home of Antioch College, took pride in the town's liberalism, and when word spread that two white barber shops refused to serve black customers, even though these were long-standing policies, students and residents sprang to action. In 1960, the campus chapter of the NAACP initiated a test case against Squire's and Lewis Gegner's barber shops. Lawrence Rubin, a white student, served as president of this predominately white chapter. Black and white students entered the shops and demanded service. Squire capitulated, but Gegner would not be moved. "You know I don't cut Negro hair," he told the black student.

The ACLU assisted in charging Gegner for violating Ohio's public accommodation statute. Gegner's defense attorney painted him as a hardworking, independent business owner and the ACLU as a communist-leaning, un-American organization set to infringe on individual liberties. The defense also pulled out a surprise star witness: a black barber who catered to Yellow Spring's black community. He testified that "black hair" required special training because it differed from "white hair." Rubin believed this testimony was self-serving because he stood to gain customers. Yet the prosecution had a star witness of its own who would challenge Gegner's claim of not being able to cut curly hair. Professor David Epstein testified that he had gotten his haircut at Gegner's shop. Epstein lowered his head and showed the court his "full head of tight, dark, kinky curls."[12] This damning testimony revealed to the jury that Gegner possessed the skills to cut curly hair and he violated state law by refusing to cut blacks' curly hair. They found Gegner guilty and fined him one dollar—hardly a punitive judgment—which had no effect on him or his business.

Meanwhile, the Ohio Civil Rights Commission ordered Gegner to accommodate black customers. The commission based its ruling on a law that had become effective in October 1961 requiring any business to serve all customers regardless of race, creed, or color. Common Pleas Judge Warren C. Young ruled against this section of the law and threw out the commission's order to Gegner, rendering it unconstitutional. Young reasoned that a barber must have special training, pass a state examination, and be licensed. Ultimately, he agreed with Gegner that compelling him to serve black customers when he did not know how to cut their hair abridged his inherent freedom to operate his trade.[13] The problem with the judge's reasoning was that Gegner did pass a state examination and was indeed licensed.

In the aftermath of Gegner's appeal, students continued to pressure him to serve all customers. The organizers and demonstrators were mostly white students from Antioch. They had been unsuccessful in convincing black students from neighboring Wilberforce University and Central State College, two historically black colleges and universities, to join the protests. Otha Nixon had recently moved to Yellow Springs after he graduated from Central State. He commuted every day to Dayton, where he worked as a teacher. He read in the *Yellow Springs News* that Antioch students were picketing Gegner's shop. Intrigued by the demonstrations, Nixon attended the meetings held by the Antioch Committee for Racial Equality (ACRE). He was not motivated to join the demonstrations as a move to secure Gegner as his barber. Nixon did not even frequent the local black barber shop because he disliked the way this barber cut his hair. In fact, a friend from college continued to cut Nixon's hair. The local black barber, though, seemed miffed that Nixon was involved in the protests. "Why are you doing this, when you can come here and get your haircut," the barber asked him. Nixon replied, "Man, I'm doing it because he won't cut my hair. That's why. And, it's wrong." One of a few black participants, Nixon offered to recruit black students from Wilberforce and Central State. The ACRE needed blacks' involvement to prevent authorities from marginalizing their campaign as one that lacked the support of the very people they proposed to be fighting for. Pragmatically, they needed black men to seek haircuts inside the shop. Nixon obtained permission from Charles Wesley, noted historian and president of Central State, to "go into the cafeteria and speak to the students and tell them that we needed black participation at Gegner's." Wesley, like other black college presidents who faced the reality that their students participated in the sit-in movement, provided unofficial support, telling Nixon, "Don't tell them I gave you permission."[14] As their numbers increased, students staged two major demonstrations at Gegner's in 1963 and 1964; in between the two, they picketed the shop every Saturday.

Nixon entered Gegner's shop with another black student and a white student, and went directly to Gegner for a haircut. Gegner refused and told him to leave, an order that Nixon ignored. Since they had planned this test, there were tons of students and police outside the barber shop. The police forcefully removed him from the shop. As Nixon remembered these details in 2009, he became overcome with emotion as he recalled the events of that day. When the police dragged him out of the shop he "started singing 'We Shall Overcome.' I cried . . . got emotional, limp, couldn't walk . . . they had to carry me." The police took him to the jailhouse but did not arrest him.[15] After this incident, the publicity began to pick up as newspapers across the country reported on the demonstrations.

The 1964 demonstration probably drew the most publicity because the police engaged in a southern-style strategy of resistance that would have made Eugene "Bull" Connor proud. Nixon remembered this as the "biggie" where "they had police dogs, fire hoses, fire engines, and tear gas. They had their billy clubs. They had these redneck police from the other surrounding counties." Rubin recalled that "hundreds of Antioch students and others held a mass protest" in front of Gegner's shop. Those "others" comprised black students from Central State and Wilberforce. Typical of protest decorum, male and female students dressed in their Sunday finest for the demonstration. The fire engines and dogs indicated to them that this might be a violent battle. It is unclear what precipitated the police charging into the crowd, but they started grabbing the students and, according to Nixon, "dislocating or breaking their thumbs." The students were "screaming and hollering, and people were running, and the tear gas started, the water hose started . . . and they were trying to throw us into cars." The cloud of tear gas watered students' eyes and the students began to vomit. The police arrested 108 students that day. The *Yellow Springs News* office was next door to Gegner's shop, offering their photographers intimate access to the escalating violence, which they captured and documented in the paper the following day. To avert further protests, Gegner closed his shop until the Ohio Supreme Court ruled on his appeal against the Civil Rights Commission order that he serve black customers.[16]

The demonstrations at Gegner's barber shop revealed fissures within white communities that often sat hidden behind public expressions of liberalism. While the coalition of police officers from surrounding counties acted as ambassadors for Bull Connor, Yellow Springs police chief James McKee, a black man, generally supported the demonstrations as long as they remained peaceful and nonviolent. Many Yellow Springs residents supported the demonstrations as well. Nixon remembered Yellow Springs as a very liberal, "hippie" town. His reference point for liberalism was that "there were a lot of mixed marriages."[17] Members of the village council, though, viewed the demonstrations differently. They were concerned that the town's liberal image would be tarnished. Nixon did not recall Jim Crow rearing its head in any other space in the town. Hundreds of students demonstrating in Yellow Springs did not fit well with the liberal image held by black and white residents; Yellow Springs was not supposed to be Birmingham. The village council did not support the demonstrations because it wanted to keep the national spotlight off the town, especially considering the contentious and violent demonstrations in the South.[18]

More broadly, the challenges that black students faced—in Yellow Springs and other college towns—in getting a haircut illuminate the racial and spatial politics of grooming. On one hand, barbers correctly pointed out that there are different hair types. "Straight," "curly," and "tightly coiled" are the three most common hair types, each requiring different grooming methods. For example, barbers can cut straight hair with a comb and scissors. These two instruments are insufficient to cut tightly coiled hair because the hair grows in various directions. Instead, clippers are used for tightly coiled hair because they can rapidly cut the hair close. White and black barbers have historically acknowledged these differences. Yet, white barbers appropriated this biological difference to mark tightly coiled hair as inferior.

For barbers, race thus did the work of organizing hair type, but hair also did the work of categorizing race. By articulating different hair types as "Negro hair" or "white hair," barbers collapsed the biological differences of hair type onto racial groups. The term "white" or "Caucasian" hair seldom appears in the historical documents because it was the standard by which all others were judged. Therefore "Negro hair" was marked as other, abnormal, and requiring "special" training to learn how to cut. White barbers associated blackness with kinky hair. Hair texture is hereditary, but multiple genes control it. Genetic variation prevents direct correlations between race and hair type.[19] Yet, the history of interraciality complicates these essential notions of blackness and hair type. Many black men sported hair just as straight as that of white men, yet white barbers excluded black men with straight hair right along with men who had tightly coiled hair. By articulating their exclusion policies based on a preferred niche in catering to a particular hair type, white barbers engaged in a discourse that relied on objective and race-neutral language that, at its core, was anything but objective and race-neutral.

The intimate environs of college towns left the increasing, but still small, number of black students with the responsibility of navigating campus, town, and racial politics. Black students sought to claim campus space by attempting to desegregate their campus barber shops, and they found a segment of white students and student organizations interested in assisting them. The coalition of black and white students demonstrated that the desegregation of white barber shops went beyond the existence and proximity of black shops. Indeed, white barbers' ideologies of race and hair type informed activists that this desegregation struggle was intended to dismantle white supremacy.

Acts of Convenience and Consciousness in Urban Travel

Black students may have found the scarcity of black shops and the unwillingness of white barbers to groom them in small towns across the country, but
the challenge of conveniently getting a haircut in any shop was not easily
mitigated in the city, either. Unlike in small towns, black-owned barber shops
anchored black neighborhoods in every major city. For many black men, the
barber shop was a regular destination in their Saturday routine. They had a
chance to get their weekly haircut, talk with their regular barber, and play
the dozens or a game of chess with other men hanging out in the shop. Yet,
some men simply wanted a haircut, from any barber, and they searched for
the closest shop regardless of the barber's race. Black students at urban college and university campuses could relate to the challenges of distance their
college-town counterparts faced when looking for the closest barber shop,
which more often than not was white. The conflicts between black men and
white barbers in the city reveal blacks' insistence on claiming their freedom
of movement by pushing the boundaries of segregation.

Chicago was a case in point. In June 1948, Joffre Stewart, a black student
at Roosevelt College downtown, walked a few doors from the college to get
a shave and haircut at Leone's Barber Shop. Stewart could have traveled to
one of the many black barber shops on the South Side, but assuming he had
been coming from campus, Leone's was a stone's throw away. The barber told
him he could not be served because he needed an appointment. Stewart went
back three times over the course of six months, each time being turned away.
As a member of CORE, Stewart was familiar with the strategies of direct action. On January 3, 1949, he enlisted Jack Fooden, a white member of CORE
and graduate student at the University of Chicago, to enter the shop first, and
Stewart would follow a few minutes later. Fooden got seated without difficulty and without an appointment. Stewart then entered and again was refused even though Fooden relinquished his chair to him. At this point, the
barber announced the shop was closing and the men would have to leave.
Stewart and Fooden attempted this strategy a few more times until, on the last
occasion, the barber called the police. Instead of arresting the barber for violating the Illinois civil rights law, the police arrested Fooden for "disturbing
the peace" and Stewart for "resisting an officer." The police took both men to
the Central Police station and booked them on disorderly conduct. With trial
set for the following week, Fooden was released on a twenty-five-dollar bond,
but Stewart elected to remain in custody until the police, or "representatives
of violence," as he called them, discharged him. CORE reported that police

regularly beat and kicked Stewart while he was imprisoned. Authorities placed him in the Bridewell Prison hospital for refusing to walk, and Stewart claims he was repeatedly slapped and clubbed while in the hospital. He was eventually taken to a psychopathic hospital, where he remained up to and through his trial so that officials could "determine his sanity." Stewart and Fooden contacted the American Civil Liberties Union (ACLU) on January 20 for assistance with the trial the next morning. With little preparation, Sanford Wolff appeared in court on their behalf. Wolff obtained a finding of not guilty for Fooden, while the presiding judge, Oscar Kaplan, dismissed the charges against Stewart because he had been assigned to the County Psychopathic Hospital.

The issue of Stewart's mental health raised other concerns.[20] Stewart's family and friends in CORE expressed deep concerns that he had been placed in a mental facility because authorities believed he had to be crazy to resist and not cooperate at the time of arrest and throughout his imprisonment. Stewart's family, however, claimed the psychiatrist intimated that Stewart would become more aggressive in his "crusade for human rights," as a manifestation of his schizophrenic state.[21] Stewart was eventually paroled from the mental facility to his mother, but being committed to a mental institution seemed an unlikely end result for trying to get a haircut a few steps from one's college campus. It is unclear if Stewart's initial attempt was a conscious act of resistance or simply an act of convenience. As this instance and others, including the debate surrounding Rosa Parks's intentions, demonstrates, African Americans' frustrations with Jim Crow's indignities in everyday life had a way of blurring the line between conscious and convenient acts of resistance in public places.[22] Nonetheless, authorities in the Stewart case made the message clear: he had to be crazy to attempt to desegregate a white barber shop and be uncooperative with authority.[23]

Stewart was among the few black students who led the battle for barber shop desegregation in the North. These campaigns were small and fairly easy to organize, requiring at a minimum one black and one white protester. By World War II, eighteen northern states had passed civil rights legislation prohibiting discrimination in public places of accommodation, providing students the legal infrastructure to stake their protests. Protesters appealed to barbers to change their policies and to the state to enforce its laws. As historian Thomas Sugrue points out, protests against commercial Jim Crow did not require mass mobilization, as did protests against job discrimination.[24] Public accommodations protests in the North received little media coverage in larger cities, so it is no surprise that these protests in small college towns were treated similarly. The black press, however, made note of public accommodations protests that occurred across the country, including the barber shop campaigns. Even without the southern-style Jim Crow signs, northern activists faced little difficulty demonstrating that Jim Crow reared its head in their restaurants, swimming pools, hotels, and barber shops.[25] These were the battlegrounds of northern public accommodations struggles, whereas southern student activists targeted lunch counters. Yet did African Americans really care about a desegregated barber shop?

White shops bypassed southern activists' radar. Civil rights workers in the South routinely placed themselves in danger by registering to vote, sitting at a lunch counter, attempting to desegregate a school, or staging a march. But if black activists in the South had challenged white barbers to desegregate their shops by attempting to get a shave, it would have added new meaning to "putting one's neck on the line for freedom." Langston Hughes used his witty, race-conscious literary character Simple to illuminate this tenuous space within the larger national black freedom movement. Simple reasoned, "It would take a brave black student to sit-in at a white barber shop in Memphis, Jackson, Toogaloo, Birmingham, Atlanta, or anywhere else. Did you say non-violent? With all the love he has got in his heart, I have never read in no newspaper where Rev. Martin Luther King has gone into a white barber shop down South and said, 'I love you, barber. Cut my hair.' Martin Luther King has got more sense than that. He knows prayer might not prevail in no white barber shop in Birmingham. Or in Boston, either."[26] Hughes used a little creative license in suggesting that there were no barber shop sit-ins, but his larger point spoke to the marginal place of barber shops in local desegregation campaigns.

If anyone understood the significance of black barber shops in urban America and the ways that segregation had organized the city, it was certainly Horace Cayton, Jr. In 1930, Cayton had co-authored, with St. Clair Drake, *Black Metropolis*, the monumental book on black Chicago. In the summer of 1946, Cayton lived on an estate outside of Saratoga Springs while writing another book. One August morning, he found himself in a predicament where he needed a haircut, but there was no black barber shop in town. He was planning to drive into Saratoga Springs to "see if I can find a colored barber to cut my hair."[27] With this trip on his mind, Cayton focused one of his regular columns in the *Pittsburgh Courier* on black men's challenges of getting a haircut at their convenience. "One of the most annoying things about being colored," Cayton began his column, "is the difficulty one has getting his hair cut. Of course, this difficulty doesn't present itself when [one] lives in the Negro communities of such cities as New York, Chicago, Pittsburgh, Detroit, etc. One picks out the cleanest shop and the most amusing barber and goes there on Friday or Saturday, according to his individual schedule. But when you move out of the Negro settlements your [troubles] begin." In Cayton's assessment, black men faced a challenge if they lived in a place with no "Negro Colony," which probably meant no black barber shop.[28]

This sojourn to a black community for a haircut, in Cayton's view, amounted to an "awful waste of time," especially when he had to travel from Long Island to Harlem every two weeks. While staying with friends in Long Island during the first part of the summer, he would follow this procedure for his haircut journey:

> I got up at six o'clock in the morning and caught an early train to New York. Ate breakfast at the station and then I proceeded to Harlem where, after waiting my turn for approximately an hour, I would get my hair cut. It would then be about lunch time and I would eat and spend the afternoon at some picture gallery. Then I would go to a show and later—if fortunate or unfortunate, it's just how you look at it—I might have a date to go out dancing. I would then have to stay overnight and take the early morning train back to Long Island. All in all, the hair cut would cost me about twenty-eight hours of time and any where from fifteen to thirty dollars—according to whether I had a date.

Cayton summed up the cost of his bimonthly haircut journeys as a "right steep price to pay for being colored." To be sure, he cared little about going to a white barber shop because, as he wrote, he would "much prefer a Negro barber, not only for reasons of racial solidarity, but also because I have the feeling that perhaps a Negro barber knows how to cut my hair better than would one of the other group." It annoyed Cayton that he, unlike white men, had to make a "pilgrimage" to New York City for a fifteen- or twenty-minute haircut. Cayton concluded that, "other things being equal," he would only patronize a black barber. But, considering the time and money that he invested in getting a haircut while living on Long Island, he did not see things as being equal.[29]

If traveling in small towns and big cities across America posed dilemmas for black men in finding a trusted barber to trim their locks, then international travel increased their level of uncertainty. "Only once have I had a white person cut my hair," Cayton noted, "and that was in France. I entered the barber shop on that occasion with both conscious and unconscious fear for I realized that was the only thing that I had done in France that I had never done in America."[30] Nonetheless, Cayton's barber shop experience in Paris substantiated perceptions for him that France was a country without racial prejudice; a sentiment that several African American soldiers, entertainers, and writers had posited since World War I.

Langston Hughes employed his fictional protagonist Simple to explain the racial politics of international travel and the challenges of getting a haircut. In "Haircuts and U.S.A.," published in December 1962, Simple lauded Europe as a place where blacks could sit in a white barber's chair without incident. Simple's friend John Williams had won the "sweepstakes" and traveled to France, Italy, and Spain. One of the most memorable aspects of his trip was being able to get a haircut anywhere. "That is certainly not true in the U.S.A.," Simple noted, "where a Negro has to look for a colored barbershop—just like in most towns down South he still has to look for a colored restaurant in which to eat, a colored hospital in which to die, and a colored undertaker to get buried by, also a colored cemetery to be buried in. They have no such jackassery in Europe."[31] Being able to get a haircut in Europe made the white barbers in Paris seem less prejudiced because of how they treated their black patrons. More than getting a haircut, getting a shave seemed to be the true marker of racial trust. Simple contended, "Here in the United States to get shaved a white barber is liable to cut a colored man's throat instead of trimming his beard. I have never heard tell of no sit-ins in no barber chairs in America."[32] Yet by 1962, there had been several sit-ins, or shave-ins, at various colleges across the country. If Hughes was not aware of these campaigns, he was certainly aware of the problems that the small number of black college students had in getting haircuts in these small towns. Simple noted that his dentist's son was one of the few black students at a small college in Ohio. Local white barbers refused to cut their hair, claiming lack of training, thus sending these students forty miles to Toledo. Hughes was likely referring to the Antioch case. Simple remarked that "if white Americans can learn how to fly past Venus, go in orbit and make telestars, it looks like to me white barbers in Ohio could learn to cut colored hair. But since they also might cut my throat, I prefer to go to Paris, to get my hair cut there. . . . Even here in Harlem, I thank God for Paris barbers. Amen!"[33] Most black men would have disagreed with Simple in suggesting that he much preferred to travel to Paris to have his hair cut by a white barber. The thought of traveling and receiving a haircut anywhere was a liberating idea for some.

If Europe offered black travelers a sense of rebirth beyond the "restrictive bonds of ethnicity, national identification, and sometimes even race itself," as Paul Gilroy suggests, I argue that blackness and black culture were not necessarily something to escape.[34] Hughes emphasizes this rebirth in Europe as a way to illuminate the racial restrictions and volatility in the United States. Blacks were not attempting to escape black shops; they just wanted the option of going to any shops as a marker of their freedom. The everyday complications of navigating landscapes beyond black public spaces heightened travelers' senses when they submitted control to allow non-black barbers to groom their hair.

Black domestic and international travelers had to consider the complications of gaining access to basic necessities during their journeys, such as places to be groomed, to eat, and certainly to sleep. Although one could go without a haircut for an extra week or two, restaurants and hotels caused much greater concerns. The 1937 publication of *The Negro Motorist Green-Book* provided "the Negro traveler information that will keep him from running into difficulties, embarrassments, and to make his trips more enjoyable" in Jim Crow America.[35] Black travelers relied on black restaurants and hotels to accommodate them during their travels. *The Negro Motorist* also included a small listing of barber shops in each city. These listings were far from comprehensive, partly because proprietors had to pay to have their businesses listed. Again, haircuts were easier to negotiate, but the comments of international travelers suggest that getting a haircut in a white barber shop abroad illuminated the state of Jim Crow back home. Black men could, and indeed often did, go their entire lives without stepping foot inside a white barber shop without feeling "segregated" because they much preferred a black shop. Unlike other public spaces, barber shops never adorned Jim Crow signs because custom did the work of ordering these spaces.[36] The barber shop's private and intimate space encouraged black and white men to congregate in racially homogeneous shops. Beyond the interior of the shops, the structure of segregation meant that black shops were located in black neighborhoods— areas white men might only frequent at night in red light districts. White shops were more spread out across urban areas, which meant that if white men did not want to, they did not have to go to a black shop, even though they could. In contrast, local black travelers faced inconveniences outside of black communities. Even though black men preferred black shops, they resented passing up a white shop to avoid humiliation.

Similar to the proprietors of campus shops, white barbers expressed concern that serving black customers would drive away their existing white customers, but the central issue in desegregating barber shops rested on how white barbers viewed hair type as a racial marker and how the state viewed the blurred lines between discrimination and service differentiation. Here, too, barbers expressed concerns about the perceived difficulties in cutting "kinky" hair. In the fall of 1960, Charles Flott, Jr., an eight-year-old resident of Uniondale, Long Island, ventured into Angelo's Barber Shop at 523 Uniondale Avenue for a haircut. Flott was very light-skinned, but when the barber discovered Flott was black, he increased the price to five dollars. Angelo Mustachio, the proprietor, had posted a sign in his shop which read "Kinky Haircut—$5." The barber raised the price in accordance with the shop's policy, which suggested that kinky hair took more work to cut, and thus required a higher fee. It is unclear if the barber realized Flott was black while he cut his hair or afterward. Based on a photo of Flott, his hair was quite curly, adding to the barber's confusion according to notions of kinky hair. Flott's skin was light enough that the barber could not determine his race. For white barbers, when skin color failed to do the work of race, hair type picked up the slack. Flott's parents filed a complaint against Mustachio with the State Commission Against Discrimination (SCAD). After a public hearing, Elmer A. Carter, chairman of SCAD, ordered Mustachio to remove the sign and to immediately cut black patrons' hair, with equal quality and rate extended to white customers.[37]

White barbers argued that they did not discriminate based on race, yet their clumsy use of hair type as a marker of exclusion proved race to be at the center of their clientele choice. Their emphasis on appearance as a signal of race made their attempts to categorize the "colored" from the "uncolored" fraught with erroneous judgment. A barber at the Greyhound Bus Station Terminal Barber Shop in Detroit thought he saw a light-skinned Negro entering his barber shop, and promptly told him "haircuts are only given by appointments." The several barbers who stood idle claimed to be waiting for their customers. The "Negro" that the barber rejected was Kamal Kapur, an exchange student from India who was attending Syracuse University at the invitation of the U.S. Government. Before Kapur left Michigan for Syracuse, he shared the incident with a Birmingham, Michigan, businessman, who in turn informed the Detroit Commission on Community Relations. Richard

V. Marks, commission director, remarked, "This is certainly a mark against our foreign affairs relations . . . and this type of thing is certainly not good." The shop manager admitted that the shop did not serve "black Negroes," and apparently he did not serve "Indian Negroes" either, but he agreed to write a letter of apology. The *Pittsburgh Courier* ran an article about the incident with the title "A Mistake? Deny Indian Haircut for Negro Looks."[38] Did the barber refuse Kapur because he looked black, or was Kapur simply black enough to be excluded?

White barbers drew on the category of "Negro" to racialize all men of color even if their hair was not "kinky." Filomeno "Phil" Coronada Ortega, a pitcher for the Los Angeles Dodgers, was surprised to be turned away from a downtown barber shop in Vero Beach, Florida. In 1961, Ortega, a "full-blooded American Indian," was rejected from this barber shop because the barber did not serve Negroes. If the barber had trouble seeing that Ortega was not a Negro, the Dodgers also had trouble seeing he was not Mexican. In the 1960s, the Dodgers believed Ortega could help them expand their market into the Latino community. While Dodgers vice president Buzzie Bavasi attempted to "Mexicanize" Ortega, Ortega much preferred to highlight his Yaqui Indian background, thus thwarting all attempts at racial marking. He identified himself as Indian, the Dodgers marked him as Mexican, and the barber marked him as Negro. Ortega, and his Indian-Mexican-Negro self, ultimately had to find a black barber shop for his haircut.[39] This barber may have followed baseball. Believing Ortega to be Mexican, he may have refused him on this basis and not his perceived blackness. When white barbers excluded those they perceived to be Latino and men who identified themselves as Latino, they omitted any particular reference to their Latin heritage by employing "Negro hair" to racialize all colored men. Yet this silence should not suggest that the Latino identity of these customers played no role in their discrimination, or that white barbers saw them as black. Instead, white barbers saw them as Latin-Negroes, an identity needing no distinction because perceived hair type grouped colored men into one category. White barbers articulated their exclusion of "Negroes," regardless of race or nation, based on their "kinky hair," which was also an attempt to deemphasize race to centralize hair and skill.[40]

African Dignitaries and Cold War Haircuts

In the post–World War II period, African immigrants and visiting diplomats faced similar difficulties in getting a haircut in the shop of their choice. They were more likely to walk into white barber shops because they lacked the same affinities for black barber shops as African Americans. Yet, as they would soon find, white barbers made no distinction based on nationality; race and hair texture were evidence enough. In 1959, Dr. Tigani El Mahi, a Sudanese psychiatrist, traveled to Pennsylvania to give a lecture at the University of Pittsburgh. When he entered the Hotel Webster Hall and requested a haircut, Frank Paolozzi "cupped his hands over his face and shied away," showing no interest in serving him.[41] Because Dr. El Mahi had traveled to the United States as part of a university-sponsored visit, and not a diplomatic mission, his exclusion failed to receive adequate attention and outcry. This would not be the case just one year later with a new presidential administration and the continuing decolonization of Africa. The high stakes of excluding African diplomats had significant implications for American credibility in Cold War politics.

When African dignitaries met the indignities of Jim Crow, the State Department, particularly the Kennedy administration, stood prone to embarrassment and worried about fumbling diplomatic relations with a new bloc of independent African nations. In the first eleven months of 1960, seventeen African nations achieved independence from their colonial powers. With a growing number of newly independent nations came a growing number of ambassadors who visited the United States. On June 26, 1961, Malick Sow, the first ambassador to the United States from the newly independent nation of Chad, drove from the United Nations in New York along Route 40 to Washington, D.C., to present his credentials to President Kennedy. Along the way, Sow stopped at a diner for coffee, but he was turned away because the diner did not serve blacks. Sow related to the State Department that these incidents of racial discrimination "make normal relations between the United States and African countries very strained." These words were not lost on the State Department, which well knew that Jim Crow would undermine diplomatic relations with African countries.[42] The State Department received numerous complaints from diplomats who were refused service, particularly in restaurants and barber shops, because these were public places of necessity. In fact, the *New York Times* reported on June 9, 1963, that State Department officials "said at least twenty African diplomats, including three or four Ambassadors, had complained that during the last 18 months they had been discriminated against in Washington barbershops." Pedro A. San Juan, director of special protocol services, conceded that these incidents "cannot be dismissed with an apology," but he failed to assert how he would handle the matter.[43] These diplomats quickly realized that this unwelcome mat was not reserved only for them; black American residents had the same trouble. Yet most black residents probably would not have considered it trouble because they much preferred a black barber shop. Marguerite Cartwright of the *Pittsburgh Courier* believed that the increasing presence of African dignitaries was contributing to a decline of racial discrimination. She noted that the Hotel Taft in New Haven, Connecticut, "fired its barber for his refusal to serve Dr. Edwin Barclay of Liberia, who was a guest at the hotel."[44]

Yet Washington, D.C., would continue to be the proving ground for African dignitaries' reception into the United States. Prince Godfrey K. Katanywa, a visiting student from Uganda studying public administration under the auspices of the International Training Division of the Agency for International Development, became acquainted with Jim Crow's tonsorial parlor when his hair screamed out for a trim. On March 16, 1964, Katanywa entered the Investment Building Barbershop at 1010 15th Street N.W., in downtown Washington, D.C., for a haircut. Instead of getting a haircut, he met resistance from the barbers in the shop. One barber told Katanywa that he "could direct me to a colored area on 14th St." in the Shaw black business district.[45] In response, Katanywa lodged a formal complaint with the State Department.

The incident outraged newspaper reporters, congressmen, and the State Department. Three days after the incident, Baker Morten of the *Washington Afro-American* retraced Katanywa's footsteps to investigate the issue. When he entered the Investment Building Barbershop and asked for a haircut, the proprietor, Rene Nezet, first told him he did not need a haircut. Next, Nezet turned to his five "tonsorial experts," as Baker referred to them, to ask if any of them would cut his hair—a question that received no response. Finally, Nezet leveled with Baker and told him, "I'll lose 50 per cent of my business if I cut colored people's hair. If the law required all barbershops to serve colored people I would also."[46] Representative Charles Diggs Jr., from Michigan, used this incident to push for tougher legislation prohibiting discrimination in barber shops. Diggs had a history of supporting economic boycotts. In August 1963 he organized a buy-in campaign in Detroit to encourage blacks to support a black-owned supermarket in an effort to fuel economic development.[47] In D.C. he was supporting a consumer protest. "It is a monstrous insult," Diggs proclaimed, "that a barber can refuse service to Negro diplomats but can take in any bum off of Washington's skid row who has the right fee and color."[48] Reaching the same conclusions as Representative Diggs, State Department officials stressed the need for regulations prohibiting such discrimination.

Yet, the District of Columbia already had legislation on the books—legislation that many referred to as the "lost laws" because they were so widely disregarded that many people assumed there were no existing laws in place to prohibit racial discrimination in public places of accommodation.

Corporation counsel Chester Gray encouraged Katanywa to apply for a warrant under the District of Columbia's Civil Rights Act of 1872, which many people believed stood as the necessary regulation in place to deal with such discrimination. As discussed in Chapter 2, an African American had invoked the 1872 act to request a warrant against a barber for refusing to cut his hair, although in that case the barber was black. But because barber shops were not listed among the scheduled public places, the Police Court had denied him the warrant. Nearly a century later, Gray believed that "when a barber flatly refuses to cut a person's hair on grounds of race or color, he is in violation of the act of 1872."[49] A new regulation to prohibit racial discrimination in barber shops had been drafted in 1963, but it had yet to pass. The State Department prompted Washington, D.C., officials to consider new legislation for this "hair-raising problem." The new law, according to Gray, "is designed to stymie barbers from having excuses such as 'I don't know how to cut the hair of colored people.'"[50] He said the 1872 law covered refusals of service but failed to protect against the myriad of possible excuses for not rendering service. Gray perceived the new law as a way to "meet modern conditions." The law would provide for suspension or revocation of licenses, require all barbers to learn how to cut all types of human hair, and require every barber shop to have a manager who can be held accountable for its policy. The White House requested the Board of Commissioners to delay issuing an antidiscrimination law for barber shops in light of the pending federal civil rights bill in Congress. Gray believed provisions concerning racial discrimination in barber shops were in the civil rights bill.[51] Ten days after denying Katanywa a haircut, Nezet changed his policy and issued an apology. He agreed to extend "the best possible service" to all future customers.

He argued that he did not intend to discriminate against Katanywa, but only intended to protect his business. Particularly, he explained that his barbers were not trained to "cut the hair of colored patrons."[52] Washington, D.C., officials stood prepared to implement their own antidiscrimination legislation if Congress rejected the proposed federal legislation or passed a weak version.

In some cases, labor regulations and civil rights legislations worked in tandem to protect the rights of African Americans to get a haircut in any barber shop they stepped into. Ironically, the white-dominated barbers union had worked tirelessly to professionalize barbering by lobbying for state licensing laws requiring apprentices to attend barbering school, master the anatomy of the body, and be examined by a state board. This emphasis on skill, efficiency, and sanitation had undergirded their politics of professionalization at the turn of the century. Black barbers resisted these proposed regulations because they believed white barbers would use these instruments to ultimately push them out of the field. By the mid-twentieth century, however, the tide had turned. White barbers were now claiming they had no skill to cut black men's hair. This excuse for exclusion flew in the face of many state officials who questioned what it meant to be a licensed barber. In 1957, California municipal judge Bill L. Dozier awarded the Reverend Archie Manley two hundred dollars because barber Robert Murrillo refused to cut Manley's hair on account that he had not been trained on "colored hair." Judge Dozier balked at the excuse, stating, "A licensed barber must learn to cut a Negro's hair."[53] In 1965, the Pennsylvania Human Relations Commission charged Richard Draper, Jr., with unlawful discriminatory practices in violation of the provisions of the Pennsylvania Human Relations Act for refusing to give Carl Brown of West Chester a haircut. Barber Louis Grimaldi testified during the commission hearings that barbers needed neither special training nor special tools to cut blacks' hair. The commission concluded that a barber with fifty years of experience, like Draper, should possess the training to cut all types of hair, and required the Draper Barber Shop to render services to all patrons regardless of race, color, creed, ancestry, or natural origin.[54]

In 1963, the commissioners of Washington, D.C., considered new regulations to revoke the license of any barber who pleaded lack of skill in cutting "kinky" hair as a reason to deny service to black customers.[55] Approximately two hundred people, mostly barbers, packed a room in the District Building on August 16 to participate in a public hearing before the District commissioners to discuss proposed regulations forbidding racial discrimination in barber shops and requiring barbers to cut "all types of human hair."[56] Walter B. Lewis, assistant executive director of the Washington Urban League, testified that barbers who serve nonwhites were able to cut all types of hair because blacks have a wide range of hair textures, suggesting the white barbers would be more well-rounded if they branched out beyond their homogenous white clientele. He proclaimed, "Any protest or inability to cut, or inconvenience in cutting hair, when nonwhites are involved is based not upon the technical requirements of the craft but upon prejudice and discrimination."[57]

Most perplexing to Lewis and other supporters of new regulations was that racial discrimination by barbers had long been prohibited under the District's public accommodations law but went unenforced. Charles J. Bovello, secretary-treasurer of Local 239 of the predominately white barbers union, refuted charges of discrimination. He testified that he told his members to serve black customers, but only after a warning that they lacked the necessary skill and that the customers should assume responsibility for the quality of the haircut, releasing the barber of any liability. Daniel L. O'Connor, attorney for Local 239 and Chapter 396 of the Associated Master Barbers, claimed it would take approximately six months for white barbers to learn how to cut blacks' hair.[58] As the District commissioners considered the testimonies, the White House requested they delay a decision to avoid "jeopardizing a few votes in Congress in the battle on civil rights legislation."[59]

The state stood squarely at the intersection of barber shop discrimination, where licensing regulations merged with civil rights legislation to address the professional labor issues of skill and training alongside the moral and political issues of racial exclusion. After the U.S. Supreme Court ruled the federal 1875 Civil Rights Act unconstitutional in 1883, northern states passed their own civil rights laws that prohibited discrimination in public places of accommodations; some of these states listed barber shops in the schedule of places subject to the law. Most southern states, however, failed to follow suit. As a practical matter, northern protesters had laws on the books to challenge discrimination in barber shops. In 1963, Governor Bert Combs of Kentucky issued an executive order prohibiting discrimination in public places of accommodation and "other places that are licensed or supervised [like] barber shops and beauty parlors." Those that failed to comply were subject to having their licenses revoked and businesses shut down.[60] Despite Governor Combs's bold move, southern congressmen stood in solidarity against President Kennedy's proposed civil rights bill. Although lunch counters and waiting rooms were the major battlegrounds of desegregation campaigns in the South, the idea of an integrated barber shop was not lost on one prominent southerner. Alabama governor George Wallace remarked after Kennedy's assassination that the civil rights bill "destroys private property rights all over the country and would put a federal policeman in every beauty shop and every barber shop in California as well as Alabama."[61] Despite southern congressmen's battle to prevent the passage of the 1964 Civil Rights Act, exemplified through their fifty-four days of filibuster, on July 2, Lyndon Johnson signed the act, which prohibited discrimination in public places of accommodation.[62] The act was a significant milestone for African Americans in dismantling Jim Crow, yet all public spaces were not treated equal. If the 1964 Civil Rights Act was supposed to be a legislative success in the struggle against Jim Crow, no one told white barbers, because they continued to exclude men they marked with kinky hair.

The act failed to adequately address the particular issues of exclusion in barber shops. Title II of the act addressed public accommodations, but like the 1875 act, it failed to include barber shops in its list of public places. Nonetheless, white barbers argued that they did not deny access based on race, which would have been prohibited under the Civil Rights Act. They instead said that they refused clients based on hair type or their lack of ability to cut certain types of hair. This labor and business discrimination would not have come under the act, still leaving a void for cities like Washington, D.C., that had been waiting, indeed told to wait, for the federal act to alleviate the daily humiliations of black people.

When the anticipated 1964 act failed to adequately address barber shop discrimination in Washington, D.C., the District commissioners passed a 1965 rule prohibiting discrimination by District barbers. Commissioner Walter N. Tobriner said, "We are sure that the barbering profession will cooperate with these new amendments and that the barbers of the District will provide their usual high level of service to all who have need of their skills, regardless of race or color."[63] Tobriner also noted that the 1872 Territorial Act rendered discrimination in barber shops illegal, but the only remedy was criminal prosecution, which was considered impractical in curbing discrimination and was rarely enforced. The new regulation provided for additional enforcement mechanisms through the District's licensing body. Commissioners made special provisions for barbers who claimed they lacked the skill to cut blacks' hair by requiring them to acquire the additional "training" to accommodate all hair types. The new regulation would not be effective until September 13, giving barbers ample time to go back to school. The Board of Education offered barbers an opportunity to register for a free barbering clinic for the additional training at Chamberlain Vocational High School on Potomac Avenue between 13th and 14th Streets S.E.[64] "Cut against the grain . . . that's it . . . straight back . . . and then down instead of up," instructed Benjamin Thornton, who led the clinic in the evenings between 6:30 and 9:30 p.m. "Cut in the part with the sharp edge of the clippers . . . you'll have to press down harder . . . then comb a little . . . that's it. . . . He just wants a shape-up . . . use the blade at the top of his forehead . . . then all the way around."[65] Black boys

between the ages of five and eighteen answered the call to give barbers heads
to practice on in exchange for free haircuts. On the first night, barbers came
from various sections of the city. But, according to Thornton, a large portion
of the fifty barbers who registered as of June 25 were black. Some of them
had been working in shops that served only whites, so they took advantage
of the opportunity to "brush up" on cutting "Negro hair." Other black barbers
signed up to learn more about cutting "white people's hair." On the first night,
at least, they stood idle without practice-customers.[66] These new standards
were reflected in the practical component of the examination for a barbering
license. All barbers were now required to bring in both a white and black subject to demonstrate their proficiency in cutting different hair types. Political
officials changed District laws, and industry officials changed licensing requirements to desegregate white barber shops. It is unclear how many white
barbers enrolled in the course to brush up on their skills to learn to cut curly
hair, or if "overnight they acquired the necessary skill and, presumably, the
esoteric instruments to enable them to barber the kinky head of the Negro."[67]

White barber shops were not the only sites of conflict. The past practices of
color-line barbers had not quite faded, resurrecting late nineteenth-century
debates within black communities about entrepreneurial motive and racial
justice. Color-line barber shops had become scarce by the mid-twentieth century, but some of these shops still existed as late as the 1960s, particularly in
the South. After Alonzo Herndon died in 1927 and left his shop to his employees, they continued to groom exclusively white men in the downtown
Atlanta shop. In fact, in late November 1965 fourteen black demonstrators
from the Southern Christian Leadership Conference staged a protest. They
sat in all of the barber chairs and demanded service, but were denied.[68] F. D.
Cooper, a black barber and owner, noted the 1964 Civil Rights Act excluded
barber shops not attached to hotels. After mounting pressure, he relented and
agreed to serve fellow African Americans if, according to *Jet* magazine, "not
too many of *them* flood the shop at one time" (emphasis in the original).[69]
A black barber shop in Birmingham, Alabama, during the 1960s welcomed
only white men. This seemed to simply be their business policy, because these
barbers would get their own haircuts in black-owned and patronized barber shops, such as Magic City, in the Fourth Avenue business district. These
urban shops escaped sustained protests at a time of intense civil rights organizing, but at least one rural, college-town shop was not so lucky.

Ralph W. Johnson of Davidson, North Carolina, the son of a light-skinned
barber who groomed only white patrons, continued not only in his father's

profession, but also in the ways of Jim Crow. Johnson described himself as "light in complexion, and my hair was straight, a fact which made me suspect at the outset among my youthful black peers."[70] Four years after the 1964 Civil Rights Act had passed, Johnson had not changed his policy of denying service to African Americans in his barber shop. He claimed he felt captive to a "social practice that had held me in its vicious tentacles and heaped injustices and deprivations upon my head for the whole of my life, and for all of the generations of my Negro forebears."[71] He had attended a segregated school and had other brushes with Jim Crow that he believed tied him to the black community despite his business policy. Johnson believed the Davidson community understood his precarious position in a small southern town, until white and black protesters demanded change.

The first week of April 1968 was a tumultuous one both for Johnson in his small, college-town barber shop and for the nation. On Tuesday afternoon, April 2, two black men with dark suits, white shirts, and neckties entered Johnson's barber shop, an occurrence that greatly puzzled him. "Since it was well settled that Negroes and white people were not served in the same barber shops," Johnson recalled, "it was unusual for Negroes to enter the shop unless they had a personal reason for seeing someone there."[72] Johnson recognized the two men, who usually dressed in work clothes. One was an employee of Davidson College, and the other was employed in "local industry." The two men walked the length of the shop, to where Johnson was sitting in the back, and asked him for a haircut. He replied that he could not cut their hair, yet he remained bewildered as to why these men were requesting service in his shop when they knew this went against local custom. After the rebuffed customers exited the shop, three white male Davidson College students entered, introduced themselves, and questioned Johnson on his policy of discrimination. He expressed two familiar explanations for refusing black patrons, dating back to the nineteenth century: the custom of segregation, and the potential loss of white patrons.[73]

Johnson's assessment of the situation rested on an outdated assumption: that local people accepted the order of things. Despite the palpable impact of the civil rights movement throughout the country, he reasoned that black people understood that he merely followed the customs of Jim Crow, a system that white people had prescribed. Since black residents had not protested his barber shop until this moment, Johnson could not fathom why they expressed their disagreement when they "knew" the customs and laws of North Carolina. As for the white students, Johnson thought it was absurd that they would question his policy since "separation of the Negro and white races was at the insistence of white people and enforced by laws of their making."[74] He assumed these students were southerners, which may or may not have been the case. In recalling these events in his memoir, Johnson repeatedly absolved himself of his decision to conform to Jim Crow customs in his shop. Johnson asserted his right and independence as a business owner to select his customer base, yet he also yielded to the preferences of his white patrons to keep that base white. While Johnson could not understand why these protesters questioned him on a policy that was well established, he additionally failed to grasp the fact that the tide had already turned across the nation, and that the civil rights movement had come to Davidson.

The protests against Johnson's barber shop commenced after he refused to give haircuts to the two black men. From the beginning, Davidson College students formed the core of the picketers. They distributed leaflets on campus urging students to boycott Johnson's shop to pressure him to change his policy because they had "no recourse in the courts" since "barber shops are not covered under the Civil Rights Act."[75] When two African students enrolled in the College prior to the passing of the Civil Rights Act, the administration secured an agreement from local businesses to make concessions to accommodate them. After the act passed, a small number of African Americans had enrolled in the college, and they too benefited from the special concession. Therefore, the five black students at Davidson College could go to Johnson or, as Johnson referred to it, "the only other barber shop in town"— owned by Hood Norton, a black barber and Johnson's estranged uncle, who also groomed only white patrons—to get a haircut, but the black residents of Davidson were turned away.[76] Hood's shop was not the only other shop in town; Davidson had a third shop "exclusively for Negroes." In fact, some black barbers who worked with Johnson and Hood during the day would work at the black shop in the evenings. As the students carried out their pickets in front of Johnson's shop, news spread to neighboring Charlotte and Winston-Salem, which brought an increasing number of people to the scene in opposition and support.

Johnson's memoir was silent on the regional and national civil rights and black power movement as he recalled the protests surrounding his barber shop April 2 through April 4, but he could not overlook the national response to the assassination of Martin Luther King, Jr., on April 4 because African Americans, even in small-town Davidson, expressed deep frustration and anger. Johnson believed he "was the focal point upon which my fellow

Negroes centered their hatred and hostility." That evening, someone hurled a rock at Johnson's shop window, an act that Johnson associated with the protests. The following day, an increasing number of African Americans joined the picket line. Even inside Johnson's shop, his barbers began to urge him to reconsider his racial exclusion policy, one to which they had no commitment. They were more connected with Davidson's black community than Johnson because they had been cutting black men's hair at night. They talked with some of the picketers when they went to work in the morning, and probably got an earful when they went to work in the black shop at night.[77] One barber claimed he had been threatened by a group of blacks because he continued to work in the shop.[78] On Saturday, April 6, Johnson's regular customers, particularly those from neighboring areas, had to wade through this sea of protest to get inside the shop. Although many of them scorned the protesters, they told Johnson they would still patronize the shop if it was integrated, but Johnson did not put much stock in their commitments.

King's death failed to provide Johnson any perspective on desegregation and the larger aims of the black and white protesters. "Forgotten was the fact that I, too, was a Negro," Johnson reasoned, "and had been for all my life subjected to the same restraints that were imposed on other Negroes."[79] He firmly believed that the white students at Davidson College "had done this to me because I was a Negro, and that in so doing they were continuing the old practice of putting a nigger in his place."[80] However, Johnson had forgotten that King put his life on the line to rid the country of racial injustice. Most striking about Johnson's case is neither that a black barber excluded black customers in the late 1960s, nor that black protesters demonstrated against a member of their race, but that Johnson failed to understand his historical moment. The civil rights movement had swept through the North and South, freedom fighters had been assassinated, major civil rights legislations had passed, and yet Johnson clung to Jim Crow because in a very fundamental way Jim Crow made him who he was, for better and worse. Not even King's death proved powerful enough to move Johnson beyond the color line.

Johnson refused to yield to the demands of the protesters because of his stubborn sensibilities and economic concerns. He accepted the power of his patrons to demand a shop that served only whites, but dismissed white and black protesters' calls to integrate. Ultimately, Johnson feared he would lose his white customers if he desegregated the shop. In the end, however, he decided to yield because of the pressure his own barbers put on him to change his policy. The mounting pressure they received from the black community had taken its toll on them. Johnson acknowledged that his business would go under without his barbers. In 1968, it was difficult to find black barbers who were willing to work in a shop that exclusively groomed white men. On May 7, Johnson instructed one of his barbers to cut the hair of another employee, symbolizing a new day in Johnson's barber shop. One barber noted, "It's something that had to be done, and I'm glad he did it. It takes a lot of pressure off us, the employees, and I think we will profit by it."[81] Johnson did not indicate the percentage of his white customers that continued to patronize the shop, but he had much to say about the "new element." He disapproved of the behavior of his new black clients, citing intoxication as a source of rowdiness. It could certainly be that these customers were not intoxicated at all, but that Johnson was not accustomed to the loud, "unruly" conversations and banter among black men who gathered in barber shops. In any case, Johnson disapproved so strongly that he consulted his barbers about reversing his policy and prohibiting black customers again. When his barbers rejected the idea, Johnson, probably still bitter and resentful, decided to close his shop rather than continue to groom a black working-class clientele. After forty-seven years of grooming white men and only three years of grooming black men, Johnson closed his shop on November 15, 1971.[82] Johnson's barber shop illuminates the strange career of desegregation where the practice of segregation lived beyond major civil rights legislations and was implemented by some blacks who felt caught in Jim Crow's web. It reveals the significance of an enduring system of discrimination that limited the life decisions of black communities by law and custom. Despite Johnson's history, it was mostly white barbers who pulled the levers of discrimination, and they employed age-old ways of seeing race to do it.

Domestic and international travel illuminated issues that black men and women took for granted: getting a haircut from someone other than their trusted barber or beautician could bring out racial bias based on hair type. Most black men had not considered frequenting a white barber shop until they found themselves a great distance from a black shop. In the case of African immigrants and visitors, they did not share the same affinities for black barber shops that African Americans harbored, which left Africans deeply insulted and the State Department considerably embarrassed. The struggles to desegregate white barber shops exposed what was difficult to see in other efforts to desegregate public places of accommodation, education, and transportation: the civil rights and black power movements were not attempts to close the social distance between blacks and whites; they were movements to dismantle white supremacy and ensure that black people had choices and control over their daily lives.[83] A majority of black men preferred to frequent black barbers, but this affinity for a black public space did not give white barbers the green light to exclude customers of color based on social and biological constructions of race. Non-essentialist notions of race and the conveniences of travel informed these calls for desegregation. Black college students entered white barber shops for haircuts just as they entered lunch counters for hamburgers, and bus depots to sit in any section of the waiting area. In 1961, Ella Baker wrote an article titled "Bigger Than a Hamburger," where she argued that the movement to desegregate lunch counters had nothing to do with consumers' desires to eat hamburgers at the Woolworth's next to white consumers, because the hamburgers were not that good anyway.[84] Instead, these college students struggled for the right to equal treatment and justice in public places of accommodation. Baker's reflections on the sit-in movement resonated with the goals of the larger black freedom movement. The movement to desegregate white barber shops, to appropriate Baker's words, was bigger than a haircut, offering a complex episode in the struggle for equal rights and access.

CHAPTER 6

The Culture and Economy of Modern Black Barber Shops

S TOKELY Carmichael, activist and chairman of the Student Nonviolent Coordinating Committee, believed that his "nappy African hair" saved him from the "cocoon of willed 'innocence' in which white America famously entombed its youth during the fifties." When Carmichael and his family moved to Amethyst Street in the Morris Park/ White Plains Road area of the Bronx, New York, in 1953, he recalled being the only black family in this predominately Italian and Irish neighborhood. His school and church were conveniently close by, even though he was one of only two black children there. When his Trinidadian father took him around to the neighborhood barber shops, the Italian and Irish barbers claimed they could not cut his hair. Until he left for college at Howard University, he would "have to go into Harlem every two or three weeks to have [his] hair cut."[1]

Carmichael immediately noticed the differences between the Italian and Irish shops in the Bronx and those in Harlem. "For one thing, everyone and everything, even to the pictures on the walls, was black, or at least not white," he fondly remembered. He went to a popular shop on 145th Street between Seventh and Eighth Avenues. "So, I often had to wait my turn in the chair. This became the one time in my life that I actually enjoyed sitting around waiting for anything."[2] While he waited, he heard the cacophony of voices with Caribbean accents and the "bluesy folks" rhythmic speech of black men from the South. According to Carmichael, those who moved in and out of the shop included "old Garveyites, race men, street players, black Republicans *and* Black Muslims, nationalists of all descriptions, and the rappers, poets, and wordmen who seemed to talk simply for the joy of hearing their own voices." It was in this Harlem barber shop, not school or church, where he learned of the *Brown* decision and the Emmett Till lynching. In short, this black barber shop "was a necessary corrective, an early window into an African-American worldview and sensibility."[3] While those white barbers in the Bronx were not clamoring to cut Carmichael's hair, it was just as well, because the black barber shop gave him something a white shop could not offer: a space in which to experience black culture and collective history, not to mention a decent haircut.

If the scattered campaigns to desegregate white barber shops were bigger than a haircut, so were the everyday decisions of black men to file into black barber shops. Whites had tried to frame blacks' exclusion, or the necessity for segregation, in terms of social space. The 1896 *Plessy v. Ferguson* decision sanctioned de jure segregation, separating black and white train passengers, lunch counter patrons, and school children. Responding to this social and physical distance definition of segregation, many civil rights activists and everyday residents believed that integration, or a closing of this distance, would mark the measurement of racial progress. But what would happen to the progress internal to black communities? The integration of Major League Baseball in 1947 marked the decline of the Negro Leagues. The *Brown v. Board of Education* decision in 1954 left black teachers wondering if they would be out of jobs. De jure desegregation did not equal de facto integration because black barber shops functioned as part of the black commercial public sphere where the integration of white shops had no bearing on the patronage of black shops. They stood as symbols of a racial economy immune to many of the larger geographical and ideological shifts that integration encouraged. As a private space in the public sphere, black barber shops provided more than haircuts. For those who believed integration was the ultimate goal, places such as black churches, beauty parlors, and barber shops illuminated the ambiguities of integration and black public spaces.

Black barber shops were unaffected by the larger desegregation movement because the intimate nature of the space willingly brought black men to the shops to see their particular barber or socialize with familiar faces. They were not there because of, or even in spite of, Jim Crow. Individual choice determined the difference between separation and segregation.[4] Black men chose to congregate in barber shops with other black men. They went to black barbers to get their haircut in the covatis style or to get their Afro trimmed. While there, they likely discussed local, national, and international issues of the day: boxer Sonny Liston's bouts, nightlife, Martin Luther King's campaign in

Birmingham, or Shirley Chisholm's campaign for U.S. president. It would have been a strange and paradoxical sight to see a line of black men waiting to have their Afros trimmed by a white barber, while engaging each other about black life and politics. Since most African Americans did not consider haircuts commodities, the racial value of the barber shop as a public space extended beyond its grooming service to include community formation and engagement.

These shops may have been about more than haircuts where men regularly congregated, but barbers did not want people to *forget* about the haircuts either. Black men saw economic security in both barbering as a profession and the shop as a space. Whether they cut hair full-time or only on weekends, in the barber shop or on their front porch, they thought men would always need and want haircuts. It was much easier for a man to shave himself with a safety razor than it was for him to cut his own hair. While some men entered barbering solely as a trade to rely on in difficult times, other men took their profession quite seriously. In the process of shaving and cutting men's hair, barbers believed they were making them look presentable to a larger public. In essence, black barbers argued they were grooming a race of men to face the challenges of Jim Crow America. Barbers' ideas of economic security also rested in the shop as a public space. To keep men coming back to the shop, barbers had only to provide satisfactory haircuts and a welcoming space. Men developed relationships with their barber first and the larger waiting public of the shop second. Changing hairstyles in the post–World War II period proved that haircuts would in fact not always be in demand and customers had their own ideas of racial grooming. Throughout the postwar period, barbers continuously had to negotiate the ways changing hairstyles could threaten their business with the black community's social and political investment in particular hairstyles that required little cutting.

Black barber shops in the postwar period served as critical commercial public spheres for African Americans across the country. As entrepreneurs, shop owners took advantage of their independence to actively support civil rights campaigns and open their shops to movement business. It was not uncommon for owners, especially those who were self-described activists, to use their shops to conduct meetings or distribute literature on protest campaigns. Barbers acted as conduits in facilitating democratic engagement, but at times their receipts took priority over giving black men a place to hang out and talk politics. Barbers contended with the politics and economy of the barber shop as African Americans' hairstyles and the racial politics of hair changed between the 1940s and 1970s. The discourse around desegregation and integration revealed what many barbers well understood: it was actually good for business that men were comfortable talking, arguing, and debating about various issues in the shop. The hopes and challenges of barber shops as a place where men could become entrepreneurs, get the latest hairstyle in black communities, or discuss politics demonstrates how African Americans could support integration and prefer separation or willing congregation. This paradox reveals a narrative about the everyday politics of black cultural economies.

The Postwar Generation of Black Barbers

Beginning in the 1930s and continuing through World War II and the early civil rights movement, a new generation of black men entered barbering. Barbering was a shining light amid dismal economic opportunities. Many of them had been drafted into the military to protect democracy abroad when their own rights at home needed protection. They returned looking for social change, but most immediately and materially they needed jobs. By now, most states had licensing laws, which, among other things, required that aspiring barbers spend a minimum number of hours in a barber college. While white barber colleges were slow to admit African Americans, many black barber colleges emerged between 1930 and 1950. Although there were more barriers to entry for this new generation, owning a barber shop was still a viable path to entrepreneurship and economic independence. In fact, barber shops were among the most common black businesses in cities in the mid-1940s. Between 1944 and 1946, Joseph Pierce, professor of mathematics at Atlanta University, served as research director for the Project for Business Among Negroes to study the state of African American business and business education. Although Pierce's sample was limited mostly to southern cities, it provides a useful glimpse into the operation of barber shops and other businesses. Pierce reported that barber shop owners averaged 8.1 years of general education, with a median age of 46.8 years, compared with 50 years, 41 years, and 36 years for undertakers, cleaning shop owners, and beauticians, respectively. The median annual numbers of barber shops, beauty shops, cleaning shops, and undertakers were 2,350; 2,025; 2,775; and 8,250, respectively.[5] World War II veterans would change these numbers considerably. The postwar generation would get through high school, and certainly barber college. In many instances, their entrepreneurial ambitions began before they held apprenticeships or entered barber college when they cut hair on the porch or shined shoes in a barber shop.

Black World War II veterans returned from the war poised to take advantage of the Selective Service Readjustment Act, also known as the G.I. Bill of Rights, enacted to help reintegrate veterans into civilian life. With the assistance of the federal government and the G.I. Bill, millions of veterans born in the 1920s purchased homes, enrolled in college, and established businesses. African Americans benefited from the G.I. Bill on a significantly lesser scale and unequal basis compared with their white counterparts. De facto quotas limited access for a majority of African Americans qualified for higher education. During the late 1940s, the number of African Americans enrolled in higher education in the North and West did not exceed five thousand. Ninety-five percent of black veterans who used their higher education benefits attended historically black colleges. Yet precollegiate vocational education and on-the-job training formed a major part of the G.I. Bill's educational component.[6] Although most black veterans were eager to get training in such fields as electrical work, machinery, and carpentry, some veterans used their G.I. Bill education vouchers to attend barber college. Black veterans with G.I. vouchers formed the majority of students at the white-owned Lincoln Barber School, located on Broad and Master Streets in north Philadelphia.[7] As of 1944, Henry Morgan had two government contracts for Tyler Barber College. The Vocational Rehabilitation Department contracted Morgan to train thirty-five to sixty students, and the Veterans Administration (VA) contracted him to train veterans.[8]

Veterans did not necessarily prefer barbering, but they could not overlook the security it offered. When Ernest Myers returned from the war, a career in barbering seemed all but destined. His father and two uncles owned a shop in Washington, D.C. that Myers used to clean up. Yet he rejected the family business because he was not keen on standing up all day. Instead, he had his mind set on becoming a dentist. Even though dentists too had their stretches of standing, a dentist certainly carried more prestige than a barber. When the person who was going to pay his way through dental school died, Myers opted for a more affordable school: barber college. Under the G.I. Bill he was able to attend Armstrong High School, a black school that housed the central barber college for African Americans in the city. He worked as a waiter at Walter Reed Hospital during the day and went to barbering school at night. After completing the program and receiving his master barber license, he joined the Eagle Barber Shop at 2800 Georgia Avenue.[9] Like Myers, Earl Middleton of Orangeburg, South Carolina, could not dismiss the security in barbering. He had cut hair for extra money on Saturdays as a teenager. Two of his uncles had barbered at the famed Herndon's Barber Shop before they retired. After Pearl Harbor, Middleton volunteered for the U.S. Army Air Corps. During the three years he spent at the Maxwell Field near Montgomery, Alabama, he cut other soldiers' hair in the evenings and on weekends. "When I returned home to Orangeburg in 1946," Middleton recalled, "barbering was my easiest route to earning a living. I knew I didn't want to teach, and I didn't want to preach."[10] While he continued to look for other opportunities, he opened a barber shop.[11] Middleton's barbering skills traveled with him throughout his life, providing the security that was so elusive for many black men in the postwar period.

The veterans in barber shops were not just those men standing behind the barber chair; they also included customers and men who just wanted to hang out and talk. Because of scarce jobs and exclusion from returning-soldier transition programs, they had time to congregate in barber shops, bars, and other public spaces.[12] The time they spent in the barber shop was often spent discussing questions of race, inequality, and resistance. The owner played a central role in how, or if, his shop was used as a "movement halfway house."[13] Since many shop owners were themselves veterans, they understood the need for a space to not only gather and talk, but also organize and resist. In postwar Monroe County, North Carolina, Robert Williams and other black veterans collectively negotiated their return to civilian life in the Jim Crow South. Most of these veterans worked during the day and attended VA-sponsored classes at night. Williams and his classmates often "congregated in the local barbershop," where they developed "a tightly knit camaraderie." At the shop of Booker T. Perry, a World War I veteran, they talked about the contempt they faced from white administrators when attempting to collect their federal benefits.[14]

In June 1946, Perry and his customers were probably not talking about benefits, but rather the fate of Benny Montgomery's life. On Saturday afternoon, June 1, Montgomery, a World War II veteran and sharecropper, asked his white landowner for his wages to get his father's car repaired. The landowner was so angry at this request that he proceeded to kick and slap Montgomery. Furious, Montgomery cut the landowner's throat with a pocketknife. The Ku Klux Klan wanted to lynch him before a trial could take place, but authorities escorted him out of Monroe to prevent this from happening. He was tried, convicted, and sentenced to death. On March 28, 1947, Montgomery died in the gas chamber. When the state shipped his remains back to Monroe for the burial, the Klan pronounced their determination to reclaim the body stolen from *them* one year ago. Black World War II veterans met at Perry's barber shop to organize a strategy to protect Montgomery's body. According to historian Tim Tyson, "When the Klan motorcade pulled up in front of Harris Funeral Home, forty black men leveled their rifles, taking aim at the line of cars." The Klan drove off without firing a shot.[15] This shop, then, was a fitting space to organize that direct resistance. Perry's role as shop owner should not be minimized. He could have suggested that the men meet elsewhere to divert attention away from his shop. But these men were not strangers—they had developed relationships with each other inside the shop, so they met where they always met. This time, talk turned into action.

James Armstrong could relate to Perry and Robert Williams. Armstrong returned to Birmingham, Alabama, from military service in World War II embittered by the lack of freedom at home he had been fighting for abroad, and like other barber shop owners, he had the economic freedom to fight for his social and political freedom. En route to barber school every night, he had to endure long waits for the bus, which often passed him by or drove off after he paid his fare and attempted to reenter at the back. By the 1950s, Armstrong owned a barber shop on the west side of town. He prospered but grew tired of the racial injustice in the city. After hearing Fred Shuttlesworth, minister and co-founder of the Alabama Christian Movement for Human Rights, advocate for resistance and freedom at a mass meeting on June 5, 1956, at Sardis Baptist Church, Armstrong was moved to action. Shortly thereafter, he joined "the ushers," the nonviolent (though armed) security force charged with protecting movement leaders. In this very public and defiant role, Armstrong worried about threats to his family and property, but as an entrepreneur, he did not worry about economic reprisals.[16]

Black barbers in small southern towns were particularly conscious of their economic independence from rural whites. For one, they witnessed the way landowners routinely reprimanded or simply fired sharecroppers for attempting to register to vote or signing a petition. Barbers acknowledged their economic autonomy as a central factor in openly supporting the NAACP and organizing protest campaigns.[17] In 1941, the NAACP became a small force in Orangeburg, South Carolina. "Of course," barber John Brunson recalled, "many of us did not publicly join up with the NAACP until later years because everybody in the system was basically of the mind that it was something that would get you in trouble. I became affiliated with the NAACP in 1952. There were very few people in it at that time. And as the years went by, more persons started affiliating with the NAACP. They were persons who

were like myself who were not beholden to employment by the white establishment. Like, for instance, school teachers and other people who worked for
white folks, they would not come anywhere near it. And in retrospect, you
couldn't blame them, because they had to have some means of employment."[18]
Despite these economic concerns, more people risked their jobs and livelihoods, not to mention their lives, fighting for justice. These everyday economic considerations of protest were not the sexy stuff of social movements,
but understanding how African Americans thought about jobs and freedom
sheds light on how activists made decisions about protest.

The autonomous spaces of barber shops were important assets in activist barbers' political work, but the shops or the barbers' property or family
were subject to white retaliation. Brunson's status as an entrepreneur partially shielded him from economic reprisals, but the White Citizen's Council
sought retribution against him by going after his wife. In 1955, after the *Brown
v. Board of Education* decision, African American residents petitioned the
Orangeburg school board for integration of the public schools. Brunson
remembered:

> I was the person who led the petition movement to get several
> people signed up. The white citizen's council attempted to impose
> economic sanctions on those who signed the petition to get them
> to take their names off. Well, my wife was teaching school during
> that time. And for two different years, they held up her contract
> because of my activities. Everybody else got their contract but her.
> But then, near the time for school to be out, she was issued a con-
> tract. This was on two occasions. So they were not successful in get-
> ting her because I was not beholden to them because I was working
> in the barbershop right there and not connected with the white
> establishment.[19]

The Citizen's Council obtained copies of the petition and found out each person's connection to a white employer, whether they were teachers or industrial workers. White employers would either demand their black employees
to take their names off the petition or simply fire them. For fear of losing their
jobs, many people who signed the petition took their names off. Although it
is not apparent how Brunson's wife finally received her contract, and he may
have overstated his position in the council's failure to fire her, she appears to
have been the scapegoat for his organizing work.

Throughout the black freedom movement, meeting spaces were critical for debating, planning, and organizing. As owners and facilitators of black institutions, ministers, barbers, beauticians, and fraternal orders opened their doors. In William Hughes's Crystal Barber Shop in Durham, North Carolina, customers could not stop talking about the student sit-ins, which four college students sparked sixty miles west in Greensboro.[20] In Greenwood, Mississippi, barbers Reverend Louie Redd and Charles Golden were among the organizers of the Greenwood chapter of the National Association for the Advancement of Colored People. They were among a number of other black businessmen or otherwise independent black workers who assisted Greenwood activists— they gave organizers free haircuts.[21] In August 1962, Redd gave the Student Nonviolent Coordinating Committee desk space in his barber shop because their previous office had been burglarized in order to deter them from continuing their voter registration movement.[22] As a business owner, Redd had the autonomy to take in SNCC members, and his involvement in movement politics compelled him to do so. But meeting in the barber shops was not always the best move. When SNCC members Stokely Carmichael and Marion Barry were enrolled at Howard University in the early 1960s, "they'd always meet each other in [the Eagle Barber Shop on Georgia Avenue], then go down to" Carmichael's house. Ernest Myers, the shop owner, recalled they were worried about "people telling what they were getting ready to do! They come in there and sit down and get a haircut . . . but when all of 'em got there they [would leave]."[23] Myers recalled that many Howard students, professors, and administrators (including the presidents, from Mordecai Johnson to Franklyn Jenifer) frequented Eagle between 9 A.M. and 2 P.M., while people from the surrounding neighborhood came by after 3 P.M., which was likely after work hours. The student activists looked to more grassroots spaces to organize, compared with traditional spaces such as the church, to exercise caution and control.

The barber shop was no Howard or Fisk University, but class was in session in several shops across the country. In fact, Brunson, like Carter G. Woodson in the 1930s, considered it a source of education. Brunson asserted that school was in session when men gathered inside the barber shop. "I'll say this too about being in the barbershop is that you can learn more in a barbershop than you can in all the schools they've got in this country. You interact with the high and the mighty. You're in contact with people with all kinds of information and they impart information. People would just talk naturally to talk. They'd talk to a barber just like they'd talk to a priest or something. They have problems or if there are not problems, they just talk. And you learn. If you have a mind to learn, you can learn a whole lot. And this . . . I got educated in the barbershop."[24] While Brunson did not indicate what kind of education he received in the shop, he suggests it was more egalitarian than the formal training of school.

The kind of education Brunson received could easily be very political in nature. In Paul Robeson's regular column, "Here's My Story," in *Freedom* in the early 1950s, he would casually mention conversations he was actively engaged in or overheard in his barber shop about electoral politics or the expansion of U.S. capital investment abroad.[25] That he mentioned these conversations without note suggests they were common. Owning a barber shop provided activists a steady stream of men to discuss local politics and recruit for organizing campaigns. In 1954, Curtis C. Bryant became branch president of the NAACP in Pike County, Mississippi, and was a key figure in local grassroots politics. Bryant worked for the railroad most of his life while actively participating in the union. He also owned a barber shop on his property next to his home. As historian Charles Payne put it, Bryant ran a "barber shop *cum* library in his front yard," where customers could read "radical" literature such as black newspapers and magazines, NAACP material, and political broadsides.[26] Joe Martin, of McComb, Mississippi, remembered Bryant's barber shop as the place where he got his political education:

> My first involvement was with the NAACP Youth Council. . . . The local president [of the NAACP], Mr. C. C. Bryant, was a barber and I got my hair cut down there. And he would have all kind of materials about different projects going on in the civil rights movement. While waiting for my hair to be cut, I would read the books. So as the place went on there, I got informed about what was going on in the country, as well as in the world, about the black struggle. I was very impressed as a young man with Medgar Evers. So, I got involved with the NAACP Youth Council at a very early age, around the ninth or tenth grade, but I was familiar with him in the eighth grade. They had some books about him, and then I was able to get some information, still through the barbershop, about Patrice Lumumba and South Africa and things like that. So I was informed about the struggle long before it got here, through books and local people.[27]

Martin linked Bryant's activism with the radical literature in his barber shop. Bryant did not divorce his work with the NAACP—his politics—from his work at the shop—his business. Martin did not patronize Bryant's shop to learn about the movement, but since Bryant made the information available for his customers, Martin got a political education when he intended only to get a haircut. Few people would have expected anything less in this shop. In fact, the shop was bombed because of Bryant's involvement with the NAACP and voter registration campaigns. This did not deter him from inviting Bob Moses, a member of the SNCC, to begin voter registration drives in southwest Mississippi, an invitation Moses accepted.[28] At the barber shop, political discourse could draw people, like Martin, into political action.

The political leanings of the shop owner often had a direct relationship to the level of political *activity*—outside of political *conversations*—that took place inside the barber shop. Discussing political candidates is a form of democratic engagement. Julia Lucas remembered discussions of voting regularly taking place in her Durham barber shop.[29] Some barbers, like William Lomax of Richmond, were more aggressive in transforming conversations on voting to voter registration. Lomax was actively involved in the NAACP and the Crusade for Voters in Richmond. He regularly talked about both organizations and encouraged everyone in his shop to join. In fact, he kept membership cards on hand to sign people up on the spot. Lomax went further than this. The Crusade for Voters reproduced the poll tax lists, which were public knowledge, and distributed them to the local barber and beauty shops. William Ferguson Reed, one of the founders of the Crusade for Voters, recalled, "We had signs made [that said] don't talk politics in here if you don't vote. And under that we had the poll tax list so that the barbers would be encouraged to vote and register themselves so that when anybody got in a political discussion the first thing they would do is go to the book to see whether you are qualified to make a statement or not."[30] Lomax remembered this requirement just as Reed had outlined. "Anybody that came in and started talking politics, we'd get their full name and put 'em in the book. If they were registered they could continue talking politics; if they were not registered, we told 'em, said, 'Look, you can't talk politics in here because you're not a registered voter.'" He claimed that some men would march right down to City Hall to pay their $2.50 to register.[31] The same sign hung in the window of James Armstrong's barber shop in Birmingham, Alabama: "If You Don't Vote, Don't Talk Politics in Here." It is unclear if Armstrong had any connection with Richmond barbers or beauticians or the Crusade for Voters, but the barbers in both cities wanted to connect black men's engagement in political discourse inside the barber shops with a charge for them to be more politically active when they left. Armstrong's and Lomax's barber shops, like many other black shops, provided an economic base for barbers to be politically active and provided their customers with a private space in the public sphere to engage in politics.

The politics of barber shops, however, were far more complicated than barbers being independent of whites or shops offering a democratic space for political conversations. For one, barbers were not completely independent of whites, particularly those in states with a licensing law. Barber licensing boards controlled the distribution and renewal of licenses. Citizens had the power to report a shop owner for unsanitary conditions, illegal activities, or any other infraction that would result in an investigation of the shop. In Virginia's case, there was no state law, but Richmond had a municipal law. Many state laws were more lenient toward rural shops, which may not even have been subject to these laws at all. However, there is no evidence suggesting that a state barber board was called in under the guise of investigating the conditions of a shop due to an owner's involvement in civil rights work. Yet, beyond white people or the state, a closer look at black customers reveals a more complicated story about barber shops and political discourse. To be sure, the level of the shop owner's political activity had an impact on the level of organizing that took place in his shop. Many black barbers were reminded, or had to remind their customers, that their barber shop was not just a public space, it was a business. Black barbers had to balance the social and political uses of their shops as public spaces with their own economic objectives of making a profit and staying in business.

Leander Blount of Brooklyn, New York, understood the politics and profits of the barber shop all too well. In the early 1950s, he grew more cautious about discussing racial politics with his customers because he was concerned that potential conflicts would drive them from the shop. Mr. Blount owned a barber shop on Reid Avenue, now called Malcolm X Boulevard, in the Bedford-Stuyvesant neighborhood. When asked to comment on "political" issues discussed in his shop, Blount expressed an expansive definition of politics, which included everyday racial politics, and underscored the fine line between politics and profits. Even sports had a political bent. "I was cutting a customer's hair one day," he recalled, sitting in his chair looking out of the shop window, "and I was going on and on about how I like the [New York] Yankees. He just listened. He didn't say anything. And you know, after that he never came back to my shop." Mr. Blount clarified his suspicion: "There were no blacks on the Yankees. So, after that I just don't talk politics. I stay right in the middle of the road."[32]

Blount's fondness of the Yankees ran counter to most black New Yorkers in the early 1950s. The most successful and profitable franchise in professional sports, the Yankees were riding high, with five consecutive world championships between 1949 and 1953. With little economic incentive to integrate, the club signed an occasional black player to its farm system. Yet, the Brooklyn Dodgers and the New York Giants had integrated their teams in 1947 and 1949, respectively. Black baseball fans took the Yankees to task for their slow pace to integrate at the major league level. In 1952, the Bronx County American Labor Party led a picketing campaign at Yankee Stadium to protest the team's unwillingness to sign black players. Most African Americans viewed the Yankees as a racist organization. When questioned on the NBC program *Youth Wants to Know*, Jackie Robinson affirmed that he believed the Yankees executives were prejudiced and said that "there are thousands upon thousands of people in Harlem who feel the same way." Not until 1955 did the Yankees promote former Kansas City Monarch Elston Howard as the first black ballplayer to join their major league roster.[33] In the early 1950s, however, to be black and root for the Yankees was tantamount to being black and voting for Strom Thurmond over Harry Truman in the 1948 presidential election.

Blount's response reveals his broad understanding of politics and his concerns for negotiating his business and political interests. Barbering instructional manuals encouraged a student to connect with his customer; however, they typically discouraged him from talking about religion and politics for fear of losing business. Although Blount was not talking about "politics," he discovered that the boundaries of political discourse were blurred. If to engage in controversial topics meant potentially losing customers, Blount decided his business must come first.

At the core, the business of barbering in the postwar period was about cutting hair, yet the two most memorable and politically charged hairstyles of this era did not actually involve much haircutting. Changing hairstyles among black men shaped the political economy of black barber shops. The "conk," "process," "Afro," and "natural" brought matters of politics and business into direct connection and often in conflict. Barbers held various opinions of these hairstyles, but they remained committed to giving men what they wanted. Some barbers, however, considered themselves not only groomers of men, but also architects of black male appearance. They were doing more than making men look good; they were making *black men* look good, acceptable, and employable. Black barbers' perceptions of race and class shaped their views, if not their service offerings, on politically inflected hair-styles. The men who entered barbering in the mid-1950s and early 1960s were more concerned about job security than grooming black male respectability.

Barbering was an accessible trade in the formal or informal economy. Henry Jones learned to cut hair in the early 1940s from his uncle, who served as the neighborhood barber for black children and "older folks" in rural South Carolina. Like many African Americans who wanted to bypass the formali-ties of a shop, his uncle cut hair out of his house. As his uncle got older, he began to send more customers to Jones, but Jones saw no future in barbering. With no other employment prospects, in 1949 he migrated to the Bedford-Stuyvesant community in Brooklyn, New York, to live with his aunt. He fol-lowed thousands of other black southerners who moved north during the second Great Migration.[34] He worked in a factory making shoes but cut hair on the side to make ends meet. He quickly realized that his income from cut-ting hair in a shop on Fridays far outpaced his industrial wages. "Once you get into business [for] yourself," he thought, "you work harder for yourself, make more [money]."[35] He eventually opened his own shop in Bedford-Stuyvesant in 1964. Robert Dexter shared Jones's aspiration for economic security, and he, like millions of other African Americans in the twentieth century, was willing to move in search of it. After finishing high school in West Virginia in 1960, Dexter spent four years shining shoes in barber shops, but he wanted so much more for himself. Mining had declined in the mid-1950s, leaving him few op-tions. He had hoped to find better opportunities in Cleveland. When he ar-rived, however, he found jobs "hard to come by" and hard to keep. In January 1962, he opted for the job security offered by the U.S. military. Dexter stayed in the military for only two years before being discharged. Upon his discharge, he worked a number of odd jobs to save his money for barber college. Dexter attended Erma Lee's Barber and Beauty College on 55th and Central, the only black barber college in Cleveland. This was also the only barber college in the city that offered night school to accommodate working students.[36]

Many African Americans struggled with the decision to pursue a "practi-cal" (that is, industrial or vocational) or a liberal arts education long after Anna Julia Cooper, Booker T. Washington, and W. E. B. Du Bois debated these prospects between 1890 and 1915.[37] Some African Americans who entered four-year colleges and universities in the 1960s did not hesitate to leave higher education for vocational learning. James Spruill left Bowie State Teachers College after two years to attend barber school because "one of the students was cutting hair on campus, and he was also cutting at the race track ... [and] he was making money." Spruill enrolled in Harris Barber College in Raleigh, North Carolina. He graduated in 1964, got his license, and took a job in Washington, D.C., in a shop with a former Harris classmate.[38] Lloyd Howerton spent one year at Virginia State College in Petersburg, but when he got married he immediately dropped out to enter barbering school, which offered better opportunities. Barbering seemed to him a ticket to success, because growing up in Clarksville, Virginia, he "noticed the black barber there" who "had a nice home, family well-kept and everything, always has new cars ... he was doing fine." Howerton enrolled in the Turpin School of Technology in Richmond in 1964 for a six-month course to receive a barbering license.[39] While this was a black trade school, its barber shop's clients were white, so he trained on straight hair. His first job, however, was at a shop with a black clientele. He quickly learned that a comb and scissors were insufficient with curly hair. Howerton remembered Turpin as being the only black barbering school in Richmond, but other barbers in the area said they had trained at Maggie Lena Walker High School, which had a college preparatory, general, and vocational course in barbering.[40]

Eugene Fleming was one of those Walker graduates, and his journey from high school, to college, and then into the barber shop was quite similar to Howerton's. When Fleming finished high school, he too went to Virginia State. During that year, he and his girlfriend were expecting a child together, so they got married, which motivated Fleming to leave college to work. He began shining shoes at the Reynolds Metal Company, and then he got a job dumping trash. He spent and saved his money. One of his major purchases was a new 1961 Chevrolet, which made his boss mad because he only had a 1959 Chevy. Fleming believes this was the central reason his boss tried to fire him on several occasions. Fleming had a habit of leaving work early to watch Muhammad Ali fight. His boss would routinely greet him with extra work the next day. He knew his boss had it out for him, so he was not surprised when he was fired in May 1963. But, two months earlier, Fleming had purchased a barber shop on Lombardi Street for approximately three hundred and fifty dollars. Strikingly, he knew nothing about barbering before he purchased the shop. He hated working for white people and wanted to open a business, any business, for himself. His uncle encouraged him to open a barber shop because of the low startup costs. He reminded Fleming that in addition to learning the trade, he needed to be committed to the business and his customers.[41] While this may have been sage advice, Fleming entered the profession at a time when new hairstyles made these two interests difficult to reconcile.

From the 1920s to the 1960s, many urban black men commonly processed their hair—resulting in a style known professionally (in the entertainment and the grooming industries) as the "process" and on street corners as the "conk." Regardless of the name they were essentially the same hairstyle, but the process was styled in the barber shop and the conk at home. The style comprised straightened hair "that was often combed into a swirl of waves atop the forehead."[42] Like the zoot suit, the conk came to represent the urban and rebellious. When Malcolm X visited the black section of Roxbury in Boston, he was entranced by the "sharp-dressed young 'cats' who hung on the corners and the poolrooms, bars and restaurants, and who obviously didn't work anywhere. . . . I couldn't get over marveling at how their hair was straight and shiny like white men's hair; Ella told me this was called a conk."[43] The style was a hallmark of black entertainment that in the 1940s and 1950s was associated with superstars like Nat King Cole, Duke Ellington, and Sugar Ray Robinson. Many up-and-coming black entertainers and youth processed their hair to achieve a level of coolness. Otis Williams, a co-founder of the vocal group The Temptations in early 1960, remembered his teenage years in the 1950s as a moment of honing his craft as a musician, which included his public presentation. "As I got more serious about my singing group, I became more interested in perfecting my image. I had to be cool and back in the mid-fifties that required a process."[44] Black musicians leveraged black cultural aesthetics as capital to build their own financial capital by connecting to their fan base. Black barbers helped groom this image of cool that entertainers needed. "That was big time if you did an entertainer's hair," barber Paige West, Jr. of Philadelphia remembered fondly. "I know one guy who worked in north Philly who did [Nat] King Cole's hair. Man you couldn't get in his shop."[45] Young people flocked to barber shops to emulate the styles of black entertainers they thought were cool. "I used to process my hair when I was younger," former Black Panther Party member Aaron Douglass recalled. "That was the thing, process and put the conk in your hair. You used to want to be like Jackie Wilson and Marvin Gaye. Blacks used to identify with the black entertainers."[46]

Younger barbers welcomed the new hairstyle because it had a price like any other commodity and they could charge much more for processing than for a haircut. Between 1951 and 1954, West worked as an apprentice in his brother-in-law Buddy Young's barber shop at 1707 South Street in Philadelphia. At first, West just cut hair, but then young customers started coming for a process. "When I first started barbering," he remembered, "a haircut was

Figure 18. Barber and customer with conked hair. *Beauty Culture-Barbershops 1950s*, Courtesy of the Photographs and Prints Division, Schomburg Center for Research in Black Culture, The New York Public Library, Astor, Lenox and Tilden Foundations.

seventy-five cents, children were twenty-five cents. Then it [adult haircuts] went up to $1.50. You know how many heads you got to cut [to see a profit]. Then I went to New York, and I met a guy who was working in a shop called Golden Glover, and that's all they did in there was process. I stayed there for awhile until I got the knack of it."[47] George Gainford, Sugar Ray Robinson's boxing trainer, owned the Golden Glover Barber Shop, with Robinson's financial backing, on the west side of Seventh Avenue between 123rd and 124th Streets in Harlem. Because of Robinson's fame, Golden Glover was a very popular place to get a process. "To get a haircut in George's barber shop," Robinson recalled, "you had to make an appointment three days in advance."[48] West was definitely in the right place to learn the new style. When he returned to Philadelphia, he continued to work with his brother for "another year, processing and cutting hair." With his new skill, his processing business increased significantly. Clients who wanted processing came mostly on the weekends, which shifted West's usual barbering customers to weekdays. The process hairstyle took an hour and a half to complete, so customers who wanted a simple haircut faced a long waiting time on the weekends. Other barbers noted similar business decisions to accommodate haircuts and processes. At Hortense Williams's barber shop in Norfolk, Virginia, barbers cut hair on one side of the shop and processed on the other.[49]

The conk was traditionally done at home because working-class men could not afford to consistently have it done at a shop, due to the significant time investment and cost. Additionally, the homemade version lasted three to four weeks. The homemade recipe was a concoction of lye and potatoes that could straighten the hair and form it into the desired style. Critics of the conk believed the lye damaged hair. The popular saying went: "Conkolene rules the world, takes the knot and makes it curls, if your hair becomes bald, conkolene did it all."[50] This line between the homemade conk that could damage the hair and the professional process done at the shop went far beyond issues of professionalism and healthy hair.

Men spent considerable time having their hair straightened and curled—everyday grooming rituals for many women—to sport a hairstyle that was supposed to represent their masculinity. Sociologist Maxine Craig has argued that marginalized heterosexual men turned "the flowing feminine waves of processed hair" into a badge of street masculinity or cutting-edge hipness. Black male entertainers drew on their celebrity status, which required them to stay trendy, and their financial means to justify the hair-beautifying attention. Street corner hustlers could rely on their masculine street credibility to dismiss questions about their neatly styled curls. Class was also important in how men understood their manliness through their conk. On the one hand, the conk became associated with the unemployed and street corner hustlers. On the other hand, working-class men could demonstrate their manliness by going to a shop to have their hair professionally styled. This act demonstrated to a broader public that they could afford it, whether true or not.[51]

When West began processing hair in Young's shop, the waiting public shifted noticeably. Young disliked the process because he claimed it brought in "riffraff." "He was used to older men coming in there his age," West believed. "And with processing, the younger guys were coming in and he didn't like it. [That was] one of the main reasons I got my own business, because he wasn't satisfied with young guys coming in here." Young associated the process with a certain class of black youth. According to West, the young men were not disrespectful to or confrontational with the older men, but "it was the idea of four and five young guys sitting in there talking their talk; the older guys talking about Jackie Robinson . . . and the young guys talking about Jackie Wilson."[52] The conflict was less likely about the congregation of young and old or the conversations about Robinson and Wilson. The conflict was more likely about Young's perceptions of the process and black youth respectability. When West left Young's shop in 1954, he took the young clientele with him and opened his own shop across the street.

Although West, and many other barbers, adjusted to the fashion, a select group of black barbers in Richmond argued that a steady stream of unskilled men were opening processing shops, which threatened the livelihoods of a long-standing black barbering community. They went so far as to help the white barbers union to revive a dead letter: a state licensing law. William Lomax helped reestablish the Barbers Protective Association (BPA) in 1962. The BPA had actively resisted proposed licensing laws in the 1930s. But now, there were new barbers and new concerns. Lomax served the association in various capacities from district supervisor, president of the local, and chairman of the board of the state unit. He remembered the BPA as a key organization that helped black barbers fight discrimination and help them get their "proper rights." But when asked what discrimination the BPA helped black barbers overcome, he invoked white and black barbers. "The white barbers . . . wanted separation," he remembered. "Basically, they wanted to put black barbers out of business for waiting on white patrons. They didn't care about black barbers waiting on black patrons."[53] The continuity between black barbers' assessments from the 1930s to Lomax's from the 1950s and 1960s is startling. They were a generation removed, but they sized up white barbers' motives just the same. In the postwar period, the BPA had intended to protect black barbers from discriminatory treatment.

Lomax and the BPA had other concerns that better explain why they championed a licensing law. As barbers in an unregulated state, black barbers in Virginia believed the popularity of the process encouraged more men to open commercial shops in their state because they did not need a license, which meant untrained stylists were likely to charge below-market rates. "You had black barbers and black hair stylists in New York, New Jersey, up north, that would come down to Richmond and work," William Lomax recalled, "so the only way we could stop that was we got the state of Virginia to institute a barber licensing law in [1962]. During that time men wore processes, you know, they got their hair straightened and waved and whatnot."[54] Lomax processed hair in his own shop, including that of a number of entertainers. Strikingly, he did not remember the state, or the licensing law, as the medium of protection, but rather the organized body of black barbers. "We needed the Barber Association to protect us, and we were instrumental in getting the barber licensing law passed." Barbers reestablished the association to protect prices, and they had a difficult time convincing younger barbers to join. "Some guys had shops in your own neighborhood that would cut for seventy-five cents or a dollar under you, so we got this organization . . . so we could all charge the same thing," barber Benjamin Thompson recalled.[55]

As mentioned earlier, Lomax was active with the Crusade for Voters, founded in 1956 to increase blacks' participation in Richmond's political process. So he understood the racial politics behind the proposed law in the state, but the economic politics were equally as important. Untrained "stylists" from the North processing hair at lower rates was reason enough for Lomax to join white barbers in calling for legislative protection. Stylists from the North served as scapegoats for any barbers who charged below market rate. Thompson remembered that "we could never get Eugene [Fleming] in there."[56] Fleming had not migrated from the North, but he had recently opened a shop after the law passed, did not have a license, and charged lower prices until he became up to speed on his skills. He said he received little help from the BPA in figuring out how to get a license, and perhaps the BPA resented him for keeping prices at seventy-five cents when they raised theirs to $1.25.[57] Whether they were dealing with new owners in the field or itinerant stylists, the BPA organized across the state to promote economic security within their ranks.

After decades of failure, longtime proponents of barbering legislation had reintroduced the bill in 1962, but they placed the State Health Department, instead of a barber board, in charge of inspecting barber shops, which passed the House and Senate and became a law.[58] The governor then appointed one African American, Lewis Knight of Newport News, to a one-year term on the barber board, and four white members to two- or three-year terms. The law included a grandfather clause that exempted people already practicing as barbers and beauticians from sitting for the exam.[59] "Finally, they brought in a bill so mild that it was passed," Virginius Dabney recalled in an interview in 1975. "My colored barber tells me that it doesn't bother him at all; it's purely for inspection of the shops by the health department, which is the way it ought to be. I think they have a board with two whites and one colored and they are not discriminating against anybody."[60] The BPA acted as a key opponent of the legislation in the 1930s because it believed white competition stood to benefit. In the early 1960s, however, a growing number of black competitors caused the BPA to rethink how the state could be useful to it.

While the BPA of Virginia attacked the economic consequences of the process hairstyle, a far greater number of African Americans began to debate the racial politics of processed hair, particularly as Afros emerged. Malcolm X recalled his first conk as a sign of racial hatred: "On top of my head was this thick smooth sheen of red hair—real red—as straight as any white man's. . . . [The conk was] my first really big step toward self-degradation."[61] These kinds of sentiments spilled over into barber shops. In West's shop in the late 1960s, customers argued daily whether black men with processed hair desired to be white. On many occasions, the "black is beautiful" rhetoric of the black consciousness movement provided the context for these arguments where Afros were the counterpoint to processes. Despite the "black is beautiful" movement, West later argued that Afros were nothing more than political statements. "You could march or be a freedom fighter with a process or a bush. You weren't any blacker if you cut your process. A person is entitled to do what they want to with their [hair] and still be a black person, think black and act black. But, who am I to tell them."[62] For West, the politics of processing reflected the politics of his profits. He was not countering the black consciousness movement because, frankly, it made perfect political sense, but a hairstyle did not mark one's identity. Barbers' perceptions of hair that represented popular styles or political statements underscored their political ideologies and concerns for profitability. West worried that the 1968 song by Hank Ballard, "How You Gonna Get Respect (When You Haven't Cut Your Process Yet)," would certainly "kill processing." Ballard sang, "Get that mess outta your hair, and wear your natural do/ And I'm gonna bet on my dear life respect gonna come to you."[63] Ballard acknowledged the popularity of the process, but he said it was a new day and African Americans should be proud of their natural hair. In the mid-1960s, the artificial process gave way to the natural Afro. The natural hairstyle served as a public, visible symbol of blackness and black power.

Part of the black power movement, the black consciousness movement helped African Americans enhance a group culture and facilitate the development of a positive group identity on their own terms by merging activist and cultural politics.[64] In the early 1960s, natural hairstyles expressed signs of self-love and black pride. Frantz Fanon's *Wretched of the Earth* (1961) and Malcolm X's *Autobiography of Malcolm X* (1965) fueled the black consciousness movement's emphasis on personal and political transformation. These texts can be considered the bibles of the black power movement because many young revolutionaries such as Huey Newton, and thousands of everyday activists, used them as standard reading for the revolution. *Wretched of the Earth* resonated well with black activists because Fanon's discussion of the psychological consequences of colonialism convinced members of the SNCC and others that they must overcome the psychological consequences of slavery symbolized in their style of dress and straightened hair. *The Autobiography of Malcolm X* told a similar narrative of transformation from street corner hustler to leader, from his self-described moment of "self-degradation" that his conk symbolized to his moment of consciousness. When African Americans read Malcolm's autobiography, they could relate to his struggles to fashion a political identity.[65]

The Afro's origins actually begin not in a black nationalist moment, but rather in the au naturel fashion moment of the late 1950s and early 1960s. Women such as musicians Odetta, Abbey Lincoln, and Nina Simone, and artist and writer Margaret Burroughs, wore short to medium Afros. Many black women admired the au naturel look at New York art shows, which Lincoln attended. Although women with the au naturel style were also often politically active, the Afro at this point symbolized more of a fashion statement partly because of the connections with downtown chic, and perhaps partly because this was initially a women's style.[66] By the mid- to late 1960s, Afros became symbols of resistance and protest. A large population of Afro wearers included young people who were active in student sit-ins, participated in the urban rebellions, and lived apart from their parents. Men tended to represent these symbols of resistance even though women were equally active. Many in this younger generation wanted not only to *engage* in political protest but also to *look* politically conscious. Many young activists in SNCC, the Black Panther Party, and even less radical organizations such as CORE and the NAACP wore Afros. Jesse Jackson, civil rights activist and founder of Operation PUSH and the Rainbow Coalition, remembered, "I feel that the way I wore my hair was an expression of the rebellion of the time."[67] The black uprisings that occurred in the Watts neighborhood of Los Angeles and in other cities rendered visible black rage, resistance, and the Afro. Afros grew out of political activism, which created a connection between direct action and aesthetic resistance. Some African Americans believed that simply by wearing an Afro, a symbol of protest, they too were involved in the move-ment.[68] While images of men tend to represent militancy, it is Angela Davis and her iconic Afro who most people celebrate when thinking about direct rebellion and hair. From Lincoln to Davis, women who sported Afros took greater revolutionary leaps because of the politics of feminine beauty that were tied to long hair and commercial products. If men missed a few haircuts, they could inevitably see an Afro staring at them in the mirror. Ultimately, while historian Robin Kelley argues that African Americans withdrew from the marketplace by not using chemicals (the commodity-based economy), it is important to note that barbers wondered if they would also withdraw from the barber shop (the service-based economy).[69]

Afros changed the political economy of the shop as style and statement shaped consumption patterns and shop talk. Paige West recalled that Afros "broke my heart" because many of his loyal customers wanted their process taken out. Customers often made "excuses" because they worried about their relationship with him. According to West, one customer said his "grand-mother was here from Alabama and she hadn't seen him since he was four years old and he wanted her to remember what he looked like. I said man how long did it take for you think that up. Just get your head cut, that's all." West and other barbers tried to combat the move away from processing by offering a solution called the blowout, which exaggerated the Afro, but it failed to pro-duce significant results. West said, "It's either a bush or it's not a bush."[70] West met heated criticism during this transition from the artificial process to the natural Afro. One customer who did not have a process asked West, "What are you gonna do when black people stop trying to act like they're white and stop getting their hair straight?" "Well," West responded, "I'll do what I have to do." Afros lasted longer than he expected, but he contends that the natural hairstyle did not hurt his business.

But some barbers were hurt—and badly. "The Afro ran a whole generation of barbers out of business," remembered Art McCoy, owner of the Super Fly barber shop in East Cleveland, and "put them on the unemployment lines." "There were a lot of 'For Sale' signs," recalled Nat "Bush Doctor" Mathis, a black hairstylist in Washington, D.C., in the 1970s. "A lot of barber shops didn't know how to style it."[71] Henry Jones of Bedford-Stuyvesant lamented that in the early 1970s, Afros nearly put him out of business because customers came to the shop less frequently.[72] Even those who still came to the shop came only for shapeups. "So, therefore," Howerton, of Washington, D.C., explained, "you [were not] getting the price of a full haircut. When you do a shapeup versus a haircut, that's less money."[73] Many barbers could not earn a decent income, which forced them to leave barbering in search of other means of work.[74]

As their client base shrank, some barbers attempted to respond to these market shifts by implementing new business strategies to keep customers, such as focusing on commodity products to enhance the Afro. Nat Mathis, who called himself a hairstylist rather than a barber, went on a local television station to prove he could give anyone a bush. His model was a white housewife with straight blonde hair. On camera, Mathis permed the white woman's hair, blew it out, cut it, and shaped it until she had a large bush. This marketing stunt earned him the title "Bush Doctor."[75] If he could transform straight hair into an Afro, he figured he could convince anyone of his skills to style an Afro from any starting point. "It seems ironic," Clinton Simpson of Birmingham, Alabama, asserted, "but we made more money than we were making when they were wearing [hairstyles] low." Barbers saw opportunities with the chemical blowout. "A chemical blowout," Simpson explained, "is where you put the relaxer in there, and comb it through until the texture gets just in that wavy pattern, shampoo it out, get the hair dryer, and blow it. It makes the hair look double the size it is, plus it looks natural."[76] This appealed to customers who wanted their Afros to look bigger.

Simpson was not alone in seeing more business from people asking to get less hair cut off. Some men and women went to the shop every two weeks to at least get it shampooed or shaped. Like several barbers, James Crawford of Cleveland noted that when people came into his Glenville area shop to have their Afros shaped, he just did what they wanted, without disdain, but rather "with respect."[77] "Business was booming," Randolph Arthur in Bedford-Stuyvesant recalled. "They let their hair grow, and I just fell right into it. I changed my styles; whatever the customer wanted, that's what I gave them. Every two weeks most of the people would be in here to trim it up. If you let it get too long, it didn't look good. They wanted Afros, so we gave it to them."[78] Barbers who were willing to accommodate the new hairstyle could at least stay afloat. Eugene Fleming of Richmond simply adjusted by learning how to pick and round the hair out. "We kind of perfected a way to cut it," he recalled. "So, we didn't lose no money. But I had run across a lot of the older men that . . . were outgunned."[79] Many barbers also charged more to style Afros. In Washington, D.C., they raised the price of a haircut from ten dollars to twelve dollars.[80] Barbers' principal duties were to cut hair. Therefore, many were slow to respond to customers with mountains of hair on their heads who did not want their hair cut, but just wanted a trim. Barbers proactively encouraged men and women to come to the shop more often to shape their Afros. In fact, beauticians grew a bit concerned because women with Afros started going to barbers to have their hair shaped or the back of their necks lined.[81] Barbers argued that many people were wrong to believe they did not have to keep their Afros well groomed.[82]

In James Alan McPherson's 1977 short story "The Faithful," he explores the barber's role in crafting how black men represented themselves. John Butler, a barber and preacher, loses business because he refuses to trim the Afro in any way, shape, or form. Butler is aware of the black consciousness movement, but he believes black youth mimicked white youth in growing out their hair. "These whites have bullshitted our young men," Butler proclaims. "Now, me, I'm as proud as the next man. But our boys didn't stop gettin' haircuts until these white boys started that mess. That's a fact. Wasn't no more than a couple of years ago, they'd be lined up against that wall on a Saturday night, laughin' at the white boys. But as soon as they see these white kids runnin' round wild, all at once, they hair ain't long enough no more." Butler takes the power away from black youth in wearing Afros by arguing it was a mere imitation of white youth's long hair. When a young boy requests a haircut in the Afro style, Butler cuts it in the schoolboy style. Butler's actions outrages the boy's father, who refers to the schoolboy style as that of a "plantation negro." Just as the boy's father believed his son's hair was a reflection of his identity (or the identity his father wanted for him), Butler also believed in the power of appearance. "You can shape a boy's life by what you do to his hair."[83] Butler refuses to change with the new hairstyles because he believes young black boys and men should be clean cut. There were hundreds of John Butlers across the country. Generational divides, personal politics, and barber shop economics played a role in barbers' feelings about Afros. But profession played an even bigger role, because black barbers were responsible for how black men looked when they walked out of the barber shop and entered a hostile white world.

By the time McPherson produced this story, the Afro had faded, but for shop owners, the damage was done. If they did not go out of business, they lost many of their barbers who turned to other work.[84] "When Afros went out of style," according to Henry Jones of Brooklyn, "people started getting haircuts again. But, there were so few barbers. I was crazy busy all the time."[85] Jones and other barbers said little about the politics of Afros and naturals. They remember that moment not for the debates about protest or "plantation negroes" but rather for the debates about dollars and cents.

Barbers groomed individual men and boys, but they also believed they were grooming a race. Whether they were activist barbers or calculating capitalists, grooming a race meant different things to different barbers. Some questioned how whites would respond to men with an Afro and its associated politics, and whether Afro wearers would get jobs. The black consciousness movement partially responded to this external, white approval of personal appearance. Other black barbers defined their roles as groomers of race through the political activity they fostered in their shops. For them, the barber shop provided a space to shape men's hair and minds. Black barbers were not a monolithic class of workers and entrepreneurs, and black barber shops were not monolithic spaces. Yet, increasing receipts and political consciousness were not necessarily mutually exclusive.

Black men were unlikely to have the same freedom to talk and learn about racially progressive issues in white shops. Moreover, they could not receive an Afro blowout or shapeup at a white shop, because this act would have undercut the very reason for maintaining an Afro. And barbers were well aware of the cultural and political value of their shops to black communities. In fact, black culture was good for business. So when a small few called for white shops to desegregate and the prospects of integration became more real, black barbers did not flinch, and black customers had no plans to venture across the color line in any significant numbers to get a haircut.

The Meanings of Congregation and the Black Commercial Public Sphere

Beginning in the 1960s, black newspaper reporters filled their columns with commentaries on integration. In 1963, Harry Ferguson, a writer for the *Chicago Defender*, assessed the progress of cities that were moving toward "completely integrating." He noted that "two threads of fact run through the reports" from cities on integration. The first was that African Americans had been slow to use the public accommodations they had gained access to. Second, "Barber shops and beauty parlors still are segregated for reasons not readily apparent. One theory is that Negroes prefer to take their business to members of their own race and that all women are reluctant to change hair dressers once they have found one they like. But the Negro appears to be making progress everywhere in the field of public accommodations."[86] Barbers and beauticians developed personal relationships with their patrons. And, yes, "once they have found one they like," they were unlikely to switch, especially to a white shop. In 1963, as discussed in the previous chapter, white barbers had not opened the doors to black customers. When they did, most blacks still preferred visiting black shops.

In 1964, *Chicago Defender* columnist Al Duckett sat among a number of people at the Down Home Barber Shop in Brooklyn, New York. While Duckett awaited his turn in the barber's chair, he talked with a fellow customer, whom he called Big Mouth, about the place of barber shops in the era of integration. Big Mouth told Duckett he was not ready for integration, but not in the way segregationist "Senator [James] Eastland means it when he says it." Eastland, from Mississippi, staunchly opposed integration and the civil rights movement. To explain what he meant, Big Mouth recalled a vacation he and his "Old Lady" took to Los Angeles. "I had not had a chance to get a haircut before leaving dear old Brooklyn," Big Mouth recounted, "and I was looking most uncool around the back of the neck. I figured the least one of my race could do so long as these white folks were paying us so much attention was to look presentable." He went to the lobby of the "integrated" hotel they had been staying at and asked a black bellhop, whom Big Mouth called "one of those Negroes who have become fully integrated," where the "colored part of town" was so he could go get a haircut. Because the bellhop directed him to the hotel barber shop, he assumed it had a black barber. "When I got there, however, I saw no folks [of] my kind dressed in those little white coats and cutting hair. Like usual, the only representative in there was a young, brown cat, hitting some licks on a white man's shoes." When he asked the shoeshine worker if there was a black barber at the shop, he told Big Mouth there was not, but any of the barbers would cut his hair. Big Mouth considered the bellhop and the shoeshine worker "too integrated." Duckett asked Big Mouth if he was satisfied with his haircut from the white barber. "Are you mad?" Big Mouth exclaimed. "Maybe they have gotten to the place where they want to cut my hair, but I have not got to the place where I trust them to do so. I don't have the kind of hair for experiments. No sir, I got right into a cab and told the driver to take me to the colored section. I got me a haircut almost as fine as I could get right here in Brooklyn in the Down Home Barber Shop."[87]

For Duckett, Big Mouth's preference ran counter to the goals of integration. Duckett argued, "You are proving the argument of segregationists who say the Negro wants to stay with his own people—looking for the colored section." But for Big Mouth, the colored section and its black barber shop provided a comfortable and familiar place. Away from home, he still believed he could find a comparable shop to accommodate him, saying, "I don't ever want to become so integrated that I can't find the colored section." Integration had its limits; Big Mouth was "more interested in the cause of [his] hair."[88] In the months before Congress passed the Civil Rights Act of 1964, Big Mouth raised a critical issue that few people questioned: what would integration bring? The passage of this monumental legislation further encouraged black communities to believe in the promise of racial progress. But, the "colored section" was not a placeholder until some better day, or better space, arrived in a new, integrated society. The goals of integration and the tenets of the black public sphere were not mutually exclusive, but in many ways they were symbiotic. African Americans fought for the rights to direct their own consumption and leisure behaviors, but they also understood that the maintenance of black cultural production should continue to be controlled by black people.

Black public discourse about integration led to widespread discussions on what many viewed as a "segregated economy." In 1968, the *Chicago Defender* warned readers about the unintended economic consequences of integration. "As black people become increasingly free to patronize whomever they please," the paper argued, "rather than being restricted to purchases in the 'ghetto,' the Negro entrepreneur finds himself in trouble," resulting in an "unwanted intrusion [by white entrepreneurs] into the Negro market."[89] However, the two businesses the paper cited as susceptible to losing black clients to white counterparts, morticians and beauticians, were actually less likely to lose their customers than say, grocers. Like barber shops, these enterprises relied on black culture to sustain them. African Americans had particular ways of exercising "homegoing" rituals to mark the passing (not the dying) of a loved one. As Karla Holloway points out, African American communities preferred open-casket viewing that allowed them to touch and kiss the deceased, and express one's grief in response to the "emotional power of the presence of the deceased." Open caskets also memorialized racial violence against black bodies, as exemplified by Emmett Till's mother's directive that the world should see "what they had done to my child." Black morticians reaped a

financial gain from open caskets because they made additional money em-
balming the deceased for public viewing, but they also understood that this
practice was central to African American memorializing.[90]

Culture did similar work in beauty shops as well. When black women went
to black beauty parlors, they sought particular kinds of hairstyles that they
trusted their beauticians could style. In addition to getting their hair styled in
particular ways, they sat next to other black women from various networks
(work, church, the neighborhood, organizational affiliations). These were
not simply captive clients forced to patronize these black businesses. These
businesses functioned as important institutions in the development of black
community.

The black service economy had a different relationship to black communities than black commodity-based economies, so integration affected them
differently. Price mattered in commodity exchanges. When faced with the decision to purchase toilet paper from a small black-owned store and the much
larger A&P, black consumers were likely to decide based on price, although
the softness of the paper might be an additional consideration in this case. But
price was only one factor in consumer services, which depended on intimate,
trusting relationships between entrepreneurs and customers. The emotional
experience of the exchange determined the likelihood of a repeat transaction.
Black customers, therefore, were more likely to switch from supporting black
grocers, clothing stores, and gas stations than they were to switch from supporting black churches, funeral homes, beauty shops, and barber shops.

The black beauty industry provides a prime example of how service and
commodity-based economies faced integration because it served both markets. Unlike barbering and barber shops, most black women entered the beauty
culture industry not to open shops and style hair, but to sell hair care products
where the shop helped serve those ends. The pioneers of the industry mar-
keted and sold a system.[91] Beauty shops, then, provided the brick-and-mortar
structures to organize the system. The many commodity products—straight-
ening comb, permanent press, and so on—represented the core of the
industry. In the post–World War II period, black entrepreneurs produced innovative products to straighten hair, hair weaves and wigs, and hair relaxers.
Johnson Products, founded by black businessman George Johnson, was the
most successful black hair care manufacturer during this period. His Ultra
Wave, Ultra Sheen, and Afro-Sheen products helped the company post $40
million in sales in the mid-1970s. In 1971, Revlon began marketing its products
to black consumers, a campaign that intensified throughout the 1970s. Other

companies such as Alberto-Culver and Gillette followed suit and gained traction in the market. In response, black companies appealed to racial solidarity to urge black consumers to support black businesses. In 1981, black-owned companies formed the American Health and Beauty Aids Institute to think innovatively about how to bring back black consumers, such as stamping a logo, the "Proud Lady Logo," of a silhouette of a black woman with three layers of hair on their products to indicate that a black firm produced it.[92] White manufacturing companies may have competed for black consumer dollars, but white beauty shop owners made no effort to bring black women into their beauty shops. In other words, white firms welcomed black consumer dollars, but they did not welcome them in their shops, and black women were not beating down their doors either. Black women were comfortable with their particular beauticians and thought little about switching to a white beautician for the sake of "integration." Black manufacturing companies lost ground in the black beauty industry, but black beauty shops remained among the leading black businesses in cities across the country. Black barber shops lacked the same history of commodity production, but they too maintained their black customers in the era of desegregation.

Black barber shops did face tangible concerns of a changing urban environment in the late 1960s and 1970s. First, shop owners, like other business owners, were caught in the line of fire during the urban rebellions of the time. Although the discontented focused their wrath on white businesses in their communities, black entrepreneurs nervously stood by their shops and stores to protect the means of their livelihoods. Many black owners placed signs in their windows that read "Black Owned" to alert an angry crowd that they were not part of the problem and should not be a target. More important, black owners meant the signal of blackness to indicate a sense of solidarity. When African Americans took to the streets in West End Richmond after Martin Luther King's assassination, Eugene Fleming stood by his shop and told frustrated crowds, "Hey, this building belongs to a soul brother." This worked—the crowds bypassed his shop.[93] Others took this a step further by putting "Soul Brother" on a sign in the shop window. James Spruill, barber in Washington, D.C., remembered white business owners putting the soul brother sign in their windows too.[94] In the aftermath of the rebellions in the mid to late 1960s, barber shop owners found themselves in business districts that had been destroyed. White proprietors took their insurance money and fled, along with the white residents who lived nearby. The broken glass and burned-out buildings made these neighborhoods look like disaster areas, making them ripe for urban reform. Unfortunately, the destruction made them susceptible to "urban renewal" projects against their will.[95]

Urban renewal—or, as many black residents labeled it, "Negro removal"—directly affected barber shops. To be sure, urban renewal did not create a moment of crisis for black barber shops, but it did cause concern for owners who were asked to close their doors and patrons who were forced to consider a new shop and a changing neighborhood.[96] The architects of highways in major cities exercised the state power of eminent domain to demolish neighborhoods and their business districts for the "public good" of connecting central business districts to growing suburban communities, and redeveloping devastated neighborhoods at the expense of those who remained. Historian Thomas Sugrue argued, "Small stores that relied on neighborhood patronage could not simply up and relocate elsewhere and expect that their clients would follow."[97] Because black barber shops were service-based enterprises driven by intimacy and trust, barbers actually could expect their clients to follow, if the shop did not move out of reach. For example, Eugene Fleming had to relocate his shop on Lombardi Street in Richmond because the state was building the Downtown Expressway. He moved approximately four blocks away to Idlewood Street.[98] In fact, he had been working on the new shop when the 1968 riots broke out. Fortunately for barber shop owners, the costs of relocating were minimal. Their services were still in demand. Their shops were still important, if not more important, in maintaining community in the face of demolition. In effect, commercial and church buildings could be demolished, but structures do not do the work of community formation; they simply facilitate it. So it would have been imperative for a displaced barber shop to relocate in order for residents to maintain that sense of the community that may have stood in a liminal state of dispersion through urban renewal but could be renewed through institutional connection. Nonetheless, it was still difficult for an owner to leave a location he had owned for twenty or thirty years. Hugh Hollins of Tulsa, Oklahoma, fared well in the relocation, but it was emotionally tough. "When Urban Renewal came through there and bought us black businesspeople out," he remembered, "I had to move out to the 46th and Cincinnati area of Tulsa. It was alright out there. I had a nice little shop, but it was nothing like the shop I had on Greenwood all those years. I sure did love Greenwood in the old days."[99]

Black barber shop owners lacked the kind of large-scale capital needed to anchor or rebuild black communities, but there were so many of them that they anchored communities in a different way. Black power advocates and urban activists advocated for black self-sufficiency that placed black entrepreneurs in a position to help community development. In an era when "black capitalism" operated as both a federally backed initiative and a grassroots strategy of economic self-development, entrepreneurs grappled with extended support from white commercial and political institutions and the calls for separatism without extensive capital.[100] Black-owned banks and emerging community development corporations attempted to lead the way in this endeavor to control the destinies of their communities.[101] While black nationalists and scholars recognized that there were large numbers of barber shops in urban areas, they dismissed them in discussions of economic development because they were small businesses. But unlike many other businesses, barber shops were closest to the idea of a "race enterprise" that black activists such as W. E. B. Du Bois wrote about in the 1930s, Malcolm X lectured about in the 1960s, and grassroots activists advocated in the 1960s and 1970s. A majority of black people went to black barber shops and spent their money there by getting a haircut, playing the numbers, or buying merchandise from a traveling salesman. Moreover, the community of people that frequented the shop contributed to the sense of "development" that more capitalized enterprises were attempting to bankroll.

The paradox of barber shops within black cultural economies is that they were not functions of segregation even though mostly African Americans patronized them. Black barbers supported one of the civil rights movement's goals of achieving integration, but they understood better than most people that integration did not mean a retreat from black communities or black culture. The major legal victories of the postwar period—the *Brown* decision, the Civil Rights Act of 1964, and the Voting Rights Act of 1965—generated optimism and hope that American society was on its way to becoming fair and just. Black barbers used their resources to further the struggle for equal rights even when many people within the movement stopped getting their hair cut to embrace the cultural resistance of that movement. The newly opened doors represented spatial access and affirmation of human dignity. Barbers knew their customers *might* gain access to white shops, but they also knew they could *not* get the latest culturally specific haircut or watch *Soul Train* on Saturday morning in those shops. Black culture would continue to be the value that black barbers and their shops offered. Part of the black cultural economy, barbers and their shops remained important professionals and institutions in black communities in the post–civil rights and black power eras.

Epilogue

SINCE the 1970s, barbering has continued to be a viable vocation for African Americans, and barber shops are still as plentiful as churches. But many of the barbers I interviewed for this book who entered the field in the late 1950s and 1960s lament that there seems to be a decline in professionalism in black barber shops. Particularly, they question younger barbers' commitment to treat the shop as a business instead of a side job, even though for some of them, barbering is indeed one of many jobs they hold down. These veteran barbers chide their younger colleagues for showing up late, using profane language, or playing loud music. While I suspect these issues occasionally crop up, the major question is, do African Americans who entered barbering in the 1980s and 1990s think about their trade and the shop differently than previous generations?

The film *Barbershop 2: Back in Business* raised similar concerns in 2004. The sequel was much less controversial than the first film, and it delved more into history and the kinds of generational changes this book has illustrated. The film incorporated two flashbacks to establish the radical history of Calvin's barber shop in the 1960s that illuminates the position of black barbers and their shops within black communities. "My life began the summer of July 4, 1967, when your father gave me a break," Eddie recalled to Calvin Jr., the current owner of the shop. Eddie first entered Calvin Sr.'s shop on that July evening when he was running from two white police officers on the South Side of Chicago. He dashed into the back door of a building, which happened to be Calvin's shop. Much to the surprise of Calvin Sr. and another barber, Eddie rushed through the door and pretended to rob the shop, without a gun. A heated exchange lasted a few minutes until the two officers ran inside. Eddie jumped into Calvin's barber chair and pleaded with him to "pretend like you're cutting my hair." This haircutting "front" was meant to mark Eddie's presence in the barber shop to deceive the police. Much to Eddie's dismay, Calvin actually cuts Eddie's conk to authenticate the front. Calvin could have turned Eddie over to the police, but instead he covered for Eddie and eventually gave him a job in the shop. This scene establishes Calvin's commitment to the South Side and Eddie's commitment to Calvin's barber shop.[1]

A second flashback in the movie complicates Calvin's shop as a place of both business and politics. When a former barber-turned-political aide scheduled a photo opportunity for an alderman inside the barber shop, Calvin Jr. opposed the idea, saying, "We don't do politics in here, this [is] a place of business. This ain't no damn community center." This statement caught Eddie's attention because it sounded similar to something Calvin Sr. said thirty years earlier. Eddie recalled a moment in the late 1960s when the Black Panther Party met inside Calvin's shop. One of the organizers addressed the members, saying, "When the FBI gassed the Black Panther house, we found a place to meet today. Thank you, Calvin." Calvin looked up from cutting a customer's hair and glanced at Eddie, to suggest that Calvin did not agree to the meeting. Calvin's facial expressions also suggest that he disagreed with the rhetoric of the Black Panther Party (BPP) organizers.[2] Whether or not Calvin agreed to the meeting or the rhetoric, he allowed the BPP to continue their work in his shop. The BPP held their meeting in public, but in the racial privacy of a black barber shop. These two flashbacks and the entire movie address the triangular relationship between black barbers, patrons, and surrounding communities. These relationships have a long and complicated history that illuminates the social history of service work and service consumption, and the private use of public spaces.

From the 1830s to the present, African Americans have come to barbering with diverse expectations. Each generation remade its stake in the profession and the shop in their own images and historical moments. Some became barbers because they worked in their father's shop as youngsters, and later inherited the shop. Most balked at the idea of working for someone else. Barbering allowed them to control their own time and labor. Yet, others simply learned barbering as a survival trade, something to fall back on when times got tough. Any given shop could have all of these barbers working side by side. Therefore, the death of professionalism is probably more perception than reality.

There have been some fundamental changes and challenges to black barber shops in the post–civil rights era. Some of the challenges ostensibly begin in barber college. All barber colleges teach the fundamentals of the trade (tools, techniques) so that students can successfully pass the licensing exam, but few teach students about the fundamentals of business. In essence, barber colleges are designed to teach students to work in a barber shop, not own one. But this has not stopped black entrepreneurs from opening their own shops. As with any line of business, training, vision, resources, and location determine a new shop's viability. The small, three-chair shop with photos of civil rights and black power activists and black entertainers lining the walls are either sustained by young barbers intent on carrying on a piece of history, or replaced by the six- to ten-chair shop and unisex salon that takes appointments. The chess and checker boards have been replaced with video games. Waiting customers can now opt out of the direct social interaction if they much prefer social media through their cell phones. While there is no black equivalent to Supercuts, a black barber shop franchise may not be too far off. While technology helps businesses innovate and become more efficient, the very local shops rooted in black communities that provide a space for organic and unpredictable consumer desires actually define the brand of these businesses.

Because the access to owning a barber shop is still relatively open, many urban neighborhoods across the country have several shops lining their commercial corridors. These shops are likely to have people hanging out inside, and possibly outside. This practice is not new. Photographs of black barber shops in the 1950s and 1960s often capture two or three people standing in front of the shop. These shops were, and to some extent still are, located next to beauty salons, nail shops, or restaurants. People make their rounds in and out of many of these small businesses to say hello, purchase lunch, or play the lottery. But urban economic developers cringe at the sight of, particularly, young black men hanging out on the street, even in front of a barber shop. In fact, many developers in small towns (like Poughkeepsie, New York) and major cities (like Chicago, Illinois) would prefer to see fewer barber shops so they can attract other businesses.

While revitalization committees might not like young black men spilling out of barber shops, black health care advocates have seized the opportunity to capture the attention of the shops' waiting public. Since 2006, the Black Barbershop Health Outreach Program has traveled to more than five hundred black barber shops across the country to screen black men for diabetes and hypertension, provide preventative education on chronic diseases such as prostate cancer, and offer resources for health services. Health care professionals routinely partner with black churches, but since men, compared with

women, are less represented in God's house on Sunday morning, professionals also bring their services to the place men frequent regularly on Saturdays.
Strikingly, the initiative has branded itself around the barber shop culture. In
fact, the website is simply blackbarbershop.org, with no mention of health.[3] I
suspect part of the strategy is to normalize health awareness and health education to encourage black men to make doctors, as their barbers are, fixtures
in their lives. Similar initiatives are taking place in beauty shops as well. These
black health care professionals join a long line of black entrepreneurs, professionals, and politicians who have attempted to partner with barbers in order
to get in front of their customers.

While this may seem like an isolated initiative, we need only look to the
2008 presidential campaign to think about how black barbers and barber
shops are situated in American society. For the first time in American history, the public was deeply interested in where a presidential candidate got his
haircut, and reporters went to black barber shops to get black men's opinions
on the candidate. The nation cared very little about where George Bush or Bill
Clinton got their haircuts, save for commenting on candidate John Edwards's
four-hundred-dollar trim. The media and the public drew on black barbers,
barber shops, and hair as symbols and vehicles of black culture to connect
Barack Obama to black communities. When it became apparent that Obama
was a serious contender for the Democratic nomination, several newspaper
reporters rushed to barber shops to poll African Americans' public opinion.
The barber shop served as the testing ground to understand the hot-button
issue of whether or not the black community accepted Obama's blackness.

Even as the press flocked to barber shops, Obama himself tapped into
barber and beauty shops to appeal to the black electorate. Much has been
written about Obama's first presidential campaign and the ways he incorporated his community-organizing experience into grassroots electoral politics.
The pitch for the South Carolina for Barack Obama Beauty & Barber Shop
Program began, "When Barack Obama first came to Chicago, he didn't know
a soul. One of the first places he found a sense of community was in a small
barber shop on Chicago's South Side, and he's been going there ever since."
Volunteers had the option to go into beauty or barber shops to facilitate
conversations about Obama, organize a "drop-by" with a field organizer, or
distribute literature in the shop.[4] Historically, black ministers have been key
arbiters of political campaigns because of their leadership of black congrega-
tions. Obama's campaign staffers visited hundreds of shops across the country because they recognized that barbers and beauticians serve the same role

outside of the church. Barbers see multiple generations of men come through their shops. But, also, every Saturday there is likely to be a group of people waiting around, ripe for campaign information.

Once elected, President Obama was forced to alter his everyday rituals, which included his regular trips to the Hyde Park Hair Salon and Barber Shop to see his barber, Zariff, on the South Side of Chicago. Again, the barber shop of a president-elect has never received so much attention—and concern. On November 12, just days after he was elected, the *Chicago Tribune* ran an article titled "Security to Keep Obama from Favorite Barbershop."[5] Instead of sitting in Zariff's chair in front of a large glass window in an urban area, Obama would have to wait for Zariff to travel to him. Unlike William "Billy Bud" Fleurville (Lincoln's barber in Illinois) and George Myers (McKinley's barber in Ohio), Zariff remained Obama's barber after he was elected president. The focus, then, on barbers and barber shops had less to do with Obama than with the role barbers continue to play in black communities. In the end, the barber-customer relationship is much more fluid and long lasting than the shop's waiting public. Zariff grooms the president to face the nation, which includes the youngest of America's citizens. Just five months into his first term, Obama faced a five-year-old African American boy, Jacob Philadelphia, who wondered if Obama's hair was like his own. The boy remarked that people often told him he and the president had the same haircut. In fact, Jacob's mother regularly took him to the barber shop where he would request a haircut just like Obama's. The president bent down and insisted that Jacob see for himself if they had a haircut in common. This indelible image was taken in the Oval Office, not a barber shop, and Zariff is nowhere to be seen; however, the barber's work of grooming race is no less present in this moment of racial and national belonging.

The history of black barbers and barber shops, as commercial public spaces, offers important lessons about the character of American democracy. Barber shops join the millions of small businesses that are central to the American economy. They build their businesses through individual and community networks to help shape people's perceptions of themselves. They perform a service for their customers; they do not serve them. Moreover, in this technological era, it is comforting that people still gather to talk, debate, and argue about politics or the mundane. Barber shops help facilitate community formations that are important for local neighborhoods and critical for barbers, who remain trusted members of black communities.

This book suggests that individual and collective interests need not be diametrically opposed. As workers and artists, barbers facilitate a system of

Figure 19. The son of a White House staffer touching President Obama's hair. Official White House Photo by Pete Souza.

production that is both economic and cultural. Inside of the barber shop, the cultural production extends beyond shaves and haircuts into larger arenas of discourse and masculinity. Black barber shops continue to operate as spaces of resistance, where barbers can reap the fruits of their labor, patrons can express themselves with particular hairstyles, and waiting public can engage in conversations particular to black communities with other African Americans. While some barber shops are more progressive than others, they symbolize the ways a shop owner's financial independence and political consciousness and a community's culture and congregation can facilitate African Americans' individual and collective dreams and realities of freedom.

My dreadlocks did not survive the publication of this book. Just as I had exercised my freedom to grow them, I felt free to cut them off myself, but Zariff gave me a shape-up in the Hyde Park shop where he works. Like young Jacob Philadelphia, who felt connected to President Obama through a haircut, and by extension more connected to the nation, I too now personally understand how black barbers and their shops can become conduits of black community formation and national belonging.

Notes

Preface

1. Melissa Harris-Lacewell and Quincy T. Mills, "Truth and Soul: Black Talk in the Barbershop," in Melissa Harris-Lacewell, *Barbershops, Bibles, and BET: Everyday Talk and Black Political Thought* (Princeton, N.J.: Princeton University Press, 2004), 162–203.

2. *Barbershop*, directed by Tim Story (Beverly Hills, Calif.: MGM Home Entertainment, 2002), DVD.

3. Quincy T. Mills, "'You Don't Look Groomed': Rethinking Black Barber Shops as Public Spaces," in Benjamin Talton and Quincy T. Mills, eds., *Black Subjects in Africa and Its Diasporas: Race and Gender in Research and Writing* (New York: Palgrave Macmillan, 2011), 77–94.

Introduction

1. *Colored American*, October 20, 1838.

2. *Colored American*, October 20, 1838.

3. On Samuel Cornish and the *Colored American* see Leslie Harris, *In the Shadow of Slavery: African Americans in New York City, 1626–1863* (Chicago: University of Chicago Press, 2003).

4. *Colored American*, October 20, 1838.

5. See Harris, *In the Shadow of Slavery*; Leslie Alexander, *African or American? Black Identity and Political Activism in New York City, 1784–1861* (Urbana: University of Illinois Press, 2008).

6. William H. Grier and Price M. Cobb, *Black Rage* (New York: Bantam, 1968), 88. See Fred M. Holycross, "The American Barbershop: Changing Gender Roles and the Modification of Masculinity," master's thesis, University of Notre Dame, 1990; Trudier Harris, "The Barbershop in Black Literature," *Black American Literature Forum* 13, no. 3 (Autumn 1979): 112–118; Melissa Harris-Lacewell and Quincy T. Mills, "Truth and Soul: Black Talk in the Barbershop," in Lacewell, *Barbershops, Bibles, and BET: Everyday Talk and Black Political Thought* (Princeton, N.J.: Princeton University Press, 2004); Craig Marberry, *Cuttin' Up: Wit and Wisdom from Black Barber Shops* (New York: Doubleday, 2005). For representations of black barbers in popular culture, see Vorris L. Nunnley, *Keepin' It Hushed: The Barbershop and African American Hush Harbor Rhetoric* (Detroit: Wayne State University Press, 2011); *Barbershop*, directed by Tim Story (Beverly Hills, Calif.: MGM Home Entertainment, 2002), DVD; and *Barbershop 2: Back in Business*, directed by Kevin Rodney Sullivan (Beverly Hills,

Calif.: MGM Home Entertainment, 2004). In 2006, Music Television (MTV) launched *The Shop*, a reality show based in Mr. Rooney's Barbershop in Jamaica, Queens, New York. The former UPN situation comedy *Cuts* focused on the barber-beauty salons emerging in urban areas at the turn of the twenty-first century.

7. Joseph B. Bibb, "The Barber Shop Chord," *Pittsburgh Courier*, October 23, 1943.

8. In *Structural Transformation of the Public Sphere: An Inquiry into a Category of Bourgeois Society*, trans. Thomas Burger with the assistance of Frederick Lawrence (Cambridge, Mass.: MIT Press, 1989), Jürgen Habermas conceptualized the public sphere as a discursive arena in which citizens deliberate about matters of "public concern" and "common interests." Nancy Fraser outlined four problematic assumptions in Habermas's concept. First, it is possible for socially unequal citizens to deliberate in the public sphere. Second, one comprehensive public is a necessary condition for greater democracy. Third, private interests should have no place in discourses in the public sphere. Fourth, civil society and the state must be separate to have a functioning democratic public sphere. Scholars of counterpublics have rejected Habermas's bourgeois conceptualization of the public sphere as liberal and universal. Fraser and Mary Ryan argue that the masculine bourgeois public was not *the* public, but there existed numerous competing counterpublics. See Nancy Fraser, "Rethinking the Public Sphere: A Contribution to the Critique of Actually Existing Democracy," and Mary Ryan, "Gender and Public Access: Women's Politics in Nineteenth Century America," in Craig Calhoun ed., *Habermas and the Public Sphere* (Cambridge, Mass.: MIT Press, 1992), 109–142, and 259–288. Scholars of the African American experience have also pointed out the limited reach of Habermas's bourgeois public sphere, arguing that it cannot be applied wholesale to black public life because they were historically excluded from the kinds of deliberative spaces Habermas studied. They too called attention to counterpublics. On the black public sphere and counterpublics, see Evelyn Brooks Higginbotham, *Righteous Discontent: The Women's Movement in the Black Baptist Church, 1880–1920* (Cambridge, Mass.: Harvard University Press, 1993); Elsa Barkley Brown, "Negotiating and Transforming the Public Sphere," in The Black Public Sphere Collective, ed., *The Black Public Sphere: A Public Culture Book* (Chicago: University of Chicago Press, 1995); Michael Dawson, *Black Visions: The Roots of Contemporary African American Political Ideologies* (Chicago: University of Chicago Press, 2001); Melissa Harris-Lacewell, *Barbershops, Bibles, and BET: Everyday Talk and Black Political Thought* (Princeton, N.J.: Princeton University Press, 2004); Catherine R. Squires, "Rethinking the Black Public Sphere: An Alternative Vocabulary for Multiple Public Spheres," *Communication Theory* 12, no. 4 (November 2002): 446–468.

9. Higginbotham, *Righteous Discontent*, 10.

10. George Schuyler interview with William Ingersoll, June 6, 1960, in *The Reminiscences of George S. Schuyler, 1962* (Alexandria, Va.: Alexander Street Press, 2003), 179.

11. George S. Schuyler, *Black and Conservative: The Autobiography of George S. Schuyler* (New Rochelle, N.Y.: Arlington House, 1966); George S. Schuyler, *Rac(e)ing to the Right: Selected Essays of George S. Schuyler*, ed. Jeffrey B. Leak (Knoxville: University of Tennessee Press, 2001).

12. For Higginbotham, the market economy had no bearing on the essential functions of the black church; therefore, she retained this distinction from Habermas's idea of the public sphere. "The public sphere in Habermas's sense," Nancy Fraser points out, "is not an arena of market relations but rather one of discursive relations, a theater for debating and deliberating rather than buying and selling." Fraser, "Rethinking the Public Sphere," 111. The debating and deliberating and buying and selling were quite central to modern black barber shops.

13. Douglas Bristol, *Knights of the Razor: Black Barbers in Slavery and Freedom* (Baltimore:

Johns Hopkins University Press, 2009). Bristol published the first scholarly monograph on a historical account of African American barbers. He examines black barbers' experiences as businessmen in the eighteenth and nineteenth centuries to argue that they fostered fraternal bonds and established a tradition of mutual cooperation. Because he focuses on a "tradition," he overstates the continuities and dismisses conflicts among barbers. *Knights of the Razor* charts a fine course for thinking about black men's perseverance to build businesses despite the confines of slavery and the constrictions of black citizenship. Urban historians mention barber shops when accounting for black urban community formation. See Allen Spear, *Black Chicago: The Making of a Negro Ghetto, 1890–1920* (Chicago: University of Chicago Press, 1967); David Katzman, *Before the Ghetto: Black Detroit in the Nineteenth Century* (Urbana: University of Illinois Press, 1973); David Gerber, *Black Ohio and the Color Line* (Urbana: University of Illinois Press, 1976); Kenneth Kusmer, *The Ghetto Takes Shape: Black Cleveland, 1870–1915* (Urbana: University of Illinois Press, 1976); Richard Thomas, *Life for Us Is What We Make It: Building Black Community in Detroit, 1915–1945* (Bloomington: Indiana University Press, 1992). Juliet E. K. Walker discusses black barbers within the context of their entrepreneurial acumen and prowess. See Juliet E. K. Walker, *History of Black Business in America: Capitalism, Race and Entrepreneurship* (New York: Macmillan, 1998), and Juliet E. K. Walker, ed., *Encyclopedia of African American Business History* (Westport, Conn.: Greenwood Press, 1999).

14. On black insurance companies, see Merah Stuart, *An Economic Detour: A History of Insurance in the Lives of American Negroes* (New York: Wendell Malliett and Company, 1940); Walter Weare, *Black Business in the New South: A Social History of the North Carolina Mutual Life Insurance Company* (Urbana: University of Illinois Press, 1973); Alexa Benson Henderson, *Atlanta Life Insurance Company: Guardian of Black Economic Dignity* (Tuscaloosa: University of Alabama Press, 1990); Robert C. Puth, *Supreme Life: The History of a Negro Life Insurance Company* (New York: Arno Press, 1976); Robert Weems, *Black Business in the Black Metropolis: The Chicago Metropolitan Assurance Company, 1925–1985* (Bloomington: Indiana University Press, 1996). On black beauty business and culture, see Tiffany Gill, *Beauty Shop Politics: African American Women's Activism in the Beauty Industry* (Urbana: University of Illinois Press, 2010); A'Lelia Perry Bundles, *On Her Own Ground: The Life and Times of Madam C. J. Walker* (New York: Scribner, 2001); Noliwe M. Rooks, *Hair Raising: Beauty, Culture, and African American Women* (New Brunswick, N.J.: Rutgers University Press, 1996); Julie A. Willett, *Permanent Waves: The Making of the American Beauty Shop* (New York: New York University Press, 2000); Julia Kirk Blackwelder, *Stylin' Jim Crow: African American Beauty Training During Segregation* (College Station: Texas A&M Press, 2003). On sports, see Neil Lanctot, *Negro League Baseball: The Rise and Ruin of a Black Institution* (Philadelphia: University of Pennsylvania Press, 2005).

15. Indeed, recent scholarship on the black cultural economy offers a fresh and innovative look at black entrepreneurial culture and public engagement. See Gill, *Beauty Shop Politics*; Adam Green, *Selling the Race: Culture, Community, and Black Chicago, 1940–1955* (Chicago: University of Chicago Press, 2007); Davarian Baldwin, *Chicago's New Negroes: Modernity, the Great Migration, and Black Urban Life* (Chapel Hill: University of North Carolina Press, 2007); Leslie Brown, *Upbuilding Black Durham: Gender, Class, and Black Community Development in the Jim Crow South* (Chapel Hill: University of North Carolina Press, 2008); Andrew W. Kahrl, *This Land Was Ours: African American Beaches from Jim Crow to the Sunbelt South* (Cambridge, Mass.: Harvard University Press, 2012).

16. Davarian Baldwin offers a similar term, "marketplace intellectual life," to explore the intellectual engagement of the black working class through consumer-based amusements.

The marketplace intellectual life, he argues, was a sphere "where cultural producers, critics, and patrons engaged the arena of commercial exchange to rethink the established parameters of community, progress, and freedom." See Baldwin, *Chicago's New Negroes*, 9.

17. Zephyr L. Frank, *Dutra's World: Wealth and Family in Nineteenth-Century Rio de Janeiro* (Albuquerque: University of New Mexico Press, 2004); Brad Weiss, *Street Dreams and Hip Hop Barbershops: Global Fantasy in Urban Tanzania* (Bloomington: University of Indiana Press, 2009).

18. See Earl Lewis, "To Turn as on a Pivot: Writing African Americans into a History of Overlapping Diasporas," *American Historical Review* 100, no. 3 (June 1995): 765–787.

19. Eric Sundquist, in his discussion of the shaving scene in Herman Melville's *Benito Cereno,* introduced the concept of "shaving-time" to mark a suspended historical moment that "pointed toward a future of black ascendancy." I have expanded his concept to mark an ever-changing moment that centers the grooming process within the dynamic interrelations among barbers, patrons, and publics. See Eric Sundquist, *To Wake the Nations: Race in the Making of American Literature* (Cambridge, Mass.: Belknap Press of Harvard University Press, 1993), 162.

20. On the hidden transcript see James C. Scott, *Domination and the Arts of Resistance: The Hidden Transcript* (New Haven: Yale University Press, 1990); Robin D. G. Kelley, "'We Are Not What We Seem'; Rethinking Black Working-Class Opposition in the Jim Crow South," *Journal of American History* 80, no. 1 (June 1993): 75–112.

21. See Jeff Wiltse, *Contested Waters: A Social History of Swimming Pools in America* (Chapel Hill: University of North Carolina Press, 2007); Kahrl, *This Land Was Ours.*

22. My discussion of "willing congregation" during segregation is taken from Earl Lewis, *In Their Own Interests: Race, Class, and Power in Twentieth-Century Norfolk, Virginia* (Berkeley: University of California Press, 1991).

23. See Stephanie Shaw, *What a Woman Ought to Be and to Do: Black Professional Women Workers During the Jim Crow Era* (Chicago: University of Chicago Press, 1996); Adam Fairclough, *A Class of Their Own: Black Teachers in the Segregated South* (Cambridge, Mass.: Belknap Press of Harvard University Press, 2007).

24. On gender as a cultural process, see Joan W. Scott, *Gender and the Politics of History* (New York: Columbia University Press, 1988). On gender and the development of American labor and business, see Ava Baron, ed., *Work Engendered: Toward a New History of American Labor* (Ithaca: Cornell University Press, 1991); Kathy Peiss, "'Vital Industry' and Women's Ventures: Conceptualizing Gender in Twentieth Century Business History," *Business History Review* 72, no. 2 (Summer 1998): 218-241.

25. See E. Anthony Rotundo, *American Manhood: Transformations in Masculinity from the Revolution to the Modern Era* (New York: Basic Books, 1993); Michael Kimmel, *Manhood in America: A Cultural History* (New York: Free Press, 1996); Gail Bederman, *Manliness and Civilization: A Cultural History of Gender and Race in the United States, 1880–1917* (Chicago: University of Chicago Press, 1995); and Martin Summers, *Manliness and Its Discontents: The Black Middle Class and the Transformation of Masculinity, 1900–1930* (Chapel Hill: University of North Carolina, 2004).

Chapter 1. Barbering for Freedom in Antebellum America

1. Amasa Delano, *A Narrative of Voyages and Travels in the Northern and Southern Hemispheres: Comprising Three Voyages Round the World Together with a Voyage of Survey and Discovery in the Pacific Ocean and Oriental Islands* (Boston: E. G. House, 1818).

2. William Richardson, ed., *Melville's "Benito Cereno": An Interpretation with Annotated Text and Concordance* (Durham, N.C.: Carolina Academic Press, 1987), 37.

3. Eric Sundquist, *To Wake the Nations: Race in the Making of American Literature* (Cambridge, Mass.: Belknap Press of Harvard University Press, 1993), 156.

4. Christopher Freeburg, *Melville and the Idea of Blackness: Race and Imperialism in Nineteenth-Century America* (New York: Cambridge University Press, 2012), 95.

5. Higginson quoted in Sundquist, *To Wake the Nations*, 159. See also Tilden G. Edelstein, *Strange Enthusiasm: A Life of Thomas Wentworth Higginson* (New Haven, Conn.: Yale University Press, 1968), 211.

6. Quote from Benjamin Henry Latrobe, *Latrobe's View of America, 1795–1820: Selections from the Watercolors and Sketches,* ed. Edward C. Carter II, John C. Van Horne, and Charles C Brownell (New Haven, Conn.: Yale University Press, 1985), 120. See also Shane White and Graham White, "Slave Hair and African American Culture in the Eighteenth and Nineteenth Centuries," *Journal of Southern History* 61, no. 1 (February 1995): 46–47.

7. On plantation culture, see John Blassingame, *The Slave Community: Plantation Life in the Antebellum South* (New York: Oxford University Press, 1979), 105–191; Stephanie Camp, *Closer to Freedom: Enslaved Women and Everyday Resistance in the Plantation South* (Chapel Hill: University of North Carolina Press, 2004), 12–92.

8. Quoted in White and White, "Slave Hair and African American Culture," 45; Ayana Byrd and Lori Tharps, *Hair Story: Untangling the Roots of Black Hair in America* (New York: St. Martin's Press, 2001), 16.

9. James Williams, interview by Irene Robertson, n.d. *Born in Slavery: Slave Narratives from the Federal Writers' Project, 1936–1938,* Vol. 2: *Arkansas Narratives*, part 7, Manuscript Division, Library of Congress, *American Memory*, 9 November 2002, http://memory.loc.gov.

10. William J. Anderson, *Life and Narrative of William J. Anderson, Twenty-four Years a Slave; Sold Eight Times! In Jail Sixty Times!! Whipped Three Hundred Times!!! Or The Dark Deeds of American Slavery Revealed. Containing Scriptural Views of the Origin of the Black and of the White Man. Also, a Simple and Easy Plan to Abolish Slavery in the United States. Together with an Account of the Services of Colored Men in the Revolutionary War—Day and Date, and Interesting Facts.* (Chicago: Daily Tribune and Job Printing Office, 1857), 14.

11. John Brown, *Slave Life in Georgia: A Narrative of the Life, Sufferings, and Escape of John Brown, a Fugitive Slave, Now in England,* ed. Louis Alexis Chamerovzow (London, 1855), 111–112.

12. William Wells Brown, *Clotel; or The President's Daughter,* ed. M. Giulia Fabi (London: Partridge & Oakey, 1853; repr., New York: Penguin Books, 2004), 8.

13. Historian Walter Johnson points out that this kind of grooming for the slave market helped create the fantasies sellers and planters traded. See Walter Johnson, *Soul by Soul: Life Inside the Antebellum Slave Market* (Cambridge, Mass.: Harvard University Press, 1999).

14. Bill Reese, interview by Sadie B. Hornsby, June 19, 1939, "I Cater to Colored People," ed. Sarah H. Hall and John N. Booth, *The American Slave: A Composite Autobiography,* gen. ed. George P. Rawick, Vol. 4: *Georgia Narratives*, part 2 (Westport, Conn.: Greenwood Press, 1977), 512 (hereafter Reese interview).

15. Ira Jones, interview by Grace Monroe, n.d., *The American Slave: A Composite Autobiography,* gen. ed. George Rawick, Supplement Series I, Vol. 5: *Indiana and Ohio Narratives* (Westport, Conn.: Greenwood Press, 1977), 100.

16. Edwin Adams Davis and William Ransom Hogan, *The Barber of Natchez* (1954; repr., Baton Rouge: Louisiana State University Press, 1973), 56. Free black and enslaved children who had no guardian were often ordered by local courts to serve apprenticeships with black

artisans. In 1808, Georgia established such a law that required free blacks between the ages of eight and twenty-one and without a guardian to be bound out as apprentices. In 1854, the Georgia legislature dropped the threshold to five years of age. Donald Grant, *The Way It Was in the South: The Black Experience in Georgia* (Athens: University of Georgia Press, 1993), 67. For further information on forced-child apprenticeship and the work life of enslaved children, see Karin L. Zipf, *Labor of Innocents: Forced Apprenticeship in North Carolina, 1715–1919* (Baton Rouge: Louisiana State University Press, 2005); Wilma King, *Stolen Children: Slave Youth in Nineteenth-Century America* (Bloomington: Indiana University Press, 1995).

17. Isaac Throgmorton, interview, 1863, Canada, *Slave Testimony: Two Centuries of Letters, Speeches, Interviews, and Autobiographies* ed. John Blassingame (Baton Rouge: Louisiana State University, 1977), 432–433 (hereafter Throgmorton interview).

18. *William Johnson's Natchez: The Antebellum Diary of a Free Negro,* ed. William Ransom Hogan and Edwin Adams Davis (Baton Rouge: Louisiana State University Press, 1951), 27–30 (hereafter Johnson, *Diary*); James Maguire, interview by Henry Bibb, 1851, *Slave Testimony*, 274–75 (hereafter Maguire interview).

19. Jacqueline Jones, *American Work: Four Centuries of Black and White Labor* (New York: W. W. Norton, 1998), 254. In 1838, Frederick Douglass, a fugitive slave at the time, could not find a job as a caulker in New Bedford, Massachusetts. He recalled in his narrative that "such was the strength of prejudice against color, among the white caulkers, that they refused to work with me, and of course I could get no employment." See Frederick Douglass, *Narrative of the Life of Frederick Douglass, An American Slave, Written by Himself,* ed. David W. Blight (1845; reprint, Boston: Bedford Books of St. Martin's Press, 1993), 118. For a discussion of labor discrimination in the antebellum urban North, see Jones, *American Work,* 246–272; Leonard Curry, *The Free Black in Urban America* (Chicago: University of Chicago Press, 1981), 15–22; David Montgomery, *Citizen Worker: The Experience of Workers in the United States with Democracy and the Free Market During the Nineteenth Century* (Cambridge: Cambridge University Press, 1993); Sean Wilenz, *Chants Democratic: New York City and the Rise of the American Working Class, 1788–1850* (New York: Oxford University Press, 1984). On labor competition and racialization see David R. Roediger, *The Wages of Whiteness: Race and the Making of the American Working Class* (London: Verso, 1991); Eric Lott, *Love and Theft: Blackface Minstrelsy and the American Working Class* (New York: Oxford University Press, 1993).

20. Douglas Bristol, *Knights of the Razor: Black Barbers in Slavery and Freedom* (Baltimore: Johns Hopkins University Press, 2009), 28–29.

21. Ira Berlin, *Slaves Without Masters: The Free Negro in the Antebellum South* (New York: Pantheon Books, 1974), 235–236; see also Juliet E. K. Walker, *History of Black Business in America: Capitalism, Race, Entrepreneurship* (New York: Macmillan, 1998), 107.

22. John Russell, "The Free Negro in Virginia, 1619–1865" (Ph.D. diss., Johns Hopkins University, 1913), nn. 108, 151.

23. Luther Porter Jackson, *Free Negro Labor and Property Holding in Virginia, 1830–1860* (New York: Atheneum, 1969), 76, 98.

24. William Howard Russell, *My Diary North and South,* Vol. 1 (London: Bradbury and Evans, 1863), 73.

25. John S. Powell, interview by Susie R. C. Byrd, n.d. [circa 1934], Federal Writers' Project, 1936-1938, reprinted in *Talk About Trouble: A New Deal Potrait of Virginians in the Great Depression,* ed. Nancy J. Martin-Perdue and Charles L. Perdue, Jr. (Chapel Hill: University of North Carolina Press, 1996), 278.

26. 1850 U.S. census, population schedule, Richmond, Henrico County, Virginia, sheet 247,

dwelling 179, family 200, Ruben West household; National Archives microfilm publication M432, roll 951; digital image, Ancestry.com, http://www.ancestory.com (accessed 2 January 2013). 1860 U.S. census, population schedule, Richmond, Henrico County, Virginia, sheet 44, dwelling 202, family 338, Ruben West household (listed as RM West); National Archives microfilm publication M653, roll 1352; digital image, Ancestry.com, http://www.ancestory.com (accessed 2 January 2013).

27. Davis and Hogan, *The Barber of Natchez*, 19–22.

28. Johnson frequently gambled on horse races. See Davis and Hogan, *The Barber of Natchez*, 32–37.

29. Brown, *Clotel*, 24–25.

30. Brown, *Clotel*, 25.

31. Gregg D. Kimball, *American City, Southern Place: A Cultural History of Antebellum Richmond* (Athens: University of Georgia Press, 2000), 43.

32. Joe William Trotter, *River Jordan: African American Urban Life in the Ohio Valley* (Lexington: University Press of Kentucky, 1998), 40.

33. Molly W. Berger, "A House Divided: The Culture of the American Luxury Hotel, 1825–1860," in Roger Horowitz and Arwen Mohun, eds., *His and Hers: Gender, Consumption, and Technology* (Charlottesville: University of Virginia Press, 1998), 45.

34. Berger, "A House Divided," 45; see also Jacqueline S. Wilkie, "Submerged Sensuality: Technology and Perceptions of Bathing," *Journal of Social History* 19, no. 4 (Summer 1986): 649–650.

35. Richard L. Bushman and Claudia L. Bushman, "The Early History of Cleanliness in America," *Journal of American History* 74, no. 4 (March 1988): 1225; Marilyn Thornton Williams, *Washing "The Great Unwashed": Public Baths in Urban America, 1840–1920* (Columbus: Ohio State University Press, 1991), 5–21.

36. *Pittsburgh Gazette*, May 14, 1833; *Pittsburgh Gazette*, June 14, 1833.

37. Laurence A. Glascoe, ed., *The WPA History of the Negro in Pittsburgh* (Pittsburgh: University of Pittsburgh Press, 2004), 57–58.

38. *Harris Business Directory* for 1839 (Pittsburgh, Pennsylvania), 14, quoted in Walker, *History of Black Business*, 107; See also William Switala, *Underground Railroad in Pennsylvania* (Mechanicsburg, Pa.: Stackpole Books, 2001), 85.

39. Paul N. D. Thornell, "The Absent Ones and the Providers: A Biography of the Vashons," *Journal of Negro History* 83, no. 4 (Fall 1998): 287.

40. Loren Schweninger, *Black Property Owners in the South, 1790–1915* (Urbana: University of Illinois Press, 1990), 50.

41. Davis, *The Barber of Natchez*, 34–35.

42. Cyprian Clamorgan, *The Colored Aristocracy of St. Louis*, ed. Julie Winch (Columbia: University of Missouri Press, 1999), quoted in Walker, *History of Black Business*, 107.

43. Gary Nash, *Forging Freedom: The Formation of Philadelphia's Black Community, 1720–1840* (Cambridge, Mass.: Harvard University Press, 1988), 254–259. On the sexual politics of amalgamation and its anti-abolitionist rhetoric see Peggy Pascoe, *What Comes Naturally: Miscegenation Law and the Making of Race in America* (New York: Oxford University Press, 2009), 47–74; Leslie Harris, *In the Shadow of Slavery: African Americans in New York City, 1626–1863* (Chicago: University of Chicago Press, 2003), 170–216.

44. Elise Lemire, *"Miscegenation": Making Race in America* (Philadelphia: University of Pennsylvania Press, 2002), 106–107. Lemire argues the customer was perhaps painted to be an abolitionist, based on his Quaker-like dress and the fact that his "desire for equality . . . would have paved the way for his own economic and perhaps literal bloodletting." This reading goes

against the interracial collaboration between black and white abolitionists of the time, as well as whites' concerns about this interaction.

45. On black dandyism see Monica L. Miller, *Slaves to Fashion: Black Dandyism and the Styling of Black Diasporic Identity* (Durham: Duke University Press, 2009).

46. Clamorgan, *The Colored Aristocracy of St. Louis*, 46, 52.

47. Clamorgan, *The Colored Aristocracy of St. Louis*, 45–63.

48. Russell, "Free Negro in Virginia," 151. See also Marie Tyler-McGraw and Gregg D. Kimball, *In Bondage and Freedom: Antebellum Black Life in Richmond, Virginia: An Exhibition at the Valentine Museum, Richmond, Virginia, February 11, 1988–September 13, 1988* (Richmond, Va.: Valentine Museum; distributed by the University of North Carolina Press, 1988).

49. Johnson, *Diary*, see entries for the months of October 1839, 268–271, and July 1840, 284–288.

50. James Buchanan, *Black Life on the Mississippi: Slaves, Free Blacks, and the Western Steamboat World* (Chapel Hill: University of North Carolina Press, 2004), 13, 67–68.

51. James Thomas, *From Tennessee Slave to St. Louis Entrepreneur: Autobiography of James Thomas*, ed. Loren Schweninger (Columbia: University of Missouri Press, 1984), 85.

52. Johnson, *Diary*, January 15, 1848, 604; September 12, 1850, 743. For additional references to his barbers leaving to work on steamboats, see pages June 2, 1847, 571; and August, 25, 1849, 661.

53. Johnson, *Diary*, July 5, 1836, 126–127.

54. Johnson, *Diary*, January 8, 1841, 314; and January 15, 1851, 770–771.

55. William Still, *The Underground Rail Road: A Record of Facts, Authentic Narratives, Letters, &c., Narrating the Hardships, Hair-Breadth Escapes and Death Struggles of the Slaves in their Efforts for Freedom, As Related by Themselves and Others* (Philadelphia: Porter & Coates, 1872), 449.

56. Throgmorton interview, 432–433.

57. Jackson, *Free Negro Labor and Property Holding in Virginia*, 197. See also Kimball, *American City, Southern Place*, 138-140.

58. Larry Koger, *Black Slaveowners: Free Black Slave Masters in South Carolina, 1790–1860* (Jefferson, N.C.: McFarland, 1985), 37–38. Also see Michael P. Johnson and James L. Roark, *Black Masters: A Free Family of Color in the Old South* (New York: W. W. Norton, 1984).

59. Koger, *Black Slaveowners*, 96.

60. The six barbers were Reuben West, Richard C. Hobson, John Ferguson, George P. Gray, George Ruffin, and Richard W. Henderson. See Jackson, *Free Negro Labor and Property Holding in Virginia*, 220.

61. Russell, *Free Negro in Virginia*, 95n, 151.

62. Johnson, *Diary*, December 24, 1835, 87; and December 27, 1835, 88.

63. Johnson, *Diary*, February 7, 1841, 317. Historian Douglas Bristol reads these acts from Johnson's perspective, which completely obscures the ways his apprentices navigated their bondage. To explain "William & John & Bill Nix's" decision to stay out after 10 P.M., Bristol claims the surplus funds Johnson allowed them to keep from a day's receipts "apparently went to their heads." Bristol describes Johnson's relationship with Bill Winston, his enslaved apprentice, as one of paternalism. He claims, "Winston viewed Johnson as a surrogate father," and describes Winston's unsavory behavior (such as altercations with other apprentices) as "independent streaks" that could be "trying at times" for Johnson, who had to perform his "role as disciplinarian" by slapping and whipping Winston and other apprentices when they did not "behave." Johnson may have had affection for Winston, possibly hoping to groom him into a successful barber like himself, but Winston was still enslaved. The problem with

paternalism is that it usually privileges the master's good will. Bristol, *Knights of the Razor*, 46–47.

64. On paternalism, see Eugene Genovese, *Roll, Jordan, Roll: The World the Slaves Made* (New York: Vintage Books, 1974). A number of scholars have criticized the paternalism framework of the master-slave relationship. See Manisha Sinha, "Eugene D. Genovese: The Mind of a Marxist Conservative," *Radical History Review* 88 (Winter 2004): 4-29; Johnson, *Soul by Soul*, 24-29; James D. Anderson, "Aunt Jemima in Dialectics: Genovese on Slave Culture," *Journal of Negro History* 61, no. 1 (1976): 99-114; Michael Tadman, "The Persistent Myth of Paternalism: Historians and the Nature of Master-Slave Relations in the American South," *Sage Race Relations Abstracts* 23 (February 1998): 7-23; George Frederickson, "The Skeleton in the Closet," *New York Review of Books*, November 2, 2000, 61-66; Michael Tadman, *Speculators and Slaves: Masters, Traders, and Slaves in the Old South* (Madison: University of Wisconsin Press, 1989); Kathleen M. Brown, *Good Wives, Nasty Wenches, and Anxious Patriarchs: Gender, Race, and Power in Colonial Virginia* (Chapel Hill: University of North Carolina Press, 1996), esp. 328-334.

65. Johnson, *Diary*, February 23, 1836, 103.

66. Johnson, *Diary*, July 24, 1840, 286-287.

67. Johnson, *Diary*, August 10, 1840, 289; September 12, 1841, 347; October 1, 1842, 406-407; January 26, 1843, 424; August 14, 1843, 444; August 23, 1843, 445-446; August 24, 1843, 446; and December 19, 1843, 467-468.

68. Johnson, *Diary*, January 1, 1844, 470.

69. Davis and Hogan, *Barber of Natchez*, 91.

70. Johnson, *Diary*, October 5, 1841, 350; October 9, 1841, 351.

71. Richard C. Wade, *Slavery in the Cities; The South, 1820-1860* (New York: Oxford University Press, 1964), 274–275; Savannah, Minutes of the Council, October 15, 1822, Mss., City Hall, Savannah, Georgia. Black workers were also pushed out of unskilled jobs in the South, though primarily in cities with large Creole populations like New Orleans, Savannah, or Mobile, or border cities such as Baltimore or Richmond.

72. Brenda Buchanan, "'The Art and Mystery of Making Gun Powder': The English Experience in the Seventeenth and Eighteenth Centuries," in *The Heirs of Archimedes: Science and the Art of War Through the Age of Enlightenment*, ed. Brett D. Steele and Tamera Dorland (Cambridge, Mass.: MIT Press, 2005), 233-274.

73. Briston, *Knights of the Razor*, 81; Wade, *Slavery in the Cities*, 40-43; "Barbershop Ordinance for Slaves, Lashes for Penalties, about November 1, 1856," *Interesting Transcriptions from the City Documents of the City of Mobile for 1859-1869*, Washington, D.C.: Works Progress Administration, Municipal and Court Records Project, 1939, 197.

74. Quoted in Richard Wade, *Slavery in the Cities: The South, 1820-1860* (New York: Oxford University Press, 1964), 48–49.

75. Bobby Lovett, *The African-American History of Nashville, Tennessee, 1780-1930* (Fayetteville: University of Arkansas Press, 1999), 11–12; Schweninger, *Black Property Owners in the South*, 50.

76. *Autobiography of James Thomas*, 1-8; John Hope Franklin and Loren Schweninger, *In Search of the Promised Land: A Slave Family in the Old South* (New York: Oxford University Press, 2006), 11-45; Lovett, *African-American History of Nashville*, 10-11.

77. Ira Berlin, *Slaves No More: Three Essays on Emancipation and the Civi War* (Cambridge: Cambridge Univerity Press, 1992), 138-147.

78. *Autobiography of James Thomas*, 1-8; Lovett, *African-American History of Nashville*, 10-11.

79. Jackson, *Free Negro Labor and Property Holding in Virginia,* 23.

80. Loren Schweninger ed., *Race, Slavery, and Free Blacks: Series I, Petitions to Southern Legislatures, 1777–1867* microfilm (Bethesda, Md.: University Publications of America, 1999), Mississippi, 1829, reel 03, frame 0367; quote from Virginia, 1837, reel 20, frame 0548. See also Virginia, 1815, reel 17, frame 0775, 1834, reel 20, frame 0116, 1836, reel 20, frame 0419; Texas, 1839, reel 15, frame 0082, 1842, reel 07, frame 0169 (hereafter *Race, Slavery, and Free Blacks*).

81. These concerns were certainly not limited to barbers. In 1850, Harriet Cook, a black washerwoman, received the support of thirty-nine white men to remain in Loudoun County, Virginia, arguing, "It would be a serious inconvenience to a number of the citizens of Leesburg to be deprived of her services as a washerwoman and in other capacities in which in consequence of her gentility, trustworthiness and skill she is exceedingly useful." For white patrons, Cook was "exceedingly useful" as a "gentile" service worker. Jones, *American Work,* 203–204.

82. Quoted in Judith Kelleher Schafer, *Becoming Free, Remaining Free: Manumission and Enslavement in New Orleans, 1846–1862* (Baton Rouge: Louisiana University Press, 2003), 135.

83. *Race, Slavery, and Free Blacks,* North Carolina, 1833, reel 06, frame 0387.

84. Maguire interview, 274–275. Eliza Potter, a free black northern hairdresser, often traveled to New Orleans to dress hair. She met there an enslaved hairdresser, Louise, who "was sold five different times, for a thousand dollars each time, and, by each of her owners, promised her freedom whenever she had made the thousand dollars and given it to them." With each owner, as soon as Louise saved 85 to 90 percent of the amount to purchase her freedom, he sold her to another slave owner, starting the cycle again. According to Potter, Louise "lost her reason, and is now a lunatic." See Eliza Potter, *A Hairdresser's Experience in High Life,* (Cincinnatti, 1859), 253–254.

85. Still, *The Underground Railroad,* 335.

86. Still, *The Underground Railroad,* 150–152.

87. Throgmorton interview, 434–436.

88. As historian Richard Wade has noted, "Cities offered some slaves an uneasy sanctuary from the master, as well as a springboard to freedom beyond." Wade, *Slavery in the Cities,* 218.

89. John Hope Franklin and Loren Schweninger, *Runaway Slaves: Rebels on the Plantation* (New York: Oxford University Press, 1999), 185–187.

90. H. Robert Baker, *The Rescue of Joshua Glover: A Fugitive Slave, the Constitution, and the Coming of the Civil War* (Athens: Ohio University Press, 2006); *Fugitive Slaves and American Courts: The Pamphlet Literature* ed. Paul Finkelman (New York: Garland Pub., 1988).

91. Franklin and Schweninger, *Runaway Slaves,* 80. On slave runaways, see also Blassingame, *The Slave Community,* 192-222.

92. Still, *The Underground Railroad,* 427–428.

93. Benjamin Drew, *A North-Side View of Slavery. The Refugee: or the Narratives of Fugitive Slaves in Canada. Related by Themselves, with an Account of the History and Condition of the Colored Population of Upper Canada* (Boston: John P. Jewett and Company, 1856), 85.

94. Brown thought England was near New Orleans because he heard people say it was "only just across the water." John Brown, *Slave Life in Georgia: A Narrative of the Life, Sufferings, and Escape of John Brown, a Fugitive Slave, Now in England,* ed. Louis Alexis Chamerovow (London: W. M. Watts, 1855), 100-101.

95. Buchanan, *Black Life on the Mississippi,* 45; J. Blaine Hudson, "Crossing the Dark Line: Fugitive Slaves and the Underground Railroad in Louisville and North-Central Kentucky," *Filson History Quarterly* 75, no. 1 (Winder 2001): 33–83.

96. James Forten to William Lloyd Garrison, May 6, 1832, in C. Peter Ripley, ed., *Black*

Abolitionist Papers, Vol. 3 (Chapel Hill: University of North Carolina Press, 1991), 85–86n5, 88–89. Cassey was treasurer of the American Moral Reform Society.

97. *Register of Trades of the Colored People in the City of Philadelphia and Districts* (Philadelphia: Merihew and Gunn, 1838), 6-7.

98. Harris, *In the Shadow of Slavery,* 170–216.

99. Switala, *Underground Railroad in Pennsylvania,* 82; Glascoe, ed., *The WPA History of the Negro in Pittsburgh,* 59.

100. In *Black Bostonians: Family Life and Community Struggle in the Antebellum North* (New York: Holmes & Meier, 1979), James and Lois Horton suggest that black customers frequented Peter Howard's barber shop in Boston for shaves, but the shop was also a space where patrons and other members of the community exchanged pertinent news. They further claim that abolitionists could often be found discussing the abolition movement in Howard's shop, which was also a station on the Underground Railroad. They cite John Daniels, *In Freedom's Birthplace,* for this information; however, Daniels does not actually provide a source citation for his discussion of Howard. Therefore, there is no clear evidence that black customers actually frequented Howard's shop. It is certainly possible they did because white abolitionists may not have cared one way or the other. Nonetheless, I am left to believe that Horton and Horton assumed Howard's shop was the kind of bustling space for black men that they are today. They do cite a Civil War pension record of a veteran who enlisted in a Massachusetts black regiment in another black barber's shop. This shop might have been read alongside Howard's shop. See Horton and Horton, *Black Bostonians,* 36–37, 142n48; John Daniels, *In Freedom's Birthplace* (New York: Arno Press, 1969), 57.

101. Switala, *Underground Railroad in Pennsylvania,* 86.

102. Switala, *Underground Railroad in Pennsylvania,* 88.

103. Benjamin Quarles, *Black Abolitionists* (New York: Oxford University Press, 1969), 145.

104. Joseph A. Borome, Jacob C. White, Robert B. Ayres, and J. M. McKim, "The Vigilant Committee of Philadelphia," *Pennsylvania Magazine of History and Biography,* 92, no. 3 (July 1968): 351.

105. Quarles, *Black Abolitionists,* 37.

106. Frederick Douglass, "Persecution on Account of Faith, Persecution on Account of Color: An Address Delivered in Rochester, New York, on January 1851," *North Star,* January 30, 1851 reprinted in *The Frederick Douglass Papers: Series One: Speeches, Debates, and Interviews Volume 2: 1847-54,* ed. John W. Blassingame (New Haven, Conn.: Yale Univesity Press, 1982), 296. See also Erasmus Wilson, ed., *Standard History of Pittsburg, Pennsylvania* (Chicago: H. R. Cornell and Company, 1898), 821.

107. "Fugitive Slave Excitement in Manchester, N. H.—Fatal Affray," *New York Times,* June 13, 1854.

108. Still, *The Underground Railroad,* 106–107.

109. Trotter, *River Jordan,* 45; Harris, *In the Shadow of Slavery,* 171.

110. Emma Lou Thornbrough, *The Negro in Indiana Before 1900: A Study of a Minority* (Bloomington: Indiana University Press, 1985), 105.

111. "George DeBaptiste, His Death Yesterday-Sketches of His Active and Eventful Life-He Was Formerly a Servant of President Harrison-His Connection with the Underground Railway-His Efforts to Rescue Negroes from Slavery," *Detroit Advertiser and Tribune,* February 23, 1875; Thornbrough, *The Negro in Indiana Before 1900,* 42; David M. Katzman, *Before the Ghetto: Black Detroit in the Nineteenth Century* (Urbana: University of Illinois Press, 1973), 14.

112. *Autobiography of James Thomas,* 74, 90.

113. Quote from Wendell Phillips Dabney, "Rough Autobiographical Sketch of His Boyhood Years," (typscript, n.d.), 67, Ohio Historical Society, Columbus; see also Matthew L. Cushman, "Free Black Barbers in Antebellum Richmond: A Cut Above the Rest" (unpublished paper, Virginia Commonwealth University, 2004).

114. Dabney, *Rough Autobiographical Sketch,* 83.

115. Dabney, *Rough Autobiographical Sketch,* 84.

116. Dabney, *Rough Autobiographical Sketch,* 121.

117. Harris, *In the Shadow of Slavery,* 97–98, 231–232.

118. Henry Bradshaw Fearon, *Sketches of America: A Narrative of a Journey of Five Thousand Miles Through the Eastern and Western States of America: Contained in Eight Reports Addressed to the Thirty-nine English Families by whom the Author was Deputed, in June 1817, to Ascertain Whether Any, and What Part of the United States Would be Suitable for Their Residence: With Remarks on Mr. Birkbeck's "Notes" and "Letters"* (London: Longman, Hurst, Rees, Orme, and Brown, 1819), 58–60; Leon F. Litwack, *North of Slavery; The Negro in the Free States, 1790-1860* (Chicago: University of Chicago Press, 1961), 181.

119. Isaac Candler, *A Summary View of America Comprising a Description of the Face of the Country* (London: T. Cadell, 1824), 284, quoted in Candler, *Summary View of America,* 284, quoted in Jones, *American Work,* 285.

120. David Walker, *Walker's Appeal to the Coloured Citizens of the World, but in particular, and very expressly, to those of the United States of America* (New York: Hill and Wang, 1965), 29.

121. Walker, *Walker's Appeal,* 232; Litwack, *North of Slavery,* 175.

122. *Report of the Proceedings of the Colored National Convention, Held at Cleveland, Ohio, on Wednesday, September 6, 1848* (Rochester: John Dick, North Star Office, 1848), 5, quote from 13 (hereafter Colored National Convention, 1848) in Howard Holman Bell, *Minutes of the Proceedings of the National Negro Conventions, 1830-1864* (New York: Arno Press, 1969); see also Patrick Real, *Black Identity and Black Protest in the Antebellum North* (Chapel Hill: University of North Carolina Press, 2002), 35–36.

123. Colored National Convention, 1848, 17; Litwack, *North of Slavery,* 174; Harris, *In the Shadow of Slavery,* 234.

124. Colored National Convention, 1848, 5; Real, *Black Identity and Black Protest,* 35.

125. Colored National Convention, 1848, 19.

126. *Anti-Slavery Bugle,* August 24, 1850, quoted in Joan R. Sherman, *Invisible Poets: Afro-Americans of the Nineteenth Century* (Urbana: University of Illinois Press, 1974), 42.

127. Martin Delany, *The Condition, Elevation, Emigration, and Destiny of the Colored People of the United States* (1852; repr., New York: Humanity Books, 2004), 145–146.

128. Delany, *The Condition, Elevation, Emigration, and Destiny of the Colored People,* 44, 46, 192-193. Barbers valued education as much as Delany. Black barbers either educated their children in the business of barbering or used their remuneration from barbering to send their children to school. In the early 1840s, Fountain Lewis Sr. arrived in Cincinnati and gained a job in a Frenchman's barber shop. When his employer moved from the city, Lewis took over the shop. His son, Fountain Jr., entered the business with him when he came of age. As men of means, black barbers had the resources to send their children to school. Accoding to historian Nikki Taylor, in Cincinnati's First Ward, which was heavily populated with black barbers in 1850, 83 percent of barbers' children attended school. See Nikki Marie Taylor, *Frontiers of Freedom: Cincinnati's Black Community, 1802-1868* (Athens: Ohio University Press, 2005), 134. For these Cincinnati barbers, their occupation presented black men with a multitude of possibilities, which included formal education in school and informal education in their

barber shops. Yet, many black leaders debated the respectability of barbering as a manly profession in a free society.

129. William Wells Brown, *The Black Man, His Antecedents, His Genius, and His Achievements* (New York: Thomas Hamilton, 1863), 152.

130. *Pennsylvania Freeman*, September 29, 1853, 154.

131. Sherman, *Invisible Poets*, 43. On Whitfield's writings see James Monroe Whitfield, *The Works of James M. Whitfield: American and Other Writings by a Nineteenth-Century African American Poet*, ed. Robert S. Levine and Ivy G. Wilson (Chapel Hill: University of North Carolina Press, 2011).

132. "Proceedings of the Convention, Of the Colored Freemen of Ohio, Held in Cincinnati, January 14, 15, 16, 17, and 19, 1852," in Philip S. Foner and George E. Walker, eds., *Proceedings of the Black State Conventions, 1840-1865*, Vol. 1 (Philadelphia: Temple University Press, 1979), 277, quoted in Litwack, *North of Slavery*, 181. On the call for blacks to acquire wealth see "Proceedings of the Convention, Of the Colored Freemen of Ohio," in *Proceedings of the Black State Conventions*, 276. African Americans at a Pennsylvaia convention passed a similar resolution in 1865. See "Proceedings of the State Equal Right' Convention, of the Colored People of Pennsylvania, Held in the City of Harrisburg, February 8th, 9th, and 10th, 1865, Together With a Few of the Arguments Presented Suggesting the Necessity for Holding the Convention, and an Address of the Colored State Convention to the People of Pennsylvania," in *Proceedings of the Black State Conventions*, 156-157.

133. First quote from Frederick Douglass, "Learn Trades or Starve," *Frederick Douglass' Paper*, March 4, 1853; second quote from True Wesleyan, "The Liberty Party," *Frederick Douglass' Paper*, March 4, 1853.

134. Joe Trotter, *River Jordan: African American Urban Life in the Ohio Valley* (Lexington: University Press of Kentucky, 1998), 17; Harris, *In the Shadow of Slavery*, 250; Herman D. Bloch, "The New York City Negro and Occupational Eviction, 1860-1910," *International Review of Social History*, 5, no. 1 (1960): 28; Robert Ernst, *Immigrant Life in New York City, 1825-1863* (New York: King's Crown Press, 1949), 104, 216.

135. Bloch, "The New York City Negro and Occupational Eviction," 30; Horton and Horton, *Black Bostonians*, 77-78.

136. "Make Your Sons Mechanics and Farmers—Not Waiters, Porters, and Barbers," *Frederick Douglass' Paper*, March 18, 1853. See also Harris, *In the Shadow of Slavery*, 240-241.

137. Quotes from "Learn Trades or Starve," *Frederick Douglass' Paper*, March 4, 1853; "Letter from Benjamin Coates," *Frederick Douglass' Paper*, March 11, 1853.

138. "Mr. Uriah Boston," *Frederick Douglass' Paper*, April 1, 1853; "Uriah Boston Again," *Frederick Douglass' Paper*, April 15, 1853. For background on Boston see Ripley, ed., *Black Abolitionist Papers*, Vol. 3, 279-280.

139. Uriah Boston, "Mr. F. Douglass Sir.," *Frederick Douglass' Paper*, April 22, 1853.

140. Lewis Woodson, "Doing Something," *Frederick Douglass' Paper*, October 28, 1853.

141. Robert J. Cottrol, *The Afro-Yankees: Providence's Black Community in the Antebellum Era* (Westport, Conn.: Greenwood Press, 1982).

142. Ripley, ed., *The Black Abolitionist Papers*, Vol. 4, 278-280; Philip S. Foner and George Walker, eds., *Proceedings of the Black State Conventions, 1840-1865*, Vol. 1 (Philadelphia: Temple University Press, 1979), 7-15, 80-89; *Proceedings of the National Convention of Colored People and Their Friends, Held in Troy, N. Y., on the 6th, 7th, 8th and 9th October, 1847* (Troy, NY: Steam Press, 1847) in Bell, ed., *Minutes of the Proceedings of the National Negro Conventions*; "The Meeting," *The Colored American*, June 6, 1840; "A Call for a Convention of the Colored Inhabitants of the State of New York," *The Colored American*, July 4, 1840; "Poughkeepsie," *The*

Colored American, July 25, 1840; "Celebration of West India Emancipation in Poughkeepsie," *The Colored American,* August 21, 1841. See also the following articles in *Frederick Douglass's Paper:* "Nominations for Members of State Council," October 28, 1853; "Statement of Votes Cast for Members of N.Y. State Council," December 23, 1853; Uriah Boston, "Friend Douglass: Dear Sir—Allow me to Present a Few Thoughts," April 20, 1855; "Classified Advertisements: Call for a State Convention of the Colored People of the State of New York," July 27, 1855; quote from "The Troy Convention," September 14, 1855; "Meeting of the Colored Citizens," October 5, 1855.

143. "Death of Uriah Boston," *Dutchess Courier,* June 16, 1889; *Boyd's Poughkeepsie Directory, Containing the Names of the Citizens; A Business Directory; Record of the Rebellion of 1861, With Sketches of American and Other Wars; And an Appendix of Much Useful Information* compiled by Andrew Boyd (Poughkeepsie: Andrew Boyd, 1862), 139.

144. *Vail's Poughkeepsie City Directory for 1874-1875,* compiled by J. P. A. Vail (Poughkeepsie: Vail and Co., 1874), 32; *Vail's Poughkeepsie City Directory for 1880-'81,* compiled by J. P. A. Vail (Poughkeepsie: John P. A. Vail and Co., 1880), 31; 1850 U.S. census, population schedule, Poughkeepsie City, Dutchess County, New York, dwelling 266, family 355, Uriah Boston household; National Archives microfilm publication M432, roll 497; digital image, Ancestry. com, http://www.ancestory.com (accessed 28 March 2011); 1880 U.S. census, population schedule, Poughkeepsie City, Dutchess County, New York, Enumeration District 054, sheet 28, dwelling 214, family 306, Uriah Boston household; National Archives microfilm publication T9, roll 825; digital image, Ancestry.com, http://www.ancestory.com (accessed 28 March 2011).

145. Xiomara Santamarina points out in her reading of Potter's book that "in her representations of her work Potter appears at an advantage relative to her white female employers not as their racial subordinate: her experience serves to display the foibles of her 'betters.'" Santamarina, *Belabored Professions: Narratives of African American Working Womanhood* (Chapel Hill: University of North Carolina Press, 2005), 112.

146. Potter, *A Hairdresser's Experience in High Life,* 27.

147. Potter, *A Hairdresser's Experience in High Life,* 68–69, 201–202.

148. Potter, *A Hairdresser's Experience in High Life,* 163.

Chapter 2. The Politics of "Color-Line" Barber Shops After the Civil War

1. Zora Neale Hurston, *Dust Tracks on a Road, an Autobiography* (1942; repr., New York: HarperCollins, 1995). The 1918 city directory lists three shops: 714 14th Street, N.W.; 1312 F Street, N.W.; 429 12th Street, N.W. The 1919 district city directory listed only four shops owned by Robinson, all of them located downtown: 1312 F Street, N.W.; 416 12th Street, NW; 1743 Pennsylvania Ave., N.W.; and 1410 G Street, N.W. Whether Hurston slightly exaggerated or Robinson decided to list only his marquee shops, the average barber did not own a chain of shops. See *Boyd's Directory of the District of Columbia 1918* (Washington, D.C.; R. L. Polk and Company, 1918), 1869; *Boyd's Directory of the District of Columbia 1919* (Washington, D.C.: R. L. Polk and Company, 1919), 1945.

2. Hurston, *Dust Tracks on a Road,* 134–135. Robinson lived at 1762 U Street, N.W.

3. Hurston, *Dust Tracks on a Road,* 136.

4. On patron-client relations see S. N. Eisenstadt and Louis Roniger, "Patron-Client Relations as a Model of Structuring Social Exchange," *Comparative Studies in Society and History* 22, no. 1 (January 1980): 42-77; James C. Scott, "Patron-Client Politics and Political Change in Southeast Asia," *American Political Science Review* 66, no. 1 (March 1972): 91-113. On the "etiquette of civility" and patron-clientage see William Chafe, *Civilities and Civil*

Rights: Greensboro, North Carolina, and the Black Struggle for Equality (New York: Oxford University Press, 1980). See also Beth Bates Thompkins, *Pullman Porters and the Rise of Protest Politics in Black American, 1925-1945* (Chapel Hill: University of North Carolina Press, 2001).

5. Eric Foner, "The Meaning of Freedom in the Age of Emancipation," *Journal of American History* 81 (1994), 435–460.

6. Tera Hunter, *To 'Joy My Freedom: Black Women's Lives and Labors After the Civil War* (Cambridge, Mass.: Harvard University Press, 1997); Myra B. Young Armstead, *"Lord, Please Don't Take Me in August": African Americans in Newport and Saratoga Springs, 1870-1930* (Urbana: University of Illinois Press, 1999).

7. W. E. B. Du Bois, *The Philadelphia Negro: A Social Study,* centennial ed. (1899; Philadelphia: University of Pennsylvania Press, 1996), 144.

8. Lorenzo J. Greene and Carter G. Woodson, *The Negro Wage Earner* (Washington, D.C.: Association for the Study of Afro American Life and History, 1930), 31.

9. David A. Gerber, *Black Ohio and the Color Line, 1860-1915* (Urbana: University of Illinois Press, 1976), 68–71.

10. George C. Wright, *Life Behind a Veil: Blacks in Louisville, Kentucky, 1865-1930* (Baton Rouge: Louisiana State University Press, 1985), 39; Ira Berlin, *Slaves Without Masters: The Free Negro in the Antebellum South* (New York: Vintage Books, 1974), 384; Thomas Holt, *Black over White: Negro Political Leadership in South Carolina During Reconstruction* (Urbana: University of Illinois, 1977), 15–16; Eric Foner, *Freedom's Lawmakers: A Directory of Black Officeholders During Reconstruction* (New York: Oxford University Press, 1993).

11. On the black elite, see Willard Gatewood, *Aristocrats of Color: The Black Elite, 1880–1920,* (1990; repr., Fayetteville: University of Arkansas Press, 2000); Jacqueline Moore, *Leading the Race: The Transformation of the Black Elite in the Nation's Capital, 1880–1920* (Charlottesville: University Press of Virginia, 1999); Kevin Gaines, *Uplifting the Race: Black Leadership, Politics, and Culture in the Twentieth Century* (Chapel Hill: University of North Carolina Press, 1996).

12. Bill Reese, interview by Sadie B. Hornsby, ed. Sarah H. Hall and John N. Booth, "I Cater to Colored People," *The American Slave: A Composite Autobiography,* gen. ed. George P. Rawick, vol. 4, *Georgia Narratives,* part 2, 513 (hereafter Reese interview).

13. Andrew R. McCants, *John Merrick: A Biographical Sketch* (Durham: The Seeman Printery, 1920), 31–32; Walter B. Weare, *Black Business in the New South: A Social History of the North Carolina Mutual Insurance Company* (Urbana: University of Illinois Press, 1973), 20–80; Booker T. Washington, *The Story of the Negro: The Rise of the Race from Slavery* (New York: Doubleday, Page, 1909), 37.

14. Alexa Benson Henderson, *Atlanta Life Insurance Company: Guardian of Black Economic Dignity* (Tuscaloosa: University of Alabama Press, 1990), 21–23.

15. George A. Myers and James Ford Rhodes, *The Barber and the Historian:The Correspondence of George A. Myers and James Ford Rhodes, 1910-1923* ed. John A. Garraty (Columbus: Ohio Historical Society, 1956), xv–xviii; Gerber, *Black Ohio and the Color Line,* 82; *Cleveland Directory for the Year Ending June 1880* (Cleveland: The Cleveland Directory Company, 1879), 557; The Ohio Historical Records Survey Project, Service Division, Work Projects Administration, *Historic Sites of Cleveland: Hotels and Taverns,* (Columbus: The Ohio Historical Records Survey Project, August 1942, 615.

16. Holt, *Black over White,* 15–16; Foner, *Freedom's Lawmakers.*

17. On black women's political leadership at the turn of the twentieth century, see Elsa Barkley Brown, "Negotiating and Transforming the Public Sphere: African American

Political Life in the Transition from Slavery to Freedom," in *The Black Public Sphere: A Public Culture Book* (Chicago: University of Chicago Press, 1995), 111–150; Ann Gordon with Bettye Collier Thomas, eds., *African American Women and the Vote, 1837–1965* (Amherst: University of Massachusetts, 1997); Glenda Gilmore, *Gender and Jim Crow: Women and the Politics of White Supremacy in North Carolina, 1896–1920* (Chapel Hill: University of North Carolina, 1998); Evelyn Brooks Higginbotham, *Righteous Discontent: The Women's Movement in the Black Baptist Church, 1880–1920* (Cambridge, Mass.: Harvard University Press, 1993).

18. Reese interview, 513.

19. Reese interview, 515.

20. George Knox, *Slave and Freeman: The Autobiography of George L. Knox*, ed. Willard Gatewood (Lexington: University Press of Kentucky, 1979), 186 (hereafter Knox, *Autobiography*).

21. Du Bois, *The Philadelphia Negro*, 346.

22. W. Scott Hall, "The Journeymen Barbers' International Union of America" (Ph.D. dissertation, Johns Hopkins University, 1936), 69.

23. W. E. B. Du Bois, ed., *The Negro in Business; Report of a Social Study Made Under the Direction of Atlanta University; Together with the Proceedings of the Fourth Conference for the Study of the Negro Problems, held at Atlanta University, May 30–31, 1899* (Atlanta: Atlanta University, 1899), 9, 16.

24. Fred M. Holycross, "The American Barbershop: Changing Gender Roles and the Modification of Masculinity" (master's thesis, University of Notre Dame, 1990), 15–16; Richard A. Plumb and Milton V. Lee, *Ancient and Honorable Barber Profession* (Indianapolis: Barbers, Beauticians, and Allied Industries International Association, 1974), 18–19.

25. Reese interview, 515-516.

26. See advertisements in Andrew F. Hilyer, *The Twentieth Century Union League Directory: A Compilation of the Efforts of the Colored People of Washington For Social Betterment* (Washington, D.C., 1901), 17.

27. Alonzo Herndon, Barber Shop Ledger, 1902, Alonzo Herndon unprocessed collection, The Herndon Home, Atlanta, Georgia.

28. On urbanization and the New South, see Don Doyle, *New Men, New Cities, New South: Atlanta, Nashville, Charleston, Mobile, 1860–1910* (Chapel Hill: University of North Carolina Press, 1990); David Goldfield, *Region, Race, and Cities: Interpreting the Urban South* (Baton Rouge: Louisiana State University Press, 1997); Blake McKelvey, *The Urbanization of America, 1860–1915* (New Brunswick, N.J.: Rutgers University Press, 1963); Howard Rabinowitz, *Race, Ethnicity, and Urbanization* (Columbia: University of Missouri Press, 1994). On Atlanta as a New South city, see James Michael Russell, *Atlanta, 1847–1890: City Building in the Old South and the New* (Baton Rouge: Louisiana State University Press, 1988), especially 232–258.

29. Quote from McCants, *John Merrick*, 32. See also Leslie Brown, *Upbuilding Black Durham: Gender, Class, and Black Community Development in the Jim Crow South* (Chapel Hill: University of North Carolina Press, 2008), 36, 153.

30. *Atlanta City Directory, 1889* (Atlanta: R.L. Polk & Co., 1889), 990; Joseph O. Jewell, *Race, Social Reform, and the Making of a Middle Class: The American Missionary Association and Black Atlanta, 1870-1900* (Lanham, Md.: Rowman & Littlefield, 2007), 71-72; Allison Dorsey, *To Build Our Lives Together: Community Formation in Black Atlanta, 1875-1906* (Athens: University of Georgia Press, 2004), 51.

31. Henderson, *Atlanta Life Insurance Company*, 21–23.

32. McCants suggests that Merrick owned two shops for black patrons; however, no other sources account for these shops. McCants, *John Merrick*, 32–34, 39–40. Historian Walter B.

Weare, in *Black Business in the New South*, asserted that Merrick's white patrons "thought of him more as the competent Negro businessman than as 'John, the white man's barber.'" Weare, *Black Business in the New South*, 20–80.

33. Herndon Biographical Statement, Herndon Family Papers, quoted in Carole Merritt, *The Herndons: An Atlanta Family* (Athens: University of Georgia Press, 2002), 34–35.

34. "Betts, Atlanta's Oldest Barber, Is Now Dead," *Atlanta Constitution*, November 19, 1901; Merritt, *The Herndons*, 35.

35. Ad reprinted in Edward R. Carter, *The Black Side: A Partial History of the Business, Religious and Educational Side of the Negro in Atlanta, GA.* (Atlanta, 1894), image insert after p. 184; "Bob Steele is Dead," *Atlanta Constitution*, August 31, 1899.

36. Merritt, *The Herndons*, 36.

37. Henderson, *Atlanta Life Insurance Company*, 21–23; Alexa Benson Henderson, "Atlanta Life Insurance Company—Alonzo Herndon and Norris Bumstead Herndon," and Juliet E. K. Walker, "Insurance Companies," both in Juliet E. K. Walker, ed., *Encyclopedia of African American Business History* (Westport, Conn.: Greenwood Press, 1999), 39, 297.

38. His other lenders included businessman H. S. Blossom; Robert Rhodes, brother of James Ford; A. L. Johnson; W. Chisholm; and H. R. Groff. Gerber, *Black Ohio and the Color Line*, 308, 345; The Ohio Historical Records Survey Project, *Historic Sites of Cleveland: Hotels and Taverns* (Columbus: The Ohio Historical Records Survey Project, 1942), 327; "George A. Myers Gone!" *Cleveland Gazette*, February 8, 1930. Myers's ledger lists the nine men who financially assisted him in opening the barber shop. Quote from George Myers to James Rhodes, March 15, 1921, in Myers and Rhodes, *Barber and Historian*, 126–127.

39. Christopher Robert Reed, *Black Chicago's First Century*, Vol. 1: *1833–1900* (Columbia: University of Missouri Press, 2005), 202.

40. Charles Chesnutt, *The Colonel's Dream* (New York: Doubleday, Page, 1905), 21.

41. Chesnutt, *Colonel's Dream*, 79.

42. Chesnutt, *Colonel's Dream*, 80.

43. Chesnutt, *Colonel's Dream*, 84.

44. Chesnutt, *Colonel's Dream*, 84.

45. "The Doll" was originally submitted to *Atlantic Monthly* in early 1904, but was not accepted for publication. It was later published in *The Crisis* in 1912.

46. Sylvia Lyons Render, ed., *The Short Fiction of Charles W. Chesnutt* (Washington, D.C.: Howard University Press, 1981), 409.

47. Render, ed., *Short Fiction of Charles W. Chesnutt*, 412.

48. Martin Summers's discussion of the consumerist model of masculinity describes Forsyth's actions in Tom's shop. Summers, *Manliness and Its Discontents*.

49. This practice is what Homi Bhabha calls the duality of overlooking; the simultaneous process of surveillance and disavowal. Homi Bhabha, *The Location of Culture* (New York: Routledge, 1994), 236.

50. Knox, *Autobiography*, 9–10.

51. Knox, *Autobiography*, 107–108.

52. Hurston, *Dust Tracks on a Road*, 132.

53. *Xenia Gazette*, October 10, 1873.

54. Quoted in Howard Rabinowitz, *Race Relations in the Urban South, 1865–1890* (New York: Oxford University Press, 1978), 196 and Leon Litwack, *Trouble in Mind: Black Southerners in the Age of Jim Crow* (New York: Alfred A. Knopf, 1998), 142–143.

55. The Republican-dominated Congress enacted the 1866 act, over President Andrew Johnson's veto, to counteract the Black Codes that southern states imposed on newly freed

slaves. The act granted them citizenship rights such as to sue, make contracts, give evidence in court, and enter property transactions.

56. Eric Foner, *Reconstruction: America's Unfinished Revolution, 1863-1877* (New York: Harper & Row, 1988), 504–505; "Equal Rights," *Harpers Weekly*, January 20, 1872; "The Virginia Legislature," *New York Times*, January 6, 1874; "North Carolina Politics—Civil Rights," *New York Times*, June 1, 1874; "The Civil Rights Bill," *New York Times*, June 8, 1874.

57. *U.S. Statutes at Large*, XVI, 27, April 9, 1866, and, quote from, *U.S. Statutes at Large*, XVIII, March 1, 1875, 335, in Richard Bardolph, ed., *The Civil Rights Record: Black Americans and the Law, 1849-1970* (New York: Thomas Y. Crowell Company, 1970), 46–47, 54–55. On the Civil Rights Act of 1875 see Foner, *Reconstruction*, 532–534; James M. McPherson, "Abolitionists and the Civil Rights Act of 1875," *Journal of American History* 52, no. 3 (December 1965): 493–510; Bertram Wyatt-Brown, "The Civil Rights Act of 1875," *Western Political Quarterly* 18, no. 4 (December 1965): 763–775. For a detailed discussion of hotels and the Civil Rights Act, see A. K. Sandoval-Strausz, "Travelers, Strangers, and Jim Crow: Law, Public Accommodations, and Civil Rights in America," *Law and History Review* 23, no. 1 (2005); and Sandoval-Strausz, *Hotel: A History* (New Haven, Conn.: Yale University Press, 2007).

58. On the passage of the Civil Rights Act of 1875, see "The Civil Rights Bills: The Bill as Passed by the House Yesterday," *New York Times*, February 6, 1875; "Civil Rights Discussed," *New York Times*, February 28, 1875.

59. In most states, such as Kentucky and Tennessee, whites opposed the Civil Rights bill and proprietors vowed to disregard it. Some believed blacks were "decent" enough not to agitate on the issue. To prevent lawsuits, the Tennessee legislature abolished the right to sue for being "excluded from any hotel or public means of transportations, or place of amusement" to sue. Coincidentally, on March 23, 1875, Tennessee passed a law that gave a proprietor great latitude to exclude "any person, whom he shall for any reason whatever, choose not to entertain, carry, or admit, to his house, hotel, carriage, or means of transportation or place of amusement." Tennessee was the only Confederate state to escape Radical Reconstruction because it complied with congressional requirements to show repentance and profess loyalty to the Union. Wright, *Life Behind a Veil*, 55–58. For Tennessee's Jim Crow law, see *Acts of Tennessee, 1875* (ch. 130), 216, in Bardolph, ed., *Civil Rights Record*, 82–83.

60. "Threatened Prosecution of a Colored Barber in Washington for Refusing to Shave Two Colored Men," *New York Times*, March 6, 1875; "A Colored Barber Refuses to Operate Upon Another Colored Man," *New York Times,* March 20, 1875.

61. On Stewart's racial classification see 1880 U.S. census, population schedule, Washington, District of Columbia, Enumeration District 38, sheet 32, dwelling 245, family 292, Carter Stewart household; National Archives microfilm publication T9, roll 122; digital image, Ancestry.com, http://www.ancestry.com (accessed 2 January 2013). On Stewart and racial politics in D.C. during Reconstruction see Kate Masur, *An Example for All the Land: Emancipation and the Struggle over Equality in Washington, D.C.* (Chapel Hill: University of North Carolina Press, 2010), 154, 162

62. Laws of the District of Columbia, June 20, 1872, ch. 51, pp. 65–66, in Constance McLaughlin Green, *The Secret City: A History of Race Relations in the Nation's Capital* (Princeton: Princeton University Press, 1967), 109. On the 1872 law, see also Masur, *An Example for All the Land*, 229–230.

63. In Chicago, March 1875, two African Americans demanded, and were granted, seats in the "dress-circle" at McVicker's Theatre. A *New York Times* article concluded that J. H. McVicker, the white proprietor, faced a dilemma: "They do not want to lose the patronage of

fashionable people, nor can they afford to pay a heavy fine several times a night by refusing to obey the law." In Trenton, New Jersey, Horace Deyo and Henry Oregue were refused the opportunity to play pool at Peter Katzenbach's billiard saloon, which was attached to Trenton House hotel. The two men filed a complaint with U.S. Commissioner Shreve, who in turn dismissed the complaint on the grounds that saloons did not fall under the Civil Rights Act. According to the commissioner, this billiard room, like a barber shop in a hotel, was separate from the hotel business and "is a private business with which the law does not and cannot interfere." For northern struggles, see "Various Notes of Interest from Chicago—The Civil Rights Bill," *New York Times*, March 14, 1875; "City and Suburban News—Trenton" and "Civil Rights in Trenton," *New York Times*, March 26, 1875. See also the following *New York Times* articles: "Working of the Civil Rights Bill—A Test Case in this District," April 22, 1875; "Civil Rights in Pullman Cars," April 21, 1875; "Colored Children in the Schools—An Important Decision by a Brooklyn Judge," September 14, 1875; "A Case Under the Civil Rights Act," November 23, 1883.

64. "Editorial Article 5—No Title," *New York Times*, March 7, 1875.

65. See Jane Dailey, *Before Jim Crow: The Politics of Race in Postemancipation Virginia* (Chapel Hill: University of North Carolina Press, 2000), 84-88.

66. Benjamin F. Butler, "Gen. Butler on the Civil Rights Bill," *Harper's Weekly*, April 24, 1875.

67. Butler, "Gen. Butler on the Civil Rights Bill."

68. 43 Congressional Record 940 (1875) (statement of Rep. Benjamin Butler), quoted in A. Leon Higginbotham, Jr., *Shades of Freedom: Racial Politics and Presumptions of the American Legal Process* (New York: Oxford University Press, 1996), 96.

69. James Bryce, *American Commonwealth* (New York: Macmillan, 1909), 502–503.

70. Higginbotham, *Shades of Freedom*, 96–97.

71. Reverend J. C. Price, "Does the Negro Seek Social Equality," *Forum* 10 (January 1891): 562–564, quoted in Charles Wynes, *Race Relations in Virginia, 1870–1902* (Charlottesville: University of Virginia Press, 1961), 117–118.

72. As Nell Irvin Painter has pointed out, sex most effectively rallied white supremacists, regardless of class, to protect white womanhood from black men in the public sphere (politics, public accommodations, and public communications). To put it another way, the rhetoric of social equality meant race mixing and associating as equals, which would lead to black men having sex with and marrying white women. This widespread sexually charged rhetoric of social equality effectively united whites against equal rights and equal movement. See Nell Irvin Painter, "'Social Equality,' Miscegenation, Labor, and Power," in Norma V. Bartley, ed., *The Evolution of Southern Culture* (Athens: University of Georgia Press, 1988), 47-67.

73. For civil rights cases brought to court regarding jury discrimination, see "The Virginia Civil Rights Cases," *New York Times*, April 12, 1879; education, "The Civil Rights Bill—The Mixed School Question," *New York Times*, September 15, 1874.

74. Justice John Marshall Harlan was the sole dissenter. Civil Rights Cases, 109 U.S. 3 (1883), in Bardolph, ed., *Civil Rights Record*, 68–72. For newspaper accounts of the decision, see *New York Times*, "Civil Rights Cases Decided" and "The Civil Rights Act Void," October 16, 1883, "The Civil Rights Decision Regarded as a Step Backward," October 17, 1883.

75. In its 1885 Civil Rights Act, the Tennessee legislature made allowances for Jim Crow: "nothing herein contained shall be construed as interfering with the existing rights to provide separate accommodations and seats for colored and white persons at such places." See *Acts of Tennessee, 1885* (ch. 68), 124–125, in Bardolph, ed., *Civil Rights Record*, 126–127.

76. Massachusetts's 1885 civil rights legislation was amended to its 1865 and 1866 legislation;

it was amended again in 1895. New York State passed its civil rights legislation in 1873, and amended it in 1881, 1893, and 1895. Nebraska's 1885 legislation was amended in 1893. Iowa and Connecticut amended their 1884 laws in 1892 and 1905, respectively. Maine, New Hampshire, and Vermont did not enact civil rights legislation. See Leslie A. Schwalm, *Emancipation's Diaspora: Race and Reconstruction in the Upper Midwest* (Chapel Hill: University of North Carolina Press, 2009), 175-217.

77. *Illinois, Laws* (1885), 64, and (1897), 137, in Spear, *Black Chicago*, 41–42; *Public Acts of Michigan, 1885* (ch. 130), 131–32, in Bardolph, ed., *Civil Rights Record*, 128–129; Kenneth Kusmer, *A Ghetto Takes Shape: Black Cleveland, 1870-1915* (Urbana: University of Illinois Press, 1976), 53, 59; David M. Katzman, *Before the Ghetto: Black Detroit in the Nineteenth Century* (Urbana: University of Illinois Press, 1973), 98. Pennsylvania's law, enacted in 1887, did not list barber shops in its schedule. Laws of Pennsylvania (1887), 130–131; Du Bois, *Philadelphia Negro*, 418; Frank Quillin, *The Color Line in Ohio: A History of Race Prejudice in a Typical Northern State* (Ann Arbor, Mich.: G. Wahr, 1913), 104.

78. "Republican Makes Point Against Race Man," *Cleveland Gazette*, October 27, 1883; "J. W. G., Who Can Tell," *Cleveland Gazette*, December 1, 1883.

79. "From the Queen City: A Representative of the Gazette Visits Colored Barber Shops," *Cleveland Gazette*, June 14, 1884. On Ross's racial classification see 1870 U.S. census, population schedule, Cincinnati, Hamilton County, Ohio, sheet 147, William Ross household; National Archives microfilm publication M593, roll 1211; digital image, Ancestry.com, http://www.ancestry.com (accessed 2 January 2013).

80. Quoted in W. Laird Clowes, *Black America: A Study of the Ex-Slave and His Late Master* (London: Cassell & Company, 1891), 102. Robinson later became an ardent supporter of Booker T. Washington and publicly supported women's suffrage in the *National Baptist Magazine*. See Louis Harlan and Raymond Smock, eds., *The Booker T. Washington Papers, 1895–1898* (Urbana: University of Illinois Press, 1972); Higginbotham, *Righteous Discontent*, 147–148.

81. "From the Queen City: A Representative of the *Gazette* Visits Colored Barber Shops," *Cleveland Gazzette*, June 14, 1884.

82. "From the Queen City: A Representative of the *Gazette* Visits Colored Barber Shops." See also "To Whom Shall We Turn?" *Cleveland Gazette*, April 10, 1886; Gerber, *Black Ohio and the Color Line*, 80–81.

83. "The Detroit 'Plaindealer' on Colored Barbers," *Cleveland Gazette*, November 17, 1883.

84. Quotes from "Knox as a Race Man," *Indianapolis World*, September 24, 1892. On Levi Christy and the *Indianapolis World*, see Knox, *Autobiography*, 24-25; Thornbrough, *Negro in Indiana*, 384-385, 388.

85. R. H. C., "J. V. C., of Pittsburgh, Gets an Answer on the Barber Question," *Cleveland Gazette*, December 8, 1883. This letter was in response to J. V. C.'s letter in the *Gazette* on December 1, 1883.

86. Juliet E. K. Walker uses this term to understand the ways slaves and free blacks navigated the racial constraints of the market economy. See Juliet E. K. Walker, "Prejudices, Profits, Privileges: Commentaries on 'Captive Capitalists,' Antebellum Entrepreneurs," *Essays in Economic and Business History* 8 (1990): 399–422.

87. C. H. C., "Barber Question—An Answer to R. H. C. by a Fellow Citizen," *Cleveland Gazette*, December 15, 1883.

88. "Encouraging," *Western Appeal*, St. Paul, April 30, 1887, in Philip S. Foner and Ronald L. Lewis, eds., *The Black Worker: A Documentary History from Colonial Times to Present*, Vol. 4: *The Black Worker During the Era of the American Federation of Labor and the Railroad Brotherhoods* (Philadelphia: Temple University Press, 1979), 273.

89. Francis H. Warren, comp., *Michigan Manual of Freedmen's Progress* (Detroit, 1915), 123 quoted in Katzman, *Before the Ghetto,* 98.

90. George Nash to Harry Smith, August 9, 1897, reel 2, frame 33, George A. Myers Papers, 1890-1929 (microfilm) Ohio Historical Society, Columbus, Ohio (hereafter Myers Papers).

91. Richard R. Wright to George Myers, October 9, 1897, reel 2, frame 631, Myers Papers.

92. Myers to Green, January 28, 1903, John P. Green Papers, Western Reserve Historical Society, Cleveland, Ohio (hereafter Green Papers). There is no evidence of the interaction of white and black customers in the barber shop, not to mention the nature and dynamics of the discourse.

93. George Campbell, *White and Black: The Outcome of a Visit to the United States* (London: Chatto & Windus, 1879), 299.

94. Paul Laurence Dunbar, *The Sport of the Gods* (New York: Penguin Putnam, 1999), 1.

95. Dunbar, *Sport of the Gods*, 37.

96. Dunbar, *Sport of the Gods*, 38.

97. Dunbar, *Sport of the Gods*, 36.

98. Blair Kelley notes a similar point in noticing barbers were key leaders in the Savannah 1906 streetcar boycotts. See Blair L. M. Kelley, *Right to Ride: Streetcar Boycotts and African American Citizenship in the Era of Plessy v. Ferguson* (Chapel Hill: University of North Carolina Press, 2010), 175.

99. In addition to Myers, George Knox of Indianapolis was an influential barber who was actively involved in Republican politics. He used his newspaper, the *Indianapolis Freeman*, as a mouthpiece for both racial equality and the Republican Party. He used his barber shop as a place to gauge the political winds by engaging with his white patrons from the Democratic and Republican Parties.

100. George Myers to James Ford Rhodes, March 8, 1920, and February 16, 1923, in Myers and Rhodes, *Barber and Historian,* 123, 146; Gerber, *Black Ohio and the Color Line,* 345–347; Felix James, "The Civic and Political Activities of George A. Myers," *Journal of Negro History* 58, no. 2 (April 1973): 168.

101. James, "The Civic and Political Activities of George Myers," 169.

102. George Myers to Charles Kinney, July 30, 1896, reel 1, frames 428-429, Myers Papers; Charles Kinney to George Myers, July 31, 1896, reel 1, frame 430, Myers Papers.

103. Carlos Stone to George Myers, September 30, 1896, reel 1, frames 514-515, Myers Papers.

104. Tyler to Myers, October 13, 1896, reel 1, frames 533-534, Myers Papers. In a letter to Myers, Tyler urged him to stop "hustling" as hard in political business and tend to his barbering business. See Ralph Tyler to George Myers, August 3, 1896, reel 1, frames 440-441, Myers Papers.

105. Myers received a flood of letters from northern and southern blacks asking him to put in a good word with Hanna or McKinley. For examples, see Tyler to Myers, October 23, 1896, reel 1, frames 550-551; H. M. Daugherty to Charles Cottrill, July 29, 1897, reel 1, frame 963; J. E. Hawkins to Myers, December 7, 1896, reel 1, frames 640-642; Charles Ferguson to Myers, June 22, 1897, reel 1, frames 209-210; Ralph Tyler to Myers, August 24, 1896, reel 1, frames 472-473; Tyler to Myers, July 28, 1897, reel 1, frames 960-961; E. A. Brown to Myers, August 14, 1897, reel 2, frame 68; Henry Arnett to Myers, August 5, 1897, reel 2, frame 9; Arnett to Myers, August 6, 1897, reel 2, frames 11-12; George Jackson to Myers, August 14, 1897, reel 2, frames 58-67; George Bailey to Myers, August 21, 1897, reel 2, frames 90-91; Samuel Huffman to Myers, September 14, 1897, reel 2, frame 176, all in Myers Papers. Despite Myers's work organizing black voters, Hanna delivered few patronage positions (primarily to black

southerners). Myers remained loyal to the party, but he acknowledged the ways the leader-ship slighted him and black voters. See Henry Vortriede to Myers, September 29, 1897, reel 2, frame 520; George Waldorf to Myers, November 4, 1897, reel 2, frame 764; John Porter (president's secretary) to Myers, November 8, 1897, reel 2, frame 775; John Porter (president's secretary) to Myers, March 23, 1898, reel 3, frame 41; Marcus Hanna to Myers, March 25, 1898, reel 3, frame 49; John Lynch to Myers, March 26, 1898, reel 3, frames 50–51; J. S. Rodgers (Private Secretary of Governor Bushnell) to Myers, February 26, 1897, reel 1, frame 794, all in Myers Papers. See also George Myers to John Green, June 10, 1898, and Myers to Green, May 28, 1901, Green Papers.

106. R. McCants Andrews, *John Merrick: A Biographical Sketch* (Durham, N.C.: Press of the Seeman Printery, 1920), 39–40; Weare, *Black Business in the New South*, 32–38.

107. For further discussion of mutual aid societies and the founding of black insurance companies, see M. S. Stuart, *An Economic Detour: A History of Insurance in the Lives of American Negroes* (New York: Wendell Mallett and Company, 1940); James H. Browning, "The Beginnings of Insurance Enterprise Among Negroes," *Journal of Negro History* 22, no. 4 (October 1937); J. H. Harmon, A. G. Lindsay, and C. G. Woodson, *The Negro as a Business Man* (Washington, D.C.: Association for the Study of Negro Life and History, Inc., 1929; repr., College Park, Md.: McGrath, 1969); Robert E. Weems, Jr., *Black Business in the Black Metropolis: The Chicago Metropolitan Assurance Company, 1925-1985* (Bloomington: Indiana University Press, 1996), 119–124; Juliet E. K. Walker, ed., *Encyclopedia of African American Business History* (Westport, Conn.: Greenwood Press, 1999); Juliet E. K. Walker, *The History of Black Business in America: Capitalism, Race, Entrepreneurship* (New York: Macmillan/Prentice Hall International, 1998), 187–193.

108. Weare, *Black Business in the New South*, 12–15.

109. Walker, *History of Black Business in America*, 187–88.

110. Brown, *Upbuilding Black Durham*, 123.

111. Quoted in Weare, *Black Business in the New South*, 30–31; Brown, *Upbuilding Black Durham*, 117.

112. Quoted in Gilmore, *Gender and Jim Crow*, 105–106; Brown, *Upbuilding Black Durham*, 61–62; Litwack, *Trouble in Mind*, 312–313; Edmonds, *Negro and Fusion Politics in North Carolina* (New York: Russell and Russell, 1951), 158–177.

113. Gilmore, *Gender and Jim Crow*, 106–113; Brown, *Upbuilding Black Durham*, 63–65.

114. Andrews, *John Merrick*, 159–160 quoted in Weare, *Black Business in the New South*, 23.

115. According to Richard Sherman, McKinley was silent on "sensitive" issues, such as the "southern way of life," which accepted blacks' subservience, to create sectional harmony, par-ticularly after the Spanish-American War. See, Richard B. Sherman, *The Republican Party and Black America from McKinley to Hoover, 1896-1933* (Charlottesville: University Press of Virginia, 1973), 12–22.

116. Gilmore, *Gender and Jim Crow*, 113–118; Litwack, *Trouble in Mind*, 314. Myers be-lieved the government should prioritize domestic affairs over foreign affairs. He believed, "I am under the opinion that this country should demonstrate its ability to protect their own citizens within its own domain—especially when some are a part and partial of this govern-ment—(Baker at Lake City, S.C.) before interfering with other Governments about the treat-ment of their subjects. Plainly speaking that we should 'first cast the mote out of our own eye.'" See George Myers to John Green, May 3, 1898, Green Papers.

117. Quoted in Sherman, *Republican Party and Black America*, 13. Ida B. Wells, *Crusade for Justice: The Autobiography of Ida B. Wells,* ed. Alfreda M. Duster (Chicago: University of Chicago Press, 1970), 257–258; Barbara Blair, *Though Justice Sleeps: African Americans,*

1880-1900 (New York: Oxford University Press, 1997), 329. On the Afro-American Council see Shawn Leigh Alexander, *An Army of Lions: The Civil Rights Struggle Before the NAACP* (Philadelphia: University of Pennsylvania Press, 2012); Benjamin Justesen, *Broken Brotherhood: The Rise and Fall of the National Afro-American Council* (Carbondale, Ill.: Southern Illinois University Press, 2008).

118. Reverdy C. Ransom to George Myers, June 10, 1899, reel 3, frame 527; Ralph Tyler to Myers, November 16, 1898, reel 3, frame 341, both in Myers Papers.

119. George Myers to John P. Green, December 9, 1898, Green Papers. The actual letter to Senator Hanna is in Myers Papers but is unreadable.

120. George Myers to John P. Green, December 28, 1898, Green Papers.

121. Marcus Hanna to Myers, December 15, 1898, reel 3, frame 362, Myers Papers.

122. One hundred and fifty people rallied on Myers's lawn in opposition to McKinley. There is no evidence of the racial mix of the crowd. See George Myers to Charles Dick, August 23, 1900, reel 4, frame 362, Myers Papers. On Myers's continued work for the party, see Myers to Dick, August 21, 1900, reel 4, frames 238-240, Myers Papers. He also looked to shed favorable light on the party as he requested Henry Arnett, of the Recorder of Deeds office, to "examine the records of the War Department for language used by Theodore Roosevelt in compliment-ing the bravery, valor and commendable conduct of the colored troops which participated in the Cuban campaigns." Arnett's replied, "THERE IS NO SUCH RECORD [his emphasis]. The fact of the matter is, all that Colonel Roosevelt has said he has said outside the official reports." See Henry Arnett to Myers, September 13, 1900, reel 4, frame 331, Myers Papers.

123. Two months before the election, Henry Arnett informed Myers that black voters in West Virginia and Indiana were gaining interest in the Democratic party because of the "fail-ure of the President to say one word against the lynchings and southern 'negro eliminating' laws being enacted in the South." See Henry Arnett to George Myers, September 1, 1900, reel 4, frames 298-300, Myers Papers.

124. George Myers to John Green, December 7, 1900, Green Papers.

125. Gerber, *Black Ohio and the Color Line,* 353-363.

126. George Myers to William McKinley, November 15, 1900, reel 4, frame 420, Myers Papers. He sent a copy of the letter to John P. Green and asserted, "I now feel as if I have done my duty." November 15, 1900, Green Papers; Sherman, *Republican Party and Black America,* 12-16. Even after this letter, Myers wrote Charles Dick in the House of Representatives per-taining to an investigation of southern disfranchisement: Charles Dick to Myers, December 16, 1901, reel 4, frame 1007, Myers Papers. Mississippi began the disfranchisement movement among southern states in 1890, followed by South Carolina in 1895, Louisiana in 1898, and North Carolina in 1900.

127. Myers to McKinley, November 15, 1900, reel 4, frames 420-421, Myers Papers.

128. George Myers to John Green, May 17, 1901, Green Papers.

129. "Organization. Prominent Men from Over the State Meet in Columbus to Effect One—George A. Myers Presides and Delivers Opening Address," *Cleveland Journal,* May 21, 1904.

130. Tyler to Myers, October 18, 1898, reel 3, frame 315, Myers Papers.

131. Kusmer, *A Ghetto Takes Shape,* 3-31.

132. Marcus Hanna, *Socialism and the Labor Unions: WM. McKinley as I Knew Him* (Boston: The Chapple Publishing Co., 1904).

133. Weare, *Black Business in the New South,* 51-81; Quincy T. Mills, "Black Wall Street," in Walker, ed., *Encyclopedia of African American Business History,* 81-82; John Sibley Butler, *Entrepreneurship and Self-Help Among Black Americans* (Albany: State University of New York

Press, 1994); W. E. B. Du Bois, "The Upbuilding of Black Durham," *World's Work* 23 (January 1912); Clement Richardson, "What Are Negroes Doing in Durham?" *Southern Workman* 42 (July 1913); Booker T. Washington, "Durham, North Carolina, a City of Negro Enterprises," *Independent* 70 (March 30, 1911).

134. Quoted in Weare, *Black Business in the New South*, 96.

135. Henderson, *Atlanta Life Insurance Company*, 13–17 (quote from 17); Merritt, *The Herndons*, 75–77; Dorsey, *To Build Our Lives Together*, 112.

136. Wade Aaron Aderhold and John Crew were central executives in the Union Mutual Relief Association of Atlanta. W. L. G. Pounds organized and managed the Royal Benevolent Insurance Association. Edward Howell was head of the National Laborers' Protective Union. Benson, *Atlanta Life Insurance Company*, 44–45.

137. Benson, *Atlanta Life Insurance Company*, 46–56.

138. "Postscript by W. E. B. Du Bois," *Crisis* 34 (September 1927): 239, quoted in Merritt, *The Herndons*, 77.

139. Merritt, *The Herndons*, 72–77. Herndon and Norris are pictured in the photo of the founding members of the Niagara Movement. On the Niagara Movement, see Alexander, *An Army of Lions*.

140. *Atlanta Independent*, February 26, 1925, quoted in Benson, *Atlanta Life Insurance Company*, 42.

141. Carter, *The Black Side*, 188.

142. Walter White, *A Man Called White: The Autobiography of Walter White* (New York: Viking, 1948), 9. See also Merritt, *The Herndons*, 85–86.

143. "In Race Riot Many Negroes Are Killed," *Atlanta Journal*, September 23, 1906.

144. Thomas Gibson, "The Anti-Negro Riots in Atlanta," *Harper's Weekly* 50 (July–December 1906); *Atlanta Constitution*, "Chased Negroes All Night," September 23, 1906; Dorsey, *To Build Our Lives Together*, 156.

145. "In Race Riot Many Negroes Are Killed." Decatur Street was the black entertainment district. Black-owned shops on this street were more likely frequented by black customers. "Died in Barber's Chair," *Atlanta Constitution*, November 6, 1901.

146. "The Atlanta Massacre," October 4, 1906, Atlanta History Center. The editor believed it was unsafe to print the author's name.

147. "Negro Barber Shops Are Closed," *Atlanta Journal*, September 25, 1906.

148. Myers to Rhodes, February 16, 1923, in Myers and Rhodes, *Barber and Historian*, 146.

149. Merritt, *The Herndons*, 115–124.

150. Hurston, *Dust Tracks on a Road*, 136.

Chapter 3. Race, Regulation, and the Modern Barber Shop

1. *New York Age*, June 15, 1905; Alfred Holt Stone, *Studies in the American Race Problem* (New York: Doubleday, Page, & Company, 1908), 157–58.

2. Wendell P. Dabney, *Cincinnati's Colored Citizens: Historical, Sociological and Biographical* (Cincinnati: Dabney Publishing Company, 1926), 184–185. Vallombrosa was a monastery near Florence built in 1038 and was surrounded by beech and firs.

3. Henry C. Dotry, *New York Age*, May 23, 1891.

4. Ninth Census of the United States, 1870; Tenth Census of the United States, 1880; Eleventh Census of the United States, 1890; Twelfth Census of the United States, 1900; Bureau of the Census, *Thirteenth Census of the United States: 1910*, Vol. 4: *Population* (Washington, D.C.: Government Printing Office, 1910).

5. Manuel J. Vieira, *The Tonsorial Art Pamphlet: Origin of the Trade, The Business in America and Other Countries, Its Rise and Progress* (Indianapolis: Pub House Print, 1877), 57–58.

6. John Higham, *Strangers in the Land: Patters of American Nativism, 1860–1925* (New Brunswick, N.J.: Rutgers University Press, 1955), 14–15; Hartmut Keil and John B. Jentz, eds., *German Workers in Industrial Chicago, 1850–1910: A Comparative Perspective* (DeKalb: Northern Illinois University Press, 1983), 7–9; Harmut Keil and John B. Jentz, eds., *German Workers in Chicago: A Documentary History of Working-Class Culture from 1850 to World War I* (Urbana: University of Illinois Press, 1988), 1–4; Matthew Frye Jacobson, *Whiteness of a Different Color: European Immigrants and the Alchemy of Race* (Cambridge, Mass.: Harvard University Press, 1998), 43–44.

7. Sunday laws generally specified that "all labor on Sunday excepting the works of necessity and charity" was illegal and subject to penalty. On the politics of Sunday laws, see Kyle G. Volk, "Majority Rule, Minority Rights: The Christian Sabbath, Liquor, Racial Amalgamation, and Democracy in Antebellum America" (Ph.D. diss., University of Chicago, 2008). Barber shops were traditionally exempt from Sunday laws because shaves and haircuts were "works of necessity," "Victory for Sunday Openers: Chicago Barbers' Shops Need Not Close the First Day of the Week," *New York Times*, November 17, 1895; W. Scott Hall, "The Journeymen Barbers' International Union of America" (Ph.D. diss., Johns Hopkins University, 1936), 89–91. For cases declaring Sunday-closing laws applicable to barbers, see *State v. Frederick* (1885) 45 Ark. 348; *State v. Nesbit* (1898) 8 Kan. App. 104; *State v. Sopher* (1903) 25 Utah 318; *State v. Linsig* (1916) 178 Iowa 484. The United States Supreme Court ruled it applicable in *Petit v. Minnesota* (1900) 177 U.S. 164. For cases declaring Sunday-closing laws not discriminatory, see *People v. Bellet* (1894) 99 Mich. 151; *People v. Havnor* (1896) 149 N.Y. 195; *Breyer v. State* (1899) 102 Tenn. 103; Ex parte Northrup (1902) 41 Ore. 489; *State v. Bergfeldt* (1905) 41 Wash. 234; *McClelland v. Denver* (1906) 36 Colo. 486; *Stanfeal v. State* (1908) 78 Ohio St. 24. For further information, see the American Law Reports, 20 ALR 1114, 1117, and the following articles in the *New York Times*: "Sunday Shaving in Georgia: Decision of an Atlanta Judge in a Test Case—Prisoners Discharged," July 14, 1878; "The Liquor Law in Long Branch," July 1, 1890; "New Rules for Barbers: They Must Now Work Until 6 O'Clock on Sundays and Holidays," February 3, 1893; "Brooklyn Barbers," June 2, 1895; "Two Peekskill Barbers Fined" and "Arrested Barbers Discharged: Brooklyn Justices Would Not Consider the Complaints of Violation of the Sunday Shaving Law," June 4, 1895; "Barbers and the Constitution: In the Hobach Case, in Brooklyn, the Government Defends the Collins Shaving Law" and "Enforce the Law and Get It Changed," July 6, 1895; "Collins Law Again in Courts: Barber Havnor Argues That It Is Unconstitutional" and "Abuse of Legislative Power," July 12, 1895; "Barbers Working in Saloons: A Novel Way to Get Around the Sunday Anti-Shaving Law in Brooklyn Tried with Success," December 9, 1895; "A Question of Wisdom, Not Power," February 9, 1896; Nelson J. Flowerdew, *Sunday Blue Laws and Other Blessings* (Los Angeles: Pacific Press, 1914).

8. "'Barbers First, Americans Always': Brooklyn Bosses Who Think the Collins Law Will Help Their Dignity," *New York Times*, June 14, 1895.

9. "Barbers Want Reforms: Tonsorial Schools and Italian Shops Their Grievances," *New York Times*, January 11, 1897.

10. Quoted in Stone, *Studies in the American Race Problem*, 158; "Exigent Domestic Service Question," *New York Age*, September 28, 1905.

11. Garrett Weaver, "The Development of the Black Durham Community, 1880–1915" (Ph.D. diss., University of North Carolina, Chapel Hill, 1987), 353.

12. Lester C. Lamon, *Blacks in Tennessee, 1791–1970* (Knoxville: University of Tennessee

Press, 1981) 140–141; John Dittmer, *Black Georgia in the Progressive Era, 1900–1920* (Urbana: University of Illinois Press, 1980), 38; William A. Crossland, *Industrial Conditions Among Negroes in St. Louis*, (St. Louis: Press of Mendle Printing Co., 1914), 68; Lorenzo J. Greene and Carter G. Woodson, *Negro Wage Earner* (New York: AMS Press, 1970), 94–96.

13. George C. Wright, *Life Behind a Veil: Blacks in Louisville, Kentucky, 1865–1930* (Baton Rouge: Louisiana State University Press, 1985), 82. Quotes from Stone, *Studies in the American Race Problem*, 168.

14. "From the Queen City. Mascotte Gives a Glowing Description of Willis B. Ross' New Tonsorial Parlors," *Cleveland Gazette*, January 17, 1885.

15. Dabney, *Cincinnati's Colored Citizens*, 184.

16. W. W. Snypp, "The Best Barber Shop in America," *Southern Workman* 56 (March 1927): 119–122. Booker T. Washington made note of the telephone service and a female stenographer during his last visit to Myers's barber shop. See Washington, *The Story of The Negro: The Rise of the Race from Slavery* (New York: Association Press, 1909), 199–200.

17. Snypp, "The Best Barber Shop in America," 119.

18. See Kristin L. Hoganson, *Consumers' Imperium: The Global Production of American Domesticity, 1865–1920* (Chapel Hill: University of North Carolina Press, 2007). While Hoganson's book focuses on American households, her discussion of the consumption of imports and cosmopolitanism is relevant to barbers' efforts to create palatial shops for their patrons.

19. Daniel Lucas, "Tonsorial Artists," in *Proceedings of the National Negro Business League: Its First Meeting Held in Boston, Massachusetts, August 23 and 24, 1900* (Boston: J. R. Hamm, 1901), 243.

20. Dittmer, *Black Georgia in the Progressive Era*, 37–38; Alexa B. Henderson, *Atlanta Life Insurance Company: Guardian of Black Economic Dignity* (Tuscaloosa: University of Alabama Press, 1990), 23; Franklin M. Garrett, *Atlanta and Environs: A Chronicle of Its People and Events*, Vol. 1 (New York: Lewis Historical Publishing Company, 1954), 609.

21. Nancy Dawson, "Hair Care Products Industry," in Juliet E. K. Walker, ed., *Encyclopedia of African American Business History* (Westport, Conn.: Greenwood Press, 1999), 283–284.

22. Russell B. Adams, Jr., *King C. Gillette: The Man and His Wonderful Shaving Device* (Boston: Little, Brown, 1978), 49–48.

23. Mic Hunter, *The American Barbershop: A Closer Look at a Disappearing Place* (Mount Horeb, Wis.: Face to Face Books, 1996), 121; Krumholz, *History of Shaving and Razors* (Bartonville, Ill.: Ad Libs, 1992); Adams, *King C. Gillette*, 56.

24. John Moore, interview by Travis Jordan, November 14, 1938, "The Moore Family," Federal Writers' Project (microfiche) (Ann Arbor, Mich.: University Microfilms International 1980).

25. See Richard Corson, *Fashions in Hair: The First Five Thousand Years* (London: Peter Owen, 1965).

26. William Leach, *Land of Desire: Merchants, Power, and the Rise of a New American Culture* (New York: Vintage Books, 1993), esp. 112–150 (quote from 146).

27. "Mass Meeting of the German Journeyman Barbers," *New York Times*, June 22, 1869, and "Barbers' Mass Meeting—Hours of Labor and Wages," *New York Times,* March 28, 1870; 1880 U.S. census, population schedule, New York City, New York, New York, Enumeration District 15, sheet 21, family 243, Fred Turrell household; National Archives microfilm publication T9, roll 867; digital image, Ancestry.com, http://www.ancestry.com (accessed 2 January 2013). Tourell's name is spelled "Turrell" in the 1880 census and "Tourelle" or "Tourell" in *New York Times* articles; "Local News in Brief," *New York Times*, April 22, 1870. Like New York unions,

barbers organized locally in other states before the JBIUA. For example, see *Constitution and By-Laws of the Barbers' Protective Union of Fall River, Mass.* [1885?], Pamphlets in American History, Labor.

28. Sterling D. Spero and Abram L. Harris, *The Black Worker: The Negro and the Labor Movement* (New York: Atheneum, 1968), 53.

29. Frank X. Noschang, "Brief History of the Journeymen Barber's International Union of America," *Journeyman Barber* 15, no. 8 (September 1919): 354–355.

30. "A. C. Mendell," *Journeyman Barber* 7, no. 4 (May 1911): 125.

31. *New York Times*, December 6, 1887; Hall, "The Journeymen Barbers' International Union," 13–17.

32. American Federation of Labor, *Report of the Proceedings of the Annual Convention of the American Federation of Labor*, American Federation of Labor Convention, 1900, pp. 12–13, 22–23, 117, 129; Herbert Hill, "Race, Ethnicity and Organized Labor: The Opposition to Affirmative Action," *New Politics: A Journal of Socialist Thought* (Winter 1987).

33. "No Color Line."

34. Quote from "Notes and Comments," *Journeyman Barber* 14, no. 3 (March 1903), 57; see also Hall, "Journeymen Barbers' International," 43–44.

35. Jacob Rheinstadter, "Philadelphia, PA," *Journeyman Barber* 5, no. 11 (December-October 1909); David A. Katzman, *Before the Ghetto: Black Detroit in the Nineteenth Century* (Urbana: University of Illinois Press, 1973), 125.

36. Hall, "Journeymen Barbers' International," 16, 44; Spero and Harris note there were 800 black members in the JBIUA in 1900 and 239 black members in 1928; these figures seem significantly low. See Spero and Harris, *Black Worker*, 76.

37. "No Color Line," *Journeyman Barber* 2, no. 9 (October 1906): 220.

38. "Notes and Comments."

39. Hall, *Journeymen Barber's International Union*, 43–44; rosters of membership of Ohio from *The Barbers' Journal* 12 (September 1901): 208–257; David A. Gerber, *Black Ohio and the Color Line, 1860-1915* (Urbana: University of Illinois Press, 1976), 72.

40. "A. C. Mendell," *Journeyman Barber* 8, no. 4 (May 1912): 149.

41. "John Hart," *Journeyman Barber* 13, no. 6 (July 1917): 261.

42. *Journeyman Barber* 7, no. 4 (May 1911): 126.

43. W. E. Faverty, "Argenta, Ark." *Journeyman Barber* 9, no. 10 (November 1913): 462–463; Joe Pilgreen, "Little Rock, Ark.," *Journeyman Barber* 10, no. 4 (May 1914); W. W. Harrison, "Gulfport, Miss.," *Journeyman Barber* 10, no. 10 (November 1911): 485; "Shreveport, LA." *Journeyman Barber* 13, no. 3 (April 1917): 114.

44. Tennessee Bureau of Labor, Statistics, and Mines, *Sixth Annual Report, 1896* (Nashville, 1897), 298–299; James Jones, Jr., "Strikes and Labor Organization in Tennessee During the Depression of 1893–1897," *Tennessee Historical Quarterly* 52, no. 4 (1993): 262–263.

45. W. O. Pinard, "Success in the South," *The Barber's Journal* 10, no. 11 (November 1899): 159

46. H. B. Cheairs, "Journeymen Barbers' Union No. 79, of Nashville, Tennessee," in *Third Annual Report, 1893*, Tennessee Bureau of Labor, Statistics, and Mines (Nashville, 1894), 314–318; Jones, "Strikes and Labor Organization in Tennessee," 260.

47. *Journeyman Barber* 13, no. 11 (November 1917): 459.

48. W. E. B. Du Bois, "The Strivings of the Negro," *Atlantic Monthly* 80 (August 1897): 194.

49. "Dangerous Forces," *Colored American*, May 23, 1903.

50. First quote from correspondence from George Myers to James Rhodes, October 28, 1919, in George A. Myers and James Ford Rhodes, *The Barber and the Historian: The Correspondence*

of George A. Myers and James Ford Rhodes, 1910-1923, ed. John A. Garraty (Columbus: Ohio Historical Society, 1956), 98; second quote from George Myers to James Rhodes, August 31, 1920, in Myers and Rhodes, *Barber and Historian,* 115. Myers's position is opposite his father's ideologies as one of the founders of the Negro National Labor Union in 1869. In 1865, white carpenters in Baltimore refused to work with blacks, so Isaac Myers, along with others, established a black-owned shipyard, the Chesapeake Marine Railroad and Dry Dock Company. At the third annual convention of the National Labor Union in August 1869, Isaac Myers made an appeal for unity between black and white workers. His speech did not receive any attention, and wasting no time, four months later he founded the Negro National Labor Union. "Isaac Myers' Speech" and "Constitution of the [Negro] National Labor Union" in Herbert Aptheker, ed., *A Documentary History of the Negro People in the United States,* Vol. 2 (New York: Citadel Press, 1951), 628–636; Myers and Rhodes, *Barber and Historian,* xv–xvi. For a discussion of the Chesapeake Marine Railroad Co., see Scott Woods, "Chesapeake Marine Railway and Dry Dock Company," in Walker, ed., *Encyclopedia of African American Business History,* 134–136.

51. Kevin Gaines, *Uplifting the Race: Black Leadership, Politics, and Culture in the Twentieth Century* (Chapel Hill: University of North Carolina Press, 1996), 94–95.

52. Robert H. Wiebe, *The Search for Order, 1877-1920* (New York: Hill and Wang, 1968), 113–115; Paul Starr, *The Social Transformation of American Medicine: The Rise of a Sovereign Profession and the Making of a Vast Industry* (New York: Basic Books, 1984); Rebecca Edwards, *New Spirits: Americans in the Gilded Age, 1865-1905* (New York: Oxford University Press, 2005), 75.

53. "Sanitary Regulations of Barber Shops," *Scientific American* 89 (October 3, 1903): 245.

54. Isadore Dyer, "The Barber Shop in Society," *New Orleans Medical and Surgical Journal* (August 1905): 3.

55. Quote from Dyer, "Barber Shop in Society," 5–12. See also Hunter, *The American Barbershop,* 109–110; "Barber Shop Diseases," *Atlanta Constitution,* March 6, 1904. Also see F. C. Walsh, "New Dangers Found in Barber Shops," *Technical World Magazine,* 19 (May 1913): 354–357.

56. Tera W. Hunter, *To 'Joy My Freedom: Southern Black Women's Lives and Labors After the Civil War* (Cambridge, Mass.: Harvard University Press, 1998), 187–218.

57. Hall, "Journeymen Barbers International Union," 79.

58. Hall, "Journeymen Barbers International Union," 79.

59. "A College for Barbers," *New York Times,* June 15, 1896; "Razor Knights Aroused: Barbers' War Against Colleges in Their Trade," *New York Times,* September 27, 1896; Hunter, *The American Barbershop,* 109. Interestingly, five of the forty-five students who enrolled in the Manhattan School in 1896 were women.

60. Emil R. Rohr, *Greater Richmond Barber College* (Richmond, n.d.), Library of Virginia.

61. J. M. McCamant, *Mack's Barbers' Guide: A Practical Hand-Book For Apprentices, Journeymen and Boss, Embracing a Theoretical Course in Barbering, as well as Recipes and Formulas for Toilet Waters, Face Lotions, Crams, Salves, Pomades, Shampoos, Sea Foams, Hair Tonics, etc.* (Ogden, Utah: Wasatch Printing Co., 1908), 57–63.

62. General Laws of the State of Minnesota Passed during the Thirteenth Session of the State Legislature, Chapter 186 "An act to regulate the practice of barbering, the licensing of persons to carry on such practice, and to insure the better education of such practitioners in the State of Minnesota" (Delano: Eagle Printing Company, 1897), 346–349.

63. "Law to Regulate Barber Shops," *Philadelphia Tribune,* March 1, 1913.

64. Hall, "Journeymen Barbers International Union," 79–103; Hunter, *The American Barbershop,* 111; quote from McCamant, *Mack's Barbers' Guide,* 60–63.

65. Quotes from House Bill 180, 75th General Assembly of Ohio, 1902, Printed Bills, Legislative Services, State Archives, Ohio Historical Society, Columbus, Ohio [hereafter cited as H.B., Printed Bills, Ohio]; Seventy-fourth General Assembly, *The Ohio Manual of Legislative Practice in the General Assembly*, Part V, "Official Directory of the House of Representatives of the 74th General Assembly (Columbus: Fred J. Heer, State Printer, 1900), 481; Doug Bristol, "The Victory of Black Barbers over Reform in Ohio, 1903–1913," *Essays in Economic and Business History* 16 (1998): 253–54.

66. Myers to Marcus Hanna, February 4, 1902, reel 5, frame 21, George A. Myers Papers, 1890-1929 (microfilm) Ohio Historical Society, Columbus, Ohio (hereafter Myers Papers).

67. Unsigned to Joseph B. Foraker, February 11, 1902, reel 5, frame 44; Unsigned to Governor George Nash, February 11, 1902, reel 5, frame 46; and quote from Myers to H. M. Daugherty, February 17, 1902, reel 5, frame 53-54, all in Myers Papers. The unsigned letters are likely from Myers. See also Bristol, "The Victory of Black Barbers over Reform in Ohio," 255–256.

68. Gerber, *Black Ohio and the Color Line,* 357; Richard Sherman, *The Republican Party and Black America: From McKinley to Hoover, 1896–1933* (Charlottesville: University Press of Virginia, 1973), 1–4. Northern black politicians were aware of the importance of black voters in the Midwest in swaying an election along party lines. In correspondence with Myers, Jere Brown noted, "Our [northern blacks'] votes perpetuate and keep the party [Republican] in power in Ohio, Indiana and Illinois." Jere Brown to George Myers, June 30, 1900, reel 2, frame 66, Myers Papers.

69. Gerber, *Black Ohio and the Color Line*, 231.

70. Ralph Tyler to Myers, February 7, 1902, reel 5, frame 32, Myers Papers.

71. The Journal of the House of Representatives of the State of Ohio for the Regular Session of the 75th General Assembly, 1902 (Columbus, 1902), 563, 694.

72. "Hurt Barbers. Bill in Legislature That Will Affect Those of Our Race," *Cleveland Journal*, February 27, 1904; "Homage to Lawmakers—The Banquet Last Week a Truly Brilliant Affair," *Cleveland Journal,* May 7, 1904; H.B. 160, 76th General Assembly, Ohio, 1904; H.B. 332, 81st General Assembly, Ohio, 1915; H.B. 294, 82nd General Assembly, Ohio, 1917; H.B. 334, 86th General Assembly, Ohio, 1925; H.B. 73 and 268, 87th General Assembly, Ohio, 1927; H.B. 62, 88th General Assembly, Ohio, 1929; S.B. 129, 90th General Assembly, 1933, Printed Bills, Ohio; Bristol, "The Victory of Black Barbers over Reform in Ohio," 256–258.

73. Victor H. Kleabe, "Austin, Tex.," *Journeyman Barber* 2, no. 12 (January 1907): 296.

74. See William Carrigan, *The Making of a Lynching Culture: Violence and Vigilantism in Central Texas, 1836–1916* (Urbana: University of Illinois Press, 2006); David Oshinsky, *Worse Than Slavery: Parchman Farm and the Ordeal of Jim Crow Justice* (New York: Free Press, 1997).

75. New York was the only northern state that had not passed a licensing law at this time.

76. Con. J. Coyle, "A. C. Mendell," *Journeyman Barber* 9, no. 8 (September 1913): 355; "C. F. Foley," *Journeyman Barber* 17, no. 3 (April 1921): 111.

77. "C. F. Foley," *Journeyman Barber* 17, no. 3 (April 1921): 111; A. M. Simons, "The Barbers' Union," *Journeyman Barber* 13, no. 5 (June 1917); "Leon Worthall," *Journeyman Barber* 13, no. 6 (July 1917); "C. F. Foley," *Journeyman Barber* 17, no. 4 (May 1921): 159.

78. "William Hubbell," *Journeyman Barber* 6, no. 12 (January 1911): 372.

79. "More Barber Shops in Norfolk than in any other City in the South, Veteran Declares," *Journeyman Barber* 21, no. 2 (March 1925): 48; John J. Lloyd, "Norfolk, VA.," *Journeyman Barber* 22, no. 1 (February 1926): 23.

80. Byrd was a key architect in Virginia's "Massive Resistance" against racial integration. See Keith Finley, *Delaying the Dream: Southern Senators and the Fight Against Civil Rights, 1938–1965* (Baton Rouge: Louisiana State University Press, 2008).

81. J. A. Panella, "Virginia Barbers Form Association," *Journeyman Barber* 25, no. 8 (September 1929): 34.

82. Panella, "Virginia Barbers Form Association."

83. H. B. Hubbard, "Virginia Convention a Success," *Journeyman Barber* 25, no. 8 (September 1929): 30.

84. F. H. Norris, Letter to the Editor, *Pittsburgh Courier*, February 8, 1930.

85. "Not a Bill for Amendment," *Richmond News Leader*, January 21, 1930.

86. "Barbers Accept Substitute for Their Measure," *Richmond Times-Dispatch*, January 25, 1930; "Barbers to Continue to Fight," *Pittsburgh Courier*, March 22, 1930.

87. "To Fight Barber Bill in Virginia: Silent Action Taken," *Pittsburgh Courier*, February 6, 1932.

88. Maryland was the earliest (1904), and North Carolina and Tennessee are the most recent (1929). Virginius Dabney, "Negro Barbers in the South," *The Nation* 131, no. 3393 (July 16, 1930): 64–65.

89. Dabney, "Negro Barbers in the South."

90. See R. Volney Risner, *Defying Disfranchisement: Black Voting Rights Activism in the Jim Crow South, 1890–1908* (Baton Rouge, La.: Louisiana State University, 2010); Michael Perman, *Struggle for Mastery: Disfranchisement in the South, 1888–1908* (Chapel Hill: University of North Carolina Press, 2001).

91. "Straight Razor for the Barber Bill," *Richmond Times-Dispatch,* February 14, 1956; "Put the 'Barber Bill' to Sleep," *Richmond Times-Dispatch,* February 2, 1960.

92. Harvard Sitkoff, *A New Deal for Blacks: The Emergence of Civil Rights as a National Issue: The Depression Decade* (Oxford: Oxford University Press, 1978), 96–97.

93. "Voice of the People," *Richmond Times-Dispatch*, February 3, 1932 reprinted in and quotes from W. C. Birthright, "Answering Scurrilous Attacks Upon the Virginia License Law and Virginia Barbers," *Journeyman Barber* 28, no. 2 (March 1932): 14.

94. See the following articles in the *Atlanta Constitution*: "Negro Barber Ban Will Be Enjoined by City Chamber" and "Reconsider It," February 3, 1926; "Council to Act on Barber Ban: Reconsideration of Measure to be Sought at Special Meeting Today" and "Methodist Women Protest Barber Act," February 4, 1926; "Council Votes Public Hearing on Barber Bill: Ordinance Committee to Air Proposed Ban on Negro Shops Next Thursday" and "Citizens Protest Against Recent Barber Ordinance," February 5, 1926; "Commendable!" February 6, 1926; "An Unfair Rebuke," February 9, 1926; "Hearings on Negro Barber Ban Move Will Begin Today," February 11, 1926; "Compromise Seen on Barber Bill," February 12, 1926; "Lawyers Attack Barber Ordinance," February 13, 1926; "Abe Martin," February 15, 1926; "Negro Barber Ban Limited to White Women, Children," February 16, 1926; "Mayor Urged to Vote Negro Barber Bill," February 17, 1926; "Atlanta Chamber Plans to Enjoin Barber Measure," February 19, 1926.

95. "An Unfair Rebuke," *Atlanta Constitution*, February 9, 1926.

96. Armand May, "Citizens Protest Against Recent Barber Ordinance," *Atlanta Constitution*, February 5, 1926.

97. M. Ashby Jones, D.D., "The Negro Barber Shop and Southern Tradition," *Atlanta Constitution*, February 21, 1926.

98. See Micki McElya, *Clinging to Mammy: The Faithful Slave in Twentieth-Century America* (Cambridge, Mass.: Harvard University Press, 2007).

99. "Compromise Seen on Barber Bill," *Atlanta Constitution,* February 12, 1926; "Negro Barber Ban Limited to White Women, Children," *Atlanta Constitution,* February 16, 1926; "Atlanta Chamber Plans to Enjoin Barber Measure," *Atlanta Constitution,* February 19, 1926;

"Court Enjoins Barber Measure," *Atlanta Constitution,* February 24, 1926; "Barber Bill Writ Hearing is Put over to March 12," *Atlanta Constitution,* March 7, 1926; "Colored Barber Ordinance Invalid," *Atlanta Constitution,* September 15, 1927.

100. "See Motive in Atlanta Barber Bill," *Chicago Defender,* February 27, 1926.

101. Birthright, "Answering Scurrilous Attacks upon the Virginia License Law and Virginia Barbers," 43.

102. Work Projects Administration, *The Negro in Virginia* (New York: Hastings House, 1940), 319.

103. Quote from "Norfolk, Va., City Council Passes Ordinance Regulating Barbers: The Barbers' Ordinance," *Journeyman Barber* 29, no. 6 (July 1933): 6; see also "Norfolk, VA.," 21–22.

104. *Ordinances and Resolutions of the Council of the City of Richmond, Commencing with [the] Month of September 1934, and Ending with the Month of August, 1936* (Richmond: Old Dominion Press, 1936), 105–106; *Annual Report of the Department of Public Welfare of the City of Richmond, Va. for the Year Ending December 31, 1935* (Richmond: William Byrd Press, 1936), 151–152; "Barber Regulations Also Approved by Council, Effective at Once," *Richmond News Leader,* June 29, 1935.

105. Quote from "Norfolk, Va., City Council Passes Ordinance Regulating Barbers," *Journeyman Barber* 29, no. 6 (July 1933): 6. See also "Norfolk, VA.," *Journeyman Barber* 29, no. 6 (July 1933): 21–22; On Panella's ethnicity see 1930 U.S. census, population schedule, Norfolk, Norfolk (Independent City), Virginia, Enumeration District 79, sheet 3, dwelling 66, family 56, Joseph Panella household; National Archives microfilm publication T626, roll 2471; digital image, Ancestry.com, http://www.ancestry.com (accessed 2 January 2013).

106. "Norfolk Barbers Improve Under Ordinance," *Journeyman Barber* 31, no. 5 (June 1935): 6.

107. "Will Enforce Sanitary Law," *Richmond News Leader,* August 26, 1935; "Close Check Kept on Barbers," *Richmond News Leader,* November 30, 1936; *Annual Report of the Department of Public Welfare of the City of Richmond, Va. for Year Ending December 31, 1936* (Richmond: Clyde W. Saunders and Sons, 1937), 151–153. The *Annual Report* indicated that they inspected 3,207 barber shops. Because I do not believe there were over 3,200 barber shops in Richmond in 1936, I suspect the report was referring to initial visits and return visits.

108. Quote from "Richmond, Va., Barbers Try for Ordinance Amendments," *Journeyman Barber* 33, no.1 (February 1937): 4; first reported in "Negro Barbers Hauled to Court in Health Drive," *Richmond News Leader,* January 15, 1937.

109. See *Annual Report of the Department of Public Welfare,* 1936, 153; *Annual Report of the Department of Public Welfare of the City of Richmond, Va. for the Year Ending December 31, 1937* (Richmond: Virginia Stationery Co., 1938), 152; *Annual Report of the Department of Public Welfare of the City of Richmond, Va. for the Year Ending December 31, 1938* (Richmond: Virginia Stationery Co., 1939), 147–148.

110. *Ordinances and Resolutions of the Council of the City of Richmond, Commencing with the Month of September, 1938, Ending with the Month of August, 1940* (Richmond: Williams Printing Company, 1940), 297–300.

111. Quote from "Committee Approves Tests for Barbers," *Richmond Times-Dispatch,* August 18, 1939; *Annual Report of the Department of Public Welfare of the City of Richmond, Va. for the Year Ending December 31, 1939* (Richmond: Virginia Stationery Co., 1940), 139–140; *Annual Report of the Department of Public Welfare of the City of Richmond, Va. for the Year Ending December 31, 1940* (Richmond: Virginia Stationery Co., 1941), 77.

112. "Finds 94 Infectious Cases," *Richmond News Leader,* June 10, 1940.

113. "Denies Need of Syphilis Exams for Public Jobs," *Chicago Defender*, November 11, 1939. Other states confronted similar claims about disease-ridden barber shops. In 1930, the Massachusetts legislature ordered an investigation of barber shops by questioning doctors to find out the number of cases of diseases attributable to barber shops. The report indicated that "only a negligible amount of skin infections could be traced to [barber shops], and there seemed to be no evidence indicating that further legislation regarding licensing, regulating, or inspecting of barber shops was needed at this time in Massachusetts." The report also indicated that syphilis was not a major issue. Quoted in "Editorial, Barber Shops and Barbering," *American Journal of Public Health and the Nation's Health* 21, no. 2 (February 1931), 186. See also *New England Journal of Medicine* 202 (January 9, 1930), 89–90.

114. Pippa Holloway, *Sexuality, Politics, and Social Control in Virginia, 1920–1945* (Chapel Hill: University of North Carolina Press, 2006).

115. "'Barber's Bill' Is Sent Back to Committee," *Richmond Times-Dispatch,* December 8, 1936; "Council Kills 'Barber Bill' by Single Vote," *Richmond Times-Dispatch,* January 5, 1937; quote from "Barber Bill Goes the Way of All Others," *Richmond Times-Dispatch,* March 5, 1938.

116. "Barber Bill Goes the Way of All Others," *Richmond Times-Dispatch*, March 5, 1938. See also "Preposterous Barbers' Bill," *Richmond News Leader*, March 3, 1938.

117. "Richmond Firemen Ordered to Stop Giving Free Haircuts to Poor Children," *Richmond Times-Dispatch*, July 27, 1940.

118. "New Barber Bill Ready," *Richmond News Leader,* February 5, 1940; "Barbers to Seek Standards," *Richmond News Leader,* August 14, 1958; "Hold Fast Virginia," *Richmond News Leader,* August 6, 1959; "'Barber Bill' Passes House by 58–25 Vote," *Richmond News Leader,* February 12, 1960; "Senate Unit Barber Examiner Bill," *Richmond News Leader,* February 17, 1960, "Kayo for 'Baber Bill,'" *Richmond News Leader,* and "He Sees No Need for a Barber Law," *Richmond News Leader,* February 19, 1960.

119. Acknowledging the problems in Richmond's black community, Mayor Ambler authorized the creation of a public housing authority, an agency Bright flatly refused. Christopher Silver and John V. Moeser, *The Separate City: Black Communities in the Urban South, 1940-1968* (Lexington: University Press of Kentucky, 1995), 58–59; Roger Biles, *The South and the New Deal* (Lexington: University Press of Kentucky, 2006), 69–70.

120. "Barber Bill Action Delayed by Assembly's Committee," *Richmond Times-Dispatch,* February 11, 1944.

121. Holloway, *Sexuality, Politics, and Control*, 121.

122. "Barber Bill Action Delayed by Assembly's Committee."

123. Quoted in Frank Quillin, *The Color Line in Ohio: A History of Race Prejudice in a Typical Northern State* (Ann Arbor, Mich.: George Wahr, 1913), 148; See also Greene and Woodson, *Negro Wage Earner*, 99.

124. "A. C. Mendell," *Journeyman Barber* 7, no. 2 (March 1911): 57.

125. Quoted in Wright, *Life Behind a Veil*, 84.

126. Myers and Rhodes, *Barber and Historian*, xxiii; "His Heart Broken? It Would Seem," *Cleveland Gazette,* February 8, 1930.

127. Ronald S. Barlow, *The Vanishing American Barber Shop: An Illustrated History of Tonsorial Art, 1860-1960* (El Cajon, Calif.: Windmill Pub. Co., 1993), 13.

128. Journeymen Barbers, Hairdressers, Cosmetologists, and Proprietors' International Union of America, *Textbook: Practical and Scientific Barbering* (Indianapolis: Journeymen Barbers, Hairdressers, Cosmetologists, and Proprietors' International Union of America, 1958); Sherman Trusty, *Art and Science of Barbering* (Los Angeles: Press of the Wolfer Printing

Co., 1956); S. C. Thorpe, *Modern Textbook of Barbering: A Practical Course on the Scientific Fundamentals of Barbering for Students and Practicing Barbers* (New York: Milady Publishing Corp., 1941).

Chapter 4. Rise of the New Negro Barber

1. Paul Laurence Dunbar, *The Life and Works of Paul Laurence Dunbar* (Naperville, Ill.: J. L. Nichols, 1907), 415.

2. The vast literature on the rise of Jim Crow runs wide. I will not attempt to reference that entire literature here, but I will cite the scholarly material that has informed my thinking on what Rayford Logan termed the "nadir" in African American history. See Rayford W. Logan, *The Negro in American Life and Thought: The Nadir, 1877-1901* (New York: Dial Press, 1954); Charles Lofgren, *The Plessy Case: A Legal-Historical Interpretation* (New York: Oxford University Press, 1987); Glenda Gilmore, *Gender and Jim Crow: Women and the Politics of White Supremacy in North Carolina, 1896-1920* (Chapel Hill: University of North Carolina Press, 1996); Jane Dailey, *The Age of Jim Crow: A Norton Casebook in History* (New York: W. W. Norton, 2009); David Oshinsky, *"Worse Than Slavery": Parchman Farm and the Ordeal of Jim Crow Justice* (New York: Free Press, 1997); Grace Elizabeth Hale, *Making Whiteness: The Culture of Segregation in the South, 1890-1940* (New York: Pantheon Books, 1998); Peggy Pascoe, *What Comes Naturally: Miscegenation Law and the Making of Race in America* (New York: Oxford University Press, 2009); Blair Murphy Kelley, *Right to Ride: Street Boycotts and African American Citizenship in the Era of Plessy v. Ferguson* (Chapel Hill: University of North Carolina Press, 2010).

3. For a discussion of black ethnology, see Mia Bay, *The White Image in the Black Mind: African American Ideas About White People, 1830-1925* (New York: Oxford University Press, 2000), 189–202.

4. George Myers, "The Business World," *Cleveland Journal*, January 21, 1905. Ten years later, he made very similar statements. See Kenneth L. Kusmer, *A Ghetto Takes Shape: Black Cleveland, 1870-1930* (Urbana: University of Illinois Press, 1976), 126; George Myers, "Envy Is Race's Scourge," *Cleveland Advocate*, January 29, 1916; "Be Superlative," *Cleveland Advocate*, July 3, 1915.

5. Kevin K. Gaines, *Uplifting the Race: Black Leadership, Politics, and Culture in the Twentieth Century* (Chapel Hill: University of North Carolina Press, 1996), 95; Booker T. Washington to George Myers, June 22, 1900, George A. Myers Papers, 1890-1929 (microfilm) Ohio Historical Society, Columbus, Ohio (hereafter Myers Papers). See also Washington to Myers, July 6, 1901, reel 2, frame 784, July 25, 1901, reel 2, frame 800, December 2, 1903, reel 5, no frame number, February 17, 1904, reel 5, no frame number; Emmett Scott to Myers, July 15, 1905, reel 5, no frame number; Washington to Myers, June 11, 1907, reel 6, no frame number, and July 9, 1908, reel 6, no frame number; all letters in Myers Papers. Washington's continuous invitations suggest that Myers did not share his opinions of the League with him, but simply declined to participate.

6. Three hundred African American businesspeople and professionals attended the first meeting held in Boston. African Americans in various cities organized local chapters. Beyond the emphasis on individual business achievement, the NNBL provided a model for black business organizations. Organizations such as the National Negro Insurance Association, the National Negro Bar Association, and the National Negro Undertakers Association grew out of the Business League. See Booker T. Washington, "The National Negro Business League," *World's Work* 4 (October 1902); Kenneth Hamilton, ed., *Records of the National Negro*

Business League (microfilm) (Bethesda, Md.: University Publications of America, 1994); John H. Burrows, *The Necessity of Myth: A History of the National Negro Business League* (Auburn, Ala.: Hickory Hill Press, 1988); Louis R. Harlan, *Booker T. Washington: The Wizard of Tuskegee, 1901–1915* (New York: Oxford University Press, 1983); Juliet E. K. Walker, *The History of Black Business in America* (New York: Macmillan, 1998). W. E. B. Du Bois actually conceived of the idea a black business league at the 1899 Atlanta Conference. See Elliot M. Rudwick, "W. E. B. Du Bois and the Atlanta University Studies on the Negro," *Journal of Negro Education* 26 (Fall 1957): 475; August Meier, "From Conservative to Radical: The Ideological Development of W. E. B. Du Bois, 1885–1905," *Crisis* 66 (November 1959): 531; Julius Lester, ed., *The Seventh Son: The Thought and Writings of W. E. B. Du Bois*, Vol. 1 (New York: Random House, 1971), 251; Manning Marable, *W. E. B. Du Bois: Black Radical Democrat* (Boston: Twayne, 1986).

7. George Myers, "'Be Superlative,'" *Cleveland Advocate,* July 3, 1915 quoted in Kusmer, *A Ghetto Takes Shape*, 126. See also David A. Gerber, *Black Ohio and the Color Line, 1860–1915* (Urbana: University of Illinois Press, 1976), 465.

8. See Jacqueline M. Moore, *Leading the Race: The Transformation of the Black Elite in the Nation's Capital, 1880–1920* (Charlottesville: University of Virginia Press, 1999); James Gregory, *The Southern Diaspora: How the Great Migrations of Black and White Southerners Transformed America* (Chapel Hill: University of North Carolina Press, 2005), 121; Willard B. Gatewood, *Aristocrats of Color: The Black Elite, 1880–1920* (Fayetteville: University of Arkansas Press, 2000); Joe W. Trotter, *River Jordan: African American Urban Life in the Ohio Valley* (Lexington: University Press of Kentucky, 1998), 109.

9. Chicago Commission on Race Relations, *The Negro in Chicago: A Study of Race Relations and a Race Riot* (Chicago: University of Chicago Press, 1922), 176.

10. Grossman, *Land of Hope: Chicago, Black Southerners, and the Great Migration* (Chicago: University of Chicago Press, 1989), 66.

11. "Starkville, Miss., May 28, 1917" in Emmett J. Scott, "More Letters of Negro Migrants of 1916–1918," *Journal of Negro History* 4, no. 4 (October 1919): 436. See also "Shreveport, LA. April 20, 1917," in Scott, "More Letters of Negro Migrants," 430–431.

12. "Greenwood, Miss. April 22, 1917," in Scott, "Letters of Negro Migrants of 1916–1918," *Journal of Negro History* 4, no. 3 (July 1919): 311–312.

13. Chicago Commission on Race Relations, *Negro in Chicago*, 176.

14. For population shifts, see Bureau of the Census, *Thirteenth Census of the United States: 1910*, Vol. 4: *Population* (Washington, D.C.: Government Printing Office, 1910); *Fourteenth Census of the United States: 1920*, Vol. 4: *Population* (Washington, D.C.: Government Printing Office, 1920); *Fifteenth Census of the United States: 1930*, Vol. 5: *Population* (Washington, D.C.: Government Printing Office, 1930). For major works on the Great Migration, see Grossman, *Land of Hope*; Kimberly Phillips, *Alabama North: African-American Migrants, Community, and Working-Class Activism in Cleveland, 1915–1945* (Urbana: University of Illinois Press, 1999); Gregory, *The Southern Diaspora*; Beth Tompkins Bates, *The Making of Black Detroit in the Age of Henry Ford* (Chapel Hill: University of North Carolina Press, 2012).

15. Walker, *History of Black Business in America*, 213–217.

16. J. H. Harmon, "The Negro as a Local Business Man," *Journal of Negro History* 14 (April 1929): 116–155; Lynne B. Feldman, *A Sense of Place: Birmingham's Black Middle-Class Community, 1890–1930* (Tuscaloosa: University of Alabama Press, 1999), 9.

17. Chrisopher Silver and John V. Moeser, *The Separate City: Black Communities in the Urban South, 1940–1968* (Lexington: University Press of Kentucky, 1995), 21, 54.

18. Silver and Moeser, *The Separate City*, 20–34.

19. For work on African American migration to the Midwest during World War I, see Grossman, *Land of Hope*; Darlene Clark Hine, "Black Migration to the Urban Midwest: The Gender Dimension, 1915–1945," in Kenneth W. Goings and Raymond A. Mohl, eds., *The New African American Urban History* (Thousand Oaks, Calif.: Sage Publications, 1996); Phillips, *Alabama North*.

20. Phillips, *Alabama North*, 127–136.

21. Robert Gregg, *Sparks from the Anvil of Oppression: Philadelphia's African Methodists and Southern Migrants, 1890–1940* (Philadelphia: Temple University Press, 1993), 25–28.

22. Richard R. Wright, *Philadelphia Colored Directory, 1908* (Philadelphia: Philadelphia Colored Directory Co., 1908), 52–55, Historical Society of Pennsylvania, Philadelphia (hereafter HSP); Richard R. Wright, *Philadelphia Colored Directory, 1910* (Philadelphia: Philadelphia Colored Directory Co., 1910), 39–41, HSP; Richard R. Wright, *Philadelphia Colored Directory, 1914* (Philadelphia: Philadelphia Colored Directory Co., 1914), 26–29, HSP.

23. Grossman, *Land of Hope*, 66, 95; Melissa Harris-Lacewell and Quincy T. Mills, "Truth and Soul: Black Talk in the Barbershop," in Melissa V. Harris-Lacewell, *Barbershops, Bibles, and BET: Everyday Talk and Black Political Thought* (Princeton: Princeton University Press, 2004). For black barber shops in Chicago in 1915, see Ford S. Black, compiler, *Colored People's Guide Book for Chicago, 1915–1916* (Chicago: White Print, 1916), 7–8.

24. Grossman, *Land of Hope*, 66.

25. For example, in West Virginia, the material gains of the black middle class were tied to black coal miners' wages. When the state's black coal miners expanded in the 1920s, so too did the black middle class. See Joe Trotter, *Coal, Class and Color: Blacks in Southern West Virginia, 1915–1932* (Urbana: University of Illinois Press, 1990). For other examples of the symbiotic relationship between the black population and black business community, see Feldman, *A Sense of Place*, 87; and Earl Lewis, *In Their Own Interests: Race, Class, and Power in Twentieth Century Norfolk, Virginia* (Berkeley: University of California Press, 1991), 38–39.

26. St. Clair Drake and Horace R. Cayton, *Black Metropolis: A Study of Negro Life in a Northern City* (New York: Harcourt, Brace, and Company, 1945), 450–451.

27. Julia Lucas, interview by Leslie Brown, September 21, 1995, transcript, Behind the Veil Collection, John Hope Franklin Research Center for African and African American Documentation, Duke University (hereafter BTV), 14; *Hill's Durham (Durham County, N.C) City Directory, 1938* (Durham: Hill Directory Co., 1937), 812. Lucas interview reprinted in Anne Valk and Leslie Brown, *Living with Jim Crow: African American Women and Memories of the Segregated South* (New York: Palgrave Macmillan, 2010), 145–146. Also see Leslie Brown, *Upbuilding Black Durham: Gender, Class, and Black Community Development in the Jim Crow South* (Chapel Hill: University of North Carolina Press, 2008), 305. Charles Herndon does not appear to be related to Alonzo Herndon of Atlanta.

28. Tiffany M. Gill, *Beauty Shop Politics: African American Women's Activism in the Beauty Industry* (Urbana: University of Illinois Press, 2010); Walker, *Black Business in America*, 208–211; Davarian L. Baldwin, *Chicago's New Negroes: Modernity, the Great Migration, and Black Urban Life* (Chapel Hill: University of North Carolina Press, 2007), 54–90; A'Lelia Perry Bundles, *On Her Own Ground: The Life and Times of Madam C. J. Walker* (New York: Scribner, 2001).

29. Quoted in Julie Willett, "'Hands Across the Table': A Short History of the Manicurist in the Twentieth Century," *Journal of Women's History* 17, no. 3 (2005): 63. See also "Prize for Fastest Barber," *Chicago Defender*, November, 1, 1919.

30. "It's Alive, Boys," *Chicago Defender*, May 25, 1918.

31. Quotes from John L. Clark, "Wylie Avenue," *Pittsburgh Courier*, November 3, 1923.

32. Julie Willett, *Permanent Waves: The Making of the American Beauty Shop* (New York: New York University Press, 2000), 40–41.

33. Willett, *Permanent Waves*, 41.

34. Mme. Roberta Creditte-Ole, "Beauty Chats," *Pittsburgh Courier*, June 26, 1926.

35. "Wore Best Bob," *Pittsburgh Courier*, December 11, 1926.

36. "Southern Barber Parlor," *Richmond Planet*, August 29, 1925.

37. Chandler Owen, "Craziness, Masculinity and Desire to Cook, Young Cited as Cause for Big Fad," *Pittsburgh Courier*, March 28, 1925.

38. "The Rising Tide of Prejudice," *Pittsburgh Courier*, March 13, 1926.

39. Donald L. Grant and Jonathan Grant, *The Way It Was in the South: The Black Experience in Georgia* (Secaucus, N.J.: Carol Publishing Group, 1993), 218.

40. Enoc P. Waters, Jr., "Interview of the Week," *Chicago Defender*, September 7, 1935.

41. Waters, "Interview of the Week."

42. Beginning in the 1920s, the black beauty industry was a burgeoning field for black women looking to leave domestic service for more professional lives. Madam C. J. Walker and Annie Turnbo Malone were two pioneering black women in the beauty culture industry who provided the infrastructure for training black beauty culturalists. For information on Walker and Malone, see Noliwe M. Rooks, *Hair Raising: Beauty, Culture, and African American Women* (New Brunswick, N.J.: Rutgers University Press, 1996); A'Lelia Perry Bundles, *Madam C. J. Walker: Entrepreneur* (New York: Chelsea House, 1991); Julia Blackwelder, *Styling Jim Crow: African American Beauty Training During Segregation* (College Station: Texas A&M University Press, 2003). On the rise of beauty shops, see Willett, *Permanent Waves*.

43. Waters, "Interview of the Week."

44. "Tonsorial Artist," *Chicago Defender*, November 18, 1944.

45. Walter Barnes, "Felix Jenkins, Oil King in Monroe, LA., Banquets Walter Barnes and Band," *Chicago Defender*, December 19, 1936.

46. D. L. Batts, "Cincinnati," *Chicago Defender*, March 9, 1940.

47. James Ford Rhodes to George Myers, February 14, 1920, in Myers and Rhodes, *Barber and Historian*, 99. See also Rhodes to Myers, July 15, 1920, in Myers and Rhodes, *Barber and Historian*, 113.

48. Myers to Rhodes, March 8, 1920 in Myers and Rhodes, *Barber and Historian*, 101.

49. Myers to Rhodes, August 31, 1920, in Myers and Rhodes, *Barber and Historian*, 115.

50. W. E. B. Du Bois, "The Class Struggle," *The Crisis* (June 1921), quoted in David Levering Lewis, ed., *W. E. B. Du Bois: A Reader* (New York: Henry Holt, 1995), 555–556.

51. William H. Jones, *Recreation and Amusement Among Negroes in Washington, D.C.: A Sociological Analysis of the Negro in an Urban Environment* (1927; reprint Westport, Conn.: Negro Universities Press, 1970), 88–91 (first quote from p. 88, second quote from p. 91).

52. Joseph Richburg, interview by Mary Herbert, June 26, 1995, transcript, Behind the Veil Collection, John Hope Franklin Research Center for African and African American Documentation, Duke University, 8 (hereafter BTV).

53. H. M. Morgan, Affidavit, August 18, 1944, in Project for Business Among Negroes, Box 2, Folder 23, Atlanta University Center.

54. K. K. Lambert, "Alabama State News," *Chicago Defender*, April 20, 1935.

55. "50 Cent Haircuts are Upheld by Court," *Chicago Defender*, December 25, 1937.

56. W. Lloyd Warner, Buford H. Junker, and Walter A. Adams, *Color and Human Nature: Negro Personality Development in a Northern City* (Washington, D.C.: American Council on Education, 1941), 49–50.

57. Warner, Junker, and Adams, *Color and Human Nature*, 50.

58. Patti Sutton, "People and Events," *Chicago Defender,* February 15, 1936; "Editor Rhodes in Speech to Hamptonians," *Chicago Defender,* February 29, 1936; "Master Barbers Meet: Plan for State Conclave," *Chicago Defender,* March 7, 1936; "Philly Barbers in New Era," *Chicago Defender,* June 20, 1936.

59. Lawrence Gordon, "A Brief Look at Blacks in Depression Mississippi, 1929–1934: Eyewitness Accounts," *Journal of Negro History* 64, no. 4 (Fall 1979): 380.

60. Lucas, interview, transcript, BTV, 5.

61. Trotter, *River Jordan*, 134.

62. Trotter, *River Jordan,* 133–134.

63. Frank Crosswaith et al., "Attention Harlem Barbers," March 1939, Box 3, Folder 12, Frank Crosswaith Papers, Schaumburg Center for Research in Black Culture, New York Public Library (hereafter Crosswaith Papers).

64. Crosswaith et al., "Register Harlem Barbers," undated, Box 3, Folder 12, Crosswaith Papers.

65. Mary Poole, *The Segregated Origins of Social Security: African Americans and the Welfare State* (Chapel Hill: University of North Carolina Press, 2006), 69. For additional work on racial and gender exclusions in the Social Security Act, see Linda Gordon, *Pitied But Not Entitled: Single Mothers and the History of Welfare, 1890–1935* (New York: Free Press, 1994); Alice Kessler-Harris, *In Pursuit of Equity: Women, Men, and the Quest for Economic Citizenship in Twentieth-Century America* (New York: Oxford University Press, 2001).

66. George DeMar, "For Immediate Release," December 4, 1939; Crosswaith et al., "Register Harlem Barbers," undated, Box 3, Folder 12, Crosswaith Papers.

67. Robert Kinzer, *The Negro in American Business: The Conflict Between Separatism and Integration* (New York: Greenberg Press, 1950); United States Department of Commerce, *Sixteenth Census of the United Staes: 1940 Census of Busines* Vol. 3, Service Establishments, Places of Amusement, Hotels, Tourist Courts and Tourist Camps, 1939 (Washington, D.C.: Government Printing Office, 1942), 114.

68. Robert E. Weems, Jr., *Desegregating the Dollar: African American Consumerism in the Twentieth Century* (New York: New York University Press, 1998), 14–30.

69. W. E. B. Du Bois, "A Negro Nation Within the Nation," *Current History* 42 (June 1935): 265–270, cited in Lewis, ed., *W. E. B. Du Bois*, 563–570.

70. On economic boycotts in Cleveland, see Phillips, *Alabama North*, 190–225.

71. Suzanne E. Smith, *To Serve the Living: Funeral Directors and the African American Way of Death* (Cambridge, Mass.: Belknap Press of Harvard University Press, 2010), 48-49.

72. Lizabeth Cohen, *A Consumers' Republic: The Politics of Mass Consumption in Postwar America* (New York: Vintage Books, 2003), 41–53.

73. E. Franklin Frazier, *Black Bourgeoisie* (Glencoe, Ill.: The Free Press, 1957), 153-173.

74. "Realty Owner Sued in Vice Probe," *Chicago Defender*, January 12, 1935.

75. "Deacon Is Caught in Lottery Raid," *Chicago Defender*, April 6, 1935.

76. "Barber Held for 'Numbers,'" *Pittsburgh Courier*, October 17, 1936.

77. "Held for Numbers," *Pittsburgh Courier*, September 24, 1938.

78. For a discussion of African Americans' participation in the numbers business, see Shane White, Stephen Garton, Stephen Robertson, and Graham White, *Playing the Numbers: Gambling in Harlem Between the Wars* (Cambridge, Mass.: Harvard University Press, 2010); Victoria Wolcott, *Remaking Respectability: African American Women in Interwar Detroit* (Chapel Hill: University of North Carolina Press, 2001), 93–130; and Victoria Wolcott, "Culture of the Informal Economy: Numbers Runners in Inter-War Black Detroit," *Radical History Review* 69 (Fall 1997): 46–75.

79. Wolcott, *Remaking Respectability*, 122–123.

80. Drake and Cayton, *Black Metropolis*, 480.

81. Drake and Cayton, *Black Metropolis*, 470–494.

82. "Texas State News," *Chicago Defender*, November 16, 1935; "Huttig, Ark.," *Chicago Defender*, June 13, 1936; and James Ferrell, "Parkin," *Chicago Defender*, March 15, 1941.

83. "Defender Has Bulletin Board for War News," *Chicago Defender*, October 19, 1935.

84. For work on the black press, see Ann Field Alexander, *Race Man: The Rise and Fall of the "Fighting Editor," John Mitchell Jr.* (Charlottesville: University of Virginia Press, 2002); Armistead S. Pride and Clint C. Wilson II, *A History of the Black Press* (Washington, D.C.: Howard University Press, 1997); Henry L. Suggs, ed., *The Black Press in the South, 1865–1985* (Westport, Conn.: Greenwood Press, 1996); Roi Ottley, *The Lonely Warrior: The Life and Times of Robert S. Abbott* (Chicago: Regnery, 1955).

85. "Camden, Ark.," *Chicago Defender*, June 8, 1935; "San Mateo, Calif.," *Chicago Defender*, June 1, 1935; "Brady, Tex.," *Chicago Defender*, October 19, 1935; "Leland, Miss.," *Chicago Defender*, October 26, 1935; "Columbus, GA.," *Chicago Defender*, November 30, 1935; "Augusta, Ark.," *Chicago Defender*, December 7, 1935; "Hattiesburg, Miss.," *Chicago Defender*, December 7, 1935; "Itta Bena, Miss.," *Chicago Defender*, December 21, 1935; "Huttig, Ark.," *Chicago Defender*, February 15, 1936.

86. Direct quote from Lucas oral history in Valk and Brown, *Living with Jim Crow*, 145–146; also see unedited transcript in Lucas, interview, transcript, BTV, 15.

87. John Wilson, "Brown Bomber Again Race's No. 1 Hero," *Chicago Defender*, September 26, 1936; Allan McMillan, "Hi Hattin' in Harlem," *Chicago Defender*, September 7, 1935; Al Monroe, "Speaking of Sports," *Chicago Defender*, December 14, 1935.

88. "Joe Louis Entertains," *Pittsburgh Courier*, December 7, 1935.

89. Direct quote from Lucas oral history in Valk and Brown, *Living with Jim Crow*, 145; also see unedited transcript in Lucas, interview, transcript, BTV, 14.

90. Charley Cherokee, "National Grapevine," *Chicago Defender*, August 17, 1946, and "Father Divine Marries?" *Chicago Defender*, August 17, 1946. Many Divine followers questioned whether his former wife had actually died as he reported. For work on Divine, see Kenneth E. Burnham, *God Comes to America: Father Divine and the Peace Mission Movement* (Boston: Lambeth Press, 1979); Robert Weisbrot, *Father Divine and the Struggle for Racial Equality* (Urbana: University of Illinois Press, 1983); and Jill Watts, *God, Harlem USA: The Father Divine Story* (Berkeley: University of California Press, 1992).

91. Lucius C. Harper, "Dustin' Off the News," *Chicago Defender*, July 22, 1944.

92. Direct quote from Lucas oral history in Valk and Brown, *Living with Jim Crow*, 145; also see unedited transcript in Lucas, interview, transcript, BTV, 15.

93. *Hill's Durham (Durham County, N.C.) City Directory, 1942* (Durham: Hill Directory Co., 1942), 437.

94. Robin D. G. Kelley, *Hammer and Hoe: Alabama Communists During the Great Depression* (Chapel Hill: University of North Carolina Press, 1990), 161.

95. Kelley, *Hammer and Hoe*, 95.

96. Wendell Willkie, "Citizens of Negro Blood," *Collier's Weekly*, October 7, 1944, p. 11; Walter White, "Will the Negro Elect Our Next President?" *Collier's Weekly*, November 22, 1947, pp. 26–27; Charley Cherokee, "National Grapevine," *Chicago Defender*, October 21, 1944.

97. Once Mitchell was elected to office, he distanced himself from African Americans. He first alienated the black population by insisting that he was not in Congress to represent his race and he would not dole out patronage positions. He charged Howard University

with teaching communism on its campus and called for an investigation. Although African Americans' reception of Mitchell's bill was mixed, his tendency to deflect the pressures of racial representation caused many African Americans to distrust him and his legislative agenda. For a full discussion of Mitchell's life and political career, see Dennis S. Nordin, *The New Deal's Black Congressmen: The Life of Arthur Wergs Mitchell* (Columbia: University of Missouri Press, 1997).

98. Enoc P. Waters, Jr., "The Mitchell Bill, Bane or Blessing?: How It Is Regarded by Kelly Miller, NAACP, Barber Shop Forum," *Chicago Defender*, August 10, 1935.

99. Waters, "The Mitchell Bill."

100. Waters, "The Mitchell Bill."

101. Waters, "The Mitchell Bill."

102. Waters, "The Mitchell Bill."

103. On anti-lynching legislation, see Walter White, *A Man Called White: The Autobiography of Walter White* (New York: Viking Press, 1948); Mary Jane Brown, *Eradicating This Evil: Women in the American Anti-Lynching Movement, 1892–1940* (New York: Garland Publishing, 2000); Nancy Weiss, *Farewell to the Party of Lincoln: Black Politics in the Age of FDR* (Princeton, N.J.: Princeton University Press, 1983).

104. Mitchell's bill did not pass because of his contentious battle with the NAACP, continuous outburst, and a lack of support from the Roosevelt administration to pick sides in a black political conflict.

105. Andrew Dobson, "From Uncle Joe Dobson's Journal," *Chicago Defender*, May 18, 1935.

106. "Editorial Letter by Marcus Garvey, New York, 6 February 1923," in *The Marcus Garvey and Universal Negro Improvement Association Papers, Volume V, September 1922–August 1924* (Berkeley: University of California Press, 1986), 225-226. On W. A. Domingo, see Winston James, *Holding Aloft the Banner of Ethiopia: Caribbean Radicalism in Twentieth-Century America* (New York: Verso, 1998); Minkah Makalani, *In the Cause of Freedom: Radical Black Internationalism from Harlem to London, 1917-1939* (Chapel Hill: University of North Carolina Press, 2011), 61-62.

107. Charley Cherokee, "National Grapevine," *Chicago Defender*, July 22, 1944.

108. Carter G. Woodson, "Is the Educated Negro a Liability?" *Chicago Defender,* May 21, 1932. Woodson explored these issues further in his *Mis-education of the Negro* (Washington, D.C.: Associated Publishers, 1933).

Chapter 5. Bigger Than a Haircut

1. James Tracy, *Direct Action: Radical Pacifism from the Union Eight to the Chicago Seven* (Chicago: University of Chicago Press, 1996), 31; August Meier and Elliott Rudwick, *CORE: A Study in the Civil Rights Movement, 1942-1968* (New York: Oxford University Press, 1973), 12; George M. Houser, *Erasing the Color Line* (New York: Fellowship Publications, 1945), 26-27.

2. To be sure, the YMCA Racial Equality Committee had been meeting with local barbers since 1952 to accept black customers with no success. In late spring of 1953, the S-CHRC voted unanimously to work with the YMCA Committee and make the opening of campus barber shops to all students the top priority for the fall semester. "Cutting Color Line Gets Top Priority for Next Year," *Daily Illini*, June 17, 1953, Folder: Scrapbook 1, Harry Tiebot Papers, Special Collections, University of Illinois at Urbana-Champaign (hereafter Tiebot Papers).

3. "Cutting Color Line Gets Top Priority for Next Year."

4. "'J. C.' Caroline Thrown for Loss by Campus Barbers," Flyer, November 7, 1953, Box 3, Folder: S-CHRC, Barbershop Issue, Scrapbook 1, Tiebot Papers.

5. "The Barbershop Issue," *Daily Illini*, November 20, 1953, Box 3, Folder: Scrapbook 1, Tiebot Papers.

6. "The Barbershop Issue."

7. Earl S. Rappaport to ACLU, undated, Box 9, Folder 3, Chicago Division, American Civil Liberties Union Papers, Special Collections, University of Chicago, Chicago, Illinois (hereafter ACLU Papers).

8. Edward H. Meyerding to John Langdon, October 12, 1954, Box 9, Folder 3, ACLU Papers.

9. "Haircut Rules Are Posted by Barbershops," *Daily Illini*, May 2, 1954, Folder: Scrapbook 1, Tiebot Papers.

10. Folder: Scrapbook 1, Tiebot Papers.

11. Langdon to Meyerding, October 1, 1954, Box 9, Folder 6, ACLU Papers.

12. Lawrence Rubin, "On Serving Justice for Hair-raising Racism," *Jewish Daily Forward*, August 20, 2007, http://forward.com/articles/10548/on-serving-justice-for-hair-raising-racism/.

13. "Judge Dumps Law Forcing Barbers to Serve Negro," *Chicago Daily Defender*, May 7, 1963.

14. Otha Nixon, interview with author, May 30, 2009 (hereafter Nixon interview).

15. Nixon interview.

16. Quotes from Nixon interview; "Ohio Barber Quits After Bias Protests," *Chicago Daily Defender*, March 17, 1964.

17. Nixon interview.

18. On the Birmingham campaign, see Glenn T. Eskew, *But for Birmingham: The Local and National Movements in the Civil Rights Struggle* (Chapel Hill: University of North Carolina Press, 1997).

19. Thanks to Thomas Fisher, M.D., for this brief explanation on hair, heredity, and genetic makeup. Scholars of science and race say very little about hair and heredity.

20. Bernie Phillips, "Jailed for Haircut!" *Roosevelt Torch,* February 14, 1949, and Report on Foodin-Stewart case, untitled and undated, Chicago Division of ACLU, Box 9, Folder 6, ACLU Papers.

21. Notes on Stewart-Fooden Case, January 26, 1949; ACLU Organization Secretary to Editor of *Roosevelt Torch*, February 18, 1949; and Bernie Phillips, "Conflicting Stories Told in Stewart Case," *Roosevelt Torch,* February 21, 1949, Box 9; all in Box 9, Folder 6, ACLU Papers.

22. Douglass Brinkley, *Rosa Parks* (New York: Viking, 2000); Herbert Kohl, *She Would Not Be Moved: How We Tell the Story of Rosa Parks and the Montgomery Bus Boycott* (New York: New Press, 2005); Beatrice Siegel, *The Year They Walked: Rosa Parks and the Montgomery Bus Boycott* (New York: Four Winds Press, 1992).

23. It would be another fourteen years, until August 12, 1963, before CORE announced plans of a large-scale campaign to desegregate white barber shops, and churches. CORE planned for one black customer a day to attempt to get a haircut in a white shop. In accordance with the organization's direct action policy, they were willing to "talk things over" with the barbers before launching a public demonstration. These plans tapered off because the planning for the March on Washington for Jobs and Freedom, scheduled for August 28, consumed their time and energy. It appears they did not revisit these plans after the march because there is no mention of a campaign to desegregate white shops in the city newspapers or CORE's organizational records. "Plan Drive Against Bias in Chicago Barbershops," *Chicago Daily Defender*, August 12, 1963. See also Meier and Rudwick, *CORE*; Congress of Racial Equality Papers, microfilm, ed. August Meier and Elliott Rudwick (Frederick, Md.: University Publications of America, 1983).

24. Thomas Sugrue, *Sweet Land of Liberty: The Forgotten Struggle for Civil Rights in the North* (New York: Random House, 2008), 133–135.

25. See Jeff Wiltse, *Contested Waters: A Social History of Swimming Pools in America* (Chapel Hill: University of North Carolina Press, 2007); Victoria W. Wolcott, *Race, Riots, and Roller Coasters: The Struggle over Segregated Recreation in America* (Philadelphia: University of Pennsylvania Press, 2012).

26. Langston Hughes, "Haircuts and U.S.A.," *Chicago Defender*, December 29, 1962. On Hughes and his use of Simple in the *Chicago Defender*, see Arnold Rampersad, *The Life of Langston Hughes, Volume II: 1941-1967, I Dream a World* (New York: Oxford University Press, 1988), esp. 62-67; Langston Hughes, *Langston Hughes and the* Chicago Defender: *Essays on Race, Politics, and Culture, 1942-1962,* ed. Christopher C. De Santis (Urbana: University of Illinois Press, 1995).

27. Quote from Horace Cayton, "Personal Problem," *Pittsburgh Courier,* August 31, 1946. On black community formation in Saratoga Springs prior to the 1940s, see Myra B. Young Armstead, *"Lord, Please Don't Take Me in August": African Americans in Newport and Saratoga Springs, 1870-1930* (Urbana: University of Illinois Press, 1999).

28. Cayton, "Personal Problem."

29. Cayton, "Personal Problem."

30. Cayton, "Personal Problem"; Horace Cayton, "Around the World," *Pittsburgh Courier,* November 6, 1954.

31. Hughes, "Haircuts and U.S.A."

32. Hughes, "Haircuts and U.S.A."

33. Hughes, "Haircuts and U.S.A."

34. Paul Gilroy, *The Black Atlantic: Modernity and Double Consciousness* (Cambridge, Mass.: Harvard University Press, 1993), 18–19.

35. *The Negro Motorist Green-Book* (New York: Carson and Smith, 1937); Sugrue, *Sweet Land of Liberty*, 132.

36. On Jim Crow signs, see Elizabeth Abel, *Signs of the Times: The Visual Politics of Jim Crow* (Berkeley: University of California Press, 2010).

37. [Photo of Flott and mother in front of SCAD office, with caption] *Crisis* 67, no. 9 (November 1960): 584; "Clip N.Y's $5 'Kinky' Haircuts," *Pittsburgh Courier*, February 18, 1961.

38. "A Mistake? Deny Indian Haircut for Negro Looks," *Pittsburgh Courier*, January 30, 1960.

39. Photo insert, April 8, 1961, *Pittsburgh Courier;* Samuel O. Regalado, *Viva Baseball! Latin Major Leaguers and Their Special Hunger* (Urbana: University of Illinois Press, 1998), 176–177.

40. " 'Shave-Ins' Run into $5 Fee," *Chicago Daily Defender,* February 19, 1962.

41. George E. Barbour, "African Doctor Refused Service by Hotel Barber," *Pittsburgh Courier*, April 18, 1959.

42. Mary Dudziak, *Cold War Civil Rights: Race and the Image of American Democracy* (Princeton, N.J.: Princeton University Press, 2000), 152–153. See also Phillip E. Muehlenbeck, *Betting on the Africans: John F. Kennedy's Courting of African Nationalist Leaders* (New York: Oxford University Press, 2012).

43. "Diplomats in Capital Report Discrimination by Barbers," *New York Times,* June 9, 1963.

44. Marguerite Cartwright, "World Backdrop," *Pittsburgh Courier,* February 4, 1961.

45. Baker Morten, "No Barber Can Refuse Customer Because of Race," *Washington Afro-American,* March 21, 1964.

46. "African Prince Rebuffed Seeking Haircut in D.C.," *Washington Star,* March 19, 1964.

47. Suzanne E. Smith, *Dancing in the Street: Motown and the Cultural Politics of Detroit* (Cambridge, Mass.: Harvard University Press, 1999), 78-79.

48. "Digs Presses to End Barber Discrimination," *Washington Post*, March 19, 1964.

49. Morten, "No Barber Can Refuse Customer."

50. Morten, "No Barber Can Refuse Customer."

51. Morten, "No Barber Can Refuse Customer."

52. "Barber Changes Policy After Snubbing African," *Washington Post*, May 26, 1964.

53. "Failure to Cut Negro's Hair Costs Barber $200," *Pittsburgh Courier*, February 9, 1957.

54. "State Commission Orders Barber to Cut Negro's Hair," *Pittsburgh Courier*, November 27, 1965.

55. "D.C. May Use License Power on Barbers," *Washington Post*, June 29, 1963.

56. Paul A. Schuette, "Barbers Expected to Pack Hearing on Anti-Discrimination Proposals," *Washington Post*, August 16, 1963.

57. Paul A. Schuette, "Rule Barring Discrimination Splits Barbers," *Washington Post*, August 17, 1963.

58. Schuette, "Rule Barring Discrimination Splits Barbers."

59. Charles D. Pierce, "White House Holds Up Anti-Bias Barber Rule," *Washington Post*, November 10, 1963.

60. "Ky. Governor Bans Race Bias in Public Places," *Chicago Daily Defender*, June 27, 1963.

61. "Wallace to Continue Fight Against Rights," *Chicago Daily Defender*, January 13, 1964.

62. On the Civil Rights Act of 1964, see Clifford M. Lytle, "The History of the Civil Rights Bill of 1964," *Journal of Negro History* 51, no. 4 (Oct., 1966): 275-296; Charles W. Whalen and Barbara Whalen, *The Longest Debate: A Legislative History of the 1964 Civil Rights Act* (Cabin John, Md.; Washington, D.C.: Seven Locks Press, 1985); Hugh Davis Graham, *Civil Rights and the Presidency: Race and Gender in American Politics, 1960-1972* (New York: Oxford University Press, 1992); Rebecca Zietlow, *Enforcing Equality: Congress, the Constitution, and the Protection of Individual Rights* (New York: New York University Press, 2006), 97-127; Jason Sokol, *There Goes My Everything: White Southernerns in the Age of Civil Rights, 1945-1975* (New York: Alfred A. Knopf, 2006), 182-237.

63. "D.C. Barbers Ordered to Give Haircuts to All," *Washington Star*, June 11, 1965.

64. "D.C. Barbers Ordered to Give Haircuts to All."

65. Leonard Downie, Jr., "Barbers Schooled on Negro Haircuts," *Washington Post*, June 25, 1965.

66. "Barbershop Anti-Bias Ruling Goes into Effect Tomorrow," *Washington Star*, September 12, 1965.

67. "White Barbers and Negro Hair," *Crisis* 73, no. 3 (March 1966), 143.

68. "SCLC Protesters Sit at Negro Barbershop," *Atlanta Journal-Constitution*, November 28, 1965; "Herndon Barber Shop Closes after Picket by SCLC Members," *Atlanta Daily World*, November 28, 1965.

69. "GA Negro Barbers Finally Agree to Clip Negroes' Hair," *Jet* 29, no. 10 (December 16, 1965), 18.

70. Ralph W. Johnson, *David Played a Harp: A Free Man's Battle for Independence* (Davidson, N.C.: Blackwell Ink, Inc., 2000), 8.

71. Johnson, *David Played a Harp*, 354.

72. Johnson, *David Played a Harp*, 355–356.

73. Johnson, *David Played a Harp*, 355–356.

74. Johnson, *David Played a Harp*, 355–356.

75. Johnson, *David Played a Harp*, 361.

76. Johnson, *David Played a Harp*, 363–373.

77. Johnson, *David Played a Harp*, 400.

78. Johnson, *David Played a Harp*, 414.

79. Johnson, *David Played a Harp*, 413.

80. Johnson, *David Played a Harp*, 416.

81. Johnson, *David Played a Harp*, 434, quote from Dick Anderson, "Negro Leaders Call off Boycott, Johnson Serves Negro Customers," *Davidsonian*, May 17, 1968 reprinted in Johnson, *David Played a Harp*, 435.

82. Johnson, *David Played a Harp*, 438–449.

83. Charles M. Payne, "'The Whole United States Is Southern!': *Brown v. Board of Education* and the Mystification of Race," *Journal of American History* 91 (June 2004): 83–91.

84. Ella Baker, "Bigger Than a Hamburger," *Southern Patriot*, June 1960.

Chapter 6. The Culture and Economy of Modern Black Barber Shops

1. Stokely Carmichael, *Ready for Revolution: The Life and Struggles of Stokely Carmichael* [Kwame Ture] (New York: Scribner, 2003), 73.

2. Carmichael, *Ready for Revolution*, 73.

3. Carmichael, *Ready for Revolution*, 73–74.

4. James Farmer, *Freedom, When?* (New York: Random House, 1965), 111-128; Malcolm X, "The Ballot or the Bullet," in *Malcolm X Speaks: Selected Speeches and Statements* ed. George Breitman (New York: Grove Press, 1965), 42-43; Martin Luther King, Jr., "The Ethical Demands for Integration," in *A Testament of Hope: The Essential Writings and Speeches of Martin Luther King, Jr.* ed. James Melvin Washington (San Francisco: HarperSanfrancisco, 1991), 117-125.

5. Joseph A. Pierce, *Negro Business and Business Education: Their Present and Prospective Development* (New York: Harper, 1947), 71, 78, 82, 99.

6. Ira Katznelson, *When Affirmative Action Was White: An Untold History of Racial Inequality in Twentieth-Century America* (New York: W. W. Norton, 2005), 113-141. For additional work on the G.I. Bill, see Michael J. Bennett, *When Dreams Came True: The GI Bill and the Making of Modern America* (McLean, Va.: Brassey's, 1996); Theda Skocpol, "The G.I. Bill and U.S. Social Policy, Past and Future," *Social Philosophy and Policy* 14 (Summer 1997).

7. Paige West, Jr., interview by author, August 11, 2004, Philadelphia, Pennsylvania (hereafter West interview).

8. H. M. Morgan, Affidavit, August 18, 1944, in Project for Business Among Negroes, Box 2, Folder 23, Robert Woodruff Library, Special Collections, Atlanta University Center.

9. Ernest Myers, interview with author, April 10, 2009, Washington, D.C. (hereafter Myers interview). L. Tyson said that most of the men at Armstrong studying barbering were there on the G.I. Bill. L. Tyson, interview by author, April 9, 2009, Washington, D.C. (hereafter Tyson interview).

10. Earl M. Middleton, with Joy W. Barnes, *Knowing Who I Am: An Entrepreneur's Struggle and Success in the American South* (Columbia: University of South Carolina Press, 2008), 23–62.

11. Middleton, *Knowing Who I Am*, 65.

12. Lizabeth Cohen, *A Consumers' Republic: The Politics of Mass Consumption in Postwar America* (New York: Vintage Books, 2003), 166-173.

13. Aldon Morris, *The Origins of the Civil Rights Movement: Black Communities Organizing for Change* (New York: Free Press, 1984).

14. Timothy Tyson, *Radio Free Dixie: Robert Williams and the Roots of Black Power* (Chapel Hill: University of North Carolina Press, 1999), 54–55.

15. Tyson, *Radio Free Dixie,* 49–50. On the experiences of black returning WWII veterans and civil rights activism, see Jennifer Brooks, *Defining the Peace: World War II Veterans, Race, and the Remaking of Southern Political Tradition* (Chapel Hill: University of North Carolina Press, 2004); Steve Estes, *I Am a Man! Race, Manhood, and the Civil Rights Movement* (Chapel Hill: University of North Carolina Press, 2005); Christopher Parker, *Fighting for Democracy: Black Veterans and the Stuggle Against White Supremacy* (Princeton: Princeton University Press, 2009).

16. Armstrong was also very active in local efforts to integrate the public schools. On August 22, 1957, Armstrong and seven other black families responded to Shuttlesworth's call for families to volunteer to request that their children be reassigned to all-white schools. Armstrong's daughter and three sons could not attend Graymont Elementary, which was one and a half blocks from their home. The challengers met mob violence as they attempted to integrate the schools; all were turned away. They filed a lawsuit for school integration, and Armstrong was the number-one plaintiff. For six years, the case went through numerous delays before the U.S. district judge issued his decision. Finally, in the fall of 1963, the Graymont, Ramsay, and West End schools were ordered to desegregate. On September 3, Dwight and Floyd Armstrong registered for classes, but Governor George Wallace instructed the Alabama state troopers to close down the school. Lawyers won several injunctions preventing Wallace from continuous resistance. On September 10, the intent of *Brown v. Board of Education* was finally realized in Birmingham. Although Dwight and Floyd told their father about the daily harassment they received from white students, Armstrong was encouraged by their tenacity to stay enrolled. Frye Gaillard, *Cradle of Freedom: Alabama and the Movement That Changed America* (Tuscaloosa: University of Alabama Press, 2004), 127–129, 191–193; Townsend Davis, *Weary Feet, Rested Souls: A Guided History of the Civil Rights Movement* (New York: W. W. Norton, 1998), 84–85.

17. Black beauticians made similar claims. See Tiffany M. Gill, *Beauty Shop Politics: African American Women's Activism in the Beauty Industry* (Urbana: University of Illinois Press, 2010), 111–112.

18. John Brunson, interview by Charles Houston, Jr., July 26, 1994, transcript, Behind the Veil Collection, John Hope Franklin Research Center for African and African American Documentation, Duke University (hereafter BTV), 27. Septima Clark was one of the teachers in the South fired for working with the NAACP. Still committed to education and resistance, she began working with the Highlander Folk School. See Septima Clark and Cynthia Stokes Brown, *Ready from Within: Septima Clark and the Civil Rights Movement* (Navarro, Calif.: Wild Tree Press, 1986); Stephanie Shaw, *What a Woman Ought to Be and Do: Black Professional Women Workers During the Jim Crow Era* (Chicago: University of Chicago Press, 1996); Jacqueline Rouse, "'We Seek to Know in Order to Speak the Truth': Nurturing the Seeds of Discontent—Septima P. Clark and Participatory Leadership," in Bettye Collier-Thomas and V. P. Franklin, eds., *Sisters in the Struggle: African-American Women in the Civil Rights and Black Power Movements* (New York: New York University Press, 2001).

19. Brunson, interview by Houston, 27–28, 46. In 1966, John Brunson became president of the local NAACP.

20. William Hughes, interview with author, September 2, 2003, Durham, North Carolina (hereafter Hughes interview).

21. Black beauticians regularly offered black women free hairdos after messy battles of sit-in protests in the 1960s. See Gill, *Beauty Shop Politics,* 98.

22. SNCC members also met in Reverend Aaron Johnson's church. Reverend Johnson, a barber, and according to historian Charles Payne "the most reliable minister of the period," was the first minister to open his church to organizers for meetings. Reverend Johnson was an army veteran, an active member of the Greenwood chapter of the NAACP, a founding member of the local chapter of the Freedom Democratic Party, and a leader in the boycotts that forced downtown merchants to desegregate. White employers pressured his congregants when he allowed SNCC members to meet in his church. As his congregation dwindled, even his barbering income was insufficient to sustain him and his family. However, his church headquarters in Indianapolis started sending him money in support. See Charles Payne, *I've Got the Light of Freedom: The Organizing Tradition and the Mississippi Freedom Struggle* (Berkeley: University of California Press, 1995), 151–152, 157, 177, 188–192; Davis, *Weary Feet, Rested Souls,* 278–279.

23. Myers interview.

24. Brunson, interview by Houston, 23–24. In 1936, Brunson began his apprenticeship and continued in this position until a chair became available in 1938.

25. Paul Robeson, "We Can't Sit Out This Election," *Freedom*, August 1952 in Paul Robeson, *Paul Robeson Speaks: Writings, Speeches, Interviews, 1918-1974* ed. Philip S. Foner (New York: Brunner/Mazel, 1978), 323–325; Robeson, "Africa Calls—Will You Help?" *Freedom*, May 1953 in Robeson, *Paul Robeson Speaks*, 349–351.

26. C. C. Bryant, interview by Jimmy Dykes, November 11, 1995, transcript, Mississippi Oral History Program, University of Southern Mississippi Digital Collections (digilib.usm. edu) (hereafter Bryant interview; MOHP); quote from Payne, *I've Got the Light of Freedom*, 111–113. On Bryant, see John Dittmer, *Local People: The Struggle for Civil Rights in Mississippi* (Urbana: University of Illinois Press, 1995); Aaron Henry, *The Fire Ever Burning* (Jackson: University Press of Mississippi, 2000), 81-103.

27. Joe Martin, interview by Jimmy Dykes, November 1, 1995, transcript, MOHP.

28. Bryant interview; Payne, *I've Got the Light of Freedom*, 111–113. On Bob Moses, see also Robert P. Moses and Charles Cobb, Jr., *Radical Equations: Math Literacy and Civil Rights* (Boston: Beacon Press, 2001); Dittmer, *Local People*; and Barbara Ransby, *Ella Baker and the Black Freedom Movement: A Radical Democratic Vision* (Chapel Hill: University of North Carolina Press, 2003).

29. Julia Lucas, interview by Leslie Brown, September 21, 1995, transcript, BTV.

30. Dr. William Ferguson Reid, interview by Ronald E. Carrington, March 21, 2003, p. 8, Digital Collections, Virginia Commonwealth University Libraries, available from http:// dig.library.vcu.edu/u?/voices. On the Crusade for Voters see Christopher Silver and John V. Moeser, *The Separate City: Black Communities in the Urban South, 1940-1968* (Lexington: University Press of Kentucky, 1995), 178-181; Lewis A. Randolph, *Rights for a Season: The Politics of Race, Class, and Gender in Richmond, Virginia* (Knoxville: University of Tennessee Press, 2003).

31. William Lomax, interview by author, June 18, 2007, Richmond, Virginia (hereafter Lomax interview). Black beauticians also actively encouraged their clients to register to vote. See Gill, *Beauty Shop Politics*, 111.

32. Leander Blount, interview by author, July 28, 2004, Brooklyn, New York.

33. The Yankees were among the last four of sixteen major league teams to integrate their squads, in addition to the Philadelphia Phillies (1957), the Detroit Tigers (1958), and the Boston Red Sox (1959). See Neil Lanctot, *Negro League Baseball: The Rise and Ruin of a Black Institution* (Philadelphia: University of Pennsylvania Press, 2004), 345–349, 386–391 (Robinson quote from 391). The Boston Red Sox's slow pace to integrate its team was not

lost on black Bostonians either. Howard Bryant remembered his grandfather admonishing him in the 1980s for "rooting for the Red Sox instead of the National League Cardinals and Dodgers, teams that had embraced integration while the Red Sox had not." His grandfather scoffed, "We don't care for the Red Sox around here, because the Red Sox have never had any niggers." Though not true, his statement does highlight the team's tenuous history with black players. See Howard Bryant, *Shut Out: A Story of Race and Baseball in Boston* (New York: Routledge, 2002), vii–viii. Also see Jules Tygiel, *Baseball's Great Experiment: Jackie Robinson and His Legacy* (New York: Oxford University Press, 1983), and *Extra Bases: Reflections on Jackie Robinson, Race, and Baseball History* (Lincoln: University of Nebraska Press, 2002); Brad Snyder, *Beyond the Shadow of the Senators: The Untold Story of the Homestead Grays and the Integration of Baseball* (Chicago: Contemporary Books, 2003).

34. James N. Gregory, "The Second Great Migration: A Historical Overview," in *African American Urban History Since World War II* ed. Kenneth L. Kusmer and Joe W. Trotter (Chicago: University of Chicago Press, 2009), 19–38; James N. Gregory, *The Southern Diaspora: How the Great Migrations of Black and White Southerners Transformed America* (Chapel Hill: University of North Carolina Press, 2005); Joe W. Trotter, ed., *The Great Migration in Historical Perspective: New Dimensions of Race, Class, and Gender* (Bloomington: Indiana University Press, 1991); Arnold R. Hirsh, *Making the Second Ghetto: Race and Housing in Chicago, 1940–1960* (New York: Cambridge University Press, 1983);.

35. Henry Jones, interview by author, August 4, 2004, Brooklyn, New York (hereafter Jones interview).

36. Robert Dexter, interview by author, July 20, 2005, Cleveland, Ohio (hereafter Dexter interview); James C. Crawford, interview by author, August 16, 2005, Cleveland, Ohio (hereafter Crawford interview); Marva Wimberly, interview with author, July 26, 2005, Cleveland, Ohio (hereafter Wimberly interview); Eugene Parker, interview with author, July 26, 2005, Cleveland, Ohio (hereafter Parker interview); Leroy Wilcox, interview with author, July 23, 2005, Cleveland, Ohio (hereafter Wilcox interview). Beauticians were also required to attend a licensed beauty culture school, so some colleges housed both a beauty and barber college. Erma Lee and her husband, Clarence Lee, received a license for the Erma Lee School on October 8, 1934, and in 1936 established the Erma Lee Beauty School. Erma Lee's beauty college was an outgrowth of Elso Polo Beauty College, founded by her mother Goldena Edwards in 1918 in Pine Bluff, Arkansas. The school was opened to teach "scientific beauty culture" to black women. During the World War I era, the family closed the school and moved to Cleveland. In 1927, Erma Lee opened a beauty shop at 4728 Woodland Avenue. She built a sizable clientele and later moved to a larger space at 5512 Woodland Avenue, but her growing business needed additional operators. When the Ohio State Board of Cosmetology passed regulations, Lee saw an opportunity to train not only black beauticians, but also black barbers. See "Business Personalities You Ought to Know," *Cleveland Eagle*, February 14, 1936, Container 3, Folder 1, The Future Outlook League Records, Western Reserve Historical Society, Cleveland, Ohio; Regennia Williams, *Cleveland, Ohio*, Black America Series (Charleston, S.C.: Arcadia, 2002), 73.

37. Anna Julia Cooper, *A Voice from the South* (1892; reprint, New York: Oxford University Press, 1988); Booker T. Washington, *Up from Slavery: An Autobiography* (1900; reprint, New York: Dover Publications, 1995); W. E. B. Du Bois, *The Souls of Black Folk* (1903; reprint, New York: Oxford University Press, 2007).

38. James Spruill, interview by author, April 11, 2009, Washington, D.C. (hereafter Spruill interview).

39. Lloyd Howerton, interview by author, April 9, 2009, Washington, D.C. (hereafter Howerton interview).

40. Richmond barbers William Lomax, Benjamin Thompson, and Eugene Fleming noted they took the vocational course at Walker High School. Thompson and Lomax majored in barbering, while Fleming majored in bricklaying and plastering. Lomax interview; Eugene Fleming, interview by author, June 19, 2007, Richmond, Virginia (hereafter Fleming interview).

41. Fleming interview.

42. Maxine Craig, "The Decline and Fall of the Conk; or, How to Read a Process," *Fashion Theory* 1, no. 4 (November 1997): 404.

43. Malcolm X, with the assistance of Alex Haley, *The Autobiography of Malcolm X* (New York: Grove Press, 1965), 45.

44. Williams quote in Nick Salvatore, *Singing in a Strange Land: C. L. Franklin, the Black Church, and the Transformation of America* (New York: Little, Brown, 2005), 199.

45. Some of Paige West's customers included Dinah Washington, Sarah Vaughn, and the Drifters. West interview.

46. Maxine Leeds Craig, *Ain't I a Beauty Queen? Black Women, Beauty, and the Politics of Culture* (New York: Oxford University Press, 2002), 112.

47. West interview.

48. Sugar Ray Robinson, *Sugar Ray: The Sugar Ray Robinson Story* (New York: Viking Press, 1970), 213.

49. West interview; Hortense Williams, interview by Kisha Turner, July 17, 1995, transcript, BTV, 14–15.

50. For a critique of the conk, see Susan Willis, "I Shop Therefore I Am: Is There a Place for Afro-American Culture in Commodity Culture?" in Robyn R. Warhol and Diane Price Herndl, eds., *Feminisms: An Anthology of Literary Theory and Criticism* (New Brunswick, N.J.: Rutgers University Press, 1997), 992–1008; and Craig, *Ain't I a Beauty Queen?*

51. Craig, "The Decline and Fall of the Conk," 405–413.

52. West interview.

53. Lomax interview.

54. Lomax interview.

55. Benjamin Thompson, interview by author, June 20, 2007, Richmond, Virginia (hereafter Thompson interview).

56. Thompson interview.

57. Fleming interview.

58. "In the Senate," *Richmond News Leader,* March 5, 1962; "Once Again—the Barber Bill," *Richmond News Leader,* February 2, 1962; "House Committee Clears Barber Examiner Bill," *Richmond News Leader,* February 14, 1962; "Assembly Complete Barber Bill Action," *Richmond News Leader,* March 10, 1962; Virginia Department of Professional and Occupational Registration, "An act to regulate the practice of barbering . . . [and] to establish a Board of Barber Examiners . . . Approved April 7, 1962 (Richmond: Department of Professional and Occupational Registration, 1962), Library of Virginia, Richmond, Virginia.

59. The other appointees included Walter Trelbley of Richmond, president of the Virginia Association of Master Barbers, and J. S. Hall of Roanoke, for three-year terms, and Charles Valentine, chairman of the Alexandria Barber Board, and Edward Dancy of Petersburg, for two-year terms. For the beauticians, the term limits were also staggered: Bertrude Wooldridge of Wise, president of the Virginia Hairdressers Association, for a five-year term; Mary Hutchins of Hampton, former president of the State Association and operator of a hairdressing school, for a four-year term; Garnett Hurt of Roanoke, for a three-year term; and Mary Davis of Richmond, owner of training schools in Richmond and Roanoke, for a two-year term. "Barber, Hairdresser Boards Are Appointed," *Richmond News Leader,* June 10, 1962.

60. Virginius Dabney, interview by Daniel Jordan and William H. Turpin, June 10–13, 1975, interview A-0311-1, transcript, 71-72, Southern Oral History Program Collection, University of North Carolina, Chapel Hill (docsouth.unc.edu).

61. Malcolm X, *Autobiography*. See also Richard B. Turner, *Islam in the African-American Experience* (Bloomington: University of Indiana Press, 1997), 182; Manning Marable, *Malcolm X: A Life in Reinvention* (New York: Viking, 2011).

62. West interview.

63. Hank Ballard, "How You Gonna Get Respect (When You Haven't Cut Your Process Yet)?" (1968), on James Brown, *James Brown's Funky People*, Part 3, compact disc (UMG Records, 2000).

64. William Van Deburg, *New Day in Babylon: The Black Power Movement and American Culture* (Chicago: University of Chicago Press, 1992), 201; Jeffery O. G. Ogbar, *Black Power: Radical Politics and African American Identity* (Baltimore: Johns Hopkins University Press, 2004), 93-110; Peniel Joseph, *Waiting 'Til the Midnight Hour: A Narrative History of Black Power in America* (New York: Henry Holt, 2006); Amy Abugo Ongiri, *Spectacular Blackness: The Cultural Politics of the Black Power Movement and the Search for a Black Aesthetic* (Charlottesville: University of Virginia Press, 2010).

65. Frantz Fanon, *The Wretched of the Earth* (New York: Grove Press, 2004); Malcolm X and Alex Haley, *The Autobiography of Malcolm X* (New York: Ballantine, 1999); Marable, *Malcolm X*; Nikhil Pal Singh, "The Black Panthers and the 'Undeveloped Country' of the Left," in *The Black Panther Party Reconsidered* ed. Charles E. Jones (Baltimore: Black Classic Press, 1998), 68-69; Miriam Ma'at-Ka-Re Monges, "'I Got a Right to the Tree of Life': Afrocentric Reflections of a Former Community Worker," in *Black Panther Party Reconsidered*, 140-141; Cleveland Sellers with Robert Terrell, *The River of No Return: The Autobiography of a Black Militant and the Life and Death of SNCC* (Jackson: University of Mississippi Press, 1990), 187-188.

66. Robin D. G. Kelley, "Nap Time: Historicizing the Afro," *Fashion Theory* 1, no. 4 (November 1997): 341–344.

67. Phyl Garland, "The Natural Look," *Ebony* 21 (June 1966): 143–146; Ayana D. Byrd and Lori L. Tharps, *Hair Story: Untangling the Roots of Black Hair in America* (New York: St. Martin's Press, 2001), 55; Lloyd Boston, *Men of Color: Fashion, History, Fundamentals* (New York: Artisan, 1998).

68. Craig, *Ain't I a Beauty Queen*, 87–91, 97, 99, 106–107; Frantz Fanon, *The Wretched of the Earth* (1963; repr., New York: Grove Press, 1965); Malcolm X, *Autobiography*. On the Watts riots, see Gerald Horne, *Fire This Time: The Watts Uprising and the 1960s* (Charlottesville: University Press of Virginia, 1995).

69. Kelley, "Nap Time," 346.

70. West interview. The Afro went through many names: the "freedom," the "bush," and the "Afro."

71. Byrd and Tharps, *Hair Story*, 55, 65, 87.

72. Jones interview.

73. Howerton interview.

74. Albert Hillman, interview by author, April 12, 2009, Washington, D.C. (hereafter Hillman interview). Other barbers offered similar assessments. Spruill interview; Wilcox interview; Hughes interview.

75. Byrd and Tharps, *Hair Story*, 86–87.

76. Clinton Simpson, interview by author, June 8, 2009, Birmingham, Alabama; Spruill interview.

77. Crawford interview; Wimberly interview; Parker interview; John Fort, interview with author, August 14, 2004, Philadelphia, Pennsylvania.

78. Randolph Arthur, interview by author, July 30, 2004, Brooklyn, New York.

79. Fleming interview.

80. Hillman interview; Tyson interview; Spruill interview.

81. Phyl Garland, "The Natural Look," *Ebony* 21 (June 1966): 146; Margaret Williams Neal, interview by Rhonda Mawhood, July 19, 1993, transcript, BTV, 94–95.

82. Arletta Claire, "Naturals Can't Be Just 'Natural' They Require Grooming, Cutting," *Chicago Defender,* October 7, 1969; "Natural Reduces Barbershop Trade," *Chicago Defender,* March 28, 1970; "Some Advice for Young Men with Longer Hair," *Chicago Defender,* August 12, 1970; Spruill interview.

83. Quotes from James Alan McPherson, "The Faithful," in *Elbow Room: Stories* (Boston: Little, Brown, 1977), 67, 78. See also Herman Beavers, *Wrestling Angels into Song: The Fictions of Earnest J. Gaines and James Alan McPherson* (Pennsylvania: University of Pennsylvania Press, 1995), 56–57. White barbers faced similar challenges as black barbers when the Beatles popularized long hair.

84. On the passing of Afros, see Phyl Garland, "Is the Afro on Its Way Out?" *Ebony,* February 1973, 128–136.

85. Jones interview. James Spruill also mentioned the shortage of barbers after the Afro; Spruill interview.

86. Harry Ferguson, "Gains, Setbacks in Rights Fight," *Chicago Daily Defender*, July 29, 1963.

87. Al Duckett, "Know the Negro," *Chicago Defender*, April 4, 1964.

88. Duckett, "Know the Negro."

89. "Black Business Feels Integration Sting," *Chicago Defender*, June 22, 1968.

90. Karla F. C. Holloway, *Passed On: African American Mourning Stories, A Memorial* (Durham, N.C.: Duke University Press, 2002), 25–26; Smith, *To Serve the Living.*

91. Davarian L. Baldwin, *Chicago's New Negroes: Modernity, the Great Migration, and Black Urban Life* (Chapel Hill: University of North Carolina Press, 2007), 53–90; Kathy Peiss, "'Vital Industry' and Women's Ventures: Conceptualizing Gender in Twentieth Century Business History," *Business History Review* 72, no. 2 (Summer 1998), 235.

92. Walker, *History of Black Business in America*, 302–308; Nancy Dawson, "Hair Care Products Industry," in Juliet E. K. Walker, *Encyclopedia of African American Business History* (Westport, Conn.: Greenwood Press, 1999), 282–290; Susannah Walker, "Black Dollar Power: Assessing African American Consumerism since 1945," in *African American Urban History Since World War II*, 400-402. For a larger discussion of black consumption and white competition in the post-civil rights era, see Robert E. Weems, Jr., *Desegregating the Dollar: African American Consumerism in the Twenieth Century* (New York: New York University Press, 1998).

93. Fleming interview.

94. Spruill interview; Howerton interview.

95. Fort interview; Parker interview; Wilcox interview. On the 1968 rebellions sparked by Martin Luther King's assassination see Komozi Woodard, *A Nation Within a Nation: Amiri Baraka (Leroi Jones) and Black Power Politics* (Chapel Hill: University of North Carolina Press, 1999), 93–99; Clay Risen, *A Nation on Fire: America in the Wake of the King Assassination* (Hoboken, N.J.: John Wiley & Sons, 2009). On buisness ownership and the rebellions see, Jonathan J. Bean, "'Burn, Baby, Burn': Small Business in the Urban Riots in the 1960s," *Independent Review* 5, no. 2 (Fall 2000): 165-187.

96. Hughes interview.

97. Sugrue, *Sweet Land of Liberty*, 432.

98. Fleming interview.

99. Hugh Hollins, interviews by Eddie Faye Gates, May–August 1994, in Alan Govenar, *African American Frontiers: Slave Narratives and Oral Histories* (Santa Barbara, Calif.: ABC-CLIO, 2000), 214.

100. See Robert E. Weems, *Business in Black and White: American Presidents and Black Entrepreneurs in the Twentieth Century* (New York: New York University Press, 2009); Timothy Mason Bates, *Black Capitalism: A Quantitative Analysis* (New York: Praeger, 1973). Early critiques of black capitalism include E. Franklin Frazier, *Black Bourgeoisie* (Glencoe, Ill.: Free Press, 1957); Earl Ofari, *The Myth of Black Capitalism* (New York: Monthly Review Press, 1970); Ronald W. Bailey, ed., *Black Business Enterprise: Historical and Contemporary Perspectives* (New York: Basic Books, 1971), esp. 99-179.

101. Laura Warren Hill and Julia Rabig, ed., *The Business of Black Power: Community Development, Capitalism, and Corporate Responsibility in Postwar America* (Rochester, N.Y.: University of Rochester Press, 2012).

Epilogue

1. *Barbershop 2: Back in Business*, directed by Kevin Rodney Sullivan (Beverly Hills, Calif.: MGM Home Entertainment, 2004)

2. *Barbershop 2*.

3. The Black Barbershop Health Outreach Program, blackbarbershop.org.

4. South Carolina for Barack Obama Beauty and Barber Shop Program, https://my.barackobama.com/page/s/beautyandbarber.

5. Susan Kuczka and John McCormick, "Security to Keep Obama from Favorite Barbershop," *Chicago Tribune*, November 12, 2008.

Index

Abbott, Robert, 157
abolitionists, 17, 18, 42–45, 55–56, 265n100
Africans, 188, 203–6, 214
Afros, 217–18, 228, 236–41
Alabama, 65, 208, 221, 238, 239. *See also*
   Birmingham; Mobile; Montgomery; Selma
Alexandria, Va., 131
Allison, Ebenezer, 31
Ambler, Gordon B., 139, 140, 286n119
American Anti-Slavery Society, 17
American Bar Association (ABA), 126
American Civil Liberties Union (ACLU), 190,
   192, 197
American Federation of Labor (AFL), 120–22
American Health and Beauty Aids Institute,
   245
American Medical Association (AMA), 125, 126
Anderson, William, 19
Ann Arbor, Mich., 87
Antioch College, 192–94, 200
apprentices: enslaved, 20–21, 29–35, 259–
   60n16, 262–63n63; free blacks as, 29–30,
   259–60n16; fugitive slaves as, 41
Armstrong, James, 222, 226–27, 298n16
Arnett, Benjamin, 96
Arthur, Randolph, 239–40
Arthur Moler barber colleges, 127
Associated Master Barbers of America
   (AMBA), 166, 167, 208
Athens, Ga., 63–67
Atlanta, Ga., 68–70, 102, 127, 168, 169; barber
   shop locations in, 151, 152; barber shop
   ordinances proposed in, 135–36, 161; black
   insurance company in, 99–100; number and

composition of barbers in, 63, 113–15; race
   riot of 1906 in, 81, 102–4. *See also* Herndon,
   Alonzo
Atlanta Benevolent Protective Association,
   99–100
Atlanta Constitution, 69, 117, 118, 135–36
Atlanta Independent, 102
Atlanta Life Insurance Company. *See* Atlanta
   Benevolent Protective Association
Atlanta Mutual Insurance Association, 100, 151
Auburn, N.Y., 83

Baker, Ella, 215
Ballard, Hank, 236–37
Baltimore, Md., 64, 113, 114, 167–69
Banks, Nathaniel, 60–61
Barber and Beauty Culturists Union, Local 8,
   169–70
barber colleges, 127–28, 141–42, 219, 250–51; for
   blacks, 166, 219–20, 229–30, 300n36
Barbershop (movie), 2
Barbershop 2 (movie), 249
Barbers' Protective Association of Virginia
   (BPA), 132–33, 137, 141, 234–36
barber training, 209–10. *See also* apprentices;
   barber colleges
Barclay, Edwin, 205
Barry, Marion, 224
bathhouses, 26–27, 29, 66
beauty industry, 244–45; black, 157, 244–45,
   290n42 (*see also* black beauty shops)
Beecher, Henry Ward, 54
Benito Cereno (Melville), 15–17, 74, 75
Benson, James E., 65

Acknowledgments

M Y grandfather, Elmon Mills, was a barber on the South Side of Chicago. The moments I remember most vividly are those when he had no customers and sat in his barber's chair talking with a fellow barber or other men in the shop. I selectively forget the buzzing in my ear from the clippers that unnerved me when he cut my hair. I acknowledge him and his memory in my attempt to re-create a space he occupied Tuesday through Saturday.

I am grateful to have had a mentor during my undergraduate education who saw promise in me. As a business major at the University of Illinois at Urbana-Champaign, I enrolled in a number of history courses with Juliet E. K. Walker and her tutelage transformed me. If the prizes my research paper garnered were not enough to call into question my career aspirations, Juliet was not shy about offering sound advice that the historical profession better suited me. I am grateful I listened.

I was fortunate to be part of a vibrant intellectual community at the University of Chicago, where several scholars and friends have shaped me, and this book, in immeasurable ways. Melissa Harris-Perry (formerly Harris-Lacewell) trusted me to conduct the ethnography of Truth and Soul Barber Shop and the opportunity to co-author a chapter in her book. As I have written elsewhere, the seeds for my book were planted in that barber shop. Melissa cultivated my thinking on black politics and always provided keen insight and direction. Thomas C. Holt encouraged and championed the broad scope of this project from the start. His stories of his father, who was a barber, demonstrated his excitement and curiosity beyond the particulars of writing a book. His probing questions and unyielding support continue to inspire me. I am grateful to Jim Grossman, who went beyond the call in guiding me in the writing of history. He has always made the time to read drafts, help me navigate the profession and publishing, and hand me a crushing defeat (or lesson) on the tennis court. Yes, thanks, Jim, for reminding me that learning happens everywhere. The Center for the Study of Race, Politics, and Culture served as my institutional anchor for much of my time there. Many thanks to Michael Dawson and Cathy Cohen for bringing me on board the Black Civil Society Project and the Reproduction of Race and Racial Ideologies Workshop. I presented parts of this book to the Race Workshop and the Social History Workshop and greatly benefited from participants' comments. Julie Saville was challenging and insightful in her comments on black leadership in Reconstruction-era politics. I would also like to thank Thomas Adams, A. J. Aiseirithe, Lisa Andersen, William Balan-Gaubert, Nancy Buenger, Michael Czaplicki, Illya Davis, Christopher Deis, David Ferguson, Rosalind Fielder, Jacqueline Goldsby, José Hernández, Moira Hinderer, Mae Ngai, Mary Pattillo, Damon Phillips, Mark Rifkin, Kodi Roberts, John Rosa, Amy Dru Stanley, Jacqueline Stewart, Kyle Volk, and Ellen Wu.

Many people have read all or parts of this book at various stages. Jim Merrell read the entire text and provided such extensive comments and suggestions that he handed the manuscript back to me with his now-legendary "Guide to the Scribbles & Scrawls Besmirching Your Paper." I benefited greatly from his comments. Benjamin Talton is a remarkable colleague and friend. He was more than generous with his time in reading drafts with little turnaround time. At every step, he continued to remind me of the value of this book. Emprisia Lee helped me make the book accessible to a nonacademic audience. I am grateful to have a network of friends who have read chapters or offered sound advice that helped me develop my ideas, including Martha Biondi, Cathy Cohen, Christopher Freeburg, Janette Gayle, Jessica Graham, Sarita Gregory, Joshua Guild, Allyson Hobbs, Gretchen Long, Charles McKinney, Jessica Millward, Charles Payne, Dylan Penningroth, Barbara Ransby, Shaka Rawls, Shana Redmond, Nick Salvatore, Candice Swift, Elizabeth Todd-Breland, and Dorian Warren.

Colleagues at a number of institutions and professional conferences welcomed me at various stages of this book and helped shepherd it along. At the University of Notre Dame, Reanna Ursin, LaReine Marie-Mosely, Paul Minifee, and Sara Busdiecker composed an amazing cohort of fellows and were amazing in their engagement. Richard Pierce, Heidi Ardizzone, Ivy Wilson, Al Tillery, and Gail Bederman provided generous feedback on various chapters, which influenced this project immensely. Participants of the Gender History Group at Notre Dame pushed me on my use of manhood and masculinity. Colleagues in the history department at Binghamton University were more than welcoming during a sabbatical leave by granting me office space and inviting me to participate in their workshop series. Leigh Ann Wheeler, Nancy Appelbaum, Diane Sommerville, Melvin Dubofsky, and Howard Brown provided insightful feedback on my work. Laura Warren Hill contributed useful research assistance as she worked on her dissertation. Participants in the Seminar on the City, convened by Lisa Keller and Kenneth T. Jackson, at Columbia provided extensive comments. I also want to thank Mary Marshall Clark, Ron Grele, and the participants in the 2004 Summer Oral History Seminar at Columbia's Oral History Institute. I have presented versions of chapters at conferences and received thoughtful comments from a number of people, including Stephanie Shaw, Davarian Baldwin, Tiffany Gill, and Brandi Brimmer.

As a faculty member at Vassar College, I have been fortunate to be surrounded by a number of selfless colleagues who have provided a supportive space to think and write. My colleagues in the history department—notably, Jim Merrell, Rebecca Edwards, Miriam Cohen, and Ismail Rashid—read drafts, wrote letters of recommendation for fellowships, and offered sound advice on navigating university presses. When I returned to Vassar from a year's leave, I was pleasantly surprised to see a large Jacob Lawrence print titled "Barber Shop" hanging on the wall in the department. I pass this print on the way to my office, and I have Rebecca to thank for purchasing this wonderful piece of art not only to keep me inspired, but also to raise our students' intellectual curiosities about the past. I would also like to thank a group of then-junior faculty who formed a writing group in which we held each other accountable to keep writing. They include: Candice Swift, Laura Yow, Tyrone Simpson, Eve Dunbar, Kristin Carter, Kiese Laymon, and Light Carruyo. In the final writing stages, Sarita Gregory and Myra Young-Armstead offered critical and affirmative feedback that the manuscript was ready to leave my desk. Rachel Gorman sacrificed part of her holiday to help me clean up the endnotes during copyediting.

Many institutions extended generous support to help make this book possible. Several departments at the University of Chicago funded the initial research. The Trustees Fellowship, the Arthur Mann and the Freehling research travel grants from the History Department, and the Doolittle-Harrison Fellowship from the Office of Graduate Affairs provided critical financial support in the early stages of this project. I am especially grateful to the Center for the Study of Race, Politics, and Culture for also awarding

me research and travel funds. I would also like to acknowledge the financial
support from the Mellon Summer Fellowship and the fellow participants of
the Rethinking African American Studies Seminar convened by Ken Warren
and Adolph Reed. Many thanks to the Africana Studies Department at the
University of Notre Dame for awarding me an Erskine A. Peters Fellowship.
At Vassar, I received generous funding from the Lucy Maynard Salmon Fund
to bring this project to completion.

While this financial support was crucial to producing this book, the gen-
erosity of family and friends in offering housing, food, and other resources
was equally important. The following friends helped me stretch my research
funds by allowing me to stay at their homes during extended research trips:
Benjamin and Janie, Minkah Makalani, Somi, Alprentice Rawls, and James
and Delores Williams.

Historians are lost without librarians and archivists, and I owe a huge
thanks to many of them for their assistance. They include: Frank Conaway,
Social Sciences Bibliographer at the University of Chicago; David Smith of
the New York Public Library; Carol Merritt, Director of the Alonzo Herndon
Home in Atlanta; Janice White Sikes of the Auburn Avenue Research Library;
Wendy Chmielewski at the Swarthmore Special Collections; Mary Wilke
at the Center for Research Libraries; Beavercreek Community Library in
Yellow Springs, Ohio; and the research staff at the Western Reserve Historical
Society and the Ohio Historical Society in Cleveland, the Historical Society
of Pennsylvania, and the Library Company of Philadelphia. The librarians,
especially Carol Lynn Marshall, and interlibrary loan staff at Vassar facilitated
the unusually large microfilm requests of city directories. These directories
formed the basis of the maps in this book, and I am grateful to Boundary
Cartography for producing these final maps and helping me think about spatial representation.

Several Vassar students worked as research assistants on this project: Sam
Anderson, Dyana Boxley, Kara Conley, Guillermo Farias, Katherine George,
Hannah Groch-Begley, Luke Leavitt, Renata McAdams, Spencer Resnick,
Kyle Sullivan, and Kyle Tam. Yemi Erku provided much needed research
from Wisconsin.

I owe a huge debt to all of the barbers who shared their life histories with
me, even though I had not cut my hair in eight years at the time I spoke to
them. Thanks to the Audio Transcription Center for transcribing the oral interviews I collected. Thanks also to the many people who suggested that I
check out their barber shop.

I am indebted to Robert Lockhart at the University of Pennsylvania Press for his support and patience. His unyielding interest and commitment to this book was clear from the start. Noreen O'Connor-Abel took great care with the copy editing to improve the book. The anonymous reviewers for the press offered sound suggestions and comments that made this a much stronger book. Rachel Taube, Will Boehm, and a host of other wonderful folks at the press put in a tremendous amount of work preparing this book for timely publication. Thanks to Jim O'Brien for producing the index and providing an extra set of eyes in the final stages of the book's production.

Finally, I extend enormous gratitude to the friends and family who supported me, irrespective of the book, which essentially gave me the confidence to produce this work. Henoc Erku and Rashid Carter exhibited unyielding friendship. My family usually asked one question: "How is the book?" That simple gesture of thoughtfulness went a long way. My grandmothers, Ethel Mills and Tisha Taylor, set clear examples of conviction, strength, and humility that have influenced me. My mom, Janetta Mills, cultivated my interest in books at an early age, and my father, Ronald Mills, taught me perseverance; both were essential in completing this book. Many thanks to my brothers Deshawn, Tréance, and Elán. My wife, Gail, loved me and this book at every stage of development. She read early drafts and helped me shape the narrative. She also supported my frequent research trips and late nights at the library, and shouldered many responsibilities to free me up to work. I would like to thank my daughters, Niambi and Nahla, who accepted with grace and elation that I had "to go to the library to write a book." And, when I returned home, they routinely darted toward me with wide eyes and huge smiles screaming, "Daddy." Last, to our new arrival, Yohannes, if the women in this family shape you in the ways they have shaped me, you are in for an amazing life.